# THE
# ISO 9000
# HANDBOOK

*Edited By*

# Robert W. Peach

Published by
**CEEM Information Services ✦ Fairfax, Virginia**

# THE ISO 9000 HANDBOOK

Edited by: **Robert W. Peach**

Robert Peach and Assoc., Inc.
541 N. Brainard Avenue
La Grange Park, IL 60525-5520
Tel: (708) 579-3400; Fax: (708) 579-1620

Published by: **CEEM Information Services**

10521 Braddock Road
Fairfax, Virginia 22032
Tel: (800) 745-5565, (703) 250-5900; Fax: (703) 250-5313

## First Edition, Third Printing

Printed in the United States of America

Director, CEEM Information Services: Mark Morrow
Senior Editor: Tom Tibor
Assistant Editors: Ellen Crosby, Susan C. Hatch
Production Assistant: Leah Wilbur
Marketing Director: Darryl Graham
Design & Production: James P. Gildersleeve

ISBN 1-883337-27-5

# TABLE OF CONTENTS

# EDITOR'S PREFACE

As the 21st century draws near, American business faces expanding international competition. The economic superpowers, the United States and the Far East, will soon be joined by the unified market of the European Community.

The key to economic success in this global marketplace will be higher-quality products and services. This emphasis on increased quality is demonstrated by the growing acceptance of international quality standards, such as the ISO 9000 series standard.

Meeting and exceeding the requirements of ISO 9000 quality assurance and quality management standards is fast becoming essential in order to succeed in an evermore competitive marketplace.

The primary objective of this handbook is to compile in a single source the information that a US organization needs to understand the ISO 9000 series of quality assurance and quality management standards and initiate the process of implementing those standards. Another objective is to describe recent developments in the European Community in the areas of product standards, product certification and quality assurance.

Whatever the motivation, whether to protect sales to the European Community, to respond to the requirements of large customers, or to adopt the standard on the basis of good quality practice, there is a need to understand not only the content and use of the standard, but also the marketplace factors that are influencing adoption of the ISO 9000 series standard worldwide.

The publishers of *Quality Systems Update (QSU)* are qualified to provide the material for such a handbook. My responsibility as editor has been to work with the *QSU* staff to ensure that the contents of the handbook are accurate and unbiased.

In carrying out this process, input has been solicited from a variety of knowledgeable contributors. While many of the conditions affecting registration to the standard are constantly changing, each contributor has made every effort to be as current and as accurate as possible in discussing the subject matter of this handbook. Subscribers to *QSU* will recognize that some material contained in the Handbook has appeared in previous *QSU* issues. This material has been fully updated.

The contributors to this handbook come from a variety of backgrounds and thus reflect different points of view regarding quality system standards issues. Most of these differences are not substantive and will, we believe, contribute positively to the reader's appreciation of the broad spectrum of factors that influence the application of ISO 9000.

In a few cases, however, the opinions of the contributors conflict, or may seem to conflict. As long as the facts used by the contributors are correct, no attempt has been made to resolve these differences. Rather, such differences reflect the diverse judgments and perspectives of people throughout American industry and should contribute to the comprehensiveness of the handbook.

Underlying the increasing level of ISO 9000 registration activity is the fact that the ISO 9000 standards describe a technically sound quality system for use by manufacturing and service organizations. The standards are proving to be a valuable foundation for expanded quality practice to which principles of Total Quality Management (TQM) are applied. Many companies initially make use of the standards because of external demands — customer requirements, regulatory compliance or market competition. They soon find that meeting all requirements of the standard results in significant internal benefits and that the rewards are well worth the cost and effort necessary to become registered.

I trust that this handbook will provide the information readers need to apply the standard successfully in their own organizations and to achieve the benefits of an improved quality system, and that readers will discover that this is only the beginning of an era of continual improvement in the quality capability of all segments of commerce and industry.

*Robert Peach*

# ABOUT THE EDITOR

## Robert W. Peach

Robert W. Peach is Principle, Robert Peach and Associates, Inc., Quality Management Consultants, La Grange Park, Illinois. He has received degrees from the Massachusetts Institute of Technology and the University of Chicago.

Mr. Peach established and for over 25 years managed the Quality Assurance activity at Sears Roebuck and Company. In this capacity, he and his staff worked with quality systems at the plants of hundreds of Sears suppliers.

Mr. Peach is a Fellow of the American Society for Quality Control (ASQC), and chairs the ASQC Standards Council. Past service in the ASQC includes Vice-President, Publications Technical Editor, *Quality Progress*; and Chairman, Awards Board. Through ASQC he aided in the evaluation of contractor quality programs for NASA's Excellence Award for Quality and Productivity. He also has been an instructor in quality control in the Graduate School of the Illinois Institute of Technology, and has taught courses in quality engineering for the ASQC Professional and Technical Development Division.

For three years, Mr. Peach served as Project Manager of the Malcolm Baldrige National Quality Award Consortium, which administers the awards program managed by the National Institute of Standards and Technology. He is now a technical advisor to the award administrator. He is a member of the Executive Committee of the American National Standards Institute (ANSI) Z-1 Accredited Standards Committee on Quality Assurance, and chaired the writing of the ANSI/ASQC Z-1.15 Standard, *Generic Guidelines for Quality Systems*. He has served as a member of the ANSI International Standards Council and Certification Committee, and on the Board of the American Association for Laboratory Accreditation.

Mr. Peach is a delegate to the International Laboratory Accreditation Conference (ILAC), and is a member of the US Delegation to the ISO TC 176 Committee on Quality Assurance, where he served as Convenor of the Working Group that developed ISO Quality System Standard 9004 (ANSI/ASQC Standard Q94). He currently chairs the ASQC's Registrar Accreditation Board.

Mr. Peach has spoken over 200 times to organizations on the subject of quality management, is author of the ASQC home study course, "Successfully Managing the Quality Function," and has received the Edwards Medal of the ASQC for leadership in the application of modern quality control methods. He is a certified quality engineer and registered professional engineer in quality engineering.

# ABOUT THE PUBLISHER

## CEEM

Recent transformations in global marketplace competition and in US regulatory and legislative policy have altered many long-held business assumptions. Since 1979, CEEM has responded to this changing business climate by offering carefully tailored seminars, workshops, conferences and publications designed to provide middle and senior management with timely and accurate information.

CEEM's programs and information services cover a wide range of topics, including environmental management, ISO 9000 series quality system standards, and government regulatory compliance. Respected government and industry experts participate in discussions on topics such as the Environmental Protection Agency's (EPA) Superfund program, aboveground storage tanks, biotechnology, environmental permitting, workplace safety, risk assessment, and the Americans with Disabilities Act (ADA).

CEEM's ISO 9000 series quality system management courses, seminars and publications enjoy an international reputation. Course offerings include internal auditing processes, quality systems certification, laboratory quality assurance and automated management systems.

Conferences and seminars range from one to five days, depending on the topics and audience. While CEEM designs and sponsors many of its own course offerings, it also co-sponsors courses and seminars with respected national and international organizations. These organizations include the British Standards Institution(BSi), the Victoria Group, the American Association for Quality Systems Registration (A2QSR), the American Association for Laboratory Accreditation (A2LA), the American Management Association (AMA), the American Petroleum Institute (API), the National Association of Manufacturers (NAM), Business Publishers, Inc. (BPI), and Inside Washington Publishers.

Through its newsletters, guidebooks, handbooks, reports and videos, CEEM Information Services provides executives and managers with up-to-date information on an array of topics, including critical environmental issues, international product standards, laboratory certification, and ISO 9000 quality systems registration developments. CEEM's staff has extensive experience and expertise in conference management, journalism, marketing and training programs.

A substantial percentage of CEEM's profits is returned to improving products and services. As a result, the company has gained an international reputation for excellence. To protect its customers, CEEM offers a full money-back guarantee on all its courses, training materials and publications. An additional service available is the expertise to handle all travel arrangements through a CEEM Division, the Patriot Travel Group — providing both convenience and value. To further CEEM's mission to benefit others, at least ten percent of net profits are donated to charity. CEEM was first established as the Center for Energy and Environmental Management. Because its scope has broadened, its board of directors voted to adopt the acronym CEEM. A full mission statement is available upon request.

# BACKGROUND AND DEVELOPMENT OF ISO 9000

BY DONALD MARQUARDT

## INTRODUCTION

In 1987, the International Organization for Standardization (ISO) published the ISO 9000 Series International Standards. The ISO 9000 series comprises generic standards that provide quality management guidance as well as quality assurance requirements and guidance. The standards apply to all types of companies; they can be adapted to fit both small and large corporations in all sectors of the economy, including those that are predominantly manufacturing and those that are predominantly service sector suppliers.

While ISO publishes thousands of standards, the five documents in the ISO 9000 series (ISO 9000 - 9004) are beginning to have a growing impact on international trade. One driving force is the development of regional economic groups of nations, particularly the European Community via its *EC 1992* thrust.

## The International Organization for Standardization (ISO)

ISO was founded in 1946 to develop a common set of manufacturing, trade and communication standards. The Geneva, Switzerland-based organization is composed of 91 member countries. The American National Standards Institute (ANSI) is the United States representative to ISO.

All standards developed by the ISO are voluntary; no legal requirements force countries to adopt them. However, countries and industries often adopt and attach legal requirements to ISO standards, thereby making the standards mandatory. ISO develops standards in all industries except those related to electrical and electronic engineering. Standards in these areas are made by the Geneva-based International Electrotechnical Commission (IEC), which has over 40 member countries, including the United States.

ISO has 146 full-time staff members from 27 countries. The organization is structured into 173 technical committees, 631 subcommittees, 1,830 working groups and 18 *ad hoc* study groups. The technical committees draft the standards.

ISO receives input from government, industry and other interested parties before promulgating a standard. As of late 1991, ISO had issued 8,114 international standards and technical reports and published 68,580 pages of technical text.

The European Community has adopted the ISO 9000 series as part of its efforts to establish systems for product certification and quality systems registration. Registration involves the audit and approval of a quality management system against ISO 9001, ISO 9002, or ISO 9003 by an independent registrar, also known as a third-party registrar.

The standard has also been adopted in the United States as the ANSI/ASQC Q90 series. As of this writing, 55 countries have adopted the ISO 9000 series as a national standard, and thousands of companies worldwide have become registered to ISO 9001, ISO 9002, or ISO 9003. (Figure 1-1) As of August 1992, there were more than 400 registered sites or facilities in the United States, representing nearly 300 companies.

---

### ISO Adoption Worldwide

Countries adopting the ISO 9000 series typically assign their standards a name or number consistent with other existing national standards. The United States has adopted the ISO 9000 series as the *American National Standards Institute/American Society for Quality Control (ANSI/ASQC) Q90* series, labeling the series ANSI/ASQC Q90, Q91, Q92, Q93, and Q94. In the United Kingdom, the ISO 9000 series is designated BS 5750. The EC has adopted the ISO 9000 series as European Norm (EN) 29000.

Government bodies worldwide are also beginning to use the ISO 9000 series. In the United States, the Department of Defense (DoD) is considering replacing its MIL-Q-9858A standard with the ISO 9000 series in its existing second-party quality assurance audit scheme. The US Food and Drug Administration (FDA) has indicated its intent to incorporate ISO 9000 standards in its Good Manufacturing Practices (GMP) regulations for medical devices.

## THE EUROPEAN COMMUNITY

---

Perhaps the single most visible factor driving the acceptance of the ISO 9000 series is the effort to unify the twelve major European nations that comprise the European Community into a single internal market. These twelve full members are: Belgium, Denmark, France, Germany, Greece, Ireland, Italy, Luxembourg, the Netherlands, Portugal, Spain and the United Kingdom.

EC 92, as it is known, nominally becomes effective at midnight on December 31, 1992. The impact on trade within Europe and on trade with other countries is already being felt worldwide. In preparation for EC 92, the European Community has been developing a comprehensive framework for product certification, product standards and product testing.

Quality systems registration to ISO 9001, ISO 9002, or ISO 9003 plays an important role in this framework. The EC has adopted the ISO 9000 series verbatim; its version is the EN 29000 series. To understand fully the role of the ISO 9000 standards, it is important briefly to introduce EC 92.

## The History of the EC

The European Community (EC) originated with the 1957 Treaty of Rome, which was established to abolish tariffs and quotas among its six member states and to stimulate economic growth in Europe. (The original members of the EC were France, West Germany, Italy, Luxembourg, the Netherlands and Belgium.)

Economic growth slowed during the 1970s and early 1980s, and Europe began to fear that the US, Japanese and Pacific Rim economies would dominate the world economy of the 21st century. The European nations, with their differing technical standards and requirements, were concerned that they would fall behind. In response, the European Community, now consisting of twelve countries, called for a greater push toward a unified market and for the removal of trade barriers.

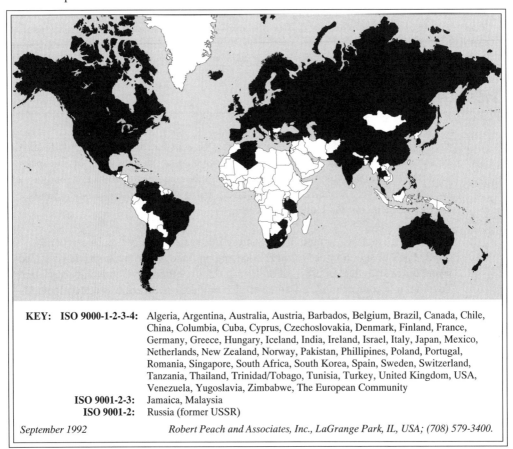

KEY:   ISO 9000-1-2-3-4:   Algeria, Argentina, Australia, Austria, Barbados, Belgium, Brazil, Canada, Chile, China, Columbia, Cuba, Cyprus, Czechoslovakia, Denmark, Finland, France, Germany, Greece, Hungary, Iceland, India, Ireland, Israel, Italy, Japan, Mexico, Netherlands, New Zealand, Norway, Pakistan, Phillipines, Poland, Portugal, Romania, Singapore, South Africa, South Korea, Spain, Sweden, Switzerland, Tanzania, Thailand, Trinidad/Tobago, Tunisia, Turkey, United Kingdom, USA, Venezuela, Yugoslavia, Zimbabwe, The European Community
ISO 9001-2-3:   Jamaica, Malaysia
ISO 9001-2:   Russia (former USSR)

*September 1992*                    *Robert Peach and Associates, Inc., LaGrange Park, IL, USA; (708) 579-3400.*

*Figure 1-1: Fifty-five countries adopt ISO 9000 series as national standards.*

The 1987 Single European Act reinforced economic unification among the EC nations. Its goal is to establish an internal market by December 31, 1992, in which there is free movement of goods, persons, services and capital.

At the same time, the EC developed a new approach to regulating products. It enlisted the aid of key European regional standards organizations[1] to develop EC-wide, "harmonized" standards. The purpose of these standards was to eliminate the jumble of standards of the individual twelve member states. The EC has drafted nearly 300 regulations to implement the Single European Act.

## European Product Certification

In the EC product certification and standards system, there are two categories of products: regulated and nonregulated.

*Regulated* products are those that have important health, safety, or environmental implications. Examples of regulated products include medical devices, personal protective equipment and construction products. For these products, the EC has implemented directives. A *directive* is the official legislation of the European Community. *Nonregulated* products are those not covered by EC legislation.

EC directives contain the minimum health, safety and environmental requirements that a product must meet. Each directive deals with a class of regulated products and spells out the essential requirements for compliance, including, in many cases, quality assurance certification. In EC terminology, "quality system certification" has the same meaning as "quality system registration" in the United States and Canada. (See box on next page.)

The procedure for complying with EC directives is called *conformity assessment.* Conformity assessment involves a number of activities that, when successfully completed, give customers confidence that products conform to all requirements.

Depending upon the requirements of a particular directive, conformity assessment can require one or more of the following: type-testing of the product, third-party audit of the quality system, testing of regular production, third-party audit of testing laboratory systems, or the manufacturer's self-declaration of conformity.

Adherence to directive requirements must be demonstrated before a regulated product can be awarded a designation known as the *EC mark* and legally be sold in the EC. (Chapter 8 describes the mark and the EC's conformity assessment procedures in detail.)

## Accreditation, Certification and Registration

Terms such as *accreditation*, *certification* and *registration* are often used interchangeably, creating some confusion. To clarify the meanings, the Conformity Assessment Committee of the International Organization for Standardization, in its *ISO/IEC Guide 2: General terms and their definitions concerning standardization and certification* defines the terms as follows:

**Certification**: Procedure by which a third party gives written assurance that a product, process or service conforms to specified requirements.

**Accreditation**: Procedure by which an authoritative body gives formal recognition that a body or person is competent to carry out specific tasks.

**Registration**: Procedure by which a body indicates relevant characteristics of a product, process or service, or particulars of a body or person, and then includes or registers the product, process or service in an appropriate publicly available list.

In Europe *quality systems certification* is used more widely than *quality systems registration*, which is the US terminology.

## The Importance of Quality Assurance

Each directive offers manufacturers options among the various conformity assessment procedures. This is known as the *modular approach.* Some of the EC directives require quality system registration. Examples include medical devices, construction products, telecommunications terminal equipment and gas appliances. The draft forms of the furniture flammability, recreational craft, cable ways and lifting equipment directives also specify quality system registration.

For other directives, quality system registration is not an absolute requirement. However, in order to ensure confidence in the quality of products circulating throughout Europe, the EC has strongly emphasized quality assurance.

Meeting the product and quality system requirements necessary for doing business in the EC poses a major challenge for those companies which produce regulated products.

In addition, marketplace incentives are driving suppliers and customers of the EC worldwide to follow the modular approach for nonregulated and regulated products. The reason is that there is economic and public relations value for a company to have a single consistent system for all products, whether regulated or nonregulated, as well as for all external audits, whether by second-party customers or by third-party registrars.

---

## The Registrar and the Registration Process

A registrar is a third-party company (i.e., a company independent of the supplier and its customers) whose business is to evaluate a supplier's quality system for conformity to ISO 9001, ISO 9002 or ISO 9003. Evaluations include an examination of the company's quality policy, quality system documentation and quality records. A key part of the evaluation is a thorough on-site audit to determine whether each required quality system element is defined, documented, deployed and consistently implemented, and that required documentation and records are current and available. Training of personnel is verified through records and on-site interviews.

When a supplier's quality system is verified to conform to the requirements of the selected standard (ISO 9001, ISO 9002 or ISO 9003) the registrar issues a certificate to the supplier describing the scope of the supplier's quality system that has been certified. The certification is then listed in a register (registration) which is available to the public. The registrar allows the supplier to display the registrar's mark on advertising, stationery, etc., as evidence that it has achieved registration.

The business of registering companies to ISO 9001, ISO 9002 or ISO 9003 began in 1987. There are several types of registrars in the United States. They include:

○ Established US companies that already provide product certification services in a specific industry sector, or quality systems certification in a specific industry sector, or both, based on standards within that industry sector

○ Established companies that have been quality systems registrars in Europe or other regions, providing certification to standards that are predecessors to the ISO 9000 series

○ New companies formed by quality experts or organizations with prior experience in related areas.

*(Chapter 4 in this Handbook discusses registrars and the registration process in detail.)*

Registration to ISO 9001, ISO 9002, or ISO 9003 is not required for nonregulated products. But the market is driving the move toward registration, and the EC adopted the ISO 9000 series because its members anticipated a process of quality systems registration by third parties.

Third-party audits place great importance on a company's quality system. Companies have two outputs: revenue and products. Financial outputs are measured by the balance sheet; products are measured by quality. Just as companies require impartial auditors to examine financial systems, they require third-party auditors to assess the quality system.

# IMPLICATIONS FOR THE US

The implications of the EC's efforts are far-reaching. The EC is systematically instructing quasi-governmental standards agencies to establish new standards and directives for every area of economic activity. This effort may create the most comprehensive product and quality standards in the world.

---

### Who Accredits Registrars?

How does a company that is seeking ISO 9000 registration know that a particular registrar is competent to conduct audits? The Dutch Council for Certification in the Netherlands (RvC) and the National Accreditation Council for Certifying Bodies (NACCB) in the United Kingdom are two quasi-governmental bodies that certify organizations to perform third-party quality system audits. The Registrar Accreditation Board (RAB) in the United States also performs this function. A number of other nations have established or are in the process of establishing accreditation schemes for registrars operating in their countries. The criteria against which to evaluate registrars are based on ISO guidelines and EC standards.

Mutual recognition of registration certificates is necessary for the smooth functioning of international trade. Mutual recognition means that a company's registration, awarded by an accredited registrar in one nation, will be accepted by the accreditation agency (and by all customers) in other nations.

Various issues regarding registrar accreditation and the mutual recognition of registration certificates are not yet settled. (Chapter 9 discusses these and related issues in detail.)

In October 1991, the seven member states of the European Free Trade Association (EFTA) signed a draft European Economic Area (EEA) treaty with the European Community to join the single market and to create a free flow of goods, services, people and capital beginning January 1, 1993. The members of EFTA are Austria, Finland, Iceland, Liechtenstein, Norway, Sweden and Switzerland. Sweden and Austria have already applied for EC membership, and more countries are certain to follow.

Interest in European integration has also extended to other countries with the signing of Association Agreements with Poland, Hungary and the Czech and Slovak Federal Republic. Therefore, the entire European Economic Area (EEA) could consist of a combined market of 375 million people in a $5 trillion annual economy.[2]

With the inclusion of other Eastern European countries and the former Soviet republics, the EC could eventually develop into an economic market of 500 to 800 million people.

The United States is the EC's biggest foreign supplier. In 1991, the US exported about $103 billion in goods to the countries of the EC.[3] About half of these exports are subject to EC-wide regulations. The US share of EC imports has been growing steadily and is now more than 16.5 percent — the largest country share of the EC import market.[4]

US companies are understandably eager to gain and maintain an economic foothold in this market. Manufacturers can foresee millions of new customers for products and services. The challenge is to meet both product and quality system standards necessary for unrestricted trade within this market.

# THE ROLE OF THE ISO 9000 SERIES

Within a national economy and in international trade, the ISO 9000 series standards have two primary roles:

**Quality Management.** The ISO 9000 series standards provide guidance for suppliers of all types of products who want to implement effective quality systems in their organizations or to improve their existing quality systems.

**Quality Assurance.** The standards also provide generic requirements against which a customer can evaluate the adequacy of a supplier's quality system.

# Development of the ISO 9000 Series

In the past two decades, "quality" has emerged as an important aspect of commerce and industry. Various national and multinational standards developed in the quality systems arena for commercial and industrial use, or for military or nuclear power industry needs. Some standards were guidance documents. Other standards were used in contracts between purchaser and supplier organizations.

In 1959, the US Department of Defense (DoD) established the MIL-Q-9858 quality management program. In 1968, the North Atlantic Treaty Organization (NATO) essentially adopted the tenets of the DoD program in the NATO AQAP1, AQAP4, AQAP9 series of standards. In 1979, the UK's British Standards Institution (BSi) developed the first commercial quality assurance system standards from its predecessors. These standards were designated the BS 5750 series, Parts 1, 2, and 3.

Despite the commonality among these predecessors to the ISO 9000 series standards, there was no real consistency until Technical Committee 176 (TC 176) of the International Organization for Standardization (ISO) issued the ISO 9000 series standards in 1987. ISO is a worldwide federation of national standards bodies (ISO member bodies). The American National Standards Institute (ANSI) is the US member body to ISO. Countries that have member bodies to ISO have national technical advisory groups representing them to ISO. In the United States, the American Society for Quality Control (ASQC) administers the Technical Advisory Group (TAG) to TC 176 on behalf of ANSI.

All ISO standards, including the ISO 9000 series, are subject to a review approximately every five years. The next revision is due in 1992. Changes to ISO 9001, ISO 9002, ISO 9003, and ISO 9004 are expected to be minor. More significant revisions are anticipated for 1996. A long-range plan devised by TC 176, called *Vision 2000*, discusses the future use of the ISO 9000 series through the year 2000. (*Vision 2000* is discussed in Chapter 7.)

ISO has developed other quality standards that offer guidance in various aspects of quality management. These include:

○ **ISO/9004-2:** *Quality management and quality system elements - Part 2: Guidelines for services*

○ **ISO/9000-3:** *Guidelines for the application of ISO 9001 to the development, supply and maintenance of software*

○ **ISO/DIS 9004-3:\*** *Quality management and quality system elements - Part 3: Guidelines for processed materials*

○ **ISO/10011-1:** *Guidelines for auditing quality systems - Part 1: Auditing*

○ **ISO/10011-2:** *Guidelines for auditing quality systems - Part 2: Qualification criteria for auditors*

○ **ISO/10011-3:** *Guidelines for auditing quality systems - Part 3: Managing audit programs*

○ **ISO/10012-1:** *Quality assurance requirements for measuring equipment - Part 1: Management of measuring equipment.*

(See Chapter 7 for details on new and proposed quality standards.)

\* Draft International Standard

These two roles are complementary. In the context of programs for quality system registration, as in the European Community, the quality assurance role is more visible, but the business values of both roles are important.

The ISO 9000 series was developed primarily for two-party contractual situations — to satisfy the customer's quality assurance requirements. The aim is to increase the confidence of customers in the quality systems of their suppliers. This is particularly important when the supplier and the customer are in different countries or when the distance between them is great. This benefit is accomplished by:

■ Establishing consistent quality practices that cross international borders
■ Providing a common language or set of terms
■ Minimizing the need for on-site vendor visits or audits.

Another aim of the ISO 9000 series is to harmonize international trade by supplying a set of standards with worldwide credibility and acceptance. However, the ISO 9000 series has assumed a larger role in both the EC and around the world.

In short, it has become accepted as a *de facto*, baseline requirement that is separate from its use within the EC-regulated industry structure. Manufacturers and service industries report that some standard contract forms now include quality system registration queries.

Why this expansion? The reasons are outlined below.

## Legal Requirements

Some companies are implementing ISO 9001, ISO 9002, or ISO 9003 because registration is a legal requirement to enter the regulated EC market or because registration helps to meet a domestic regulatory mandate.

## Contractual Requirements

Customers are requesting suppliers to become registered as a contractual requirement. Companies are being asked by their customers or purchasers of their products and services to become registered to ISO 9001, ISO 9002, or ISO 9003 as a pre-condition to placing a contractual purchase order.

In many cases, suppliers have multiple sites making the same product. When only some of the sites are registered, the supplier may be required by the customer to ship only from the registered site(s).

## Registration of Subcontractors

The ISO 9001 and ISO 9002 standards require the supplier to ensure that materials, components and other products purchased from subcontractors conform to specified requirements. As a consequence, an increasing number of companies are requiring that their subcontractors become registered, even though the ISO 9001 and ISO 9002 standards do not specifically require registration of subcontractors (sub-suppliers).

## Reduce Multiple Assessments

Another reason for the push for ISO 9000 registration is that it promises to reduce the need for multiple assessments. Customers wishing to buy products from one or more suppliers often find it necessary to audit each supplier's quality system. Suppliers, in turn, must undergo multiple assessments in order to sell to different customers. ISO 9000 registration reduces the need for multiple assessments based on the confidence that a quality system is in place.

## Legal Concerns

Legal concerns are also driving registration. Some companies register a quality system, at least in part, for the role registration may play in product liability defense. Companies that sell regulated products in Western Europe may be subject to broad product liability and safety requirements. European liability regulations are becoming more stringent and are moving toward strict liability concepts prevalent in the United States.

An EC product liability directive, for example, holds a manufacturer liable, regardless of fault or negligence, if a person is harmed or if an object is damaged by a faulty product.

In addition, an EC product safety directive requires manufacturers to monitor product safety. The possible consequences of these directives would be to require companies to document that they have an adequate production process with respect to quality systems, so as to better prove that products meet specified requirements and thereby minimize liability claims. (See Chapter 10 for a thorough discussion of the product safety and product liability directives and other legal issues.)

## The Marketplace

The greatest impetus for ISO 9000 series implementation, however, is market pressure. Companies are implementing the ISO 9000 series to keep up with competitors who are registered and to distinguish themselves from any non-registered competitors.

Part of this impetus is the worldwide trend toward quality as business becomes more global. In the past decade, quality has become a watchword for industries worldwide.

Previous national standards to evaluate quality systems originated in special commercial, industrial and military sectors. As trade increased, international quality became critical for both customers and suppliers. Suppliers wanted to demonstrate quality to their customers. Supplier companies, in turn, placed increasing value on the capability and performance of their potential sub-suppliers with regard to quality.

Until the development of the ISO 9000 series, however, quality standards were inconsistent. The publication of the ISO 9000 series has increased the international pace of harmonization and accelerated the trend toward quality as a key aspect of international trade.

## Internal Improvement

Although market pressure has stimulated many companies to seek ISO 9000 registration, other companies have done so out of a strong belief in the process. Companies that have implemented the standards have often discovered that internal improvements in facility performance and quality have lasting value at least equal to the market prestige of ISO 9000 approval. A well-established quality system can result in productivity gains and reduced costs associated with repair, rework, scrap and other inefficiencies.

The ISO 9000 standards can also be used as a foundation or a building block for implementing broader quality systems such as Total Quality Management (TQM) and for meeting more stringent quality goals such as the criteria of the Malcolm Baldrige National Quality Award in the United States.

## Concerns about ISO 9000 Registration

Despite its worldwide acceptance, the ISO 9000 series standard and the issue of ISO 9000 registration has also raised some concerns.

### Cost

Achieving registration to ISO 9001, ISO 9002 or ISO 9003 requires money and time. Preparing for registration may take six to 18 months or longer to complete, and may require a multi-person-year effort.[5] Registrar fees can exceed $10,000 to $20,000 or more per site, not including company resources invested in the registration effort.

## ISO 9000 Registration: Questions to Consider

Companies interested in seeking ISO 9000 series registration should consider the following questions:

○ Does your customer require compliance with ISO 9001, ISO 9002 or ISO 9003? If yes, does your customer require second-party or third-party assessment?

○ Are you doing business with any companies based in an EC or EFTA country?

○ Are you doing business with companies based in a non-European country that subscribe to the EC system at a national level?

○ Are you doing business with any companies that, in turn, are doing business with an EC- or EFTA-based company or with other companies based in a non-European country that subscribe to the EC system at a national level?

○ Do you wish to improve your competitive position even though your product is nonregulated or not governed by a directive?

○ Are you planning to improve your basic quality system while working towards internal quality improvement?

If the answer to any of these questions is yes, you may want to consider complying to an ISO 9000 series standard or inquire about quality system registration.

*Bud Weightman*

In some industries, companies have established a product quality baseline perceived to be above the level provided for in the ISO 9000 series. In such an industry, the ISO 9000 standards may be perceived to add cost without adding real value. However, many companies that believed their quality system exceeded the requirements for ISO 9000 registration subsequently discovered that this was not true for all elements of their systems.

## ISO 9000 as a Trade Barrier?

Standards facilitate a common international industrial language, provide consumer confidence, and promote product safety. Standards can also facilitate and encourage trade. Used improperly, however, standards can hinder worldwide trade. According to a January 1992 report by the Manufacturers' Alliance for Manufacturing and Innovation (MAPI), the ISO 9000 series could "hurt US manufacturers' competitive position in European trade." [6]

One argument says that standards adopted on a regional scale to facilitate trade within the region can produce the consequence of acting as a trade barrier. In the early 1970s, for example, Europe developed a regional certification system for electronic components. This system, in effect, became a non-tariff barrier to trade for American and Japanese manufacturers. The groups adversely affected petitioned the international electronics standards body, the IEC, to develop an international system to replace the regional one.

However, when examples like this are cited, a major misunderstanding about the ISO 9000 series is revealed. The ISO 9000 series deals only with quality systems, not with a product's technical or performance specifications. The example deals with product certification to regional technical specifications. These can become non-tariff trade barriers for suppliers in other countries that have different technical specification standards for the same class of products.

## A Level Playing Field

Another concern sometimes cited is that a level playing field can hurt high-quality companies. According to this argument, all products manufactured by ISO 9000 registered companies initially may be viewed favorably. This may benefit the manufacturer that previously produced to lower-quality standards, because now its products are viewed on a par with all others. A universal quality standard may tend to level the playing field among international competitors, benefiting European manufacturers much more than their US counterparts.[7]

This example reveals another misunderstanding regarding the ISO 9000 series standards. While the ISO 9000 series does represent a universal quality standard, there is no expectation that because two companies are both registered, the levels of each company's quality system and products are the same.

Registration means that both companies have quality systems that meet at least the scope of the stated standard (ISO 9001, ISO 9002 or ISO 9003), that each quality system element is adequate and that it is consistently deployed. There is still ample opportunity for suppliers to win in the marketplace because they offer products with better technical specifications and better conformance to the technical specifications than that of their competitors.

## The EC System Is Uncertain

The EC product certification system has also created a good deal of uncertainty, making it difficult for American companies to plan.[8] The regulatory framework is still developing. The status of directives and which products they cover is unclear, as are the conformity assessment requirements for specific products. The timetable for deciding these questions keeps shifting. Other unresolved issues have arisen as well, including the accreditation of auditors and the strictness of audits in various countries.

These are genuine problems. While they affect both European and non-European suppliers, undoubtedly the effects are somewhat more serious for non-European suppliers. However, these problems concern the procedures for **implementation** of the testing, accreditation and certification systems. They are not related to the content or structure of the ISO 9000 standards themselves.

In addition, there is the perception that the EC is exploiting the differences between the US and European standard-setting systems and government-business relation- ships to its advantage.[9] The European system is government-oriented, with an emphasis on third-party verification, while the American system is driven by the private-sector and relies mainly on manufacturers' self-declaration of conformity.

US manufacturers are not as familiar as European companies with a government-driven standards system such as the one being implemented in the European Community. This unfamiliarity with the system, coupled with the many uncertainties about the developing EC system for conformity assessment, leaves American manufacturers in the dark about how to meet various requirements. Europeans who are more familiar with the system and who have an ability to influence it may have an advantage.

American ingenuity and flexibility have always been a cultural advantage, however. Many US firms have proven their ability to become registered and to compete effectively.

# THE MOVE TO ISO 9000 IS ON

Despite the costs and the unsettled issues, the global drive toward quality system registration to the ISO 9000 standards has begun. Nations, regional bodies such as the EC, and customers worldwide are using registration to the ISO 9000 series standards as a means to differentiate quality companies from the rest in the field.

Companies deciding not to jump on the bandwagon may well find themselves running to catch up with international competition. John Hinds, the new president of International Organization for Standardization (ISO) and president of AT&T, says that US companies must understand and adopt international standards if they are to compete effectively in the world. According to quality expert Philip Crosby, "it's becoming very clear now that quality is not so much an asset *per se* as a price of getting into the game. If you don't have it, you can't play. And if you can't produce it, they won't be interested in you."

## About the Author

*Donald W. Marquardt is President of Donald Marquardt and Associates. Formerly he was the manager of the E.I. duPont Quality Management & Technology Center. He is the head of the US delegation to ISO TC 176. Mr. Marquardt chaired the writing of the ISO 9000 Standard and was a senior examiner, Malcolm Baldrige National Quality Award, 1988.*

## ENDNOTES

[1] Three main standards organizations include the Committee for European Standardization (CEN), the European Committee for Electrotechnical Standardization (CENELEC), and the European Telecommunications Standardization Institute (ETSI).

[2] Burgess, John, "Competing in a Diverse Market," *The Washington Post,* December 6, 1991: p.A1.

[3] Farren, J. Michael, "The New Europe and Global Competitiveness," *Business America,* February 24, 1992: p.2.

[4] *ibid.,* p.6.

[5] Hockman, Kymm, "ISO 9000: Opportunity or Nightmare?" *ISO 9000 News,* Volume 1, Number 1, January 1992.

[6] Meckstroth, Daniel, *The European Community's New Approach to Regulation of Product Standards and Quality Assurance (ISO 9000): What It Means for US Manufacturers,* Manufacturers' Alliance for Manufacturing and Innovation, Washington, DC, 1992.

[7] *ibid.,* p.7.

[8] *ibid.,* p.13.

[9] *ibid.*

**2**

# OVERVIEW OF THE ISO 9000 SERIES STANDARD

## INTRODUCTION

This chapter is an overview of the ISO 9000 series standard. As mentioned in the first chapter, the ISO 9000 series includes generic standards that provide quality management guidance and identify generic quality system elements necessary to achieve quality assurance. An individual company determines how these standards are to be implemented to meet its specific needs and the needs of its customers.

The ISO 9000 series cover a broad scope of quality system elements. (See box on next page.) The ISO 9000 standards are basic and uncomplicated. A company that has achieved ISO 9000 system registration can attest that it has a documented quality system that is fully deployed and consistently followed. This does not necessarily imply that it produces products whose quality is superior to that of its competitor's products.

Basically, the ISO 9001, 9002, and 9003 standards require a company to document what it does and do what it documents. To illustrate the objective of ISO documentation: if a company suddenly replaced all personnel, their replacements, properly trained, could use the documentation to continue making the product or providing the service as before. ISO 9001, 9002, and 9003 requirements do not constitute a full-fledged *total quality management* system; rather, they are a necessary foundation for such a system.

---

### Quality System Elements in the ISO 9000 Series

| | |
|---|---|
| Management Responsibility | Quality System |
| Contract Review | Design Control |
| Document Control | Purchasing |
| Purchaser-Supplied Product | Product Identification and Traceability |
| Process Control | Inspection and Testing |
| Inspection, Measuring and Test Equipment | Inspection and Test Status |
| Control of Nonconforming Product | Corrective Action |
| Handling, Storage, Packaging and Delivery | Quality Records |
| Internal Quality Audits | Training |
| Servicing | Statistical Techniques |

---

# TYPES OF STANDARDS IN THE ISO 9000 SERIES

The basic ISO 9000 series is comprised of five standards: ISO 9000, ISO 9001, ISO 9002, ISO 9003, and ISO 9004. The standards are of two types: guidance standards and conformance standards.

ISO 9000 and ISO 9004 are *guidance standards*. This means they are **descriptive** documents, not prescriptive requirements. Companies do not register to either ISO 9000 or ISO 9004. Instead, they register to one of the *conformance standards*, ISO 9001, ISO 9002 or ISO 9003. These are models for quality systems.

# GUIDANCE STANDARDS

## ISO 9000

*ISO 9000: Quality management and quality assurance standards — Guidelines for selection and use*, explains fundamental quality concepts. It defines key terms and provides guidance on selecting, using, as well as tailoring ISO 9001, ISO 9002 and ISO 9003 for external quality assurance purposes. It also provides guidance on using ISO 9004 for internal quality management purposes. It is the "road map" for use of the entire series. ISO 9000 is explained more fully below.

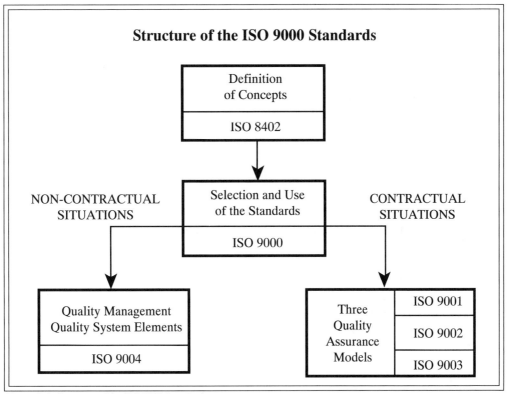

**Structure of the ISO 9000 Standards**

Definition
of Concepts

ISO 8402

NON-CONTRACTUAL
SITUATIONS

Selection and Use
of the Standards

ISO 9000

CONTRACTUAL
SITUATIONS

Quality Management
Quality System Elements

ISO 9004

Three
Quality
Assurance
Models

ISO 9001

ISO 9002

ISO 9003

*Figure 2-1: Structure of the ISO 9000 Standards.*

## Key Terms

As noted in the *Introduction* to the standard, "a principal factor in the performance of an organization is the quality of its products or services."

What is a **product**? A product is defined as "the result of activities or processes. It can be tangible or intangible, or a combination thereof." The ISO 9000 series standards classify products into generic product categories: hardware, software, processed materials and services. Note that from this broad point of view, a service is considered a product.

What is **quality**? Quality has many ordinary meanings. For example, quality often refers to "excellence" or some other subjective meaning.

# Definitions in ISO 9000

## Quality Policy

A company's quality policy is "the overall quality intentions and direction of an organization as regards quality, as formally expressed by top management." (ISO 9000, Clause 3.1) It is a key element of corporate policy.

## Quality Management

Quality management is "that aspect of the overall management function that determines and implements the quality policy." (ISO 9000, Clause 3.2) According to quality systems consultant Ian Durand, "Quality management is not separate from general management. When used effectively, quality management should be an integral part of an organization's overall management approach." That approach is designed to produce quality results for the customer.

## Quality System

According to ISO 9000, a quality system is "the organizational structure, responsibilities, procedures, processes and resources for implementing quality management." (ISO 9000, Clause 3.3) The quality should "only be as comprehensive as needed to meet quality objectives."

## Quality Control

ISO 9000 defines quality control as "the operational techniques and activities that are used to fulfill requirements for quality." (ISO 9000, Clause 3.4) Quality control is a broad concept. When referring to a sub-set of "company-wide quality control," companies should use modifying terms, such as "manufacturing quality control."

## Quality Assurance

Quality assurance includes "all those planned and systematic actions necessary to provide adequate confidence that a product or service will satisfy given requirements for quality." (ISO 9000, Clause 3.5) The purpose of quality assurance is to provide appropriate confidence that a product or service will satisfy specific quality requirements. The purpose of a quality assurance system is to prevent problems from occurring, detect them when they do, identify the cause, remedy the cause, and prevent reoccurrence. A more succinct summary is offered by Ian Durand. "The basics of a quality system," he says, "is to say what you do, do what you say, record what you did, check the results and act on the difference."

But in the quality field, the meaning is more specific. According to ISO 8402: *Quality management and quality assurance —Vocabulary,* quality is defined as

> *"the totality of characteristics of an entity that bear on its ability to satisfy stated or implied needs."*

In a contractual situation, "stated" needs are specified in the contract requirements. In other situations, "implied" needs should be identified and defined by the company. Needs are usually translated into product features and characteristics with specified criteria.

Most organizations produce products to meet specific criteria, such as technical specifications. However, as ISO 9000 notes, "technical specifications may not in themselves guarantee that a customer's requirements will be consistently met..." This realization has led to the development of "quality system standards and guidelines that **complement** relevant product or service requirements given in the technical specifications."

The ISO 9000 series embodies many of these standards and guidelines.

Section 3.0 of ISO 9000 defines five key terms necessary to understand properly the ISO 9000 series. (See box on previous page.) Figure 2-2 illustrates the relationship of these concepts.

## Quality Objectives

In Section 4.0: Principal Concepts, ISO 9000 describes an organization's three basic quality objectives. Each organization should:

- Achieve and sustain the quality of the product or service produced so as to meet continually the purchaser's stated or implied needs
- Provide confidence to its own management that the intended quality is being achieved and sustained
- Provide confidence to the purchaser that the intended quality is being, or will be, achieved in the delivered product or service provided.

## Contractual/Noncontractual Situations

Section 5.0 notes that the ISO 9000 series is intended to be used in two different situations: contractual and noncontractual.

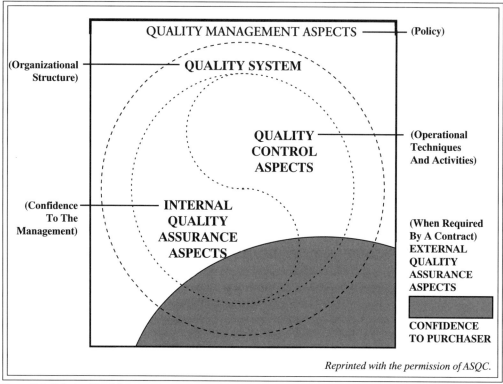

*Figure 2-2: Relationship of Concepts.*

In both *contractual* and *noncontractual* situations, an organization wants to install and maintain a quality system to strengthen its competitiveness and to achieve the needed product quality in a cost-effective way.

Additionally, in the *contractual* situation, the purchaser wants to know whether his supplier can produce products or services that consistently meet necessary requirements. According to the ISO 9000 series, in a contractual situation, both supplier and customer must agree on what is acceptable.

## Internal vs. External Quality Assurance

Section 6.0 defines the type of standards that comprise the ISO 9000 series. ISO 9000 and ISO 9004, which are guidance standards, give guidance to "all organizations for quality management purposes." These documents are used for internal quality assurance, "which are "activities aimed at providing confidence to the management of an organization that the intended quality is being achieved."

ISO 9001, ISO 9002 and ISO 9003, which are conformance standards, are used for *external quality assurance.* External quality assurance refers to:

> *activities aimed at providing confidence to the purchaser that the supplier's quality system will provide a product or service that will satisfy the purchaser's stated quality requirements.*

## Other Sections in ISO 9000

Sections 7.0 and 8.0 examine how organizations can use ISO 9004 for internal quality management purposes and how to select among the three conformance models for quality assurance (ISO 9001, ISO 9002 or ISO 9003). The guidance on selection is discussed below.

**Clause 8.3:** Demonstration and Documentation states that the quality system elements chosen by the organization "should be documented and demonstrable in a manner consistent with the requirements of the selected model."

The nature of these elements and the degree to which they should be documented and demonstrated can vary, according to criteria such as the:

- Use of the product or service
- Complexity of the design
- Complexity and difficulty of production
- Ability to judge product quality and fitness for use on the basis of final product test alone
- Safety requirements of the product or service
- Past performance of the supplier.

**Clause 8.4:** Pre-Contract Assessment, recognizes that an assessment of a supplier's quality system is performed prior to a contract to determine the supplier's ability to satisfy the requirements of the standard.

This assessment may be delegated to a third-party organization. The number or "the extent of assessments can be minimized" by using one of the ISO 9000 standards and by recognizing previous assessments.

**Clause 8.5:** Contract Preparation Aspects, discusses various aspects of contract preparation, including:

- Tailoring standards to meet the needs of specific contracts
- Review of contractual quality system elements by both parties
- Use of supplementary quality assurance requirements where necessary, such as quality plans, programs, audit plans, etc.
- Technical requirements, which are defined in the technical specifications of the contract.

# ISO 9004

*ISO 9004: Quality management and quality system elements —Guidelines,* provides guidance to all organizations for internal quality management purposes, without regard to external contractual requirements of quality assurance. ISO 9004 examines most of the quality system elements contained in ISO 9001, ISO 9002 and ISO 9003 in greater detail. It can help organizations determine the extent to which each quality system is applicable to them.

Throughout ISO 9004, "emphasis is placed on the satisfaction of the customer's need, the establishment of functional responsibilities, and the importance of assessing, as far as possible, the potential risks and benefits."

## Organizational Goals

ISO 9004 recommends each company organize itself "in such a way that the technical, administrative, and human factors affecting the quality of its products and services will be under control." The aim is to reduce, eliminate and prevent quality deficiencies.

To achieve its objectives, companies should develop a quality system that is "appropriate to the type of activity and to the product or service being offered." An effective quality system should be designed to satisfy customer needs and expectations while serving to protect the company's interests.

## Topics Covered

ISO 9004 describes elements of a quality management system. The:

> *selection of appropriate elements...and the extent to which these elements are adopted and applied by a company depends upon factors such as market being served, nature of product, production processes, and consumer needs.*

ISO 9004 covers the following general topics:

- Management Responsibility (4.0)
- Quality System Principles (5.0)
- Economics - Quality-Related Cost Considerations (6.0)
- Quality in Marketing (7.0)
- Quality in Specification and Design (8.0)
- Quality in Procurement (9.0)
- Quality in Production (10.0)
- Control of Production (11.0)
- Product Verification (12.0)
- Control of Measuring and Test Equipment (13.0)
- Nonconformity (14.0)
- Corrective Action (15.0)
- Handling and Post-Production Functions (16.0)
- Quality Documentation and Records (17.0)
- Personnel (18.0)
- Product Safety and Liability (19.0)
- Use of Statistical Methods (20.0).

The topics discussed in ISO 9004 cover the full range of quality system elements. (Guidance offered by ISO 9004, cross-referenced to the corresponding clauses in ISO 9001, will be described in Chapter 3.)

# CONFORMANCE STANDARDS

ISO 9001, ISO 9002 and ISO 9003 are models used for external quality assurance. Each standard contains a set of necessary quality system elements. ISO 9001 is the most comprehensive standard while ISO 9003 is the least comprehensive. Each model is a complete, independent document. A company should select the appropriate conformance model after a thorough assessment of its quality system needs. Table 2-1 compares the the quality system elements contained in each model.

## ISO 9001

*ISO 9001: Quality systems - Model for quality assurance in design/development, production, installation and servicing* is the most comprehensive of the conformance standards. It includes all elements listed in ISO 9002 and ISO 9003. In addition, it addresses the design, development and servicing capabilities not addressed in the other models.

ISO 9001 is used when the supplier must ensure product conformance to specified needs throughout the entire product cycle. It is used when the contract specifically requires a design effort. It is also used when product requirements are stated principally in performance terms.

ISO 9001 commonly applies to manufacturing or processing industries, but it can also be applied to services like construction, or to professional services, such as architecture and engineering. (The requirements of ISO 9001 are discussed in detail in Chapter 3.)

## ISO 9002

*ISO 9002: Quality systems - Model for quality assurance in production and installation* addresses the prevention, detection and correction of problems during production and installation. The main distinction between ISO 9001 and ISO 9002 is that ISO 9002 does not include the design function.

ISO 9002 applies to a wide range of industries whose work is based on technical designs and specifications provided by their customers. It is relevant for products that do not involve a design aspect and is used when the specified product requirements are stated in terms of an already-established design or specification.

(All clauses in ISO 9002 are in ISO 9001; therefore, they are discussed in Chapter 3.)

## ISO 9003

*ISO 9003: Quality systems - Model for quality assurance in final inspection and test* is the least comprehensive standard. It addresses only the requirements for detection and control of problems during final inspection and testing. ISO 9003 applies to organizations whose products or services can be adequately assessed by testing and inspection. Generally, this refers to less- complex products or services.

# SELECTING THE MODEL FOR QUALITY ASSURANCE

ISO 9000, Section 8.0, offers guidance to selecting the appropriate model for quality assurance. ISO 9000 lists six factors to be considered when choosing to become registered to ISO 9001, ISO 9002 or ISO 9003. The choice of which model to select depends on the functional or organizational capability required of a supplier.

| Cross-Reference List of Qualty System Elements | | | | |
|---|---|---|---|---|
| **Paragraph (or Subsection) in Q94** | | **Corresponding Paragraph (or Subsection) Nos. in:** | | |
| **No.** | **Title** | **Q91** | **Q92** | **Q93** |
| 4 | Management Responsibility | 4.1 ◆ | 4.1 ● | 4.1 ○ |
| 5 | Quality System Principles | 4.2 ◆ | 4.2 ◆ | 4.2 |
| 5.4 | Auditing the Quality System (Internal) | 4.17 ◆ | 4.16 1 | — |
| 6 | Economics—Quality-Related Cost Considerations | — | — | — |
| 7 | Quality in Marketing (Contract Review) | 4.3 ◆ | 4.3 ◆ | — |
| 8 | Quality in Specification and Design (Design Control) | 4.4 ◆ | — | — |
| 9 | Quality in Procurement (Purchasing) | 4.6 ◆ | 4.5 ◆ | — |
| 10 | Quality in Production (Process Control) | 4.9 ◆ | 4.8 ◆ | — |
| 11 | Control of Production | 4.9 ◆ | 4.8 ◆ | — |
| 11.2 | Material Control and Traceability (Product Identification and Traceability) | 4.8 ◆ | 4.7 ◆ | 4.4 ● |
| 11.7 | Control of Verification Status (Inspection & Test Status) | 4.12 ◆ | 4.11 ◆ | 4.7 ● |
| 12 | Product Verification (Inspection and Testing) | 4.10 ◆ | 4.9 ◆ | 4.5 |
| 13 | Control of Measuring and Test Equipment (Inspection, Measuring and Test Equipment) | 4.11 ◆ | 4.10 ◆ | 4.6 |
| 14 | Nonconformity (Control of Nonconforming Product) | 4.13 ◆ | 4.12 ◆ | 4.8 |
| 15 | Corrective Action | 4.14 ◆ | 4.13 ◆ | — |
| 16 | Handling and Post-Production Functions (handling, Storage, Packaging and Delivery) | 4.15 ◆ | 4.14 ◆ | 4.9 |
| 16.2 | After-Sales Servicing | 4.19 ◆ | — | — |
| 17 | Quality Documentation & Records (Document Control) | 4.5 ◆ | 4.4 ◆ | 4.3 ● |
| 17.3 | Quality Records | 4.16 ◆ | 4.15 ◆ | 4.10 |
| 18 | Personnel (Training) | 4.18 ◆ | 4.17 ● | 4.11 ○ |
| 19 | Product Safety and Liability | — | — | — |
| 20 | Use of Statistical Methods (Statistical Techniques) | 4.20 ◆ | 4.18 ◆ | 4.12 |
| — | Purchaser Supplied Product | 4.7 ◆ | 4.6 ◆ | — |

**KEY:** ◆ Full Requirement; ● Less Stringent than ANSI/ASQC Q91; ○ Less Stringent than ANSI/ASQC Q92
— Element Not Present

**NOTES:**
1. *The paragraph (or subsection) titles quoted in the table above have been taken from Q94; the titles given in parentheses have been taken from the corresponding paragraphs and subsections in Q91, Q92 and Q93.*
2. *Attention is drawn to the fact that the quality system element requirements in Q91, Q92 and Q93 are in many cases, but not in every case, identical.*

*Reprinted with the permission of ASQC.*

*Table 2-1: Cross-reference list of quality system elements.*

Companies should take into account the following six considerations:

- Complexity and difficulty of the design process
- Design maturity
- Production process complexity
- Product or service characteristics (complexity, number, criticality)
- Product or service safety
- Economic costs of the preceding factors versus the costs due to nonconformities.

After a company consults ISO 9000, it should consult ISO 9004 "in order to develop and implement a quality system and to determine the extent to which each quality system element is applicable." ISO 9004 can help every company develop a thorough internal quality assurance system.

# THE ISO 9001 STANDARD

## INTRODUCTION

ISO 9001 is the most comprehensive conformance model and includes all the clauses contained in ISO 9002 and ISO 9003. This chapter discusses the requirements of ISO 9001 in detail. It includes guidelines taken from ISO 9000-2: *Quality management and quality assurance - Part 2: Generic guidelines for the application of ISO 9001, ISO 9002 and ISO 9003*. Like ISO 9000 and ISO 9004, ISO 9000-2 is a guidance document; companies do not seek to become registered to any of these documents but rather use them for assistance when implementing ISO 9001, ISO 9002 or ISO 9003.

This chapter also includes guidance from ISO 9004 and, where appropriate, interpretation of ISO 9001 elements by experts in the field. (See p. 341 for complete biographies.) This "interpretation" takes two forms: comments by The Victoria Group, a management consulting company in the quality field; and question-and-answer interpretations which previously appeared in *Quality Systems Update* newsletter.

## Basic Definitions

It is important to define three key terms before discussing ISO 9001 in detail: supplier, purchaser and subcontractor.

A *supplier* is the organization providing a product to the customer. In a contractual situation, the supplier is the producer.

The *purchaser* is the recipient of products or services delivered by the supplier. (The 1992 version of the ISO 9000 series standard plans to use the term "customer" rather than "purchaser.")

The *subcontractor* is the organization that provides products or services to the supplier. (Note that an organization can be a supplier, a purchaser and a subcontractor at the same time.)

Differences in terminology used in ISO 9001 (and ISO 9002 and ISO 9003) compared to that used in ISO 9004 are occasionally confusing. This is brought about in part since ISO 9001, ISO 9002 and ISO 9003 contractual standards are **external**, with language expressed from the point of view of a third-party auditor. ISO 9004 guidelines are **internal**, expressed from the point of view of the company itself.

A major source of confusion is the different uses of the term "supplier." Plans for the 1992 revision of the standards include changing the ISO 9004 use of the term "supplier" to "subcontractor," to avoid the use of "supplier" entirely. This change should minimize the confusion when standards ISO 9001 and ISO 9004 are used together.

Table 3-1 charts the various ways in which these terms are used, not only in the ISO 9000 series, but also in the US DoD's military standards, the US Food and Drug Administration's Good Manufacturing Practices requirements, and in the Malcolm Baldrige National Quality Award Criteria.

# 4.0 QUALITY SYSTEM REQUIREMENTS

The main body of ISO 9001 is contained in the quality system requirements of Section 4.0. There are 20 clauses in all. The first quality system requirement is management responsibility.

| Terms Describing Purchaser/Supplier Relationships in Quality System Standards | | | |
|---|---|---|---|
| | **Companies Supplying Products/Services To You** | **Your Organization** | **Companies To Whom You Provide Products/Services** |
| **ISO 9001, 2, 3 (Contractual/ External)** | Subcontractor | Supplier | Purchaser |
| **ISO 9004 (Guidelines, Internal)** | Supplier | Company | Customer |
| **Military Standards MIL-Q-9858A MIL-I-45208** | Subcontractor | Contractor | Procurer |
| **Medical Device Good Manufacturing Practices (GMPs)** | Component Supplier | Manufacturer | User |
| **Malcolm Baldridge National Quality Award Criteria** | Supplier | Company | Customer |
| From chart developed by Dale Thanig, Nicolet Instrument Corporation. | | | |

*Table 3-1: Terms describing purchaser/supplier relationships in quality system standards.*

# ISO 9001: Key Points

The introductory clause of ISO 9001 gives an overview of the structure of the ISO 9000 series, explains the applicability of each section and emphasizes significant aspects of the ISO 9001 standard. There are several key points to note:

First, the *Introduction* states that "the alternative quality assurance models...represent three *distinct* forms of functional or organizational capability." In other words, ISO 9001, ISO 9002 and ISO 9003 do not represent three steps on a ladder of excellence but rather are separate, independent standards. The appropriate standard to use depends on the activity of the business being registered.

The introduction further explains that requirements specified in the standard are always *complementary (not alternative)* to the technical (product/service) requirements. The product specifications remain part of the requirement.

ISO 9000 series registration does not solve all problems, nor is registration a substitute for complying with the regulatory requirements of government agencies such as the US Environmental Protection Agency (EPA).

Section 1.0 states that "the requirements specified in this International Standard are aimed *primarily at preventing nonconformity* at all stages from design through to servicing." The emphasis is on prevention of quality problems. A system of prevention, monitored through all stages of design, production and servicing, is used in quality management. The language of ISO 9001 thus mirrors the tenets of Total Quality Management (TQM).

Sections 2.0 and 3.0 stress the importance of ensuring that related documents or special definitions are made clear to all readers. International Standard ISO 8402 should be used as a reference for standard quality terminology, thereby ensuring wide reader understanding.

*The Victoria Group*

# 4.1 MANAGEMENT RESPONSIBILITY

## Introduction

This clause details the responsibility of management for developing a quality system. Basically, four management responsibilities are called for:

- Establish a quality policy
- Organize personnel
- Verify quality
- Review the quality system.

## 4.1.1 Quality Policy

### *ISO 9001 Requirements*

The organization shall:

- Define quality policy, quality objectives, quality commitment
- Document the quality policy
- Make sure everyone in the organization understands, implements and maintains the policy.

### *ISO 9000-2 Guidance*

ISO 8402, *Quality Management and Quality Assurance - Vocabulary,* defines a quality policy as:

> *the overall intentions and direction of an organization as regards quality, as formally expressed by top management. The quality policy forms one element of the corporate policy and is authorized by top management.*

ISO 9000-2 recommends that management ensure the quality policy is:

- Easy to understand
- Relevant to the organization
- Ambitious, yet achievable

Commitment to a quality policy starts at the top of an organization. Management should demonstrate its commitment visibly, actively and continually.

### ISO 9004 Guidance

In Section 4.0: Management Responsibility, ISO 9004 counsels that management should:

- Define objectives pertaining to key elements of quality, such as fitness for use, performance, safety and reliability
- Consider the costs associated with all quality elements to minimize quality losses
- Ensure that appropriate levels of management define specialized quality objectives.

## 4.1.2 Organization

### 4.1.2.1 Responsibility and Authority

### ISO 9001 Requirements

The organization shall define the responsibility, authority and the interrelation of all personnel affecting the quality of product and service to customers.

This clause focuses on those personnel who must prevent the occurrence of product nonconformity, identify and record any product quality problems, recommend solutions, and verify their implementation. Finally, they must control further processing, delivery or installation of nonconforming products until the problem has been corrected.

### ISO 9000-2 Guidance

Individuals in the organization should:

- Be aware of the scope, responsibility and authority of their functions
- Be aware of their impact on product and service quality
- Have adequate authority to carry out their responsibilities
- Understand clearly their defined authority
- Accept responsibility for achieving quality objectives.

### ISO 9004 Guidance

Key points from ISO 9004, Section 4.0, suggest that management should:

- Provide sufficient resources to achieve its objectives
- Determine the level of competence, experience and training necessary
- Control all activities affecting quality

- Emphasize preventive actions to avoid occurrence of problems
- State written procedures simply, unambiguously and clearly
- Indicate methods to be used and the criteria to be satisfied.

## 4.1.2.2 Verification Resources and Personnel

### *ISO 9001 Requirements*

Management shall make sure the company has adequate resources and trained personnel to carry out any verification work. Verification activities include:

- Inspection, testing, and monitoring
- Design reviews
- Quality system audits.

The standard also requires that:

> *Verification activities shall include inspection, test, and monitoring of the design, production, installation, and servicing of the process and/or product; design reviews and audits of the quality system, processes, and/or product shall be carried out by personnel independent of those having direct responsibility for the work being performed.*

**[EDITOR'S NOTE:** *This requirement — that design reviews and audits by carried out by personnel independent of those directly responsible for the work — applies **only** to design reviews and audits of the quality system, **not** to the inspection, test and monitoring of other functions, such as production, installation and servicing. The semicolon in the exact wording of the sentence from ISO 9001 is extremely important. This issue will be addressed in the 1992 revision of the ISO 9001 standard.]*

### *ISO 9000-2 Guidance*

Effective verification requires objectivity and cooperation among those involved. Adequate verification resources and personnel can involve the following elements:

- Awareness of standards
- Adequate training
- Production schedules that allow time for inspection, testing and verification
- Appropriate equipment
- Documented procedures
- Access to quality records.

### 4.1.2.3 Management Representative

*ISO 9001 Requirements*

Management shall appoint a management representative who has authority to implement and maintain the quality system.

*ISO 9000-2 Guidance*

If the management representative has other functions to perform, there should be no conflict of interest involved.

## 4.1.3 Management Review

*ISO 9001 Requirements*

Management shall:

- Conduct regular management reviews of the system to make sure it remains suitable and effective
- Keep records of its reviews.

*ISO 9000-2 Guidance*

The scope of reviews should encompass:

- Organizational structure
- Implementation of the quality system
- Achieve quality of the product or service
- Information based on purchaser feedback, internal audits, process and product performance.

The frequency of reviews is not specified but depends on individual circumstances. In terms of follow-up, problems should be documented, analyzed and resolved. Required changes to the quality system should be implemented in a timely manner.

## Management Review

The management representative is an individual who, "**irrespective** of other responsibilities," has the duty and authority to ensure that the requirements of the ISO standard are maintained. While it does not matter who performs this task, it does matter that it be handled seriously.

Clause 4.1.3: Management Review, makes a distinction between reviewing and maintaining the quality system in a way which meets the standard. Management's role is to review and maintain the system; any suitably skilled personnel can perform the system audits.

The management review requirement is often mishandled. Management must be concerned with the overall process, not just with audit results. The following questions can serve as guidelines:

○ Is the system working effectively?

○ What are the quality metrics, both internal and external?

○ Will changes be made within the operation of the company that will radically affect the system?

○ Is technology changing in a way that necessitates rewriting documentation?

○ Is the company achieving its quality objectives?

*The Victoria Group*

# 4.2 QUALITY SYSTEM

### *ISO 9001 Requirements*

Clause 4.2 requires companies to prepare a documented quality system. This means preparing documented quality procedures and instructions and effectively implementing them. Specific elements noted for meeting this requirement are:

■ Preparation of a quality plan and a quality manual
■ Identification of controls, resources and skills necessary to achieve required quality

- Updating quality control, inspection and testing techniques as necessary
- Identification of extraordinary measurement requirements
- Clarifying standards of acceptability
- Ensuring the compatibility of the design, production, installation, inspection and test procedures
- Identifying and preparing quality records.

## *ISO 9000-2 Guidance*

The quality manual can be structured as a tiered set of documents, with each tier becoming more detailed. Quality policy would be the top tier while detailed instructions and record-keeping forms would be at the lower tier.

Quality plans define how quality system requirements will be met in a specific contract or for a specific class of products. An example might include a detailed sequence of inspections for a particular product, types of inspection equipment and quality record requirements.

## *ISO 9004 Guidance*

In Clause 4.4.4, ISO 9004 stresses that the goal of the quality system is to provide confidence that:

- The system is understood and effective
- Products and services actually satisfy requirements and customer expectations
- Emphasis is on problem prevention rather than detection after occurrence.

The quality system applies to all activities related to the quality of a product or service. These activities range from initial market research and design through to installation, servicing and disposal after use.

Marketing and design are especially important for determining and defining customer needs and product requirements.

# ISO 9000 Interpretation
## Clause 4.2 - Quality Plans

*By:* **Ian Durand,** President, Service Process Consulting, Inc.
**Joseph Tiratto,** Consultant
**Charles McRobert,** President, Quality Practitioners, Inc.
**Clyde Brewer,** Consultant

**Questions:**

What is a quality plan?
Is a quality plan mandatory?
Is a quality plan product-specific, or is it a project plan?

**Answer:**

Tiratto, Brewer, and McRobert agreed that while a quality plan is encouraged in ISO 9001 and ISO 9002, it is not mandatory. McRobert and Brewer said that quality plans are mentioned in Note (a) of Clause 4.2, but notes are not part of the requirements of the standard. Notes are interpretative, not prescriptive.

Durand indicated that the TC 176 Working Group updating ISO 9001, ISO 9002, and ISO 9003 is considering making quality plans mandatory in the next revision of these standards. The basic standards in the ISO 9000 series were published in 1987; ISO rules require a review of every standard at five-year intervals. TC 176 is working simultaneously on the next two revisions, targeted for 1992 and 1996.

Tiratto noted that a new standard is being developed by an ISO TC 176 Working Group that will contain detailed guidance on quality plans. Tiratto says the quality plan may be used either as a product-specific plan or as a project plan to define how the quality system requirements will be met.

McRobert and Brewer agreed that a quality plan can be either product-specific or a project plan. McRobert said that ISO 9004, Clause 5.3.3, contains product-specific recommendations.

Additionally, Brewer said that references for quality plans can be found in Sections 4.10.1, 4.10.2 and 4.10.3, which refer to inspection and testing. Durand noted that design and development plans are required by Clause 4.4.2.

Sections 4.1, 4.2, 4.4, 4.9 and 4.10 refer to plans or objectives. Fifteen clauses do not refer to plans. However, all of these sections do require procedures.

# 4.3 CONTRACT REVIEW

### *ISO 9001 Requirements*

It is important for the supplier thoroughly to understand the purchaser's needs. The objective of contract review is to make sure that:

■ Contracts truly reflect adequately defined and documented requirements
■ Any requirements differing from those in the statement of requirements are resolved
■ The supplier is capable of meeting the contract requirements.

Clause 4.3 requires companies to:

■ Establish and maintain procedures for contract review and coordination of contract review
■ Maintain records of contract reviews.

In a note to Clause 4.3, ISO 9001 suggests that coordination of contract review activities with the purchaser's organization is appropriate.

### *ISO 9000-2 Guidance*

The contract review process steps are:

■ Review the contract
■ Achieve agreement
■ Discuss results of contract review
■ Discuss draft quality plan (if existing).

The contract review procedure should have the following features:

■ An opportunity for all interested parties to review the contract
■ A verification checklist
■ A method for questioning the contract requirements and addressing the questions
■ A draft quality plan
■ Provision for changing the contract.

### ISO 9004 Guidance

ISO 9004, Section 7.0: *Quality in Marketing,* discusses the role of the marketing function in establishing quality requirements for the product. Marketing should determine the need for a product or service, define the market demand accurately, determine customer requirements, and communicate these requirements clearly within the company.

These product requirements can be detailed in a statement, such as a *product brief* which "translates customer requirements and expectations into a preliminary set of specifications as the basis for subsequent design work."

A product brief may include the following elements:

- Performance characteristics (e.g., environmental and usage conditions and reliability)
- Sensory characteristics (e.g., style, color, taste, smell)
- Installation configuration or fit
- Applicable standards and statutory regulations
- Packaging
- Quality assurance/verification.

The marketing function should establish an "information monitoring and feedback system…" to analyze the quality of a product or service.

---

### Clause 4.3 - Contract Review

Contract review is another area that is often poorly handled. The requirement is hardly onerous or unreasonable — all that is asked is that there is a clear understanding of what the customer wants, that what has been ordered is the same as that for which a quote has been provided, and that the supplier can actually meet those requirements. Regarding this last point, for example, do not accept a contract that calls for a two week delivery if the best that the company can meet is ten weeks.

*The Victoria Group*

# 4.4 DESIGN CONTROL

The essential quality aspects of a product, such as safety, performance and dependability, are established during the design and development phase. Thus, deficient design can be a major cause of quality problems. The sub-sections of 4.4 are:

- Design and Development Planning
- Activity Assignment
- Organizational and Technical Interfaces
- Design Input
- Design Output
- Design Verification
- Design Changes.

## 4.4.1 General Requirement

### *ISO 9001 Requirements*

Suppliers shall establish and maintain procedures to control and verify the design of the product to ensure that it meets specified requirements.

## 4.4.2 Design and Development Planning

### *ISO 9001 Requirements*

The supplier shall develop plans that identify the person(s) responsible for each design and development activity.

### *ISO 9000-2 Guidance*

Planning procedures should take into account:

- Sequential and parallel work activities
- Design verification activities
- Evaluating the safety, performance and dependability incorporated in the product design
- Product measurement, test and acceptance criteria
- Assignment of responsibilities.

### 4.4.2.1 Activity Assignment

*ISO 9001 Requirements*

The supplier shall plan and assign design and verification activities to quality staff equipped with adequate resources.

*ISO 9000-2 Guidance*

ISO 9000-2 notes that design activities should be sufficiently specific and detailed to permit effective verification.

### 4.4.2.2 Organizational and Technical Interfaces

*ISO 9001 Requirements*

Design input can come from a variety of sources. The responsibilities and authorities of these sources shall be defined, documented, coordinated and controlled. The basic requirements are to:

- Identify the interfaces between different groups
- Document, transmit and regularly review the necessary information.

*ISO 9000-2 Guidance*

To function effectively, the information procedure should establish:

- What information should be received and transmitted
- Identification of senders and receivers
- Purpose of information
- Identification of transmittal mechanism
- Document transmittal records to be maintained.

## 4.4.3 Design Input

*ISO 9001 Requirements*

Design inputs are usually in the form of product performance specifications or product descriptions with specifications. The supplier shall:

- Identify all design input requirements pertinent to the product
- Review their selection by the supplier for adequacy
- Resolve incomplete, ambiguous or conflicting requirements.

### *ISO 9000-2 Guidance*

A *design description document* can serve as a definitive reference throughout the design process. It should quantify all requirements as much as possible, with details agreed between the purchaser and supplier. The document should identify design aspects, materials, and processes that require development, including prototype testing.

## 4.4.4. Design Output

### *ISO 9001 Requirements*

Design outputs can include drawings, specifications, instructions, software and servicing procedures. Outputs of the detailed design are the final technical documents used throughout the production process. The requirements are to:

- Document design output in terms of requirements, calculations and analyses
- Ensure that design output meets input requirements, contains acceptance criteria, conforms to regulations, and identifies critical characteristics of the design.

### *ISO 9000-2 Guidance*

Design outputs are the final technical documents used throughout the process, from production through servicing. Design outputs should show how they incorporate the design input requirements.

## 4.4.5 Design Verification

### *ISO 9001 Requirements*

The supplier shall establish a design verification plan to ensure that the output meets input requirements.

### *ISO 9000-2 Guidance*

Design control measures should include design reviews, qualification tests, alternative calculations and comparisons with proven designs.

In most cases, two or more of these measures are used. Design reviews and/or type-testing may be a regulatory requirement. Design verification should involve personnel independent of those who did the work under review.

ISO 9000-2 includes many questions that the design review can address. Some of these are:

- Do design reviews satisfy all specified requirements?
- Are product design and processing capabilities compatible?
- Are safety considerations covered?
- Are the materials and/or facilities appropriate?
- Arc components or service elements standardized?
- Are purchasing, production, installation, inspection and testing plans technically feasible?
- Has software been validated, authorized and verified?
- Where qualification tests have been performed, were the conditions representative of actual use?

## 4.4.6 Design Changes

### *ISO 9001 Requirements*

Designs may be changed or modified for many reasons. Changes to design inputs shall be reviewed to determine whether they influence previously approved designs. The requirement is to: establish and maintain procedures for appropriate review and approval of design changes.

### *ISO 9000-2 Guidance*

Design changes in one component should be evaluated for their effect on the overall product. Sometimes, improving one characteristic may have an unforeseen adverse influence on another. The new design output should be communicated to all concerned and the changes documented.

### *Design - ISO 9004 Guidance*

Section 8.0: *Quality in Specification and Design,* discusses the specification and design function in detail. The overall design function should "result in a product that provides customer satisfaction at an acceptable price that enables a satisfactory return on investment for the enterprise."

The product must be "producible, verifiable, and controllable under the proposed production, installation, commissioning, or operational conditions."

## Clause 4.4 - Design Control

"Design output meets design input," sums up the entire intent of the design requirements. Clause 4.4 can be met following this suggested road map:

1. Plan what is to be done.

2. Document that plan.

3. Assign someone to review the contract and document the designated person.

4. Create an input specification which includes "acceptance criteria."

5. Follow up as progress is made and make sure that the plan is still being followed.

6. Review how the system is working with the involved employees, and document the progress.

7. At the end of the task, make sure the output matches the input.

8. Conduct tests and keep records. Do these in accordance with the "acceptance criteria" in step (4.) above.

9. Make sure that a good method of tracking changes is in place and that everyone understands the rationale for all changes made.

*The Victoria Group*

The topics covered in Section 8.0 include the following:

- Design Planning and Objectives (Defining the Project)
- Product Testing and Measurement
- Design Qualification and Validation
- Elements of Design Review
- Design Verification
- Design Baseline and Production Release
- Market Readiness Review
- Design Change Control
- Design Requalification.

These topics expand on subjects covered in ISO 9001. The results of the final design review should be "appropriately documented in specifications and drawings that define the design baseline." The quality system should provide for a market readiness review to "determine whether production capability and field support are adequate for the new or redesigned product."

ISO 9004 discusses design change control. The quality system should provide a procedure for "controlling the release, change and use of documents that define the design baseline and for authorizing the necessary work" to implement changes throughout the product cycle.

ISO 9004 stresses the need for "periodic re-evaluation" of the product to ensure that the design is still valid compared to all specified requirements.

# 4.5 DOCUMENT CONTROL

## 4.5.1 Document Approval and Issue

### *ISO 9001 Requirements*

The supplier shall:

- Establish and maintain procedures to control all documents and data
- Review and approve documents for adequacy prior to issue. The appropriate documents should be available where needed and obsolete documents must be promptly removed.

### *ISO 9000-2 Guidance*

Document control applies to all documents and/or computer records pertinent to design, purchasing, production, quality standards, inspection of materials and internal written procedures. Internal written procedures describe:

- How documentation for these functions should be controlled
- Who is responsible for document control
- What is to be controlled
- Where and when the control is to take place.

### *ISO 9004 Guidance*

ISO 9004, Section 17.0: *Quality Documentation and Records,* offers examples of the types of quality documents that require control:

- Drawings
- Specifications
- Blueprints
- Inspection instructions
- Test procedures
- Work instructions
- Operation sheets
- Quality manual
- Operational procedures
- Quality assurance procedures.

It also stresses that "sufficient records be maintained to demonstrate achievement of the required quality and verify effective operation of the quality management system." ISO 9004 gives examples of the types of quality records that require control:

- Inspection reports
- Test data
- Qualification reports
- Validation reports
- Audit reports
- Material review reports
- Calibration data
- Quality cost reports.

## 4.5.2 Document Changes / Modifications

### *ISO 9001 Requirements*

The organization shall:

- Identify changes in documents
- Review and approve changes to documents
- Establish a master list of documents to identify the current version
- Re-issue documents after a "practical" number of changes have been made.

# ISO 9000 Interpretation:
# Document Control Requirements Of The ISO 9000 Series Standard

*By:* **Charles McRobert,** President, Quality Practitioners, Inc.
**Ian Durand,** President, Service Process Consulting, Inc.
**David Middleton,** Vice-President, Excel Partnership, Inc.
**Joseph Tiratto,** President, Joseph Tiratto and Associates, Inc.

## Question:

Does ISO 9001, Clause 4.5: Document Control, cover all documents in the company or only documents covering product technical information? What are some of the general requirements of this clause?

## Answer:

The experts agreed that language used in ISO 9001, Clause 4.5: Document Control, is drafted broadly.

McRobert stressed that "a document is any means of conveying technical information concerning the product or the quality system from the conceptual phase to installation and servicing."

The list of controlled documents includes product drawings and specifications, quality manuals, procedures, process sheet specifications, recipes, formulations, purchase orders, product labels, packaging instructions, product rosters, training records, contracts, and inspection and test criteria.

Middleton noted that the "scope of the quality system should define the service provided within a company's scope of activities." Middleton said, for example, a customs clearance company should include customer notification under its controlled document plan if informing customers of delays is part of that company's scope of activities. In another example, a manufacturer of general engineered products would not need to control documents covering analysis of wage rates since that document does not directly impact product quality.

Middleton pointed out that document control is a common weak link found during third-party audits. He said this problem is usually remedied by identifying "relevant documents" (those that directly impact product or service quality) and demonstrating document control by date, review status, approval, and master list. For further guidance on the issue, Middleton suggested reading Section 17 of ISO 9004.

Tiratto noted that guidance on this issue can be found in *ISO 9000-2, Generic guidelines for the application of ISO 9001, ISO 9002, and ISO 9003*. Tiratto said this document states that document control should include "those documents and/or computer records pertinent to inspection of materials and the supplier's internal written procedures which describe the control of documentation for these functions."

Tiratto noted further that Clause 4.5 of ISO 9001 requires controls for the preparation, handling, issue and recording of changes to documents. He pointed out that this requirement "applies not only to internal documentation, but also to externally updated documentation."

---

### Clause 4.5 - Document Control

Poor document control is something that frequently lets companies down, and it is very important. ISO 9001 requires that there be a master list of every document that forms part of the controlled system, so that it is clear as to which specific documents make up that system. A master list also makes it possible for those using documents to make sure that they have the right one. It is appropriate that a master set of each document on the master list accompany that list. In addition, it is useful that copies of all documents be distributed where they are likely to be used.

Make sure that relevant paperwork and documents are where they are needed for people to do the job right. Put a system in place to ensure that when a document changes, all the old copies are removed to prevent accidental use. Also ensure that, when changes are made, either the original author makes them, or someone else who has all the relevant information.

*The Victoria Group*

---

### *ISO 9002 Guidance*

Supplier documentation is usually subject to revision. This requirement applies both to internal and external documentation, such as national standards. Organizations should consider the effect that changes in one area may have on other parts of the organization and the actions that should be taken to assess this effect. Other things to keep in mind include:

■ Planning the circulation of a change proposal to avoid disruption
■ Timing of the change implementation.

# ISO 9000 Interpretation:
## Review and Approval of Documents in ISO 9001 4.5.2

*By:* **Robert Peach,** Principal, Robert Peach and Associates, Inc.
**Joseph Tiratto,** President, Joseph Tiratto and Associates, Inc.
**Charles McRobert,** President, Quality Practitioners, Inc.
**Garnett Davis,** Operations Supervisor, Det Norske Veritas
Industry, Inc.

## Question:

Does the review and approval of documents in ISO 9001 4.5.2 have to be conducted by personnel **other** than the originator or the originating department?

## Answer:

All four experts agreed that the current version of ISO 9001 does not imply that the originator or the originating department cannot review and approve documents or changes to documents. However, all the experts did qualify the overall positive response.

According to Peach, the "intent of Clause 4.5.2 is to ensure that changes made in documents already issued follow the same approval process as conventional industry practice." Peach defined this process as a system in which a document is issued by a designated originating activity (department), before it passes through one or more approval stages. These stages may be organizationally in the same department or another department.

Meeting Clause 4.5.2 avoids the possibility of unauthorized changes being made in documents by short-circuiting the basic originator/approval process. Clause 4.5.1 makes it clear that the review / approval process is necessary for all documents."

Davis pointed to Clause 4.1.2.2 to clarify DnV's response:

"Clause 4.1.2.2 requires that design reviews and internal audits be performed by personnel independent of those having direct responsibility for the work being performed. To this end, it would not be acceptable for the same design engineer who performed the actual design development to also perform the design review and subsequent approval of the design documents."

Davis noted that the question concerning Clause 4.5.2 "is not directly related to the approval of design output documents." He concluded that the reference clarifies DnV's response.

McRobert said he agreed that no "requirement in the standard makes review and approval of a document by someone other than the originator mandatory." He did add his own caveat: "I personally believe that companies in which adequate staffing allows a document to be reviewed by others is beneficial. But where staff size or economics limits this activity, review and approval by the author is acceptable."

*(continued on next page)*

---

### ISO 9000 Interpretation:
### Review and Approval of Documents in ISO 9001 4.5.2

*(continued from previous page)*

Peach highlighted the Clause 4.5.2 phrase: "…unless specifically designated otherwise." He said that the phrase might be interpreted to "permit changes to be made in documents while circumventing the approval process." This phrase should not be a license for the supplier to decide arbitrarily that no approval for changes is required.

"On the contrary," Peach said, "if there are valid situations in which a change my be made without following the formal review justification process, those conditions should be specifically spelled out, with justification made to the registrar. The supplier is then obligated to demonstrate that the system is being followed."

#### Changes in 1992 Revisions

"Numerous appropriate situations for waiving approval exist," Peach concluded. "And it is likely that the phrase *unless specifically designated otherwise* will be carried over in the 1992 revision of ISO 9001." Peach cited one possible example where waiving the approval process might be acceptable: if a supplier had field-installation responsibilities and its qualified personnel were empowered to modify a product or practice on the spot, an approval mechanism might not be available or practical.

---

# 4.6 PURCHASING

## 4.6.1 General

### *ISO 9001 Requirements*

The supplier shall ensure that the purchased product conforms to specified requirements and regulatory requirements.

### *ISO 9000-2 Guidance*

Planned and adequately controlled purchasing procedures ensure that purchased sub-contracted products, including services, conform to specified requirements. Suppliers should establish effective working relationships and feedback systems with all subcontractors.

### *ISO 9004 Guidance*

Section 9.0: *Quality in Procurement,* discusses procurement quality in detail. The section states that "purchase materials, components, and assemblies become part of the company's product and directly affect the quality of its product." A procurement quality program should include the following elements:

- Requirements for specification, drawings, and purchase orders
- Selection of qualified suppliers
- Agreement on quality assurance
- Agreement on verification methods
- Provisions for settlement of quality disputes
- Receiving inspection planning and control
- Receiving quality records.

---

## Section 4.6 - Purchasing

The standard's use of the words *purchaser*, *supplier*, and *subcontractor* may confuse readers. The *purchaser* is the person or organization buying the goods or services produced within the system under review.

The *supplier* is the company or organization whose quality system is under discussion. The *subcontractor* is the vendor, supplier, or person from whom the company obtains materials, services, or personnel impacting the product or service the company sells.

The purchaser is **always** the party referred to as the customer. The supplier is **always** the company whose quality system is under review. The subcontractor is **always** the person from whom the supplier is buying product.

Clause 4.6 discusses the procurement operation of the company being registered. When the standard addresses the contractually required inspection of product at source or upon delivery, it refers to a customer's demand to inspect goods at the subcontractor's site before shipment to the supplier.

*The Victoria Group*

---

## 4.6.2 Assessment of Subcontractors

### *ISO 9001 Requirements*

The supplier shall:

- Select subcontractors on the basis of their ability to meet requirements
- Establish and maintain records of acceptable subcontractors
- Ensure that quality system controls are effective.

### *ISO 9000-2 Guidance*

The supplier may employ several ways for choosing satisfactory subcontractors, including:

- Reviewing previous performance in supplying similar products (including services)
- Satisfactory assessment of an appropriate quality system standard by a competent body
- Assessment of the subcontractor by the supplier to an appropriate quality system standard.

The supplier's quality records should be sufficiently comprehensive to demonstrate the ability of subcontractors to meet requirements. Factors can include:

- Product compliance with specified requirements
- Total cost for the supplier
- Delivery arrangements
- Subcontractor's own quality systems
- Performance of subcontractors (should be reviewed at appropriate intervals).

## 4.6.3 Purchasing Data

### *ISO 9001 Requirements*

The supplier shall:

- Clearly and specifically describe the product ordered in the purchasing document, including, where applicable:

  - Type, class, style, grade, or other precise identification
  - Title or other positive identification, and applicable issue of specifications, drawings, process requirements, inspection instructions, and other relevant data, including requirements for approval or qualification of product, procedures, process equipment and personnel
  - Title, number, and issue of the quality system standard that applies to the product

- Review and approve purchasing documents for adequacy of specified requirements.

### *ISO 9000-2 Guidance*

The purchasing data should define the technical product requirements to the subcon-

# ISO 9000 Interpretation:
## Assessment of Subcontractors - Ensuring an Effective System

*By:* **Ian Durand,** President of Service Process Consulting, Inc.
**Charles McRobert,** President, Quality Practitioners, Inc.
**Dennis Arter,** Senior Member, ASQC
**Robert Peach,** Principal, Robert Peach and Associates, Inc.

### Question:

What does "assessment" mean in ISO 9001, Clause 4.6.2: Assessment of Subcontractors? How does the supplier ensure that quality system controls are effective?

### Answer:

Durand noted that "in the context of ISO 9001, the term *assessment* means an evaluation with a scope that extends beyond quality requirements to include all requirements the supplier chooses to place on their selected sub-contractor" list. He said that *quality requirements* noted in the first sentence of Clause 4.6.2 could include service aspects such as "on-time delivery performance in addition to technical quality history."

In addition, Durand said the supplier might consider other factors such as the financial security, market position, interpersonal skills, and customer satisfaction policies of the subcontractor.

Durand pointed to Clause 4.10.1: Receiving Inspection and Testing, as a source of important information to "ensure that quality system controls are effective." He said that the ISO 9000 series "implicitly embeds closed-loop feedback controls throughout the quality **system**." He concluded that the "supplier should establish layered levels of measurements, analysis, problem detection, and action."

### Other Assessment Methods

McRobert agreed with Durand that technical, contractual requirements are only part of a prudent program of subcontractor assessment. McRobert listed several other possible methods of assessment, including previous history of subcontractor performance, testing of the subcontractor's product, and on-site quality system assessment. While subcontractor quality system requirements and on-site audits are not mandatory, McRobert preferred both assessment methods.

McRobert believed the clause is "poorly titled" since "assessment" in the title is described in the text as "selection based on the subcontractor's ability to meet contractual requirements." He said the title implies "that the *selection* activities comprise *assessment* for the purpose of the standard."

Arter and Peach also agreed that various methods can be used for assessment of subcontractors.

*(continued on next page)*

# ISO 9000 Interpretation:
## Assessment of Subcontractors - Ensuring an Effective System
*(continued from previous page)*

## Approved Supplier List

Arter said other possible assessment methods could include a listing in a register for a particular product line or written responses to a questionnaire. He said the process of evaluating potential suppliers must be documented in an in-house procedure and the results recorded. He noted that this record usually takes the form of an "Approved Supplier List," but it may be as simple as a notation or signature in the vendor's file folder.

The last sentence in Clause 4.6.2 calls for ensuring the effectiveness of controls. Arter called the sentence "ambiguous." He said suppliers must have a program for keeping approved suppliers on and off a list. Arter said supplier performance "needs to be evaluated on a periodic basis." He noted that some suppliers need an annual evaluation, while others might be evaluated every three years.

Finally, Arter said the effectiveness of a supplier selection process is examined through the internal audit program (ISO 9001, Clause 4.17) and the management review process (ISO 9001, Clause 4.1.3).

## Further Guidance

According to Peach, the term *assessment* as defined in the ISO 8402 standard "is more properly referred to as *quality evaluation*, and used to determine supplier quality capability." ISO 8402 states that "quality evaluation" may be used for qualification, approval, registration or accreditation purposes. Peach said further interpretation is provided by a review of British Standard 5750, Part 4, Clause 4.6.2: Assessment of Subcontractors (the British counterpart to ISO 9001), which states:

> "The supplier should be able to demonstrate that he continually reassesses subcontractors on the basis of performance during subcontracts and takes due account of such information when placing future subcontracts."

"The key," according to Peach, "is to be able to demonstrate continual or periodic reassessment of the evaluation process." He agreed with Arter, Durand and McRobert that this demonstration must be a documented system that shows the periodic review of the process, evidence of its effectiveness, and its implementation. Peach concluded the consideration of the type of product is extremely important, adding that the supplier should be able to demonstrate the process for deciding the level of content that is appropriate, considering factors such as the reliability of the purchaser, and the consequence of receipt of off-standard products.

*(continued on next page)*

---

**ISO 9000 Interpretation:**
**Assessment of Subcontractors - Ensuring an Effective System**
*(continued from previous page)*

**Conclusion**

Tiratto agreed with the conclusions of the panel, but pointed out that guidance documents have also been prepared for specific industry sectors such as chemicals and software. For example, in *ANSI/ASQC Q90 ISO 9000: Guidelines for use by the chemical and process industries*, assessment of the subcontractor's ability consistently to meet requirements may be based on the following evidence:

○ On-site assessment of subcontractor's quality and/or performance data (current and historical)
○ Trials or demonstration in the supplier's laboratories or plant. For example, the supplier may have to rely on inspection and testing when a subcontractor's appraisal is not feasible (i.e. spot purchases of bulk material)
○ Documented evidence of successful use in similar processes
○ Third-party assessment and registration of the subcontractors quality systems to an acceptable standard.

---

tractor to ensure the quality of the purchased product. This can be done by referring to other applicable information such as national or international standards or test methods.

Companies should assign responsibility for reviewing and approving purchasing data to appropriate personnel.

## 4.6.4 Verification of Purchased Product

### *ISO 9001 Requirements*

The purchaser shall have the right to verify the purchased product to make sure it conforms to specified requirements.

In some cases, verification is required at the facilities of the supplier's subcontractor. In this situation, the purchaser may extend verification to the sub-contractor's facilities.

However, verification by the purchaser does not absolve the supplier from providing an acceptable product, nor does it preclude subsequent rejection.

When verification is required at the sub-contractor's facilities, sub-contracts should include special clauses or statements to this effect.

The contract can provide that the purchaser uses the supplier's data to decide which products or services will require verification at the source, and the nature and extent of this verification.

### ISO 9004 Guidance

In Section 9.0, ISO 9004 notes that agreements with the supplier "may also include the exchange of inspection and test data" to further quality improvements. A clear agreement on verification methods can "minimize difficulties in the interpretation of requirements as well as inspection, test, or sampling methods."

# 4.7 PURCHASER-SUPPLIED PRODUCT

### ISO 9001 Requirements

The supplier shall establish and maintain procedures for verification, storage and maintenance of purchaser-supplied products.

Products that are lost, damaged or unsuitable must be recorded and reported to the purchaser.

**NOTE**: *Verification by the supplier does not absolve the purchaser of responsibility for providing an acceptable product.*

---

### Purchaser-Supplied Product

Purchaser-supplied product, as referenced in Clause 4.7, refers to items the customer provides to the supplier which are to be incorporated into the product and then returned in final form to the customer. An example of a purchaser supplied product involves a well-known supermarket chain that provided its supplier, a manufacturer of 35-mm film, with cassettes and boxes in which the film was to be packaged. Other types of purchaser-supplied products range from labels to pallets or even to railway tankers.

*The Victoria Group*

## Clause 4.8 - Product Identification and Traceability

The key words in this clause are, *Where, and to the extent that, traceability is a specified requirement….* The level of required traceability is left to the discretion of the company unless specifically called for under contractual or regulatory requirements. A company, such as one that manufactures inexpensive pencils, could decide that there is no traceability requirement at all.

This also allows the company some latitude in determining the type of traceability, encompassing, for example, traceability of materials within the factory and finished product traceability to the customer.

Product-identification requirements can also vary widely. They range from identification by serial number and full test and inspection records to virtually no identification at all. Once again, the company must decide, document its decision, and then adhere to it. Companies should realize that if there is an industry norm for identification and traceability, auditors will expect to see that norm being followed. If there is a regulatory requirement, companies are advised to follow it.

*The Victoria Group*

### ISO 9000-2 Guidance

*Purchaser-supplied product* is any product owned by the purchaser and furnished to the supplier for use in meeting the requirements of the contract. The supplier accepts full responsibility for the product while in its possession.

Purchaser-supplied product could be a service, such as the use of a purchaser's transport for delivery. The supplier should make sure that the service is suitable and should be able to document its effectiveness.

# 4.8 PRODUCT IDENTIFICATION AND TRACEABILITY

In some cases, contracts require the organization to trace specific materials or assemblies throughout the process of their development, through delivery and/or installation.

Product (and service) traceability refers to the ability to trace the history, application or location of an item or activity by means of recorded identification.

### ISO 9001 Requirements

Where appropriate, the supplier shall establish and maintain procedures for identifying the product during all stages of production, delivery and installation.

To the extent that traceability is a specified requirement, individual product, or batches thereof, must have a unique identification.

### ISO 9000-2 Guidance

There are many identification methods, including marking, tagging or documentation, in the case of a service. The identifier should be unique to the source of the operation. Separate identifiers could be required for changes in various aspects of the production process.

Traceability may require identification of specific personnel involved in phases of the operation. This can be accomplished through signatures on serially numbered documents, for example.

# 4.9 PROCESS CONTROL

## 4.9.1 General

Preventing problems by controlling the production process is preferable to discovering them at the final inspection. Process-control activities often include statistical process-control methods, procedures for accepting materials into the process, and the proper maintenance of process equipment and essential materials.

### ISO 9001 Requirements

The supplier shall:

- Identify and plan the processing steps needed to produce the product
- Ensure that the processes are carried out under controlled conditions
- Provide documented instructions for work that affects quality
- Monitor and approve necessary processes
- Observe and stipulate relevant criteria for workmanship, where practical.

## Clause 4.9 - Process Control

*Work instructions*, which are referred to in Clause 4.9: Process Control, can take the form of anything from a representative sample to a detailed written document. It is important to assess the training and skills of employees when evaluating where to make use of work instructions.

In determining the use of work instructions, the standard cautions companies to consider "where the absence of such instructions would adversely affect quality." In assessing whether an employee is correctly performing his/her job, there are three possible responses:

○ A work instruction exists that details these responsibilities
○ Records exist proving the individual was hired with a particular skill; or
○ The employee has received on-the-job training; records exist to document the training and prove it has been performed.

*The Victoria Group*

### *ISO 9000-2 Guidance*

The adequacy of production process control should take into account the adequacy of the measurement processes. When effective process control depends upon consistent operation of process equipment and essential materials, the supplier should include within the scope of the quality system the proper maintenance of such process equipment and essential materials.

### *ISO 9004 Guidance*

Sections 10.0 and 11.0 in ISO 9004 discuss quality in production and control of production. Clause 10.1 discusses planning for controlled production. Controlled conditions include "appropriate controls for materials, production equipment, processes and procedures, computer software, personnel, and associated supplies, utilities and environments."

Section 10.0 recommends that companies:

■ Conduct process capability studies to determine the potential effectiveness of a process

- Develop work instructions that "describe the criteria for determining satisfactory work completion and conformity to specification and standards of good workmanship"
- Verify the quality status of a product, process, software, material or environment
- Verify the capability of production processes to produce in accordance with specifications
- Control and verify auxiliary materials and utilities, "such as water, compressed air, electric power, and chemicals used for processing," where important to quality characteristics.

Section 11.0 offers guidance in the areas of:

- Material control and traceability
- Equipment control and maintenance
- Special processes (See ISO 9001, Clause 4.9.2, below.)
- Documentation of work instructions, specifications and drawings
- Process change control
- Control of the verification status of material and assemblies (See ISO 9001, Clause 4.12)
- Control of nonconforming materials.

## 4.9.2 Special Processes

### *ISO 9001 Requirements*

The supplier shall:

- Continuously monitor special processes to ensure that requirements are met
- Maintain records for processes, equipment and personnel.

### *ISO 9000-2 Guidance*

All products are produced by processes. Special processes are those whose results cannot be fully verified by subsequent inspection and testing of the product and where processing deficiencies may become apparent only after the product is in use. Special processes are particularly common in producing processed materials. Examples of critical product quality characteristics in this area include:

- Metal parts (strength, ductility, fatigue life, corrosion-resistance following welding, soldering, etc.)
- Polymerized plastic (dyeability, shrinkage, tensile properties)

- Bakery products (taste, texture, appearance)
- Correctness of financial or legal documents/software.

Special processes may require:

- Comprehensive measurement assurance and equipment calibration
- Statistical process control and special training.

### *ISO 9004 Guidance*

Clause 11.4: Special Processes, of ISO 9004 notes that "more frequent verification of special processes should be made" to check on the:

- Accuracy and variability of equipment used to make or measure the product
- Skill, capability and knowledge of workers
- Special environments, time, temperature or other factors that affect quality
- Certification records that are maintained for personnel, processes and equipment.

# ISO 9000 Interpretation:
## Clause 4.9.2 - Special Processes, and Chemical Producers

*By:* **Ian Durand,** President, Service Process Consulting, Inc.
**Robert W. Belfit,** President / Chairman, Omni Tech International, Inc.
**Joseph Tiratto,** President, Joseph Tiratto and Associates, Inc.
**Terry Heaps,** Project Administrator, QA Services, Vincotte USA, Inc.

## Question:

Does Clause 4.9.2: Special Processes, of ISO 9001 encompass all production processes used by chemical producers? Some auditors have affirmed that it does, basing their decision on the interpretation that all processes are "one, large, special process."

## Answer:

All four experts referred to published industry guidelines in answering this question. The American Society for Quality Control (ASQC) book, *ANSI/ASQC Q90/ISO 9000 Guidelines for Use by the Chemical and Process Industries*, was referenced by three experts.* Two experts referenced European Chemical Industry Council (ECIC) guidelines.

The experts agreed that ISO 9001, Clause 4.9.2: Special Processes, could cover all the production processes used by a chemical producer. Belfit, however, said he interprets this clause differently.

Belfit suggested that when proceeding through the registration process, a chemical producer should interview potential registrars to ascertain the possible interpretation.

### Key to Interpretation

Belfit said the first sentence of the clause is the key to interpreting the standard. Belfit illustrated his interpretation by citing the example of a product that is "manufactured under as much control and testing as possible, but requires the shipment be delayed until the purchaser has utilized the product in his process, and therefore releases the product for shipment."

Belfit said these special processes are not those generally run on a regular basis, and "therefore the processing parameters and testing parameters have not or cannot be defined precisely to ensure that the product will perform in the purchaser's application." He concluded that "special processes in the chemical industry imply that it is not possible through process control, in-process testing, or final testing to establish whether the product will perform in the purchaser's application."

On the other hand, Belfit pointed out, "the production of benzene, styrene, ethyl alcohol, polystyrene, or polyvinyladine chloride are processes that are run on a continuous basis and these are, in reality, commodity products." He said the performance of these products in the purchaser's application is predictable based on the process controls, the end-process analysis, and/or the

*(continued on next page)*

# ISO 9000 Interpretation:
## Clause 4.9.2 - Special Processes, and Chemical Producers
*(continued from previous page)*

product analysis of the final product. "These products are covered by Clause 4.9.1 in the general statement under process control," Belfit said.

### No "Find-and-Fix" Approach

Durand noted that examining the central theme of the ISO 9000 series is important in interpreting ISO 9001, Clause 4.9.2: Special Processes. He said the overall emphasis of the ISO 9000 series is on "preventing quality problems before they occur, rather than relying on 'find-and-fix' approaches."

For this reason, Durand said, "it is not unusual for registrars to look for, and prefer to find, attention given to control of all processes that affect the quality of the 'total market offering,' i.e. both the tangible goods and accompanying services."

Durand noted that "in the real world there are always trade-offs between process control and inspection and testing." He said Sections 4.9: Process Control, and 4.10: Inspection and Testing, should be considered complementary. According to Durand, this trade-off is implied in the first sentence of Clause 4.9.2.

In establishing the balance between the two approaches, Durand said such factors as the feasibility of subsequent inspection, the relative effectiveness and costs, and the specific processes and products being considered should be evaluated.

To illustrate, he noted that in some chemical industries, skilled operators assess color, granularity, texture and handling characteristics to complement process control. Durand concluded that assessing relevant factors and establishing a balance between process control and inspection requires working knowledge of the industry and the specific processes and products under consideration.

For example, Durand said that keeping levels of airborne contaminates below specified thresholds during production of solid-state devices is essential. "Complete reliance on inspection and testing is generally not a viable alternative to cleanliness and sanitation during food preparation either," Durand added. He said that both of these examples are types of chemical processes.

### Help Resources

Heaps also agreed that a case could be made for including special processes as part of all production processes. Heaps noted that "confusion may exist, if any does exist, in the manner with which auditors approach 'special processes' since there is little difference between the requirements for 'special processes,' and 'process control' in the ISO 9001 and ISO 9002 standards."

*(continued on next page)*

# ISO 9000 Interpretation:
## Clause 4.9.2 - Special Processes, and Chemical Producers
*(continued from previous page)*

Heaps said ECIC guidelines state that chemical processes may be considered special process for a variety of reasons. For example:

○ A characteristic can be measured only during the process and not in the finished product
○ A characteristic of the product changes (matures) after the product has been delivered
○ The complete characteristics of a product are not known
○ There is no satisfactory method of measuring a product characteristic.

"There may be a greater emphasis on the results of the in-process inspection and testing and calibration of the equipment used to make or test the product than may be required for a conventional process," Heaps said. Heaps cited other ECIC guidelines concerning customer requirements. For example:

○ A specification is agreed for certain characteristics inspected or tested during the process
○ Before acceptance of the contract, the product is evaluated after use in this product or process
○ The process and/or the source of raw materials is not changed without the customer's agreement
○ Specified statistical process control methods are used.

Special skills, capabilities, and training of personnel may be needed to meet any additional quality requirements. Tiratto said that "processes of the chemical process industry are generally considered special processes." He cited ECIC guidelines as a reference. In addition, Tiratto cites guidelines in *ANSI/ASQC Q90/ISO 9000: Guidelines for Use by the Chemical and Process Industries*. These guidelines include:

○ Equipment used to make or measure product
○ Operator skill, capability and knowledge
○ Environmental factors affecting quality
○ Records of qualifications.

In summary, Durand concluded, "Process control almost always makes good business sense and should be the approach of choice anyway."

* *ANSI/ASQC Q90/ISO 9000: Guidelines for Use by the Chemical and Process Industries* is available from ASQC Quality Press, 611 East Wisconsin Avenue, Milwaukee, Wisconsin 53202, 1-800-952-6587.

# 4.10 INSPECTION AND TESTING

This section looks at three areas of inspection and testing:

- Receiving
- In-process
- Final inspection.

## 4.10.1 Receiving Inspection and Testing

### *ISO 9001 Requirements*

Receiving inspection allows suppliers to verify that subcontractors are fulfilling their contractual obligations. Suppliers shall:

- Ensure incoming products are not used or processed until they have been inspected
- Verify in accordance with the quality plan and the documented procedures.

### *ISO 9000-2 Guidance*

This clause does not imply that incoming items must be inspected and tested if the supplier can use other defined procedures that would fulfill this obligation. The procedures should include:

- Provisions for verifying that incoming items, materials or services are accompanied by supporting documentation
- Provision for appropriate action in the event of non-conformities.

### *ISO 9004 Guidance*

Clause 9.7: *Receiving Inspection Planning and Controls,* notes that the "extent to

---

## Clause 4.10 - Inspection and Testing

Clause 4.10: Inspection and Testing requires little comment; it is largely self-explanatory. The one point that is worth making is that the standard does not **require** that any inspection and testing be performed. It does require that conformance can be demonstrated, but how that is done is up to the company. What is required is that there should be "documented procedures" — and that they are followed. It also requires that records be maintained.

*The Victoria Group*

which receiving inspection will be performed should be carefully planned. The level of inspection...should be selected with overall cost being borne in mind."

Clause 9.8: *Receiving Quality Records,* stresses that appropriate records should be kept to "ensure the availability of historical data to assess supplier performance and quality trends." Companies should also consider maintaining "records of lot identification for purposes of traceability."

## 4.10.1.2 Release for Urgent Production Purposes

### *ISO 9001 Requirements*

The supplier shall positively identify and record incoming product to permit recall and replacement, if necessary.

### *ISO 9000-2 Guidance*

The release of incoming product subject to recall should generally be discouraged as a matter of good quality management practice. There are two exceptions:

- An objective evaluation of quality status and solution of any nonconformities can still be implemented
- Correction of nonconformities cannot compromise the quality of adjacent, attached or incorporated items.

The supplier's procedures shall:

- Define responsibilities and authority of people who may allow incoming product to be used without prior demonstration of conformance to specified requirements
- Explain how such product will be positively identified and controlled in the event that subsequent inspection finds non-conformities.

## 4.10.2 In-Process Inspection and Testing

### *ISO 9001 Requirements*

The supplier shall:

- Inspect, test and identify product
- Establish product conformance to specified requirements
- Identify nonconforming product
- Perform in-process inspection and testing.

Processing, however, does not have to be delayed pending the results of inspection and testing as long as a system exists for identifying items that haven't been fully checked but can be recalled later.

### ISO 9000-2 Guidance

In-process inspection and testing applies to all forms of products, including services. It allows for early recognition of non-conformities.

Statistical control techniques are commonly used to identify product and process trends and prevent nonconformities. Inspection and test results should be objective, including those carried out by production personnel.

### ISO 9004 Guidance

Clause 12.2: *In-Process Inspection,* lists types of verification checks:

- Set-up and first-piece inspection
- Inspection or test by machine operator
- Automatic inspection or test
- Fixed inspection stations at intervals through the process
- Patrol inspection by inspectors monitoring specified operations.

## 4.10.3 Final Inspection and Testing

### ISO 9001 Requirements

The supplier shall carry out all specified final inspection and tests, including those specified either on receipt of product or in-process.

No product shall leave the company until every activity specified in the quality plan or documented procedure has been satisfactorily completed.

### ISO 9000-2 Guidance

Final inspection involves the examination, inspection, measurement or testing upon which the final release of a product is based. Release specifications should include all designated release characteristics.

### ISO 9004 Guidance

Clause 12.3: *Completed Product Verification,* lists two types of final production verification:

- Acceptance inspections or tests
- Product quality auditing.

Acceptance inspections are used to ensure that "items or lots produced have met performance and other quality requirements."

Product quality auditing that is performed on representative sample units may be either continuous or periodic.

## 4.10.4 Inspection and Test Records

### ISO 9001 Requirements

The supplier shall establish and maintain records that indicate whether the product has passed inspections and test procedures.

### ISO 9000-2 Guidance

Inspection and test records facilitate assessment according to specifications and are useful for regulatory requirements and possible product liability problems.

### ISO 9004 Guidance

Clause 17.0: *Quality Documentation and Records,* discusses in detail procedures for establishing and maintaining quality records, including inspection and test records.

Clause 17.3: *Quality Records,* notes that "while in storage, quality records should be protected from damage, loss, and deterioration due to environmental conditions."

## Clause 4.11 - Inspection, Measuring and Test Equipment

Clause 4.11 discusses control of inspection and test equipment and calibration. The standard requires that equipment used "to demonstrate the conformance of product to the specified requirements" be calibrated to traceable national standards. This does not mean **all** equipment.

In one example, an audit team demanded that each of 35,000 gauges and meters at a certain refinery be calibrated in a manner traceable to national standards. The company correctly calibrated only those gauges which influenced the quality of the product and those that were used to demonstate conformance to specified requirements.

Demonstrating conformance is not confined to a single site in the company. Test and inspection equipment must be under traceable calibration control at those locations or places in the process where conformance can be demonstrated. Items which can be checked using portable transfer standards do not require such rigorous records. Once this determination of requirements is made, the rest of Clause 4.11 is easy to follow.

*The Victoria Group*

# 4.11 INSPECTION, MEASURING AND TEST EQUIPMENT

### *ISO 9001 Requirements*

The supplier shall:

- Control, calibrate and maintain inspection, measuring and test equipment with marking, authorized stamps or other suitable means (whether owned by the supplier, on-loan, or provided by the purchaser)
- Use equipment in a manner to ensure that measurement uncertainty is known.

The clause spells out, in detail, the requirements for testing accuracy, calibration of equipment, handling of equipment and documentation of the checking procedures. Suppliers shall:

- Identify necessary measurements, the accuracy required and the appropriate inspection, measuring and test equipment
- Identify, calibrate and adjust all equipment
- Establish, document and maintain calibration procedures

- Ensure that equipment is capable of required accuracy and precision
- Identify equipment to indicate calibration status
- Maintain calibration records
- Assess and document the validity of previous inspection and test results when equipment is out of calibration
- Ensure suitable environmental conditions for calibration, inspection, measurement and testing
- Ensure accuracy and fitness for use when handling, preserving and storing equipment
- Safeguard inspection, measuring and test facilities.

## ISO 9000-2 Guidance

Clause 4.11 addresses the suitability of the equipment used in monitoring quality. ISO 10012-1: *Quality assurance requirements for measuring equipment - Part 1: Management of measuring equipment,* offers guidance for the management of measuring equipment. However, the guidance in ISO 10012-1 does not add to, or otherwise change the requirements in ISO 9001, except where conformance to ISO 10012-1 is required.

Measurements may include less tangible instruments, such as polling, questionnaires or subjective preferences.

The requirements of this clause also should be applied to measurements subsequent to production and inspection of a product (e.g., handling, storage, packaging, delivery or servicing).

## ISO 9004 Guidance

In Clause 13.2, ISO 9004 notes that the "control of measuring and test equipment and test methods should include the following factors, as appropriate:"

- Correct specification and acquisition
- Initial calibration prior to first use in order to validate required bias and precision
- Testing of software and procedures controlling automatic test equipment
- Periodic recall for adjustment, repair and recalibration to maintain required accuracy in use
- Documentary evidence that covers instrument identification, calibration status and procedures for all handling procedures
- Traceability to accurate and stable reference standards.

# 4.12 INSPECTION AND TEST STATUS

## *ISO 9001 Requirements*

The supplier shall:

- Identify the inspection and test status of the product throughout production and installation to ensure that only acceptable product has been used
- Identify the inspection authority responsible for the release of the conforming product.

The test status may be indicated by marking or tagging or signing, either physically or by electronic means.

## *ISO 9000-2 Guidance*

The status should indicate whether a product has:

- Not been inspected
- Been inspected and accepted
- Been inspected and is on hold awaiting decision
- Been inspected and rejected.

The most certain method of ensuring status and accurate disposition is physically to separate these product categories. In an automated environment, however, other methods can be used, such as a computer database.

## *ISO 9004 Guidance*

Clause 11.7 addresses control of verification status. Identification of verification status "may take the form of stamps, tags, or notations on shop travelers, or inspec-

---

### 4.12 - Inspection and Test Status

Inspection and test status is often misinterpreted as applying only to the inspection and test stages of an operation. In fact, this clause states that at any stage in the operation it should be possible to identify the conformity of any item. The manner in which this is accomplished is left to the company to decide.

*The Victoria Group*

tion records that accompany the product." Identification should be capable of indicating:

- Verified versus unverified material
- Acceptance at the point of verification
- Traceability to the unit responsible for the operation.

# 4.13 CONTROL OF NONCONFORMING PRODUCT

### *ISO 9001 Requirements*

The supplier shall establish and maintain a procedure to prevent the inadvertent use or installation of a nonconforming product. The nonconforming product should, where practical, be segregated.

### *ISO 9000-2 Guidance*

A nonconforming product, either an intermediate or final product or service, is one that fails to meet specifications. This applies to a nonconforming product that occurs in the supplier's own production as well as nonconforming products received by the supplier.

The procedures for controlling a nonconforming product should include:

- Determining which product units are involved in the nonconformity
- Identifying the nonconforming product units

---

### Clause 4.13 - Nonconformity

ISO 9001, Clause 1.1, states "the requirements specified in this Standard are aimed primarily at **preventing** nonconformity at all stages from design to servicing" (emphasis added). Fortunately, the authors of this standard were realists and, despite the stated intent of Clause 1.1, it has been recognized that even in the best of all possible worlds things still go wrong. The clause on nonconforming product is designed to ensure that such items are properly identified, prevented from accidental use, and that there is a formal way of deciding what to do with them.

*The Victoria Group*

---

- Documenting the nonconformity
- Evaluating the nonconformity
- Considering alternatives for disposing of the nonconforming product units
- Physically controlling the movement, storage and processing of the nonconforming product units
- Notifying all functions that may be affected by the nonconformity.

## 4.13.1 Nonconformity Review and Disposition

### *ISO 9001 Requirements*

The supplier shall:

- Define the responsibility for review and authority for the disposition of nonconforming product
- Document the disposition of the product
- Re-inspect repaired and re-worked product.

Nonconforming products may be:

- Reworked
- Accepted without repair by concession of the purchaser
- Re-graded for alternative application
- Rejected or scrapped.

### *ISO 9000-2 Guidance*

Suppliers should consider the procedures in Clause 4.13 in relationship to the risk of failure to meet purchaser requirements. Actions (a) through (d) in Clause 4.13.1 all carry degrees of risk. In the long-term, action (d) may carry the lowest risk.

**NOTE:** *ISO 9000-2 points out that while "ISO 9003 does not have a subclause dealing explicitly with nonconformity review and disposition, the guidance presented here may be helpful in the implementation of Clause 4.8 of ISO 9003."*

### *ISO 9004 Guidance*

ISO 9004, Clause 14.0: *Nonconformity,* includes the following guidance:

- Procedures to deal with nonconforming product "should be taken as soon as indications occur that materials, components, or completed product, do not or may not meet the specified requirements."

- The persons who review nonconforming items "should be competent to evaluate the effects of nonconformity on interchangeability, further processing, performance, reliability, safety and esthetics."

- "Decisions to 'pass' an item should be accompanied by authorized concessions/ waivers, with appropriate precautions."

# 4.14 CORRECTIVE ACTION

### *ISO 9001 Requirements*

The supplier shall:

- Investigate and analyze the problem
- Initiate action to avoid recurrence
- Apply controls to ensure that corrective actions are taken and are effective
- Implement and record changes in procedures resulting from corrective action.

### *ISO 9000-2 Guidance*

This clause explains what an organization must do when things go wrong. Analysis of nonconformities can be performed by using inspection and test records, process monitoring, audit observation and all other available feedback methods. Corrective action procedures should include:

- Establishing responsibility for taking corrective action
- Defining how the action will be carried out
- Verifying the effectiveness of the corrective action.

---

### **Clause 4.14 - Corrective Action**

The clause pertaining to nonconforming products is followed, logically, by a clause on corrective action. Often the weakest part of quality systems, corrective action loops are frequently designed only to address the immediate problem while failing to act to avoid its recurrence. Another common problem is that they often only deal with matters of products or services while overlooking the system. ISO 9001 Clause 4.14 addresses both the product/service and the system.

*The Victoria Group*

---

Procedures should also take into account nonconformities discovered in product that has already been shipped and designated as satisfactory.

### *ISO 9004 Guidance*

According to ISO 9004, Clause 15.0: *Corrective Action,* the

> *coordination, recording, and monitoring of corrective action related to all aspects of the organization or a particular product should be assigned to a particular function within the organization. However, the analysis and execution may involve a variety of functions, such as sales, design, production engineering, production, and quality control.*

A problem affecting quality "should be evaluated in terms of its potential impact on such aspects as production costs, quality costs, performance, reliability, safety, and customer satisfaction."

Nonconforming items should be recalled, "whether these items are in a finished goods warehouse, in transit to distributors, in their stores, or already in field use."

# 4.15 HANDLING, STORAGE, PACKAGING AND DELIVERY

## 4.15.1 General

### *ISO 9001 Requirements*

The supplier shall establish, document and maintain handling, storage, packaging and delivery procedures.

---

### Clause 4.15 - Handling, Storage, Packaging and Delivery

Clause 4.15 is fairly straightforward. The usual problem here is that once again there is a tendency to forget that these activities take place throughout the entire process, not merely at the end.

*The Victoria Group*

### ISO 9000-2 Guidance

The requirement applies to incoming materials, materials in process and finished product. The procedures should provide proper planning, control and documentation.

## 4.15.2 Handling

### ISO 9001 Requirements

The supplier shall provide a method to prevent damage or deterioration.

### ISO 9000-2 Guidance

The handling methods should include provision for the transportation unit such as pallets, containers, conveyors, etc., to prevent damage. Another factor to consider is the maintenance of the handling equipment.

## 4.15.3 Storage

### ISO 9001 Requirements

The supplier shall:

- Provide secure storage
- Stipulate appropriate receipt and dispatch methods.

### ISO 9000-2 Guidance

Suitable storage procedures should take into account:

- Physical security
- Environmental control (temperature and humidity)
- Periodic checking to detect deterioration
- Legible, durable marking and labeling methods
- Expiration dates and stock rotation methods.

## 4.15.4 Packaging

### ISO 9001 Requirements

The supplier shall control packaging, preservation and marking processes.

### *ISO 9000-2 Guidance*

The packaging procedures should:

- Provide appropriate protection against damage, deterioration or contamination as long as the material remains the responsibility of the supplier
- Provide a clear description of the contents or ingredients, according to regulations or the contract
- Provide for checking packaging effectiveness.

## 4.15.5 Delivery

### *ISO 9001 Requirements*

The supplier shall protect product quality after final inspection and test, including delivery to destination.

### *ISO 9000-2 Guidance*

For some products, delivery time is a critical factor. Procedures should take into account various types of delivery and variations in potential environmental conditions.

### *ISO 9004 Guidance*

Clause 16.0: *Handling, and Post-Production Functions,* emphasizes the need for a documented system for incoming materials, materials in process, and finished goods. Clause 16.0 also refers to the need for proper and complete installation instructions.

# 4.16 QUALITY RECORDS

### *ISO 9001 Requirements*

The supplier shall:

- Establish and maintain procedures for handling, maintaining and disposing of quality records (includes pertinent subcontractor quality records)
- Store records effectively and prevent loss or damage
- Establish and record retention times of quality records
- Make quality records available for evaluation by purchaser or his representative.

All quality records shall be legible and identifiable to the product involved.

### *ISO 9000-2 Guidance*

The purpose of quality records is to demonstrate required quality and the effectiveness of the quality system. Quality records are referred to throughout ISO 9001. Effective quality records contain direct and indirect evidence that demonstrates whether the product or service meets requirements.

The records should be readily accessible. They may be stored in any suitable form, either as hard copy or on electronic media.

Sometimes, purchasers may be required to store and maintain selected quality records that attest to the quality of products (including services) for a specified part of the operating lifetime. The supplier should provide such documents to the purchaser.

International standards do not specify a minimum time period for retaining quality records. Suppliers should consider the following:

- Requirements of regulatory authorities
- Product liability and other legal issues related to record-keeping

---

## Clause 4.16 - Quality Records

The ISO 9001 standard continually refers to the need for records to demonstrate completed actions. Clause 4.16 does not call for the creation of additional records, but points out that records must be identified, sorted, stored and maintained in a manner which makes them easily accessible.

Often, too much importance is attached to fulfilling the requirements of this clause. Contrary to popular belief, the clause does not require fireproof safes, bank-vault storage, microfiche, or other similar methods of storage. Once again, the level of protection required for records depends upon the nature of the business, as well as any contractual or statutory requirements. The records connected with the construction of a nuclear power station need to be kept somewhat longer, and under more secure conditions, than the records for making a compact disc.

Some registrars have definite ideas about record-retention times. It is a good idea to establish whether the company's record-retention policy agrees with the registrar's demands during an initial meeting. The record-retention policy should be clarified and agreed upon before the audit team arrives on-site.

*The Victoria Group*

# ISO 9000 Interpretation
## Clause 4.16 - Electronic Control of Documents

*By:* **Joseph Tiratto,** President, Joseph Tiratto and Associates, Inc.
**Robert D. Bowen,** President, r. bowen international, inc.
**Ian Durand,** President, Service Process Consulting, Inc.
**Charles McRobert,** President, Quality Practitioners, Inc.

**Question:**

Can documents be generated electronically? If so, how can they be controlled to meet the requirements of ISO 9000 series standards?

**Answer:**

All four experts agreed that generating and tracking documents electronically is allowed by the ISO 9000 series standard. Bowen said that ISO 9000 series document control principles apply equally to all media; he also pointed out four distinct advantages of electronic media:

○ **Accuracy**: Immediate on-line review of proposed changes by all knowledgeable persons and a transaction history file showing the date and nature of changes.

○ **Authenticity**: Secure sign-on functions to ensure controlled access to *read and write* functions.

○ **Completeness**: On-line edit-checks that ensure all required information is complete before a document is released.

○ **Currency**: Instantaneous removal of all obsolete documents. Uniform start-up of all concerned persons when initiating procedures or changes.

Other strengths noted by Bowen include immediate update of suppliers' documents through electronic data interchange. In addition, Bowen said, "many organizations find it easier to establish a planned review system of quality-related documents if those documents are on-line." He noted that setting up a database reminder to review documents at specified agreed-upon intervals is easy to accomplish.

**Paperless Environment**

McRobert said that he had worked with "nearly paperless" companies whose document-control systems were excellent. He agreed with Bowen's contention that electronic control of documents makes review and approval of documents and highlighting of changes easier.

McRobert noted that "some auditors with misguided zeal have requested hard copies of all controlled documents with approval signatures." He suggested that any company whose auditor suggests this approach "immediately seek relief" from this requirement.

*(continued on next page)*

---

### ISO 9000 Interpretation
### Clause 4.16 - Electronic Control of Documents
*(continued from previous page)*

Durand pointed out that controlled documents can include mechanical assembly drawings, circuit schematics, process flow charts, physical reference samples, pictures of reference samples, or video tapes illustrating proper work methods.

He agreed that using electronic media for document control has many distinct advantages. He said the complexity of such systems should not be a roadblock, pointing to the demanding access and control requirements of electronic fund transfer financial-control systems and security and administration systems.

Durand noted that a number of software programs are currently available to handle documentation and quality records of an ISO 9000-based quality system. Tiratto agreed that documents can be generated electronically in accordance with ISO 9003-Part 2: *Generic guidelines for the application of ISO 9001, ISO 9002, and ISO 9003.*

He noted, however, that in accordance with ISO 9001, 4.16, document control should include written procedures which describe:

○  How documentation should be controlled
○  Who is responsible for the control
○  What is to be controlled
○  Where and when the control is to take place.

Tiratto said the procedures should also include back-up provisions for electronically stored documents that are readily retrievable. He said back-up provision can also be electronically processed.

---

■  Expected lifetime of the product
■  Requirements of the contract.

Aside from these considerations, retaining records five to seven years is common practice.

### ISO 9004 Guidance

Clause 17.3: Quality Records, in ISO 9004 gives the following examples of quality records that require control:

■  Inspection reports
■  Test data

- Qualification reports
- Validation reports
- Audit reports
- Material review reports
- Calibration data
- Quality cost reports.

# 4.17 INTERNAL QUALITY AUDITS

### *ISO 9001 Requirements*

The supplier shall:

- Audit and evaluate all elements of the quality system regularly
- Schedule audits according to the status and importance of the activity
- Carry out audits according to documented procedures
- Document audit results and communicate them to the appropriate personnel
- Perform timely corrective action.

### *ISO 9000-2 Guidance*

The purpose of an audit is to make sure the system is working according to plan, to meet regulatory requirements, or to provide opportunities for improvement.

Auditors should be selected and assigned according to the criteria contained in ISO 9001, Clause 4.1.2.2.

---

## Clause 4.17 - Audit System

Internal quality audits were referenced in discussing the requirements of Clause 4.3: Management Review. This is the mainstay of system conformance. The quality system audit is a powerful tool for continuous improvement. The standard requires a planned, systematic process of audits to ensure that the documented system is effectively implemented and that corrective actions are taken in a timely manner. The prevention concept ensures that the system is working as planned and corrective action is taken when it is not.

*The Victoria Group*

Internal audits may also be initiated for other reasons, including:

- Initial evaluation of a system for contract reasons
- When nonconformities jeopardize the safety, performance or dependability of the products
- Verification of corrective actions
- Evaluation of a system against a quality system standard.

### ISO 9004 Guidance

Clause 5.4: Auditing the Quality System, in ISO 9004 suggests that companies formulate an appropriate audit plan that covers:

- Activities to be audited
- Qualifications of audit personnel
- Audits are taking place
- Procedures for reporting audit findings.

Internal audits should be performed in all company activities by persons independent of the activities or areas being audited.

Companies should submit documented audit findings, conclusions and recommendations to management on reporting and follow-up matters. The items that should be covered include:

- Specific examples of noncompliance
- Reasons for deficiencies
- Appropriate corrective actions
- Assessment of the implementation and effectiveness of previous corrective actions.

# 4.18 TRAINING

### ISO 9001 Requirements

The supplier shall:

- Establish maintain, and document procedures to identify training needs
- Provide appropriate training for all personnel performing activities affecting quality
- Maintain records of training.

### *ISO 9000-2 Guidance*

Training is essential to achieving quality. Training should encompass the use of and underlying rationale for the quality management approach of the supplier. The training process should include:

■ Evaluation of education and experience of personnel
■ Identification of individual training needs
■ Provision of appropriate training, either in-house or by external bodies
■ Recording of training progress and update to identify training needs.

### *ISO 9004 Guidance*

Clause 18.0: Personnel, of ISO 9004 discusses the training, qualification and motivation of personnel.

Companies should consider training of "all levels of personnel within the organization." This includes "recruited personnel and personnel transferred to new assignments."

The various levels of personnel within a company require specialized training. Executives and management require training in the "understanding of the quality system together with the tools and techniques needed" to operate the system.

Training for technical personnel "should not be restricted to personnel with primary quality assignments, but should include assignments such as marketing, procurement, and process and product engineering."

Production supervisors and workers should receive thorough training, including instruction in:

■ Proper operation of instruments, tools and machinery

---

## Clause 4.18 - Training

The training requirements of ISO 9001/9002 are very general. The choice of training required is made on the basis of appropriate education, training or experience. The company is left to decide what is appropriate, and then is asked to record that decision, follow it up and make sure that the training continues to be appropriate throughout the individual's career. Most good companies do this anyway. The standard requires that the process be documented.

*The Victoria Group*

- Reading and understanding documentation
- Relationship of their duties to quality and safety in the workplace
- Certification or formal qualification in specialized skills (such as welding)
- Basic statistical techniques.

Clause 18.3: *Motivation of ISO 9004,* looks at efforts to motivate all personnel in the organization. An effective motivation program focuses on:

- Communicating to all employees an understanding of their tasks and the advantages of proper job performance
- A continuous quality-awareness program
- A mechanism for publicizing quality achievements and recognizing satisfactory performance.

# 4.19 SERVICING

### *ISO 9001 Requirements*

The supplier shall:

- Establish and maintain servicing procedures (when required by contract)
- Verify that servicing meets specified requirements.

---

### Clause 4.19 - Servicing

Many commentators have suggested that Clause 4.19 was an afterthought — perhaps a Friday afternoon addendum on the final day that publication had to be agreed. On the contrary, the standard's drafters realized that the applications of the concept of servicing would be so diverse that it was best left to a certain degree of common sense. What is given to us by the standard is a methodology in accordance with documented procedures, and an indication that this is a contractual issue. In fact, depending upon the organization, servicing can be anything from a couple of lines in the Quality Manual to a complete organization with its own system in full compliance with ISO 9002. In the United Kingdom, there are several registered firms whose sole activity is servicing.

*The Victoria Group*

---

### ISO 9000-2 Guidance

In planning procedures for servicing, suppliers should:

- Clarify servicing responsibilities
- Plan service activities (supplier or externally provided)
- Validate design and function of necessary servicing tools and equipment
- Control measuring and test equipment
- Provide suitable documentation and instructions
- Provide backup technical advice, support, and spares or parts supply
- Provide competent, trained service personnel
- Gather useful feedback for product or servicing design.

### ISO 9004 Guidance

Clause 16.2: *After-Sales Servicing,* notes that instructions for products should be comprehensive and supplied in a timely manner. Instructions should cover assembly and installation, commissioning, operation, spares or parts lists, and servicing of products.

In the area of logistical back-up, responsiblity should be clearly assigned and agreed among suppliers, distributors and users.

# 4.20 STATISTICAL TECHNIQUES

### ISO 9001 Requirements

The supplier shall establish and maintain statistical techniques required for verifying the acceptability of the process and the product's characteristics.

### ISO 9000-2 Guidance

Statistical techniques are useful in every aspect of an organization's operation. Useful statistical methods include:

- Graphical methods to help diagnose problems
- Statistical control charts to monitor and control production and measurement processes
- Experiments to identify and quantify variables that influence process and product performance

■ Regression analysis to provide quantitative models for a process
■ Analysis of variance methods.

The documentation resulting from these methods can be used to demonstrate conformance to quality requirements.

### ISO 9004 Guidance

In Section 20.0: Use of Statistical Methods, ISO 9004 suggests that the application of statistical methods may include:

■ Market analysis
■ Product design
■ Reliability specification, longevity/durability prediction
■ Process control/process capability studies
■ Determination of quality levels/inspection plans
■ Data analysis/performance assessment/defect analysis.

---

## Clause 4.20 - Statistical Techniques

Readers schooled in concepts of statistical process control may be concerned by this brief reference to statistical techniques at the end of the standard. Statistics may be used not only for process control, but in many parts of the organization, from marketing to final inspection. While the supplier has the option of deciding whether to make use of statistical controls, the company should be aware that a registrar may consider this essential if their use in a given application has become an industry norm. The standard requires that adequate statistical techniques be used, where appropriate.

*The Victoria Group*

# ISO 9000 REGISTRATION

## INTRODUCTION

This chapter looks at the registration process. It discusses the following topics:

- What is registration?
- How to select a registrar
- Steps in the registration process
- Time and costs of registration.

## WHAT IS REGISTRATION?

Quality system registration is the assessment and audit of a supplier's quality system by a third party, known as a *quality system registrar*. The process involves an on-site visit by a team from the registrar to document facility compliance to the standard.

If the supplier's system conforms to the registrar's interpretation of an ISO 9000 series standard, the company is then registered, or *certified* to one of the ISO 9000 external quality assurance standards (ISO 9001, ISO 9002, or ISO 9003). The term *registration* is used in the United States; *certification* is used in the European Community.

# What gets registered?

ISO 9000 registration covers the quality management system of a particular company. This can mean one or several sites or facilities that are audited simultaneously.

For example, one ISO registration can encompass six sites in six different states. If these different sites are audited at the same time against the same standard, they may be covered under one registration.

Conversely, six registrations can cover six different production units of a single site. In this example, the quality management system for the production of one product may be covered under an audit and registration, but subsequent registrations would cover the quality management system of other processes or products at the same facility.

Some argue that sites in different locations should be registered separately, thereby guarding against loss of registration for all sites if only one is found to be nonconforming during a surveillance visit. Others argue that quality system registration is devalued if only part of the system, or one site within a company, is registered instead of the whole system or site.

It is the **quality system** used to **produce** a product, not the product itself, which is registered. Quality system registration does not imply product conformity. The ISO 9000 series standards don't tell companies how to run their businesses. Instead, the standards define the critical elements that must be taken into consideration to produce a quality product. It is up to the company to decide how to address these elements.

# What Is the Registration Period?

Registration is granted usually for a period of three years, though this can vary depending on the registrar. Registrars must conduct periodic surveillances of a registered site. These surveys can vary in frequency and rigor.

# HOW TO SELECT A REGISTRAR

## BY BUD WEIGHTMAN

The increasing number of companies that offer ISO 9000 series quality system registration services has made the process of selecting the best service for a particular industry or type of business a significant challenge.

Thirty-five companies offering ISO 9000 quality system registration are profiled in Appendix B of this handbook. Some of these companies have direct ties to one of the 12 EC or seven European Free Trade Association (EFTA) countries. Other companies offer ISO 9000 series quality system registration under a memorandum of understanding (MOU) with EC member country registrars. (See Chapter 9 for an explanation of MOUs and the issue of registrar accreditation)

## Choosing a Registrar

The following issues should be considered when choosing a registrar:

### Customer Market

A particular company, industry or market may influence registrar choice. Some questions to consider include:

- Does the quality system registrar specialize in registration of suppliers producing specific products?
- Is a specific European registrar required or preferred by a customer?

### Consulting and Registration: Conflict of Interest

European customer(s) may perceive a conflict of interest if a registrar offers and performs both consulting and registration services.

ISO/IEC Guide 48, *Guidelines for third-party assessment and registration of a supplier's quality system* , states in part

> *"an organization that, directly or through the agency of subcontractors, advises a company how to set up its quality system, or writes its quality documentation, should not provide assessment services to that company, unless strict separation is achieved to ensure that there is no conflict of interest."*

If a registrar offers these services directly or through an affiliate, a company should find out how the registrar separates the two activities.

## Costs

Costs associated with certification are generally based upon the size of an organization, the ISO 9000 series standard selected (ISO 9001, ISO 9002 or ISO 9003), the scope of registration (i.e., one product, a product line, an entire facility), and the location of a facility. Costs could include the following:

- Application fee
- Preparation and initial visit
- Review of quality system manual
- Review of revisions to the quality system manual
- Length of initial visit and number of auditors sent
- The number of days spent performing the formal audit
- The number of auditors sent by the registrar specifically for the assessment.

Questions to ask about registration costs include:

- Will the client be required to pay if the registrar performs a follow-up visit to verify the implementation of corrective action related to deficiencies identified during the assessment?
- Will the cost of surveillance be included in the registration fee, or will each surveillance represent an additional charge?
- How many surveillances will be performed over the life of the registration?
- How many quality system elements are covered during each surveillance?
- How long will each surveillance (or periodic inspection) last?
- What is the cost of modifying the scope of a registration?
- What is the cost of reassessment after the expiration of the original registration? Will it be the same as the initial assessment? Will it take as long as the initial assessment?
- What are the cancellation charges?
- What is the billing rate? By the man-day or by the hour? Is overtime applicable? What is the billing rate for travel time?
- Are travel expenses and lodging billed at reasonable rates? Will the registrar's auditors be traveling from a location within the United States or from Europe?

## Registrar Background Information and Company Policy

Questions to ask registrars about company policy and background include:

- How long has the company been in business?
- Is a list of previously registered companies available, with contact names and telephone numbers?
- Is a complete description of the registrar's registration system available including an application, the appeals process and a policy regarding registration suspension, withdrawal, or cancellation?
- How will clients be notified of any rule changes? Are clients permitted to comment on any of the changes? How long do clients have to implement changes once notified?
- What is the registrar's financial security? Do provisions exist if the registrar goes out of business? How would quality system registrations performed by the company be affected?
- Does the registrar require notification of any applicable customer complaints?
- Will the registrar grant quality system registration to all three standards - ISO 9001, ISO 9002 or ISO 9003? (**NOTE**: *Some registrars will not grant certification/registration to ISO 9003.*)
- What is the source of a registrar's accreditation?
- Is the source of accreditation an EC member state or a body recognized by the EC? If not, when will the accreditation entity be recognized?
- Has the accreditation entity adopted EN 45012 (Standards for certification bodies operating quality system certification)? If not, does it have plans to do so? (See Chapter 9 for an explanation of EN 45000 standards.)

Other questions to consider when selecting a registrar include:

- With which accreditation bodies in Europe does the registrar have memorandums of understanding (MOU)?
- Which US state laws govern the agreement with a registrar? Where would any legal differences occur?
- Does the registrar subcontract any of its registration activities to another organization? If so, does the subcontracted service follow the registrar's policies and regulations? Is the use of a subcontracted service agreeable?
- Does the registrar have a confidentiality agreement with the following:
  - Employees
  - Contracted assessors
  - Subcontracted organizations/personnel

- ● Members of its governing board
- ● Members of its certification committee
- ■ Does the registrar allow the use of its symbol or logo? What are the restrictions/ requirements governing its use?

## Quality System Assessment and Registration Process

Questions to ask about the quality system assessment and registration process include:

- ■ How soon can the quality system assessment be performed?
- ■ How long will the registration period last? (**NOTE:** *Normally, registrations last from one to three years.*)

Questions about the quality system manual include:

- ■ Will a controlled quality system manual be required for submission and how long will it take to review the document?
- ■ How are companies notified of quality system omissions or deviations?
- ■ How much time are companies granted to make the necessary modifications?
- ■ Must quality system manual amendments (based upon the registrar's review) be corrected and implemented prior to the assessment?
- ■ Once accepted, will a client be required to submit a quality system manual for review and approval prior to making and implementing any revisions?

## Deficiencies

Questions concerning deficiencies include:

- ■ Does a quality system have to be implemented 100 percent to receive registration?
- ■ Will a client be notified of any deficiencies in a quality system before an assessment team leaves the site? If so, will notification be verbal or written?
- ■ How much time is given to correct identified deficiencies?

## Reassessment / Surveillance

Questions about reassessment/surveillance include:

- ■ Will a reassessment or partial assessment be performed to verify corrective action implementation of deficiencies identified during the initial assessment?
- ■ Will changes/revisions in a quality system manual necessitate a reassessment?

■ Will a reassessment be required if a modification to the registration scope is requested?

■ What is the frequency of the periodic surveillances? How many quality system elements are covered during each surveillance?

## Auditor Qualifications

It is important to be aware of a registrar's auditor qualification and certification program before making a quality system registrar decision. A recognized auditor qualification/certification program ensures that manufacturers and suppliers are repeatedly audited in the same manner and at the same level of intensity. A company should make sure that the method the registrar used provides the best assessment possible.

Questions to consider when evaluating a registrar's auditor certification requirements include:

■ Does a registrar's internal training program/certification follow a specific scheme that may or may not be affiliated with a national scheme?

■ Is a registrar's quality system auditor acceptance based upon the ASQC Certified Quality Auditor (CQA) program?

■ Is participation in a 40-hour ISO 9000 lead auditor training course required?

The course may or may not be registered to a national scheme such as those administered by the United Kingdom's Institute of Quality Assurance (IQA). The IQA-administered scheme is supported by the Governing Board of the UK National Registration Scheme for Assessors of Quality Systems. This system has worldwide recognition.

### The Auditing Team

Questions to ask a registrar about its auditing team include:

■ What are the auditor's experience, training and educational requirements? Are auditor backgrounds verified?

■ Do auditors receive both ISO 9000 series and company procedures and policies prior to certification?

■ What is the standard or criteria used to certify auditors?

■ Is the standard or criteria recognized and accepted by the EC?

■ What levels of auditor certification exist (auditor-in-training/auditor/lead auditor), and what responsibilities do these auditors have during the assessment process?

■ During the assessment process, will at least one auditor be familiar with a client's product or technology?

## Published List of Registered Suppliers

If the registrar offers a list of suppliers or manufacturers it has registered, the company should ask the following questions:

- Does the list include a description, known as the *scope*, of what each product line or industry registration covers?
- What is the frequency of the list publication? (**NOTE:** The list should, at minimum, be published annually.)
- What is the charge for the list?
- Will clients be placed on a mailing list to receive the list or will a separate request be required?

## Quality System Suspension, Withdrawal or Cancellation

Questions concerning quality system suspension, withdrawal or cancellation include:

- What is the registrar's policy regarding the suspension, withdrawal or cancellation of the quality system registration?
- Will the registrar withdraw or cancel the quality system registration if a product, process or service is not supplied for an extended period of time? (The registrar should define the rules.)
- How will a client be notified of quality system registration suspension, withdrawal or cancellation?
- Will the registrar publish the quality system registration suspension, withdrawal or cancellation?

## Conclusion

The process of ISO 9000 registration can be long and is often costly. The process of selecting the best registrar for your company is important and asking the right questions is a key first step.

### About the Author

*R.T. "Bud" Weightman is President of Qualified Specialists, Inc. He is an Institute for Quality Assurance Lead Assessor and a member of the TC 176 Committee. Mr. Weightman is an ASQC Certified Quality Auditor, a certified lead auditor in the nuclear industry, and an American Petroleum Institute Lead Surveyor.*

# STEPS IN THE REGISTRATION PROCESS

BY ELIZABETH POTTS

## Introduction

The previous section discussed the process of selecting a registrar. Once the decision is made, what can and should be expected from that registrar? This section describes what to expect at each step in the process. Regardless of which registrar is selected, the registration process consists of six basic steps:

- Application
- Document Review
- Pre-Assessment
- Assessment
- Registration
- Surveillance.

## Application

To begin the registration process, all registrars require a completed application. The application will contain the rights and obligations of both the registrar and the client. It will contain such registrar rights as access to facilities and necessary information, as well as liability issues. It will contain such client rights as confidentiality, the right to appeal and complain, and instructions for the use of the registration certificate.

Clients should check conditions for terminating the application. Most applications can be terminated with 30 days written notice.

## Document Review

Once the application is completed and basic information on the company's size, scope of operations, and desired time frame for registration have been determined, the registering organization will request the company to submit documentation of its quality system.

This is generally known as a *Quality Manual*. Most registrars do not wish to see every detailed procedure the company has created at this point in the registration process. What they are looking for is the overall document that describes the quality system so that it can be compared to the appropriate ISO 9000 series standard to determine compliance. Some registrars perform this document review on-site at the facility. However, most registrars perform the review at their own offices, saving travel costs and expenses as well as the time required to host the registrar.

## Pre-Assessment

Most registering bodies recommend that a pre-assessment be conducted; some will require it. It is important when selecting a registrar that a company clarify the term *pre-assessment*. Some registering bodies use the term to mean a complete assessment, which is used to determine the current status of an operation. Others use the pre-assessment as a broad overview of a company's operations to determine its initial preparedness for a full assessment and to aid in audit planning.

In some cases, the pre-assessment is an optional step which a company seeking registration may by pass. A reputable registering body will not attempt to conduct a pre-assessment solely for the purposes of gaining additional revenue. Therefore, before a company elects not to undergo a pre-assessment, it would be wise to consider the benefits of having one conducted.

A pre-assessment could very well identify major system deficiencies (or inadequate documentation), thereby alerting the company to the need for additional preparation prior to the full assessment audit. Conversely, the company may have erroneously interpreted that certain documentation would be required, and find during the pre-assessment that the registrar would **not** require it. It should be expected that aggressive response to a perceptive pre-audit will increase the chances that the company will pass the audit on the first attempt.

A pre-assessment could result in a smaller audit team, a shorter audit, and thereby reduce overall cost of the registration process. However, be aware that if a complete pre-assessment is required by the registrar's system, another complete full assessment may also be required, with its associated time and expense, in order to be registered.

During a pre-assessment, the registrar has to be careful not to cross the line into consulting with the company. The registrar may properly evaluate the state of the supplier's quality system and documentation, and indicate clearly what will be required for registration for each ISO 9001 or ISO 9002 element. But the registrar is not to provide substantive advice and guidance to the company for the journey towards registration. A perceptive pre-assessment may identify areas in which the company might then enlist the aid of a consultant. It is not appropriate that such aid would be provided by the registrar.

## Assessment

After pre-assessment or after it has been determined that the company's documented quality system conforms to the requirements of the selected ISO 9000 standard, a full assessment is conducted. A typical assessment consists of two or three auditors who spend two to four days at a facility.

The auditors will hold an introductory meeting with company management, request escorts to assist them during the audit, hold a closing meeting to communicate any deficiencies that were discovered and probably leave a draft report containing the audit team's recommendations regarding registration.

Most registrars conduct a daily review with the client to keep them apprised of what has been detected that day and what deficiencies or findings are going to be documented. This allows the client an opportunity to respond to the stated deficiency, if desired. In most cases, all deficiencies detected, even if rectified in the course of the audit, will be reported.

During the assessment, the auditors will be interviewing all levels of personnel to determine whether the quality system as documented in the quality manual and supporting procedures has been fully implemented within the company.

## Registration

There are three possible results of an audit:

### 1)  Approval

- ■  A company will probably be registered if it has implemented all the elements of ISO 9001, ISO 9002 or ISO 9003, with only minor deficiencies detected during an assessment.

### 2)  Conditional or provisional approval

- ■  A company will probably be either conditionally or provisionally approved if:

    - ●  It has addressed all of the elements of the standard and has systems documented, but perhaps not fully implemented
    - ●  There are a number of deficiencies detected in a particular area, showing a negative trend.

■  Conditional approval requires the company to respond to any deficiencies
   noted during the time frame defined by the registering body.
■  The registering body, upon evaluation of the company's corrective action, may
   elect to perform a re-evaluation or accept the corrective action and overview
   the implementation in conjunction with subsequent surveillance visits.

### 3) Disapproval

■  The final result is disapproval, which usually occurs when a company's system
   is either very well documented but has not been implemented, or when basic
   elements of the standard such as internal auditing, corrective action or process
   control, have not been addressed at all. This situation will definitely result in a
   re-evaluation by the registering body prior to issuing registration.
■  Once a company is registered, the company receives a certificate and is listed
   in a register or directory published by registering body or another organization.

## Surveillance

It is important for a company pursuing registration to understand the duration and/or
validity of its registration. Some registering bodies have registrations that are valid
indefinitely, pending continuing successful surveillance visits. Others have registrations valid for a three-year period.

In all cases, most registering bodies conduct surveillance on a six-month schedule.
Those whose registrations expire conduct either a complete reassessment at the end
of the registration period, or an assessment that is somewhere between a surveillance
visit and a complete reassessment.

During the interval between surveillance visits, the company should continually
ensure that the quality systems that were demonstrated during the full assessment
remain in place, so that the surveillance visit will merely confirm the fact. The
internal quality audit (required by ISO 9001, Section 4.17) is a mechanism to aid in
this assurance.

However, rigorous documentation and deployment of quality practice should not
stifle continual improvement. If an improvement in practice that requires a modification in the quality systems is identified during the interval between surveillance
visits, the company should feel free to make it. The change should be specifically
documented, so that the registrar will not be surprised at the next surveillance visit.
Suppliers should work with their registrars to keep them current regarding quality-
systems changes.

## Time and Costs of Registration

The time required to implement a quality system that conforms to an ISO 9000 series standard depends on the company's current status, its commitment to the implementation of the system, and the resources it is willing to expend to implement the system. A good time frame (if a company is starting with no system or a poorly documented system) is 18 to 24 months.

The time required for actual registration depends upon the preparedness of the company and the number of deficiencies detected during the audit. Lead times are becoming increasingly critical as the demand for registration of quality systems increases. It is important, prior to choosing a registering body, to determine the resources of that registering body and whether it can meet the company's needs for registration.

There are many costs associated with registration, the first of which is actually developing and implementing the quality system. A company may elect to use only internal resources to implement the quality system, or to rely completely on the services of an outside consultant, or a combination of both approaches.

There is no guarantee, however, that registration will be achieved using any of these approaches. In fact, usually only 30 percent of companies pass a registration assessment on the first attempt.

Assessing the costs of the actual registration process should be done in great detail. When selecting a registrar, it is important that a company be totally familiar with all costs associated with the registration program. The company should ensure that it has obtained a price for application and document review and a price for a pre-assessment visit, if deemed necessary. It should also obtain the costs of the actual assessment, as well as any costs associated with issuing the registration and writing the report.

The company should be familiar with the policy of the registrar concerning the duration and cost of surveillance visits. Again, a company should know the validity period of the registration as well as any reassessment or partial reassessment costs that may be required in the future.

Furthermore, a company should be aware that some registering bodies require application fees, listing fees and registration fees in addition to those prices normally quoted for the above actions. A company must ask the registering body about all fees to ensure that the full cost of the registration is known.

In conclusion, companies should remember that they are clients of the registrar. The registrar must operate ethically. However, the client should have no fear of retribution if a complaint is necessary. The registrar should actively seek customer feedback in order continuously to improve its operations.

Furthermore, the client should feel comfortable openly discussing issues, such as scheduling and qualifications of audit teams members, with the registrar. In all cases, although the registrar cannot act as a consultant, it should be willing to guide the client through the steps of registration to ensure the maximum value service to the client.

## About the Author

*Elizabeth A. Potts is President, ABS Quality Evaluations, Inc., a third-party registrar of quality systems to a variety of standards, including the ISO 9000 series standard. Ms. Potts was most recently Quality Assurance Manager for the American Gas Association Laboratories where she was responsible for product certification follow-up inspections, ISO 9000 quality system registrations and internal quality control program development. She was also employed as a Quality Control Manager with Babcock & Wilcox, where she developed and implemented quality control programs for nuclear reactor and other defense-related components. Ms. Potts is a member of the Executive Committee of the ANSI ASC Z-1 on quality assurance and is also a member of the US Technical Advisory Group to ISO Technical Committee 176 on quality assurance and quality management. She is a registered ASQC Certified Quality Auditor (#445) and an IQA Registered Assessor.*

# IMPLEMENTING ISO 9000

BY RODERICK GOULT

## INTRODUCTION

The ISO 9000 quality assurance requirements standards represent a responsible, sensible and practical way to run a company. The basic principles are simple: say what you do, do what you say, write it down, then review and improve the process. Even if one discounts the word *quality* in the title of the ISO 9000 series standards, using the standards makes effective management sense.

Companies achieving ISO 9000 series quality system registration generally find that using the standard reduces system redundancy and improves management and communication. Some US companies complain that the ISO 9000 series is too basic or too open to loose interpretation. These firms point instead to existing company product excellence and training programs that go beyond the requirements of ISO 9000 as reasons not to invest in ISO 9000 series quality system registration.

While these companies are partially correct about ISO 9000 series limitations, an effectively structured quality management system, along with system auditing provided for in the ISO 9000 series, is a powerful quality improvement tool. This

## Making the Management of Quality Visible

Make the company policy known
- ◯ Issue a quality policy.
- ◯ Issue guidelines.
- ◯ Give training.
- ◯ Develop communications.

Demonstrate the 'quality system'
- ◯ Issue a quality manual.
- ◯ Create company procedures.
- ◯ Publish specifications.
- ◯ Lay down clear methodologies.

Declare who has authority
- ◯ Appoint a quality system representative.
- ◯ Publish organization charts.
- ◯ Have clear management structures.
- ◯ Allocate verification tasks.

Demonstrate that it all works
- ◯ Management carry out regular reviews.
- ◯ Record corrective actions.
- ◯ Review the results of audits.

Demonstrate quality of performance.
- ◯ Keep records. Carry out analyses.
- ◯ Check out all complaints.
- ◯ Track quality costs. (Not in ISO 9001/2/3.)

THE
VICTORIA
GROUP

*Table 5-1: Making the management of quality visible.*

section is a basic introduction to implementing a quality assurance system that addresses the criteria laid out in the ISO 9000 series of standards.

## Making Quality Management "Visible"

Creating a documented quality assurance management system and retaining records of that system makes quality management "visible" to the auditors. The same is true of process quality. The effectiveness of the control is seen only when records of the achievement process are analyzed. Tables 5-1 and 5-2 illustrate the overall tasks involved in making the management of quality visible and show some of the actions management can take toward that goal.

## Making the Quality of Your Process Visible

Assure Quality in Manufacture
- ○ Clear process requirements.
- ○ Job specifications.
- ○ Product specifications.

Assure Quality of Material
- ○ Documented specifications for materials.
- ○ Reviews and audits of suppliers.
- ○ Receiving inspection criteria.

Assure Quality of Process Control
- ○ Records of process activities.
- ○ Limits and tolerances defined.
- ○ Clear test and inspection documents.

Assure Quality of Process Measurements
- ○ Calibration procedures and records.
- ○ Traceable calibration standards.

Assure Quality of Deliverables
- ○ Procedures for the control of nonconforming material.
- ○ Action taken to eliminate problems, not just fix them.

Assure Quality of Delivery
- ○ Careful selection of transport vendors.
- ○ Proper storage and packaging requirements.

**THE**
**VICTORIA**
**GROUP**

*Table 5-2: Making the quality of your process visible.*

# IMPLEMENTING THE ISO 9000 SERIES STANDARDS — ASKING THE RIGHT QUESTIONS

Implementing a structured management system requires a disciplined approach, careful planning, project control, and milestone measurement. Successful implementation of an ISO 9000 series program should begin by answering four basic questions.

## 1. When Is the Anticipated Registration Date?

ISO 9000 implementation is a **process**, not a quick fix. It requires patience, training, changes of attitude, and total commitment from top management. As many companies are discovering, it requires a *paradigm shift* - a new way of looking at the role of management.

Some companies have completed the registration process in less than a year, but such an effort often requires a substantial staff commitment. A large company with a complex management structure should think in terms of at least a 12- to 18-month initial commitment.

In one instance, a 35-employee company with no previously existing quality system achieved registration in nine months. Similarly, a highly regulated company such as a pharmaceutical company, which has many existing controls in place, may have relatively little work to do to prepare for registration. Other highly regulated industries may have the same experience. Companies not operating under such strict controls, however, should not underestimate the registration timeline.

Few companies can afford to commit their resources full-time to a registration effort. Fitting the required work into busy staff schedules is also difficult, since most documentation takes two or three revisions. "Right the first time" may be the target, but it is often an elusive goal. It pays to proceed steadily and carefully. Give due consideration to every aspect of the process, including the employee who is assigned to write procedures. The person who performs a particular job is the best person to document how it is done, not that person's supervisor.

## 2. Register Part of the Organization or the Entire Organization?

If a high customer demand for registration exists for product or service A and none exists for product or service B, is registration necessary and prudent for both products?

The answer is probably **no**, unless the two products or services flow through the identical process within the company. Registration refers to the **management system**, not to the **product** resulting from that system. It is possible to have multiple systems operating within a company, producing multiple products and/or services. Managing such a situation is not easy, but sometimes it is easier than trying to operate the whole system the same way.

For example, a plastics-molding company produces high-precision items for the telecommunications industry. As a sideline it also makes small plastic toys such as those given away in cereal boxes. The telecommunication products may face market pressure for quality assurance, certification of products, and registration of the quality system. The sideline business has only one market pressure — price.

The stringent quality assurance standards on product A (high-precision telecommunication items) are not the same as those on product B (plastic toys). Therefore, the company may decide only to seek registration that covers, in its *scope statement*, the close-tolerance, high-grade injecting molding and ignores the high-volume, low-grade plastic toys. By doing so, it first registers the core business scope of the company and retains the flexibility to include other elements at a later date.

## 3. Should a Company Seek Registration to ISO 9001 or ISO 9002?

As described in Chapter 2 of this Handbook, ISO 9001 is more comprehensive than ISO 9002. ISO 9001: *Quality systems —Model for quality assurance in design/ development, production, installation and servicing*, is used when conformance to specified needs is to be ensured by the supplier throughout the entire cycle, from design to servicing. It is used when the contract specifically requires design effort and the product requirements are stated principally in performance terms.

ISO 9002: *Quality systems —Model for quality assurance in production and installation*, differs from ISO 9001 because it does not include the design function as a significant part of the organization's activity. It is used by industries that work to technical designs and specifications already provided by their customers.

The chief dilemma faced by many companies in deciding whether to register to ISO 9001 or ISO 9002 results from whether to define the term *design* in a broad or narrow sense. At one time, design encompassed only organizations which carried out original research and development. Based on that reasoning, few companies would seek the more comprehensive ISO 9001 registration.

Current concepts are different. It is generally accepted that the definition of design can be very broad. Universities and colleges can design training programs for specific curricular requirements. Banks and insurance companies design services for customers. Software houses design computer programs. A computer hardware company designs computers. However, registration bodies may not have the same definition of *design*.

To decide whether to register to ISO 9001 or ISO 9002, companies should ask two questions:

- In the continuum of the product or service offered to customers, to what extent does the design of that product or service determine the effective delivered quality and performance of the product or service supplied to the customer?

- How much control over the product or service offered to the customer is resident in the company offering the product or service?

If a company has complete control over the design of its product or service, and that control is a major factor in ensuring delivered quality, then registration to ISO 9001 is probably the correct choice.

However, if a product or service has been an integral and unchanging part of a company for many years, and the principal determining factor in ensuring the quality of the delivered product or service is the manufacturing process, then the company should choose registration to ISO 9002. A manufacturing facility whose design division is off-site can usually choose ISO 9002.

In some cases problems exist in getting the design function of a company to support a registration effort. In these situations, companies can write a *scope statement* that encompasses the entire operation, but contains a design restriction. If the registrar is willing to negotiate these restrictions, a company may specify that "at this time only the manufacturing/procurement/test…etc. areas are operating an ISO 9002-compliant system, and the design elements will be brought into an ISO 9001 system by [a specified date]."

Many companies have followed this path to ISO 9001 registration by declaring intent to embrace the design function at a later date. If design is critical to the delivered quality of a product or service, ISO 9002 can be used as a starting option, provided that the registrar concurs with an extension to ISO 9001 within a defined timeframe.

## 4. How Much Documentation Currently Exists?

In many companies, process documentation does not reside on paper, but in the collective memory of company employees. All companies have systems, but how many systems rely on the memory of trusted key staff members? If a longtime staff member is sick or leaves the job, is it really true that "everyone knows what to do?"

# ISO 9000 Interpretation:
# System Scope: Rules for ISO 9001 and ISO 9002 Registration

*By:* **Joseph Tiratto,** President, Joseph Tiratto and Associates, Inc.
**Ian Durand,** President, Service Process Consulting, Inc.
**Charles McRobert,** President, Quality Practitioners, Inc.
**Joseph Klock,** Manager, ISO Registrations, AT&T
**David L. Johnson,** Audit Manager, AT & T Quality Registrar

## Question:

Must a company with design content in its product register to ISO 9001, or can it exclude design and register to ISO 9002 given that, for registration purposes, system scope must include all company activities?

## Answer:

All five experts agreed that if design is a direct part of the process that produces a product or service, a company applying for registration would be well-advised to use the ISO 9001 standard. They were somewhat divided over the amount of influence the registrar should have in making such a decision.

McRobert said that a company with "design content in its products should not be allowed to register to ISO 9002." He noted that these companies "are selling design as part of their product and should therefore have in place an ISO 9001 system that covers design."

Durand agreed that ISO 9001 should be used by companies when production includes a design function. He noted, however, that "it is the decision of the [company] management, not the activities of the facility, that dictates the choice of the ISO quality standard used for registration."

For example, Durand noted that while he personally does not support the use of *ISO 9003: Quality systems — Model for quality assurance in final inspection and test*, at least eight facilities have been registered to ISO 9003 in the US. These include several high-tech instrumentation producers and a medical-devices producer.

Durand pointed out that registration is "almost always done at the level of a plant facility or site." He said that "unless a company's activities are confined to a single site, registration is **not** done on a company basis."

While "not all registrars may agree with the desired scope [of registration], the scope is not established by outside bodies or standards," he said. As an example, Durand cited raw-material purchasing by a corporate organization for a multi-site company. He noted that if purchasing is handled by a corporate purchasing organization and not individual plant managers, the selection of suppliers would be "outside the scope of assessment and should be so noted on the registration certificate."

*(continued on next page)*

# ISO 9000 Interpretation:
## System Scope: Rules for ISO 9001 and ISO 9002 Registration
*(continued from previous page)*

Durand emphasized that "all companies do design, even if only to design the process they use to produce the service or product." He noted that some companies choose ISO 9002 as an "intermediate step" before seeking ISO 9001 registration.

Durand found no requirement in either *ISO/IEC Guide 48: Guidelines for third-party assessment and registration of a supplier's quality system*, or in Section 8 of ISO 9000, requiring the use of a particular quality assurance model. He said the customer needs to understand the strengths and limitations of ISO 9001, ISO 9002 and ISO 9003, and then decide which standard to select.

Klock and Johnson clearly prefered that a company with design content in its product line register to ISO 9001. They both claimed, however, that ISO 9002 registration is possible—though not preferable—in some cases where there is design content.

"The standards community needs to do additional work [to clarify] responsibility for choosing the applicable standard in third-party registration. The role of the registrar in choosing a standard is not well-defined in the standards and guidelines," Klock and Johnson pointed out, adding, "in practice, the registrar represents the customer and has the responsibility to use the most applicable standard."

Klock and Johnson said that a supplier may choose to restrict products in the scope, but "generally should not exclude existing functions covered by the standard." ISO 9000 registration "assures the capability of a supplier's system to meet [specific quality] requirements, and only ISO 9001 covers design."

"Bypassing the basic design requirements of ISO 9001 may shortchange a customer who requires design work and relies on quality system registration to select competent suppliers," Klock and Johnson agreed.

Temporarily excluding design while waiting for a supplier to implement a quality system for design can pose a problem if the implementation [of ISO 9001] is unsuccessful," Klock and Johnson noted. "Such exemptions should become part of a registrar's policy after review by the managing board of customers and suppliers."

Tiratto agreed that the decision for registration to ISO 9001 or ISO 9002 is determined by the supplier who is seeking registration. Ultimately, the decision will be influenced in the marketplace by requirements that may be imposed on the supplier by customers or government regulations for certain products, such as EC directives.

More important, does management's conception of "how the system works" coincide with what really happens on the shop floor or elsewhere in the company? Not only might the process differ from the manager's conception, but it may be constantly changing without benefit of regular audit or review.

To correct this, a company should conduct a thorough review. Do sales and marketing staff follow systems to ensure that all relevant data needed is collected so that customer needs are met? Does the design staff receive all required data to meet customer expectations, and is it always in the same format? Does the design staff have control of documents and drawings? Do design procedures ensure that constraints of manufacturability, testability, maintainability, reliability and safety are considered?

In addition, a company that is trying to determine its optimum level of documentation should consider these additional questions:

- Is all the data required to procure, engineer into production, build, inspect, test, store, deliver and maintain a product provided in a consistent format?

- Do all these departments have clear instructions as to how the overall tasks are to be performed?

- Is all testing performed to the same specifications on controlled, calibrated test equipment?

- Does the company have records to prove that control exists?

These are just some of the questions companies seeking registration must address when evaluating current documentation. Many companies are shocked by the lack of positive answers to these questions.

Quality expert Phil Crosby compares the way companies operate by contrasting a game of ice hockey and the art of ballet. Despite the fact that a game of ice hockey operates by a well-defined set of rules, no two games are alike. By contrast, in a ballet, which encompasses many elements drawn together under planned, controlled conditions, every performance is essentially the same. He says that running a company can be like ballet, if planning, rehearsal, review and control are part of the corporate "score."

# GETTING READY FOR ISO 9000 REGISTRATION

The decision to implement a documented quality system based on ISO 9000 series standards affects every element of a company and will significantly change the way a company does business.

## Key Ingredient — Support from Management

A successful program must be driven by support from committed top management. Whether or not the effort of analysis and documentation is undertaken to achieve registration or is used as an internal quality management tool makes no difference in the degree of commitment or effort required.

Obtaining management support is not always easy. When the demand for registration is customer-driven, most senior executives recognize the sensible course. When this is not the case, however, the program has to be sold to them in the same way as any other venture which will require an investment in time and money.

Here are the key points to emphasize:

■ Registration enables a company to demonstrate visibly to its customers its commitment to quality
■ Registration may provide opportunities to enter markets which are open only to registered firms.

Moreover, an ISO 9000-based system will:

■ Improve the ability to collect quality metrics and thereby improve both quality and the cost of quality.
■ Enhance the ability to develop stable processes and eliminate costly surprises.
■ Improve overall business efficiency by eliminating wasteful and unnecessary duplication in management systems.
■ Be simply a better way to do business.

## Use a Project Management Approach

Once the company is committed, a project management approach should be adopted, and the process treated in the same way as any other major business undertaking.

## Assign Responsibility and Authority

The first step is to assign someone the responsibility and authority to drive the project. This person does not necessarily have to be the quality manager. The standard states that the management representative should be a person who, "irrespective of other responsibilities," ensures that the system in support of the standard is effectively maintained.

The quality manager may provide input, even if not the one selected to drive the process. This is a management system for the entire business. Every member of the firm — from the CEO to the janitors — needs to have involvement and input.

## Create a Team

Once appointed, the project manager needs a team with which to work. Volunteers should be drawn from all levels and areas of the company. To generate interest in volunteering, the project manager should undertake a program of general ISO awareness. Schedule time to enable every member of the company to attend a short (a few hours is sufficient) awareness session that explains what the ISO 9000 series standards are, how implementation will affect day-to-day work, and what the benefits will be.

## Develop Milestones

The next step is to develop a set of milestones for the process; these are outlined below. In the following example, a five-month set of milestones is described. The timeframe will vary, depending on the type of company and its existing quality system.

### *Month 1*

■ Seek good, reliable, well-informed ISO 9000 trainers for the team. Either send key members out for training or bring it in-house. Some buying hints include:

- Have the tutors helped other companies work toward successful registration?
- Have the tutors worked in ISO 9000-registered companies?

Do not use Lead Auditor training as a means of learning how to implement ISO 9000. Use a proper implementation program, or start with a two-day "What is ISO 9000?" introductory session.

■ Determine whether a consultant is going to be employed to assist the process.

Although many companies achieve ISO 9000 registration without using outside consultants, it may be a good investment to make. A consultant will be needed only to provide intermittant guidance to keep the program on track.

A consultant team should **not** do the full job of developing a company's documentation; that is the responsibility of the company itself.

In seeking a consultant, companies should find out if the consultant is a UK- or RAB-Certified Auditor. The Certified Quality Auditor (CQA) qualification from the American Society for Quality Control (ASQC) is **not** the same.

■  Has the consultant helped other companies through the process of registration to one of the ISO 9000 standards?

Companies should ask for and obtain references for the consultants they employ. A good consultant will provide them!

## Months 2 and 3

■  Conduct a business analysis.

Will the quality system be a unified system, or sectioned to reflect different business units? Analyze and decide.

■  Create a high-level flow chart.

How does the data flow through the entire business activity, from order replacement to customer delivery?

This should show the flow of information, not the activities associated with departments. It is important that this chart show what exists, not what should be.

■  Review the chart and determine whether the existing system reflects the correct information flow. If not, re-draw the flow chart and correct it.

■  Analyze those departments included in the flow chart and determine how many of them are already documented. Keep track of this information for future use.

## Month 4

■  Allocate each departmental block to an individual project team member, whose task is to begin working with employees to develop a generalized flow chart of the activities within that department. More detailed analysis comes later in the process.

■ Using the flow charts, establish a record of existing documentation.

Frequently, companies discover a significant number of written procedures already in place. Unless they are hopelessly out of date, these documents should never be discarded and should be incorporated into a new ISO 9001- or ISO 9002-based system. There is no need for duplication; companies should take advantage of and build on these pre-existing "foundations."

## *Month 5*

■ Determine what is missing for a system-wide structure of documented procedures. The system should link all departments effectively, thereby ensuring a smooth flow of information through the company. The Victoria Group calls this *gap analysis* and it will often include an audit of the active system.

Many companies employ an independent consultant to perform this audit in order to provide a more objective assessment of their system. Companies would be well-advised to check the ISO 9000 credentials of the consultant used for the gap analysis to ensure the best possible evaluation at this early stage.

■ All employees should begin to produce missing documentation. The best candidate for the task is the employee who performs the job daily. Everyone from the chief executive to the maintenance staff should be involved in flow-chart activity as well as in writing the procedures and work instructions.

A framework should be provided, and afterwards the documents should be edited to maintain a consistent style. The author of every document in the system should be the person uses it to do the job.

This is true empowerment. It gives each individual the opportunity to participate in determining how his or her particular job should be performed, and allows participation in the creation of the management system.

■ The system is complete. Verify that it meets all sections of the appropriate standard by performing a *schedule of conformity* analysis (see below). Then move into the full implementation stage of the operation.

# ELEMENTS OF GOOD DOCUMENTATION...
# HOW TO STRUCTURE DOCUMENTATION BENEFICIALLY

Documentation should help customers and auditors understand how a quality management system addresses the requirements of ISO 9001, ISO 9002 or ISO 9003.

However, companies must remember that a quality system program belongs to its creators and no other individual or organization. The process of obtaining registration must be secondary to the real-time organizational benefits of having an effective and fully functional quality system.

Quality system documentation and manuals are not required to resemble any standard or conform to any pre-ordained numbering system. Manuals do not have to use formal language or even the same tense as the standard. A quality system and its documentation should reflect the way a particular company operates.

## Layers of Structure

The first requirement in preparing a documentation system is to evaluate how the system will be structured. Quality systems have moved increasingly into the commercial arena in the last 15 years. A clear pattern for documentation has developed that may be described as current "best practice," although there are other ways to achieve the same results.

The documentation hierarchy has four tiers or layers. Each layer develops a steadily increasing level of detail about company operations and methods. These layers are shown in Figure 5-1 and consist of a quality manual, company operating procedures, work instructions, and records.

The layers in Figure 5-1 are presented as a broad-based triangle. All documentation should cascade from one level to the next to meet traceability and control requirements. Dividing the system in this way applies the political philosophy of "divide and rule" to the control of paperwork. The system should be structured so that changes at one level will virtually never affect a higher level, but may affect the levels below.

## What To Do First

Write a procedure outlining the document-control methods and practices. It is important that the control techniques be established before any attempt is made to structure a quality manual.

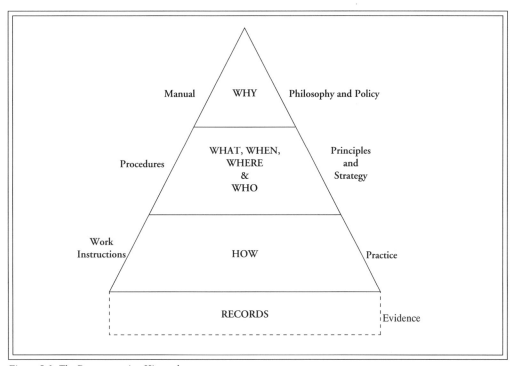

*Figure 5-1: The Documentation Hierarchy.*

What elements should be addressed in a procedure? The hierarchy diagram shows the procedure as a document that explains the *what*, *when*, *where* and *who* of the system. It will also at times describe the high-level *how*.

Questions and answers to consider when creating a procedure are:

- What should this procedure achieve? Define the scope and purpose of the document.
- Who should perform this task? Define the responsibilities by precise job title.
- What is the task? Outline and describe the task as simply as possible. Include when and where the task occurs, if appropriate.
- Are there any related activities? List any other documents directly integrated with the task.
- How is the task demonstrated? Detail the records created.

# Writing Documentation

These five questions focus and simplify the task of creating both procedures and work instructions. A procedure's scope statement enables differentiation between procedures that have company-wide application and those that are created for a single department or activity. For example, allow for differences in the complexity of document control between software engineering and the receiving department.

By applying this basic formula to the process, the documentation author is forced to think in clear, logical steps. When describing the task itself, the best approach is to create a flow chart of activity. This approach also forces a disciplined, logical approach.

## Work Instructions

These same rules should be applied to the writing of work instructions. Usually this level of documentation is machine-, task-, or product-specific. Work instructions should be written by those who know and perform the tasks. These employees should be consulted when creating the work instruction data.

Not only is this method efficient, it also creates pride of ownership in the documentation. Authors are far more likely to ensure that the documentation is current, properly applied, and that any required changes are made. This level of support from documentation-users makes it far easier to maintain.

Once created, the document must be controlled. Key elements will ensure that document control is simple and effective:

- Creating a numbering system that can flow down from procedures to work instructions and that provides a visible numeric or alphanumeric link
- Giving every document a clear and simple name
- Numbering each page of every document number in an "x of y" format where "y" is the total number of pages in the document (Example: page 3 of 18)
- Keeping a record of the document's issue or revision status clearly visible on the document itself, including brief details of any changes
- Keeping a record of the authorized holders of every document with the master copy. Establish a method for clearly identifying uncontrolled copies of documents
- Keeping the records up to date.

These same elements apply in a "paperless" computer system. Documents should be clearly identified, both in the computer and on disk.

## ISO 9000 Requirements Check

Create a *schedule of conformity* to check that every section of the relevant ISO 9000 series standard has been effectively addressed. This simple matrix (see Table 5-3) compares the documented system with the requirements of the standard being applied. It shows the section or sections of the standard addressed by each of the procedures within the system.

A useful technique in organizing the matrix lists company procedures down the shorter left-hand side of a "landscape" page and the sections of the standard across the longer top. A separate column should be provided for each of the "shall" statements in the section that are checked off as each one is addressed.

Once completed, every compulsory section of the standard should have at least one check mark against it unless it has been written out of the system. For example, Section 4.19: Servicing, of ISO 9001, might be omitted if the company has no service facility. The Quality Manual should explain all omissions; if a section is not covered, it should not be part of the system.

The matrix, which acts as a road map through the quality documentation, will also help auditors understand the system. A section of a typical matrix is shown in Table 5-3.

| Procedure Number & Name | 4.1 Management Responsibility | | | | | 4.2 Quality System | | 4.3 Contract Review | | |
|---|---|---|---|---|---|---|---|---|---|---|
| | 4.1.1 | 4.1.2.1 | 4.1.2.2 | 4.1.2.3 | 4.1.3 | 4.2(a) | 4.2(b) | 4.3(a) | 4.3 (b) | 4.3(c) |
| Quality Manual | X | X | X | X | X | X | X | X | X | X |
| Marketing MK/00 1/ Order intake | | | | | | | | X | | |
| MK/002/ Review of quotations | | | | | | | | | X | X |
| MK/003/ Pricing policy | | | | | | | | | | |
| Procurement PK/001 Pricing Quotations | | | | | | | | | X | X |

*Table 5-3: Schedule of Conformity.*

Table 5-3 highlights those procedures which could be outside the scope of the audit. For example, MK/003 in Table 5-3 deals with pricing policies and falls outside the scope.

This approach has proven quite effective. Variations of this matrix are possible and each company working on the standard will no doubt construct its own document.

# ISO 9000 IMPLEMENTATION —
# HOW TO AVOID COMMON PITFALLS

Management is committed. The ISO 9000 team has been trained. Analysis has been completed and the workforce has completed writing all the required documents which were identified by *Gap Analysis* (missing procedures needed for a system-wide structure).

But what does the management representative do with this system when it is complete and all the new documentation is neatly lined up on the bookshelf? Some fundamental questions naturally arise:

- How is the system going to be properly implemented and controlled?
- How will the management representative ensure that everyone uses all the newly assembled procedures and work instructions?
- What about changes needed because something was missing when the data were collected for a procedure or work instruction?
- How can the management team be encourage to make the review process meaningful?
- What can be done to persuade people not to mark-up "control documents"?

These and other difficult questions make the creation of an ISO 9000 system look easy. Making it happen is the difficult part. An answer does exist: the *quality system audit*. The quality system audit is a company's single-most-powerful tool for continuous improvement.

In order for the quality system to function properly, a structured audit system should be established which will encompass every element of the documented system on a regular, planned basis. Regular auditing of every aspect of the company detects any changes required in the process, as well as any deficiencies or changes required in the paperwork.

## Suggestions For Writing Documentation

In writing the text, remember the KISS principle: *Keep It Short and Simple*. Use straight-forward words and terms; do not use this documentation to demonstrate a vast and sophisticated command of the English language. Follow novelist George Orwell's suggestion to ask six questions before writing begins:

- ○ What am I trying to say?
- ○ What words will best express it?
- ○ What image or idiom will make it more clear?
- ○ Is this image fresh enough to have an effect?
- ○ Could I have put it more shortly?
- ○ Have I said anything that is ugly?

More ground rules to follow include:

- ○ Make the meaning very clear.
- ○ Sift out all irrelevant material.
- ○ Ensure that the text is grammatically correct; avoid the use of passive verbs and split infinitives.
- ○ Search out errors in spelling and punctuation.
- ○ Avoid jargon and "committee language."
- ○ Use the simplest language to convey the thought.
- ○ Use clear words and phrases.
- ○ Use short sentences.
- ○ Use punctuation thoughtfully and in a way to aid understanding.
- ○ Separate ideas into individual sentences or paragraphs.

Remember that these are documents written to enable co-workers to perform their tasks more efficiently and consistently. Also remember that documentation users are intelligent; they just have different skills. Therefore:

- ○ Do not write in an antagonistic manner.
- ○ Do not write in a condescending manner.
- ○ Do not write in a supercilious manner.

## Five Quality Failures

British quality system expert and author Lionel Stebbing describes certain fundamental problems that frequently recur during management system audits as the "Five Quality Failures." Quality system registrars report that these five problems are the most common causes of noncompliance. Good ISO 9000 consultants help their clients avoid them.

### 1. Document Control (ISO 9001, Clause 4.5)

Nearly 70 percent of all noncompliance, according to one registrar, is in the area of document control. Here are some examples of inadequate document control:

- Out-of-date versions of procedures, work instructions and engineering drawings left in areas where they are "available for use"
- Marked-up documents — urgent changes documented by writing on the master in red ink...and left that way
- Copies of important system documentation not available where needed for effective implementation of the management system
- Keeping the master set of documents in a foreman's office. This procedure may make sense in terms of control, but if the foreman locks the office at the end of the day shift, leaving the late shift staff without access to those documents, they may as well not exist!

Some of the worst offenders in document control are often the technical and engineering staffs. Frequently, and quite legitimately, the technical staff needs copies of drawings and specifications. They often write and draw on these documents as changes are developed. The practice is acceptable provided the drawing, specification or print is clearly marked with *uncontrolled copy—not to be used for production purposes* or some similar wording.

Another common problem in design and development areas is the use of outdated copies of *National Standards and Specifications.*

### 2. Calibration (ISO 9001, Clause 4.11)

The range of equipment identified as requiring calibration is frequently extensive, but if the standard is not read carefully, this list can be overextensive. The requirement is to calibrate equipment used to verify conformance: items that are for "indication only" or provide process checks but not conformity checks need not be calibrated to traceable standards.

It is important to track calibrated equipment with a good positive-recall system when items become due for recalibration. It is important that the system ensure that the person managing calibration has the freedom and authority to withdraw equipment from use when it is due for review.

Often this individual is given the responsibility for managing the calibration system, but no authority to make it work! The two things are different, and both must be in place.

Establishing a reliable calibration program is not that difficult. Several competent software programs exist which will handle the date-dependent recall requirements if loaded into continuously operational systems. Several of these programs also provide the necessary data storage on pre- and- post-calibration measurements to assist in the definition of calibration intervals.

Calibration in some way is almost mandatory when using techniques such as Statistical Process Control (SPC). If numbers are being used to generate charts, and the evaluation of those charts will be used to predict future process requirements, then the validity of the measurements made is vital.

An acquaintance of the author, involved with a subcontractor assurance program, described a visit made to one company that proudly showed an impressive range of SPC activities, covering many aspects of the operation. When questions were asked about the continued variance in the process, despite recorded corrective actions, it was discovered that none of their test equipment had been calibrated. The test results, and therefore all SPC data, were inaccurate.

## 3. Keeping Track (ISO 9001, Clause 4.12)

An inadequate "paper trail" of the status of all equipment used in the system is another common problem. Giving the user responsibility is one way efficiently to keep track of all pieces of measuring equipment contained within the system.

Whenever tests or inspections are made using equipment that is part of the calibration system, validation of calibration status should be the first item on the test or inspection report.

The second entry should be an annotation that work was stopped and the appropriate person contacted if equipment was found out of calibration. The user is the only person who can completely validate that this system works. Equipment used by field-service personnel must also be tested; it is an area that is easily overlooked.

## 4. Good Training Records (ISO 9001, Clause 4.18)

All too often the only training that is documented in many organizations is that which is provided outside the company or in-house training that takes place away from an individual's normal place of work.

Are good records available for the job-specific skills training received by each employee? Does the company routinely provide job-specific training to each employee, and if so, how? In most companies, there is a considerable amount of on-the-job training, sometimes called by names such as the "buddy" system. These forms of training can have immense value if they are properly managed, maintained and documented.

Make sure that all training is properly documented and that records exist to demonstrate who has been trained and in what skills, throughout the company.

The training syllabus may be no more than a list of skills required by an individual fulfilling a specific task. The record could be an identical list with an individual's name at the top and spaces provided for a date and signature by each skill item. A responsible individual can sign off that the requisite skill has been mastered.

Training records should be readily accessible to those who need them on a regular basis; this is not usually the human resources department but day-to-day supervisors. Wherever and however these records are maintained, ensure that they are readily accessible **where** they are required.

## 5. Planning for The Customer (ISO 9001, Clause 4.3)

The ISO 9000 series standards require *contract review* between the purchaser and supplier. Make sure evidence exists showing that a review has been made of all orders placed to ensure that the customer's requirements are clearly understood and can be met. This includes delivery and price as well as the technical ability to provide what has been requested. An obligation exists to ensure that any requirements "differing from those in the contract are resolved." (Clause 4.3)

Many businesses do not have a formal process to respond to an invitation to tender, or to a request for quote, followed by an order placement. Often, what happens is that the customer simply sends in an order for a certain number of items for delivery on a specific date.

The response from the supplier accepting the order may reflect a change in the delivery date. This is not, in and of itself, an adequate review. A mechanism should exist to ensure that any change in delivery date is negotiated and that a new date is agreed to by both parties. The process does not have to be complex, but it should happen and the record should exist.

## Review and Audit

The above discussion has identified five of the most common areas of weakness that a comprehensive and effective system of internal auditing would uncover. An inadequate procedure for internal quality system audit and review itself is a another common weakness revealed by assessments.

An internal auditing function allows a company to plan, perform and verify corrective actions. Corrective actions must happen in a closed-loop environment. Whenever a corrective action is required — whether it is a process, product or system — the proper action must be completed and the effectiveness verified. An adequate response and properly documented records prevent the problem from recurring.

The contribution made to the efficiency and reliability of a quality system by the internal audit and review process cannot be over-emphasized. Management must dedicate resources and support to this process by making the review of the results of internal audits — and the follow-up and close-out of those audits reports — a matter of high priority. It is the only way to ensure the continued reliability and effectiveness of any quality system.

# THE REGISTRATION AUDIT PROCESS

A little extra time spent preparing the entire company for a visit by an ISO 9000 series registration audit will pay huge dividends, even if the company already has a well-documented system in place or if the implementation effort began with virtually nothing down on paper.

Management team must fully understand the registration audit process. For many companies, an ISO 9000 audit will be the first experience with a detailed, objective team of auditors whose sole task is to examine the management system for compliance with a standard. Auditors have been trained to suppress personal bias and focus on facts.

The audit team does not threaten the survival of the company; no lawsuits or suspension of shipments will follow from their visit, nor will they impose changes on the system through whims, fads or fancies. The company staff need not be defensive, protective, confusing or misleading.

The structure of the accreditation and registration process in the United States, Europe, and the United Kingdom is established around a series of international standards detailing the process framework.

ISO 10011: *Guidelines for auditing quality systems*, provides guidelines for the conduct and management of an audit, and the training of auditors. ISO 10011, Part 1, not only spells out the responsibilities of the auditor and the audit manager, but also details the responsibilities of the auditee in Clause 4.2: *Roles and Responsibilities.* A company that hires a registrar to perform a facility audit commits itself to meeting the requirements contained in this section.

## Auditee's Responsibility

The ISO 10011 standard requires that the management of the company being audited (*auditee*) perform the following activities:

### Inform relevant employees about the objectives and scope of the audit

Everyone in the company is responsible for quality and, therefore, everyone should be aware of the upcoming audit. The ISO 9000 coordinator should meet with the management team to discuss what will happen during the audit.

The coordinator should explain the scope of corporate activities that will be explored by the auditors and remind management that they should be open, frank, honest and cooperative with the auditors. Team leaders should explain the auditing process. They should know that employees will be interviewed at all levels in the company and observations recorded as the audit proceeds.

### Appoint responsible members of the staff to accompany members of the audit team

The company should arrange for guides for the audit team. The guides should be members of staff who know the system and the company. Staff members who are trained and active internal auditors are excellent choices. Not only will the company gain good intelligence from these guides as the audit progresses, but such individuals will also be able to ensure that any misunderstanding or miscommunication between any auditor and the interviewee is quickly corrected.

Make guides aware that they should not answer for others, nor interrupt or try to influence the auditor unless something is going wrong. A guide who is helpful and cooperative to the auditor can help the company in making the auditor feel relaxed and comfortable with the environment.

## Provide all resources needed for the audit team in order to ensure an effective and efficient audit process

The auditors will need to spend private time together exchanging information and tracing requests as well as discussing findings. Provide a convenient room for these discussions and necessary facilities such as telephone, fax and photocopier. Make arrangements for refreshments and lunch as well. Remember: time is precious; bringing lunch in to the auditors is often the preferred choice.

## Provide access to facilities and evidential material as requested by the auditors

The audit team will require access to all areas of the company that influence the activities outlined in the registration scope statement. Do not try to refuse access to areas during the audit by claiming "commercial confidentiality." Everything the auditors see during the activity is treated as confidential. Protecting this information is an essential part of the code of conduct of the Registered Assessor (UK) or Certified Auditor (US).

If a company wants certain areas to be off-limits, these must be declared and agreed upon before the auditors arrive. Avoid surprises during the audit; they unsettle everyone and cause unnecessary tension.

As the audit progresses, the company will be asked to produce its records — from receiving inspection to management meeting minutes — to assist the auditor in seeking objective evidence of compliance. Ensure that everyone understands that material should be available to the auditors, not hidden from them. Producing records of all types is important to the process; declining access to them will damage the process. This is particularly true in the area of training records.

## Cooperate with the auditors to permit audit objectives to be achieved

The registrar wants the company to succeed as much as the company wants to succeed. Audit teams normally arrive with a positive attitude, seeking reasons for success, not reasons to be unsuccessful. When a company achieves registration, everyone is happy: the auditors, the registrar, and the company's customers.

The registration audit is the start of a long-term relationship between the registrar and the company, and like any other long term relationship, it is important to get off to a good start.

Make everyone, including security staff, aware that the audit team is going to be on-site, and what the auditors will require. One of the requirements of the ISO 9000 standard is that the Quality Policy of the company should be "understood, implemented, and maintained" at all levels of the organization. An auditor who encounters employees who do not know why an auditor is there or what he is doing may wonder how well this section has been implemented.

## Determine and initiate corrective actions based on the audit report

Once the audit is completed and the Lead Auditor has presented the team findings to the company, corrective actions may be needed. Respond promptly and effectively to these requests. The audit team leader will expect to see that a corrective action is solved, the nonconformance reported, and that the company has taken effective action to prevent recurrence.

The primary purpose of an ISO 9000-based quality system is the prevention of nonconformance at all stages. Respond to the audit finding accordingly. The standard also requires that corrective actions be effective. Ensure that the decisions taken in correcting any problems not only fix the problem and endeavor to eliminate the root cause, but provide the ability to ensure future effectiveness (i.e., will be auditable in the future).

## Explain the Process to Staff

In addition to addressing the above requirements of ISO 10011, Part 1, a company can take other actions that will make the audit effective. A key action is to explain the process clearly to all employees.

Time invested in teaching employees how to respond to auditors is time well-spent. Most people are nervous when being audited. Explaining the process in advance can help reduce nervousness and make things run more smoothly.

Make sure that each employee:

■   Understands that it is the system — not the staff — that is under scrutiny.

■ Has all the available documentation that the system says he/she should have.

■ Understands that, when asked questions, he/she should respond honestly and concisely, answering the question asked.

■ Doesn't answer the question he/she thinks the auditor **meant** to ask; doesn't volunteer masses of extra information. (It can cause problems and more often it merely confuses the auditor.)

■ Is taught to say, "I don't know," or "That isn't something I am involved with," in response to a question that goes outside his/her area of responsibility. (Most people hate to admit ignorance and will often try to answer questions about things that really are not their responsibility. This can confuse the auditor and waste time.)

■ Is taught to say, "I don't understand your question," when that is the appropriate response. They should ask for clarification when the auditor's questions aren't clearly understood.

Some auditors have difficulty in phrasing their questions in everyday language or will use the words they grew up with rather than the terms used in the company. Other auditors use formal language directly from the standard which some staff do not understand.

A company in Colorado recently experienced problems during an audit due to the way the auditors phrased their questions. According to company officials, "nonconforming material" was not a term used or understood on the shop floor.

■ Appreciates that the auditors will take notes, ask for observations to be signed, and collect some copies of "objective evidence" as they audit the facility.

The fact that something has been written down does not mean a problem exists. It is important for the comfort factor of both the auditor and the auditee that this is clearly understood.

# CONCLUSION

When all the audit reports are written and all the corrective actions taken and verified, the company will be a member of the exclusive club of registered firms. It means that management has committed to the concept of quality as a management issue, and thus to the start of the endless journey of continuous improvement. It means that the company has a more competitive opportunity in the international marketplace, and that its chances of survival in the world market are greatly enhanced, provided that the enthusiasm which took the company successfully through registration is maintained.

The registrar will return at regular intervals — typically two to four times a year — to conduct *surveillance audits*. The main effort, however, is internal. Constant vigilance by every employee to ensure the ongoing success and progress of the system is essential. Most important of all is management's constant and unwavering commitment to the path they have chosen. Remember: survival in the business world is no longer guaranteed!

## About the Author

*Roderick Goult is Chairman and Chief Executive with The Victoria Group, Ltd. He specializes in electronics, software quality and training. Mr. Goult's prior experience includes working with a number of ISO 9000 development projects on the United Kingdom's Department of Trade and Industry Quality Initiative projects and in assisting manufacturers in the United Kingdom and Sweden to obtain BABT approval. In addition, he spent six years as quality manager in AQAP-1 military communications design and manufacture. Mr. Goult is a lead assessor registered by the Governing Board of the UK National Registration Scheme for Assessors of Quality Systems.*

# ISO 9000 AND OTHER QUALITY STANDARDS

## INTRODUCTION

The ISO 9000 system standards are one of several quality system standards and guidelines developed by industry. This chapter compares the ISO 9000 standards to other well-known quality standards, including:

- The Malcolm Baldrige National Quality Award
- The Deming Prize
- Auto Industry Quality Standards
- The US Department of Defense's MIL-Q-9858A and MIL-I-45208A Standards.

# A COMPARISON OF ISO 9000 QUALITY REQUIREMENTS, MALCOLM BALDRIGE NATIONAL QUALITY AWARD GUIDELINES AND DEMING/SPC-BASED TQM PRACTICE

## BY JOEL S. FINLAY, RODC

The intent of the ISO 9000 series requirements is simple. The standard requires that a basic quality system be implemented to ensure customers that suppliers have the capabilities and systems to provide quality products and/or services.

A major goal of the Malcolm Baldrige National Quality Award (MBNQA) is to increase US competitiveness worldwide. This is consistent with W. Edwards Deming's concerns about the competitive global marketplace. In his 1986 book, *Out of the Crisis*, Deming warned that the western world needs a "transformation of the American style of management" and not merely a "reconstruction" or "revision." He further pointed out that this new way "requires a whole new structure, from foundation upward."

Comparing ISO 9000 requirements, the MBNQA guidelines, and Deming-based Total Quality Management (TQM) practices is a difficult task. To use a simple analogy, the ISO 9000 standards are like three starched, white business shirts — small, medium, and large — form-fitting but not expected to cover the whole body. MBNQA is like a giant, one-size-fits-all T-shirt with 33 pockets in which specific articles are to be placed. Deming-based TQM is like a whole wardrobe full of clothing from which the user is expected to select a set of clothing to fit his or her organization.

## Requirements of the Three Systems

### ISO 9000

ISO 9000 series requirements are clearly defined, but how the requirements are to be met is left largely to the organization. Clear documentation of all work processes affecting quality is required, but that documentation can be written as work instructions, basic training for employees, attached as a rider on a particular manufactured item or service, or even displayed as a process flow chart in a work area.

The ISO 9000 series concentrates almost exclusively on results criteria, although process criteria may meet some ISO 9000 series requirements, depending upon the lead assessor. Registering to the ISO 9000 series probably requires the least change in organizational involvement. A traditional, mass-inspection-oriented organization could readily be registered.

## MBNQA

MBNQA guidelines are clearly demarcated and the methods for meeting the guidelines fairly well-defined. MBNQA guidelines are documentation-dependent. An organization committed to basing its quality initiative upon the MBNQA guidelines must expect a high level of documentation in many areas.

MBNQA guidelines are somewhat more results-oriented than process-oriented, but the organization is required to follow both results and process criteria. MBNQA requires specific organizational involvement and change.

## Deming-Based TQM

Deming-based TQM is much more open than MBNQA or ISO 9000. It has no firm requirements other than to meet and/or exceed customer needs through an understanding of the organization and the effects of current management practices, and by the use of applied statistics. It expects the senior managers of an organization to consider management style through a scientific examination of Deming's 14 points, and then prove or disprove those points as they apply to the organization.

Deming expects senior managers to establish a controlled, customer-focused, continuously improving organization. That kind of organization has requirements, but in practice it must define these requirements in a Deming-based TQM system. That is, form should follow function. Documentation showing how processes are to be accomplished is necessary. It is up to an organization to document processes so as to communicate effectively to those who need to know. Deming-based TQM involves the most organizational involvement and organizational change of the three systems.

## ISO 9000 Compared to MBNQA

MBNQA is a larger overall system than the ISO 9000 series. Several MBNQA requirements are either not covered or receive only a cursory mention in the ISO 9000 series. Spreading knowledge about quality to other organizations is not an ISO 9000 series requirement, but it is a clear requirement of the MBNQA. The ISO 9000 series has no requirement for quality leadership benchmarking. It makes little provision for employee recognition and performance, employee morale, quality-results benchmarking, customer-relationship management, and customer-satisfaction benchmarking.

**Legend:**
- ● Highly Aligned
- ○ Somewhat Aligned
- □ Little/No Alignment
- ⊠ At Odds

Columns (Malcolm Baldrige National Quality Award Criteria):

Leadership — Senior Executive Leadership (SEL), Quality Values (QV), Management for Quality (MQ), Public Responsibility (PR)
Information and Analysis — Quality Data/Information (QDI), Quality Data Analysis (QDA)
Strategic Quality Planning — Strategic Quality Planning Process (SQPP), Quality Leadership Indicators in place (QLI), Quality Priorities (QP)
Human Resource Utilization — Human Resource Management (HRM), Employee Involvement (EI), Quality education and Training (QET), Employee Recognition and Performance Measures (ERP), Employee Well-being and Morale (EWM)
Quality Assur. of Prod./Serv. — Design/Introduction of Quality Services and Products (DIP), Process/Quality Control (PQC), Continuous Improvement (CI)

| ISO 9000 Quality Systems American National Standard | SEL | QV | MQ | PR | QDI | QDA | SQPP | QLI | QP | HRM | EI | QET | ERP | EWM | DIP | PQC | CI |
|---|---|---|---|---|---|---|---|---|---|---|---|---|---|---|---|---|---|
| **4.0 Quality System Requirements** | | | | | | | | | | | | | | | | | |
| 4.1 Management Responsibility | ● | ● | ● | | ○ | ● | ○ | | ● | ● | ● | ● | | | ● | ● | ● |
| 4.2 Quality System | | ● | ● | | ● | ● | ● | | ● | ● | ● | | | | ● | ● | |
| 4.3 Contract Review | | | | ○ | ○ | | | | | | | | | | ● | ● | ○ |
| 4.4 Design Control | | | | ○ | ○ | ○ | | | | | | | | | ● | ● | |
| 4.5 Document Control | | | | ○ | ○ | | | | | | | | | | | | |
| 4.6 Purchasing | | | | ○ | ○ | ○ | | ● | | | | | | | | ○ | |
| 4.7 Purchaser Supplied Product | | | | ○ | ○ | ○ | | ● | | | | | | | | ○ | |
| 4.8 Product Identification and Traceability | | | | ○ | ○ | | | | | | | | | | | ● | |
| 4.9 Process Control | | | | ○ | ○ | | | | | ● | ○ | ○ | | | | ● | |
| 4.10 Inspection and Testing | | | | ○ | ○ | | | | | | ○ | | | | | ● | |
| 4.11 Inspection, Measuring, and Test Equipment | | | | ○ | ○ | | | | | | | | | | ● | ● | |
| 4.12 Inspection and Test Status | | | | ○ | ○ | | | | | | | | | | ● | ● | |
| 4.13 Control of Nonconforming Product | | | | ○ | ○ | | | | | | | | | | | ● | |
| 4.14 Corrective Action | | | ● | | ○ | ● | | | | | | | | | | ● | |
| 4.15 Handling, Storage, Packaging, and Delivery | | | | ○ | ○ | | | | | | | | | | | ● | |
| 4.16 Quality Records | | | | ○ | ● | ● | ● | | | | | | | | | | |
| 4.17 Internal Quality Audits | ● | ● | ● | ○ | ● | ● | | ● | | | | | | | | ● | |
| 4.18 Training | ● | ● | ○ | | ○ | ● | ● | | ● | ● | ● | ● | ○ | ○ | | | |
| 4.19 Servicing | | | | | ● | ○ | | | | | | | | ○ | | ● | |
| 4.20 Statistical Techniques | ○ | | ○ | | ● | ● | ○ | | ○ | ○ | | ● | | | | ● | ○ |

*Table 6-1: Extent to which ISO 9000 requirements align with MBNQA guidelines.*

| 4.0 Quality System Requirements | Quality Assur. of Prod./Serv. | | | | | Quality Results | | | Customer Satisfaction | | | | | | | |
|---|---|---|---|---|---|---|---|---|---|---|---|---|---|---|---|---|
| | Quality Assessment | Documentation | Quality in support services/processes | Supplier Quality | Quality of Products/Services | Comparisons of Quality Results | Business Process, Operations and Support Service Q.I. | Supplier Quality Improvement | Knowledge of Customer Requirements and Expectations | Customer Relationship Management | Customer Service Standards | Commitment to Customers | Complaint Resolution for Quality Improvement | Customer Satisfaction Determination | Customer Satisfaction Results | Customer Satisfaction Comparison |
| 4.1 Management Responsibility | ● | ● | ● | ● | ● | ○ | ● | ● | ● | ○ | ● | ● | ● | ● | ○ | ○ |
| 4.2 Quality System | ● | ● | ○ | ○ | ● | ● | ● | ● | ○ | ● | ○ | ○ | ○ | ○ | ○ | ○ |
| 4.3 Contract Review | | ○ | | | | | | | ● | ○ | ○ | ○ | | | | |
| 4.4 Design Control | | ○ | ○ | | | | ○ | | ● | ○ | ○ | | | | | |
| 4.5 Document Control | | ● | | | | | | | | | | | | | | |
| 4.6 Purchasing | ● | ○ | ● | ● | ● | | ○ | ● | | | | | | | | |
| 4.7 Purchaser Supplied Product | ● | ○ | ● | ● | ● | | ○ | ● | | | | | | | | |
| 4.8 Product Identification and Traceability | | ○ | | ○ | | | | | | | | | | | | |
| 4.9 Process Control | ● | ● | ● | ● | ● | | ● | ○ | | | ○ | | | | | |
| 4.10 Inspection and Testing | ● | ● | ● | | ● | | ○ | ● | | ○ | | | | | | |
| 4.11 Inspection, Measuring, and Test Equipment | ● | ○ | ● | | ● | | ○ | | | | | | | | | |
| 4.12 Inspection and Test Status | ○ | ● | | | ● | | ○ | | | | | | | | | |
| 4.13 Control of Nonconforming Product | ○ | ○ | | ○ | ● | | ○ | | | | | | ● | | | |
| 4.14 Corrective Action | ● | ● | | ● | ● | ● | | | | | | | ● | ○ | ○ | |
| 4.15 Handling, Storage, Packaging, and Delivery | ● | ○ | ● | ○ | ● | ● | ○ | ● | | ● | ○ | | | | | |
| 4.16 Quality Records | ○ | ● | | | ○ | ● | ● | | | ● | ○ | | ○ | ● | ● | ○ |
| 4.17 Internal Quality Audits | ● | ● | ● | ○ | | ● | ● | | | ● | ○ | | ● | | | ○ |
| 4.18 Training | ○ | ● | ● | | | ● | ● | ○ | | ● | ○ | ○ | ○ | | | |
| 4.19 Servicing | ● | ● | ● | | ● | ● | ● | | ● | ● | ○ | ○ | ○ | | | |
| 4.20 Statistical Techniques | ○ | ● | ○ | ○ | ● | ● | | ● | | ● | ○ | | ● | ● | ● | ○ |

*Table 6-1: Extent to which ISO 9000 requirements align with MBNQA guidelines (continued).*

While the ISO 9000 series is the smaller system, there are several requirements of that series which are given limited attention in MBNQA guidelines. Document control is at the heart of the ISO 9000 series, but mentioned only in passing in MBNQA requirements. Product identification and traceability is a much larger part of ISO 9000 series requirements than in the MBNQA guidelines.

For the most part, however, the two systems cover much of the same material, although sometimes in different ways. Table 6-1 identifies the extent to which ISO 9000 series requirements align with MBNQA guidelines.

Most of the line items in Table 6-1 for each system are aligned in multiple fashion, indicated by the large number of "highly aligned" symbols. An even larger number of "somewhat aligned" symbols exist, further indicating the multiple alignment of line items in the two systems. No "at odds, potentially" symbols occur on Table 6-1.

## ISO 9000 Compared to Deming-based TQM

The ISO 9000 series has clear requirements that may or may not be particularly significant in Deming-based TQM. ISO 9000 series requirements dictate that contract review be addressed in very specific terms, while a Deming-based TQM system leaves the details entirely up to the organization. Design control, document control, and product identification and traceability are aligned with, but not required, in Deming-based TQM. Requirements in those areas are derived from specific customer needs rather than by fiat.

The ISO 9000 series has several highly specific concerns about inspection and testing that could be at odds with Deming-based TQM. Deming emphasizes that an organization should "cease dependence on inspection to achieve quality." Deming says that companies should "eliminate the need for inspection on a mass basis by building quality into the product in the first place." ISO 9000 provides for cases in which in-process control makes later inspection unnecessary, but also recognizes circumstances where inspection is needed.

The ISO 9000 series and Deming are in agreement that when inspection and testing are required, those doing the work should be trained and provided with appropriate equipment to perform the inspection or testing.

Deming urges companies to: drive out fear, eliminate slogans and exhortations, eliminate management-by-objective, remove barriers that rob people of pride in workmanship, and institute education. These points are not addressed directly in the ISO 9000 series.

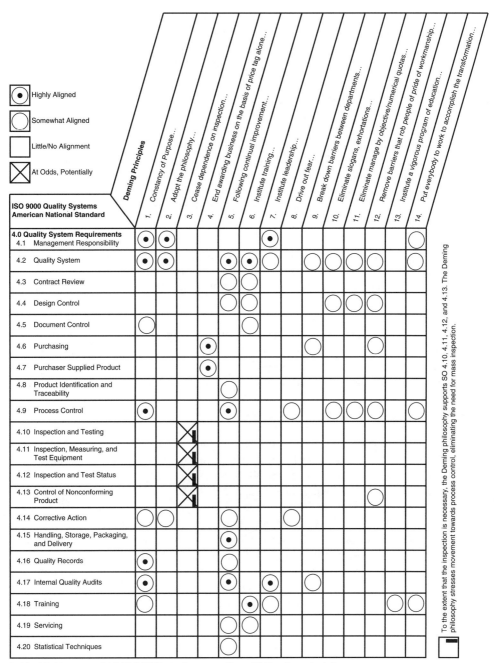

*Table 6-2: Extent to which ISO 9000 requirements align with Deming principles.*

ISO 9000 mentions statistical techniques only in passing. The basis of Deming-based TQM is statistical understanding, yet the ISO 9000 series treats statistical process control as something of an afterthought. Table 6-2 provides a graphic identification of the alignment of ISO 9000 with Deming-based TQM.

## Deming-Based TQM Compared to MBNQA

Deming-based TQM and MBNQA differ greatly in their approaches to benchmarking. Deming recommends that companies spend "time and effort focusing on what customers want and need, not what competitors are doing." Deming says that if you treat your customers right, and continuously improve in what you provide to them, your competitors will be watching you, and you will always be ahead of those competitors, because you will be continuously improving while they are trying to catch up to you.

Deming favors comparison of quality results and comparison of support-system quality results, but recommends that this comparison be made against the organization's previous record, not as a benchmarking device against competitors' results.

Deming is less concerned about measurement of customer satisfaction, and more concerned about developing a focused, continually improving relationship with customers and suppliers. While Deming supports organizational leaders helping improve public quality awareness, it is not a requirement as expressed by MBNQA.

## Comparison of Documentation and Control

The requirements for documentation are high for both MBNQA and ISO 9000. MBNQA includes elements such as benchmarking to other organizations (not required by ISO 9000) while ISO 9000 identifies specifics such as equipment calibration, only incidentally referred to in MBNQA.

Both ISO 9000 and MBNQA have high requirements for results measurement; MBNQA requires evidence of high quality, but ISO 9000 does not. The MBNQA requires process control; ISO requires documentation of process control where it exists, but does not necessarily require such control. Perhaps MBNQA does not require process control to the extent encouraged in a Deming-based TQM system. These comparisons are shown in Figure 6-1.

## Required Degree of Prescriptiveness Comparison

The degree of prescriptiveness inherent in the three approaches to quality is defined by what work is to be done and how that work is done. MBNQA guidelines spell out what must be done to attain a high score. It also spells out how each area should be approached.

The ISO 9000 series requirements define what work should be done, but offer little guidance on how the system should be set up and or how it should operate. Deming-based TQM offers little guidance on either the nature of the work or how to accomplish setting up a system. These comparisons are shown graphically in Figure 6-2.

## Theory/Application Comparison

Deming-based TQM emphasizes theory and practice to a greater degree than either MBNQA or the ISO 9000 series, and places slightly less emphasis on application.

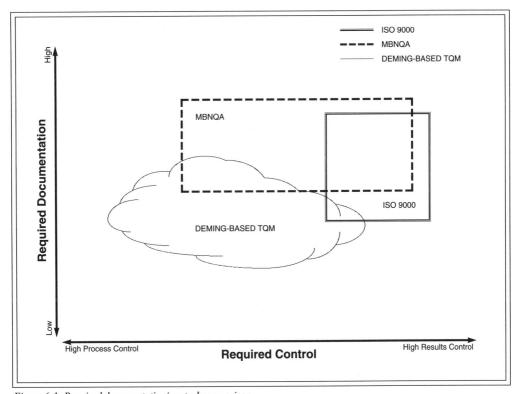

*Figure 6-1: Required documentation/control comparison.*

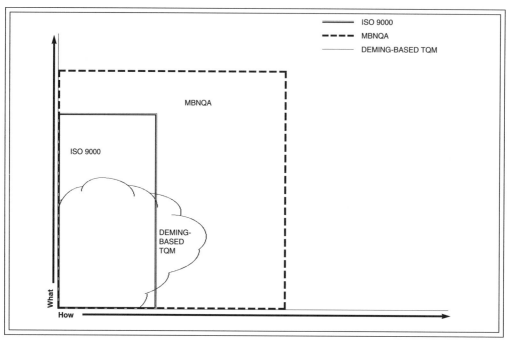

*Figure 6-2: Required degree of prescriptiveness comparison.*

ISO 9000 is a quality system based largely on traditional quality control theory, identifying elements such as design control, supplier control, process control, inspection management and training to achieve quality results for the customer.

MBNQA guidelines are a mixture of traditional theories — plus the theory developed by Crosby, Deming, Feigenbaum, Juran and others. MBNQA guidelines emphasize application of various pieces from the theories behind the approach. Figure 6-3 illustrates this graphically.

# SUMMARY

ISO 9000 series registration and instituting TQM principles are two beginnings of a quality journey.

A Deming-based TQM initiative requires the substantial commitment of personal

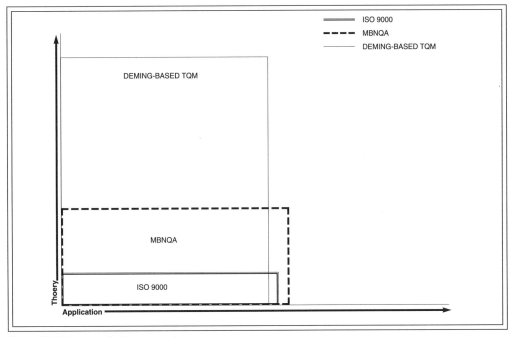

*Figure 6-3: Theory/application comparison.*

time and resources of senior managers in the transforming organization. Quality cannot be just another aspect of the business — it must become the way business is conducted.

While ISO 9000 series registration does require support and involvement by senior management, it is not nearly so demanding as a Deming-based TQM transformation initiative.

A Deming-based TQM organization creates a learning organization. This learning tenet of TQM makes selecting a Deming-based approach to TQM even more persuasive. Deming provides depth of theory as well as application. Deming points out, "There is no learning without theory." He goes on to say:

> *All theory is wrong. Some is useful. Of course all theory is wrong! If it were right, it wouldn't be theory, now would it? It would be fact. But without theory, we cannot learn. Experience alone teaches nothing. If we have a theory, then experience can help us to learn.*

After an organization has become effective through TQM transformation and has become a learning organization, the use of MBNQA quality criteria — or actually applying for the award — can be an excellent means to improve an already-effective organization. An organization that applies for the Baldrige Award is likely to put more pressure on itself than one using criteria internally.

It is a good idea for a company to spend a year working internally with the MBNQA criteria. The MBNQA criteria are self-descriptive. Even if it is difficult to measure the number of points achieved when self-scoring, the practice is worthwhile. Winning the Baldrige award should not be a company's goal. The intent should be to improve.

No matter what route a company takes on its quality journey, the most important step is the first one. In the words of Bob Killeen, retired UAW official, "I call TQM training 'retirement parties' because the fact that your company is doing TQM means it will be in business when you're ready to retire."

# REFERENCES

*ANSI/ASQC Q90-1987: American National Standard* (1987). Milwaukee, WI: American Society for Quality Control.

*ANSI/ASQC Q91-1987: American National Standard* (1987). Milwaukee, WI: American Society for Quality Control.

Deming, W. E. (1986). *Out of the Crisis.* Cambridge, MA: Massachusetts Institute of Technology Center for Advanced Engineering Study.

Deming, W. E. (1990, October). Author's notes from attending the *Quality, Productivity, and Competitive Position* seminar in Houston, TX.

Deming, W. E. (1991, October). Author's notes from attending the *Quality, Productivity, and Competitive Position* seminar in Nashville, TN.

Killeen, R. (1992, April) Notes from a presentation, *Understanding the Total Quality Movement,* sponsored by the Hubert H. Humphrey Institute of Public Affairs in Minneapolis, MN.

1992 Application Guidelines: *Malcolm Baldrige National Quality Award* Gaithersburg, MD: National Institute of Standards and Technology.

*1992 Application Guidelines: Malcolm Baldrige National Quality Award* Gaithersburg, MD: National Institute of Standards and Technology.


## About the Author

*Joel S. Finlay is a Senior Consultant with Process Management International, a Deming-based Total Quality Management consulting firm, where he has worked full-time since 1987. He has been involved in training for several Malcolm Baldrige National Quality Award winners, including Xerox and Zytec. He has assisted several companies in ISO 9000 series certification, including leading the team to certify his own company, Process Management International. He has a Ph.B. degree in communications from the University of North Dakota, an M.A. degree in small-group communication applied to the creative process, from the University of Cincinnati, and is presently a Ph.D. candidate in total quality management leadership at Walden University. Finlay is the author of more than two dozen publications, including a book on applied creativity and an edited book on organization development. He is certified as a registered organization development consultant (RODC) — only about 100 people world-wide hold the RODC certification.*

# ISO 9000/TQM/BALDRIGE COMPARISON

BY WILLIAM HARRAL

(REPRINTED FROM *QUALITY SYSTEMS UPDATE* NEWSLETTER)

## Question:

*My company has a TQM program in place and would now like to win the Malcolm Baldrige Award. How can we also sell an ISO 9000 series registration program to management? What specific benefits can be found in ISO 9000 series compliance for our company?*

## Response:

Making management aware of the complementary nature of TQM, Baldrige, and ISO 9000 registration may help to sell the program. If an organization has a TQM approach that focuses on the process and system, it is probably well-positioned to pursue ISO 9000 series registration.

Some TQM programs are "quality tools" and activity-focused without a vision or system. This is the result of the naive notion that total quality control occurs if you simply do enough things. While the Malcolm Baldrige National Quality Award has many positive aspects, it has a few shortcomings, as do all award-based endeavors. The Baldrige Award shortcomings received considerable discussion recently in *Quality Progress* and *Harvard Business Review*. To these shortcomings could be added the following:

■   As an award, the Baldrige has few winners and many "non-winners." Organizations and individuals may become frustrated and discouraged enough to abandon the TQM philosophy if a Baldrige Award attempt is unsuccessful.

■   Annual awards are temporal and become quickly dated.

■   The award focuses on the US with little attention given to global marketing.

■   No business purposes aside from advertising and marketing are supported by winning the award.

(**NOTE**: See adjoining box.)

These shortcomings are rectified if efforts to win the Baldrige award are combined with ISO 9000 series registration efforts. These benefits are:

■ Every organization that satisfies the applicable ISO 9000 model can be a "winner." As awareness of the ISO 9000 series spreads, unregistered sites may become "losers" of business and prestige.

■ Registration is perpetual, as long as requirements are satisfied.

■ ISO 9000 series registration applies globally; it has been adopted by more than 50 countries.

■ Registration supports advertising and marketing. Customer and statutory requirements may be satisfied as well. It may also provide defense against product liability cases.

---

## EDITOR'S NOTE:

The primary objective of the Malcolm Baldrige National Quality Award is not to present awards, but to develop and maintain a set of criteria that define state-of-the-art quality practice for American industry. To make this possible, Malcolm Baldrige criteria are updated each year in a scheduled workshop at which improvements to the criteria are solicited from quality professionals, experienced in the use of the criteria.

Changes are made both by clarifying wording and modifying substantive content. Consequently, significant improvement in the award criteria have been made each year since the program began in 1988. In contrast, the ISO 9000 standards are confirmed each five years; the process is underway for the first five-year revision, to be available in 1993. A structured voting process by delegates worldwide is required.

The number of companies applying for the Malcolm Baldrige National Quality Award has been remarkably low, with only 90 companies applying in 1992. However, 235,000 copies of the Award criteria were distributed during 1991, and the pace of requests continues at the rate of several hundred per week long after the deadline for submitting applications has passed. This confirms the fact that Malcolm Baldrige Award Criteria are viewed not primarily as the basis for an award, but as criteria to be pursued by American industry. To a degree, criticism of the shortcomings of the award mechanism misses the point of the process.

Developing TQM systems for clients using the appropriate ISO 9000 series model and additional customer/statutory requirements as a framework is possible and desirable. The basic framework is augmented with the necessary TQM tools and practices to pursue the organization's vision. Little additional expense or effort is required to pursue simultaneously both TQM and ISO 9000 series goals. ISO 9000-registered organizations gain the acknowledgment of being "winners" while still pursuing the elusive Baldrige Award. The dual goals are complementary since ISO 9000 registration supports 70 to 90 percent of the Baldrige criteria.

## Question:

*Does achieving the Baldrige Award preclude striving to meet the requirements of ISO 9000?*

## Response:

In 1987, our TQM clients began demanding that the ISO 9000 series be included in their quality systems. Though initially there was skepticism about such a request, in retrospect it proved to be a beneficial step for all parties concerned.

The first benefit is using an internationally recognized structure (the ISO 9000 series) for the TQM effort. TQM has a tendency to be quite individualistic and can vary depending on the background of its local champion. Dr. Jack B. ReVelle, chief statistician at Hughes Aircraft and co-chair of the ASQC TQM committee, has identified eight completely different TQM models being used by major organizations worldwide.

Consequently, promotion or portrayal of an organization as "TQM-based" or "committed to TQM" can be confusing and may be challenged. There are other advantages to using the ISO 9000 series model, complemented by customer and statutory requirements, to define a TQM framework:

■  Communication benefits from a common reference.

■  All ISO 9000 quality elements are necessary for TQM, although the identified elements and models are not sufficient to support TQM by themselves.

■  Most TQM tools, policies, philosophies and practices readily align with sections of the ISO models.

■  Second-party assessments or audits are more organized and efficient due to similar or familiar sequences in quality plan and quality system documentation.

■ System recognition to an ISO 9000 series model by a customer is more widely acknowledged and accepted than being recognized to an individual company standard (i.e., Ford's Q1, GM's Targets for Excellence, US Department of Defense's Exemplary Facility).

A growing number of organizations are subscribing to an approach that utilizes the appropriate ISO 9000 series model and augments it where necessary. This is consistent with ISO guidelines which state that the ISO 9000 standards arc mcant to complement, not replace, other requirements.

A common path to follow would include pursuing:

■ Quality system recognition through customer awards
■ ISO 9000 series registration
■ Baldrige Award using previous ISO and supplier recognitions as demonstrations of excellence.

This approach is more conservative and profitable than either pursuing the Baldrige Award alone or pursuing it as the first goal. By pursuing customer awards first, business relationships are solidified and current business is promoted. The ISO 9000 recognition expands the potential customer base to fund the costs associated with pursuit of the Baldrige. This approach also results in the Baldrige Award being the crowning achievement and amplifying earlier recognitions.

If a company achieves the Baldrige Award as its first or only award, the firm's year in the spotlight may be over before it can take full competitive advantage of the recognition.

## About the Author

*William Harral, CQE, CQA, CRE, PEIT, is director of Arch Associates, a Total Quality Management and ISO 9000 consulting and training firm. He has had 20 years experience in various engineering, manufacturing, planning and quality management positions at Ford Motor Company prior to founding Arch Associates in 1983. Mr. Harral is the author of numerous articles, books, and handbooks on quality. He is active in ASQC as senior member, was past-chair of the greater Detroit section, deputy regional director, TQM committee co-chair, and audit division counselor.*

*At Automotive Industry Action Group (AIAG) request, he currently chairs the authoring committee for a Guide for Supplier Qualification based on the ISO 9000 series. Mr. Harral holds an M.B.A. from the University of Michigan and a B.S. in industrial and systems engineering from Ohio State University. He has completed training and successfully tested for IQA Lead Assessor status.*

# ISO 9000 AND THE AUTOMOTIVE INDUSTRY

BY WILLIAM HARRAL

## Introduction

Acceptance of ISO 9000 standards in the motor vehicle industry has been driven by contractual and commercial requirements, the competitive marketplace, company policies and economics. Legislative and regulatory drivers have not previously affected this industry. However, a new EC directive may do just that.

North American automotive organizations have traditionally viewed the ISO 9000 series with skepticism. Yet that attitude may be changing.

This article discusses recent developments in EC legislation and in the US automotive industry with respect to quality system standards. (Chapter 8 discusses the EC system for product regulation in detail.)

## The EC Situation

European Community (EC) motor vehicle legislation dates to 1970 and has addressed such areas as: type approval, noise and exhaust systems, emissions, lamps and indicators, road-worthiness, passenger restraints, field-of-vision, wipers, defrosters, heaters, fuel tanks, impact protection and tire-tread depth. Most of the legislation and its amendments pre-date issuance of ISO 9000 standards.

A draft revision of the directive for type approval is now circulating within the EC for comment. It contains specific provisions for production quality control and the acceptability of registration to at least the ISO 9002 or equivalent accreditation standard. Verification of conformance to type could be provided by the certifying organization itself or by the manufacturer who would provide details of its third-party registration and scope to the certifying organization.

Tentatively, the new directive would become effective January 1, 1993, and be phased in over five years. It would become mandatory for all new vehicles in 1996 and fully effective in 1998. Several US suppliers have received letters of inquiry, requests for proposals or quotes, or other notifications from European motor-vehicle or component manufacturers referencing conformance to ISO 9000 standards. Some suppliers are already considering registration or other demonstration of conformance to the standards.

## The US Situation

A common complaint among passenger-vehicle and truck suppliers has been the difficulty and cost of complying with customer quality-system requirements. Various company standards often differ in intent, philosophy, approach and detail.

Customers have been aware of the problems but lacked a means to reach a mutually agreeable set of requirements.

At several recent conferences, leaders in the motor vehicle industry noted the problem and the benefits of increased standards. At an Automotive Management Briefing in August 1992, John McTague, Ford's vice president of technical affairs, emphasized a need for widespread recognition and acceptance of international technical product and test standards. This would minimize redundancy and non-value-added costs and increase global competitiveness.

## Big Three Agreement

A purchasing panel composed of representatives from Ford, Chrysler and GM noted current efforts by the American Society for Quality Control (ASQC) to "commonize" tactical issues — including statistical process control, failure effects mode analysis, quality planning, initial sample qualification, measurement systems and analysis. These efforts will be followed by strategic plans, or "system commonization," sometime in 1993-94.

Acceptance of and requirements for ISO 9000 series registration will be defined after the industry develops some experience and confidence with the system. This may occur by dealing with suppliers who become registered on their own initiative or for reasons other than demands from the Big Three auto makers.

## Cooperative Competition

Independent competitors are becoming more cooperative because of Deming's influence on automotive companies over the past dozen years. Other factors include European and Asian business practices, additional statutory freedom, and the non-value-added costs of suppliers that maintain different documentation systems for different customers, even if they contain similar information.

Major North American automotive manufacturers and suppliers formed the Automotive Industry Action Group (AIAG) in 1982. The group was formed to address differing requirements among the Big Three in shipping, transportation, electronic data and manufacturing support.

A project team was initiated in the 1980s to develop strategies for continuous quality improvement through leading-edge technologies and methodologies. Unfortunately, the strong automotive market at that time reinforced resistance to change and eliminated an apparent need for cooperation.

There were other reasons for resistance to change:

- Belief that differences in a quality system provide a company with a competitive advantage
- Security issues connected to third-party assessments were not acceptable, especially in light of Japan's "time to market" advantage
- Misidentification of ISO 9000 series as a European standard instead of a global standard — and a possible link to traditional European cost disadvantages
- Unfamiliarity with the descriptive rather than prescriptive approach to quality systems requirements
- Concern about abilities of suppliers and in-house quality managers to comprehend and apply specific requirements appropriate to individual quality systems based solely on ISO documents
- ISO 9000's lack of emphasis on planned continuous improvement, TQM, or other statistical methods
- Lack of understanding about the ISO 9000 series as minimal requirements to be augmented with additional requirements.

With the declining market of the 1990s, a Commonization Task Force was created between AIAG and the Automotive Division of ASQC to develop common practices on tactical and methodological issues. These included measurement system analysis, basic statistical process control, initial sample reporting, quality planning, failure effects mode analysis, and others.

As a result, manuals in each area are being developed and distributed throughout the industry, leading to reduced system costs and significant benefits to suppliers and consumers.

# AUTOMOTIVE QUALITY REQUIREMENTS STANDARDIZATION

BY BRUCE W. PINCE, ALICE A. MILES, R. DAN REID,
RUSSELL M. JACOBS, JOSEPH R. PHELAN,
AND RADLEY M. SMITH

**EDITOR'S NOTE:** *The following is an excerpt from a status report on the efforts of automotive industry to harmonize their systems for supplier total quality assessment, including the possible integration of ISO 9000 standards. The report was presented at ASQC's 46th Annual Quality Congress in May 1992.*

## Introduction

To help suppliers continuously improve, *original equipment manufacturers (OEM)* such as Chrysler, Ford and General Motors, are instituting supplier total quality assessment systems. These largely similar systems have significant differences in requirements, standards, procedures, and reporting, which cause redundant work and increase transaction costs.

The three OEMs, in collaboration with their suppliers, American Society for Quality Control, and the Automotive Industry Action Group (AIAG), have teamed up to harmonize elements of the three assessment systems.

## Situation Analysis

The traditional North American OEMs each began in the early- to mid-1980s to develop total quality systems for their suppliers. The OEMs sought to accelerate the rate of suppliers' quality improvement. These total quality management systems incorporated quality requirements and also addressed related systems and processes, such as technology, delivery, management, and commercial and financial practices.

Because each OEM had different requirements, each developed a company-unique system for its suppliers. Chrysler's "Supplier Quality Assurance" was announced in 1986. Ford's "Q1" was announced in 1981 and its extension "Total Quality Excellence" in 1987. General Motors' "Targets for Excellence" was announced in 1986. These three supplier quality assurance methods were developed prior to the promulgation of the ISO 9000 series, have a broader scope, are specific and prescriptive, and are integrated with the business practices of the OEMs to meet their individual requirements.[1]

While the three systems are similar in intent, content and process, all three systems have significant differences in requirements, standards, assessment procedures, rating systems, operating processes, nomenclature and reporting format and methods. Suppliers must deal with these differences, which impact productivity.

Standardization or harmonization of these differences will accelerate supplier quality improvement and reduce transaction costs. In July 1988, ASQC's Automotive Division Executive Council authorized a Supplier Quality Requirements Task Force. The Task Force quickly secured the three OEMs' involvement and support.

Planning sessions established Task Force requirements and scope. A Supplier Advisory Council (SAC) formed in June 1989, consisting of quality and manufacturing managers from 13 representative supplier companies.

The Task Force charter is to:

- Eliminate supplier confusion and redundancy concerning the three OEMs' assessment system reporting formats, technical nomenclature, reference manuals and process guidelines
- Reduce supplier/OEM assessment system transaction costs by eliminating waste in supplier labor and time
- Concentrate on "tactical" approaches, pursuing specific projects with definable cost/benefits, rather than a "systems approach" to commonizing assessment processes
- Focus on the quality aspects of the three systems, rather than working on their management, technology, financial and administrative elements.

A key Task Force success factor was the need for a common vision of success. (See Figure 6-4.) This vision provides for the continuance of three OEM processes in the future; but over time, however, it is expected that industry standards can be agreed upon, thereby reducing the amount of unique company-, division-, or commodity-specific requirements.

Inputs into the development of these standards include national award criteria, such as the Malcolm Baldrige Award and Deming Prize as well as the OEM requirements and other standards, such as ASME, ANSI, SAE, etc.

In October 1989, the Task Force teamed with the AIAG — a not-for-profit industry organization of more than 700 subscribing OEMs and suppliers devoted to automotive industry communication, education and systems standardization, and non-competitive technical collaboration. The team is now called the ASQC/AIAG Task Force.

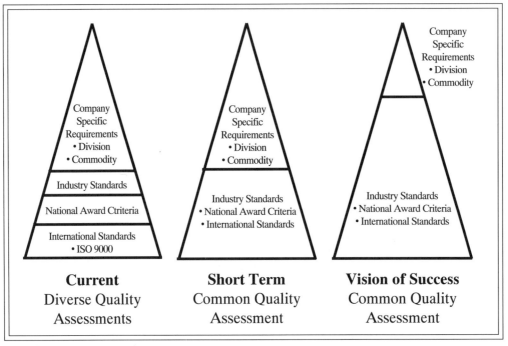

*Figure 6-4: A common vision of success.*

Work groups perform the project development. Each work group is led by an OEM representative. Work group technical experts are from the OEM's materials management, engineering and technical staffs. Supplier experts contribute technical review, comment and special skills. The SAC reflects the objectives of the supplier community, helps identify projects, generates data for project cost-benefit analysis and advises on project priorities established by the Task Force.

The Work Groups' job is to:

- Assess discrepancies originating in unique OEM internal procedures (*root causes*) or in superficial origin (*cosmetics*)
- Debate and resolve *root cause* discrepancies by getting collective OEM approval to harmonize the divergent processes inside their three organizations, or "flag" intractable remnant differences
- Adjust *cosmetic* discrepancies by agreeing on changes to nomenclature, format notation, statistical method, etc.

The Task Force then reviews the resulting draft to coordinate it with other related projects completed or underway to ensure inter-project consistency. In addition, getting "buy in" from the various constituencies in these three huge companies can require several rounds of drafts, revisions, etc.

Often, it is difficult to resolve the intractable differences that are rooted in how the OEMs **really** do business. For example, in one project, analysis showed that, while the three processes seemed superficially similar, the three OEMs all used different software systems to manage their processes.

Also, each OEM's quality and engineering organization is affected differently depending on the process being standardized. Here, no cosmetic change is possible when the consequence may be tens of millions of dollars in OEM software system changes, radical revamping of the OEM operating organization, retraining, or other changes.

ASQC has primary responsibility in reviewing the project for technical accuracy and consistency across the industry. This ASQC oversight function has materially contributed to project improvement. ASQC works with the other standards organizations (professional societies, government and international agencies, etc.), to ensure project compliance. Roll-out planning and execution is the responsibility of the OEMs.

Each OEM must find a cost-effective way to integrate the revised manual/process/report into its unique supplier assessment system. This is often a difficult task, requiring "selling" the changes inside the OEMs. These formidable cultural, organizational and operational barriers to project development and implementation are countered by several positive influences, including: everyone's desire for cost reduction through waste elimination, a mutual desire to improve quality and shorten product cycle schedules, and finally, a growing sense of community, of "being in the same boat."

## Results

In October 1990, the Task Force released the *Measurement Systems Analysis Reference Manual*[2] to 13,400 supplier addresses. Based on GM's gage reliability and repeatability manual and integrating parallel Chrysler and Ford documents, this manual can be used by any supplier to develop measurement systems data satisfying all three supplier assessment systems, and it ensures identical supplier and OEM MSA process.

A common *Initial Sample Inspection Report* has also been developed. This report warrants conformance of a supplier's initial product sample to OEM requirements, based upon statistical and operating process data. The *Report* is now undergoing gradual implementation, as each OEM revises and re-issues its quality assessment procedures.

A *Statistical Process Control Reference Manual* was released in December 1991. Based on the Ford Statistical Process Control manual, it incorporates inputs from Chrysler and GM. The ASQC Reading Team significantly altered the document, recommending more attention to "process SPC" and certain aspects of capability studies. This manual also ensures that identical SPC processes are in use in all suppliers and OEMs, and that the OEMs mutually accept the supplier data that is generated.

Five Work Groups are proceeding on the following projects: an initial sample process guideline; an advanced product quality planning process guideline; a problem identification, resolution and reporting guideline; an FMEA reference manual and a critical characteristics guideline.

Suppliers and OEM users have expressed their enthusiastic approval of this standardization and harmonization effort and its benefits.

## Conclusion

The ASQC/AIAG Task Force, working with OEMs and suppliers to harmonize OEM quality systems, has had significant early successes. The work continues and should be sustained, based on cost-effective results to date.

### About the Authors

*Bruce W. Pince*, Senior Vice President, Sandy Corporation, Troy, MI 48084.

*Alice A. Miles*, Project Manager, North American Automotive Operations, Production Purchasing, Ford Motor Company, Dearborn, MI 48121.

*R. Dan Reid*, Manager of Supplier Development, Administration, General Motors Corporation, Detroit, MI 48202.

*Russell M. Jacobs*, Component Procurement and Supplier Development, Chrysler Corporation, Detroit, MI 48232.

*Joseph R. Phelan*, Executive Director, Automotive Industry Action Group, Southfield, MI 48034 (executive on loan from Ford Motor Company).

*Radley M. Smith*, Corporate Staff Quality Engineer, Ford Motor Company, Dearborn, MI 48121.

# DOD AND THE ISO 9000 SERIES QUALITY SYSTEM STANDARDS*

BY **K.D. HOLLINGSWORTH**

## Introduction

Interest in the ISO 9000 Quality System Standards has been building since it first became evident that the US Department of Defense (DoD) was considering adopting the standards to replace MIL-Q-9858A and MIL-I-45208A. Recently, more and more presentations have been made at conferences and seminars and an increasing number of articles on the subject have appeared in newsletters and magazines.

Most of the material thus presented has been very general. DoD spokespersons have been quick to say that DoD is interested in using the standards, but they have not made clear the specific problems which must be resolved before DoD can or will make a definite commitment and begin incorporating the standards in contracts. The purpose of this article is to identify some of those problems, and to examine in detail a few of the major differences between ISO 9001/Q91 and MIL-Q-9858A.

The material below is based on the author's analysis and comparison of the referenced documents, discussions with DoD officials involved in the ISO transition effort, and information obtained at various conferences and seminars where related presentations were made by DoD officials. Speculation as to how, when or whether DoD will proceed in this area must remain just that. This article does not pretend to represent any official DoD position or plans concerning the anticipated transition to ISO 9000 standards.

PART I will identify general problems and considerations related to the use of ISO standards within DoD; PART II will point out some of the major differences between ISO 9001/Q91 and MIL-Q-9858A; PART III will discuss certification in DoD procurements; and PART IV will briefly summarize.

*See Editor's Note at the end of this section.*

## PART I — Problems and Considerations Related to the Use of International Quality System Standards Within DoD

### Adoption of the ISO 9000 Standards by DoD

By Adoption Notices, February 6, 1991, DoD formally adopted ANSI/ASQC Standards Q90 through Q94. Since the ISO 9000 series is technically identical to the Q90 series, this action, in effect, constituted DoD adoption of the ISO 9000 series standards.

Since ISO 9001 and Q91 are technically identical, and for the sake of simplicity, the remainder of this article will refer to Q91 only.

### Use of ISO 9000 Standards in DoD Contracts

There is a difference between "adopting" standards and directing that they be used. There are two conditions which must be met for the standards to be in general use in DoD contracts.

First, the standards must be adopted for use by DoD. That condition has already been met. However, adopting the standards simply provides for their listing in the DoD *Index of Specifications and Standards* (DODISS), and makes them available to DoD personnel through the publication distribution center.

Second, DoD buying offices must be directed by the *Federal Acquisition Regulation (FAR)* and *DoD Federal Acquisition Regulation Supplement (DFARS)* to use the adopted standards; this has not been done.

FAR, Subpart 46.2, provides guidelines for contracting officers to follow in the selection of appropriate quality requirements to be included in Government contracts. Within these guidelines, the FAR states that under certain conditions it is appropriate to incorporate "higher-level" quality requirements.

Although the FAR lists examples of higher-level quality requirements, it does not further prescribe the use of specific documents containing such requirements. The reason for this is that the FAR is applicable, not only to DoD, but to National Aeronautics and Space Administration and General Services Administration as well, and each of these organizations has its own "higher-level quality requirements."

At this point, the DFARS picks up and, in Subpart 246.2: Contract Quality Requirements, identifies the higher-level quality requirements documents which apply to DoD procurements. These documents are MIL-I-45208A and MIL-Q-9858A.

Therefore, although DoD has adopted the ISO 9000 series quality requirements, the DFARS directs DoD contracting officers to use MIL-I-45208A and MIL-Q-9858A. Consequently, the ISO 9000 series will not be in general use in DoD contracts until the DFARS is revised.

## *A Proposed Revision?*

A proposed revision to replace MIL-I-45208A and MIL-Q-9858A with the Q90 series has not yet been presented for consideration.

Why has a proposed revision not been presented? There are many major administrative, implementation and technical differences between the two sets of documents which have not been reconciled to DoD's satisfaction. It is doubtful that DoD will be pressured into using the ISO documents as they currently exist for the sole purpose of "going along." DoD officials will direct use of the documents when the differences have been resolved and when they believe it is in their best interest to do so.

In addition to this overall lack of direction for use of the Q90 documents, there is another serious problem which DoD has not yet worked out.

## *Three Quality System Requirements Documents*

There are three quality system requirements documents now used in DoD contracts:

- MIL-Q-9858A, Quality Program Requirements
- MIL-I-45208A, Inspection System Requirements
- FAR Clause 52.246-2, Standard Inspection Requirement.

Within the Q90 series there are also three quality system requirements documents:

- Q91, Quality Systems - Model for Quality Assurance in Design/Development, Production, Installation and Servicing
- Q92, Quality Systems - Model for Quality Assurance in Production and Installation
- Q93, Quality Systems - Model for Quality Assurance in Final Inspection and Test.

Since there are three documents in each group, it has been assumed that there is a direct correlation at each level. Unfortunately, this is not the case. Consider the following:

Although there are many differences between Q91 and MIL-Q-9858A (discussed in detail later in this article), Q91 is roughly equivalent to MIL-Q-9858A. Both documents establish Quality Program-level requirements.

The only substantive difference between Q91 and Q92 is that Q91 contains requirements for control of Design/Development and Servicing and Q92 does not. This
same difference also exists between Q91 and MIL-Q-9858A. Since MIL-Q-9858A
and Q92 both differ from Q91 in the same way, Q92 also must be roughly equivalent
to MIL-Q-9858A.

If both Q91 and Q92 are equivalent to MIL-Q-9858A, then obviously both Q91 and
Q92 are on a much higher plane than MIL-I-45208A.

Is Q93 equivalent to MIL-I-45208A? No. Q93 is used where conformance to
requirements is to be ensured "solely at final inspection and test." MIL-I-45208A is
used where technical requirements of a contract require "both in-process and final
end-item inspection…" The provisions of MIL-I-45208A greatly exceed those of
Q93.

The problem is that there is no ISO quality system requirement document which is
even close to MIL-I-45208A.

So, what is DoD to do? There are thousands of contracts which currently contain
MIL-I-45208A. If DoD replaces MIL-I-45208A with Q92, they will be adding
requirements to the contracts and the price of the product will go up. If they replace
it with Q93, DoD's confidence in product conformance will go down.

What are some possible options? They could tailor requirements out of Q92; they
could tailor requirements into Q93, or they could come up with a new standard,
possibly a modified MIL-I-45208A under a new number. This is a big problem.

And, what about the quality system requirement contained in FAR Clause 52.246-2?
Q93 greatly exceeds this standard inspection clause, so the same problem arises as
was seen with MIL-I-45208A. Should DoD change Clause 52.246-2, supplement it,
replace it, or leave it as it is?

Also, what about Q93? It doesn't fit any place in DoD's current scheme of things.
Will DoD create a niche for it, or simply ignore it?

These may not be all the problems and questions that DoD is wrestling with, but it
gives some idea of the magnitude of the decisions which must be met before DoD
will put ISO 9000/Q90 standards into use.

# PART II — Major Differences Between Q91 and MIL-Q-9858A

On the surface MIL-Q-9858A, *Quality Program Requirements*, and Q91, *Quality Systems - Model for Quality Assurance in Design/Development, Production, Installation and Servicing*, appear to be very much alike. There are, however, many differences (Note that these same differences exist between MIL-Q-9858A and Q92).

Some of the differences are major and obvious while others are minor and more subtle. All must be carefully considered, however, to be certain that the full impact on quality is known before a transition is initiated. Some of the major differences are outlined below.

## 4.1: Management Responsibility

Q91, Clause 4.1.1: *Quality Policy,* requires management to define and document policy and objectives for quality and commitment to quality, and to ensure that the policy is understood, implemented and maintained at all levels. While MIL-Q-9858A: Clause 3.1 Organization, does include management responsibilities, it does not address any of the specific responsibilities mentioned above.

Q91, Clause 4.1.2.2: *Verification Resources and Personnel,* requires the supplier (contractor) to identify in-house verification requirements and to provide adequate resources and trained personnel for their accomplishment. It also prohibits certain activities from being performed by persons having direct responsibility for the work. None of this is addressed by MIL-Q-9858A.

Q91, Clause 4.1.2.3, requires the appointment of a Management Representative who will be responsible for ensuring that the ISO requirements are met. MIL-Q-9858A contains no such specific requirement.

Q91, Clause 4.1.3, requires that records be maintained of Management Reviews. MIL-Q-9858A requires management reviews but does not require that they be documented.

Q91, Clause 4.2: *Quality System,* in a "NOTE," emphasizes the need for development of "quality plans ", and preparation of a "quality manual." MIL-Q-9858A requires written procedures, but does not mention written "plans" or a quality assurance Manual. (NOTES are for guidance only; they are not requirements)

Q91, Clause 4.3: *Contract Review,* requires that records of contract review be maintained. MIL-Q-9858A requires contract review, but does not specifically require that records be maintained.

Q91, Clause 4.4: Design Control, requires the supplier (contractor) to establish and maintain procedures to control and verify the design of the product. MIL-Q-9858A does not address design control.

## 4.5: Document Control

Clause 4.5.1 requires the supplier (contractor) to establish and maintain procedures to control all documents and data that relate to the requirements of the ISO standard. It specifically requires that such documents be reviewed and approved for adequacy by authorized personnel prior to issue.

MIL-Q-9858A, Paragraph 4.1, Drawing, Documentation and Changes, contains a requirement for validation of design and supplementary documents, but it does not require that all documents be reviewed and approved for adequacy by authorized personnel prior to issue.

Clause 4.5.2: Document Changes/Modifications, requires the supplier (contractor) to establish and maintain a master list or equivalent document to identify the current revision of documents. MIL-Q-9858A contains no such specific requirement.

## 4.6: Purchasing

Clause 4.6.2 requires the supplier (contractor) to establish and maintain records of acceptable suppliers. MIL-Q-9858A requires no such record.

Clause 4.6.3 requires the supplier (contractor) to review and approve purchase documents for adequacy of specified requirements prior to release. MIL-Q-9858A contains no such specific requirement.

Clause 4.6.4 grants the purchaser the right to perform verification at source or upon receipt."where specified in the contract." MIL-Q-9858A establishes both of these as automatic government rights.

Q91, Clause 4.7: Purchaser-Supplied Product, requires the supplier (contractor) to establish and maintain procedures for the control of purchaser-supplied product. MIL-Q-9858A, Clause 7.2.1: Government-furnished Material, contains similar requirements, but they are much more detailed than those of Q91.

## 4.8: Product Identification and Traceability

Clause 4.8 requires that, where appropriate,

> *the supplier (contractor) establish and maintain procedures for identify-*
> *ing the product from applicable drawings, specifications, or other*
> *documents, during all stages of production, delivery and installation.*

MIL-Q-9858A, Paragraph 6.1, *Materials and Materials Control,* contains a requirement for identification of raw materials, but the scope of Q91 is greater.

"Where, and to the extent that traceability is a specified requirement," individual
product or batches shall have a unique identification. MIL-Q-9858A does not
address traceability.

## 4.9: Process Control and 4.10: Inspection and Testing

Q91, Clause 4.9: *Process Control,* requires that "Special Processes" be "qualified."
MIL-Q-9858A contains no such specific requirement.

Q91, Clause 4.10: *Inspection and Testing,* specifically addresses receiving, in-
process and final inspection and testing.

MIL-Q-9858A contains similar requirements for receiving inspection and in-process
inspection in Paragraphs 6.1, *Materials and Materials Control,* and 6.2, *Production
Processing and Fabrication,* respectively. There are differences in wording, but the
requirements are essentially the same.

MIL-Q-9858A, in Clause 6.3: *Completed Item Inspection and Testing,* addresses
final inspection and test of completed products. The scope and content, however,
differ significantly from the Q91 final inspection and testing requirement.

With respect to receiving inspection, Q91 states in Clause 4.6.4: *Verification of
Purchased Product,* that the purchaser will be afforded the right to verify product
conformance upon receipt, "where specified in the contract." MIL-Q-9858A, Clause
1.2: *Contractual Intent,* grants this right automatically.

## 4.11: Inspection, Measuring and Test Equipment

Q91, Clause 4.11: *Inspection, Measuring and Test Equipment,* contains requirements
similar to MIL-Q-9858A. There are, however, some differences:

The main difference, of course, is that MIL-Q-9858A, Paragraph 4.2, *Measuring and Testing Equipment,* automatically invokes MIL-STD-45662A, *Calibration System Requirements.* Q91 does not invoke any separate calibration system requirements.

MIL-Q-9858A, Paragraph 4.4, *Use of Contractor's Inspection Equipment,* requires that contractors make measuring and test equipment available to government representatives for their quality assurance activities. Q91 does not contain such requirements.

MIL-Q-9858A, Paragraph 4.5, *Advanced Metrology,* requires that contractors identify and provide notification of any precision measurement needs exceeding the known state-of-the-art. Q91 does not address this subject.

## 4.12: Inspection and Test Status

Q91, Clause 4.12: *Inspection and Test Status,* specifically requires that records identify the authority responsible for the release of conforming material. MIL-Q-9858A contains no such specific requirement.

## 4.13: Control of Nonconforming Product

Q91, Clause 4.13: *Control of Nonconforming Product,* contains several major differences from MIL-Q-9858A, Paragraph 6.5, *Nonconforming Material.*

MIL-Q-9858A specifically states that "acceptance of nonconforming supplies is a prerogative of...the Government." Q91, Clause 4.13.1, states that "Where required by the contract, the proposed use or repair of product...shall be reported for concession to the purchaser or the purchaser's representative." In other words, MIL-Q-9858A automatically requires concession (Government approval) of all use-as-is and repair dispositions while Q91 requires concession only if required by the contract.

MIL-Q-9858A specifically states that "acceptance of nonconforming supplies...shall be as prescribed by the Government." Q91, Clause 4.13.1, does not grant any authority of this kind to the purchaser (Government).

MIL-Q-9858A requires that repair or re-work of nonconforming material be "in accordance with documented procedures acceptable to the Government." Q91 contains no such requirements.

MIL-Q-9858A requires the contractor to "make known to the Government upon request the data associated with the costs and losses in connection with scrap and with re-work..." Q91 contains no such requirements.

MIL-Q-9858A requires that the contractor provide "holding areas or procedures mutually agreeable to the contractor and the Government Representative..." Q91 does not address holding areas or procedures.

## 4.14: Corrective Action

Q91, Clause 4.14: *Corrective Action,* and MIL-Q-9858A, *Corrective Action,* both have the same intent: to identify conditions adverse to quality and to eliminate those conditions so that problems caused by those conditions will not recur. This is the intent, but a literal reading and comparison of the documents raises some interesting questions, as outlined below.

Q91, Clause 4.14 a, requires "investigating the cause of nonconforming product and the corrective action needed to prevent recurrence." This could be read that Q91 requires investigation, determination of cause, and corrective action to eliminate the cause of any and all nonconforming product. Where the nonconforming product has resulted from inherent, random variations in the process itself, satisfying such a requirement would be extremely costly, if not impossible.

MIL-Q-9858A makes it clear that corrective action is required for the detection and correction of "assignable conditions" only. Assignable conditions are what Deming refers to as "special causes," — causes which come from outside the system.

Q91, Clause 4.14 b, requires "analyzing all processes, work operations, concessions, quality records, service reports, and customer complaints..." MIL-Q-9858A requires analysis of "trends or performance of work...to prevent nonconforming product." The word "all" in Q91 implies a much larger scope than MIL-Q-9858A.

MIL-Q-9858A specifically extends the corrective action requirement to subcontractors. Q91 does not.

Q91, Clause 4.14 a, requires "investigating the cause of nonconforming product..." MIL-Q-9858A, in addition to nonconforming product, establishes "excessive losses or costs" as conditions which require corrective action. MIL-Q-9858A also makes it clear that corrective action extends to design, purchasing, manufacturing, testing or other operations.

## 4.15: Handling, Storage, Packaging and Delivery

Q91, Clause 4.15: *Handling, Storage, Packaging and Delivery* is not as wordy as MIL-Q-9858A, Clause 6.4: *Handling, Storage and Delivery,* but the requirements are essentially the same. One specific major difference is that MIL-Q-9858A requires that these activities be monitored. Q91 does not.

## 4.16: Quality Records

Q91, Clause 4.16: *Quality Records,* contains records requirements which greatly exceed those of MIL-Q-9858A, Clause 3.4: *Records.*

Q91 requires procedures for "identification, collection, indexing, filing, storage, maintenance and disposition" of quality records. It also requires that records be stored and maintained in such a way that they are readily retrievable; and that such storage facilities provide an environment which will minimize deterioration, damage or loss. MIL-Q-9858A contains none of these requirements. It makes only a general statement that records are to be maintained and used.

MIL-Q-9858A requires that quality records be made available for review by the Government Representative. Q91 requires that records be made available only "where contractually agreed" and then, only for "an agreed period."

## 4.17, 4.18, 4.19, 4.20

Q91, Clause 4.17: *Internal Quality Audits,* requires a comprehensive system of planned and documented internal audits. MIL-Q-9858A contains no such requirement.

Q91, Clause 4.18: *Training,* requires that a formal training program be established and maintained. MIL-Q-9858A does not address training.

Q91, Clause 4.19: *Servicing.* MIL-Q-9858A does not specifically address "servicing." It does, however, state in Clause 1.1, that it is applicable to all supplies or "services" when referenced in the contract.

Q91, Clause 4.20: *Statistical Techniques,* could be interpreted to state that statistical techniques are mandatory wherever they are appropriate. MIL-Q-9858A, Clause 6.6: *Statistical Quality Control and Analysis,* makes such practices optional.

"NOTES" are contained throughout the ISO. They provide guidance and clarification but are not contractual. MIL-Q-9858A contains no such extraneous material.

# Differences Keyed to MIL-Q-9858A

MIL-Q-9858A, Clause 1.2: *Contractual Intent,* establishes the Government's rights for review and evaluation of the Quality Program and for disapproval of the program if the contractor's procedures do not accomplish its objectives. Q91 does not address the purchaser's (Government's) rights to review, evaluate and disapprove the contractor's quality procedures or system.

MIL-Q-9858A, Clause 1.3: *Summary,* requires establishment of a quality program which is effective and "economical." Q91 does not address the economical aspect of a quality system.

MIL-Q-9858A, Clause 3.6: *Costs Related to Quality,* requires that the contractor maintain and use quality cost data as a management element. Q91 contains no similar requirement.

MIL-Q-9858A, Clause 7.1: *Government Inspection at Subcontractor or Vendor Facilities,* establishes the Government's right to perform inspection at subcontractor or vendor facilities. Q91, Clause 4.6.4: *Verification of Purchased Product,* affords the purchaser the right to verify product conformance at source or upon receipt, but only where that right is "specified in the contract."

# PART III — Third-Party Certification

One question which always arises in any discussion of DoD and the international standards concerns certification. Will DoD go along with the certification scheme which is followed in commercial application of the ISO standards? Some specific questions are addressed below:

## Will DoD Certify Contractors?

MIL-I-45208A and MIL-Q-9858A have been used for 28 years and DoD has never certified contractors to these documents. It is DoD policy that the assigned Government Quality Assurance Representative (QAR) will evaluate the contractor's quality program on a continuing basis. If the QAR does not find anything wrong, the program or procedures will not be disapproved. DoD has not, however, and almost certainly will not "certify," approve or provide any sort of written confirmation of the acceptability of a contractor's quality program or inspection system.

There are at least two reasons for this. First, DoD simply is not staffed to audit and certify all of the thousands of contractors it uses.

Second, a contractor could be in compliance today and not tomorrow. Considering the critical and complex nature of supplies procured under MIL-I-45208A and MIL-Q-9858A, DoD could not accept the risk of having defective supplies delivered over an extended period of time after certification and between subsequent audits.

Since these considerations will continue to exist, there is no reason to believe that DoD will change the current practice under ISO standards.

## Will DoD Accept Third-Party Certification?

There are several possibilities which depend to a great extent upon the type of procurement and the level of contractual quality requirement imposed.

If a contract is for complex, critical supplies being procured under MIL-I-45208A, MIL-Q-9858A or their ISO equivalents, then the chances of DoD accepting those supplies on the basis of a third-party certification are extremely remote, or even non-existent. The reason is the same as stated in the comments on the first question above.

If, on the other hand, a contract is for non-complex, non-critical and/or commercial supplies, the chances of accepting third-party certification improve considerably. Actually, DoD already accepts some supplies of this nature under a Certificate of Conformance (FAR 46.504). Provision would have to be made in the FAR and DFARS, of course, but it is a possibility.

This same question could also be asked relative to purchases by prime contractors from their suppliers. A single supplier may feed a large number of prime contractors. When those primes are working to contracts containing MIL-I-45208A or MIL-Q-9858A quality requirements, DoD holds each of them independently responsible for ensuring the quality of purchased materials. As a result, the supplier (say, of electronic components) may be subjected to the controls and on-site evaluations of literally dozens of prime electronic equipment manufacturers.

If such a supplier were to become certified to an accepted standard by a recognized certification body, then DoD might allow the prime contractors to present evidence of such certification as an indication of quality control at the subcontract level. This could significantly reduce the number and extent of prime contractor on-site evaluations.

Obtaining evidence of certification of a supplier, however, will not relieve the primes of their responsibilities to DoD for ensuring that all purchased supplies are in complete conformance to contract technical requirements. If DoD subsequently finds the supplies to be nonconforming, the prime will beheld responsible.

## PART IV — Summary

■ Will DoD replace MIL-I-45208A and MIL-Q-9858A with ISO standards?

Unquestionably. These documents are old and need to be updated anyway. This is an ideal time to make the change. However, the change will not be a simple one-to-one replacement; there are too many major differences. DoD will either:

● Use the existing documents with heavy supplementation

● Develop new standards based on ISO standards but tailored to meet DoD's needs.

■ Will DoD accept third-party certification?

As a basis for accepting product under prime contracts containing MIL-I-45208A, MIL-Q-9858A or their ISO equivalents, it is extremely unlikely. For other purchases, and at the subcontract level, it is possible.

■ When will DoD begin using ISO standards?

They will undoubtedly be "grandfathered-in." Consequently, even after use of the new standards is directed, the transition will occur over an extended period of time. MIL-I-45208A and MIL-Q-9858 will continue in use until existing contracts containing those requirements are completed.

As to when use of the new standards will be directed, that will depend on how long it takes DoD to resolve the differences, change the FAR and DFARS, and develop and issue implementing procedures.

## About the Author

*K. D. Hollingsworth is a quality consultant specializing in DoD contract quality assurance matters. He teaches the subject, performs audits to MIL-I-45208A and MIL-Q-9858A requirements, and assists clients in resolving problems associated with contractual quality requirements. He retired from government service in 1986 with over 30 years' experience in DoD quality assurance at regional and national levels. Immediately prior to his retirement, he was Course Director for DoD Quality Management courses. In addition, he holds provisional registration as an ISO Assessor.*

**EDITOR'S NOTE:** *This paper by K.D. Hollingsworth appeared in the April 1992 issue of Quality Systems Update (QSU). A comprehensive critical response by Paul Hassing was published in the June issue of QSU. In reference to many parts of the MIL-Q 9858A standard, Hassing has indicated that while Hollingsworth's statements are **technically** correct, current interpretation by many at DoD results in the actual application being similar, if not identical, to ISO 9001 requirements. The sections that Hassing considers affected by this practice are quality auditing, training, contract review, design, and document control. In some other cases Hassing further disagrees with Hollingsworth and considers the wording of MIL-Q 9858A to be essentially parallel to ISO 9001, specifically concerning the requirement for a management representative and the need to document management review of the quality audit.*

*In the same issue of QSU, Hollingsworth responds that he does not agree with the practice of reading into MIL-Q 9858A requirements that are not explicitly stated. Those interested in further reviewing the comments of these knowledgeable professionals should refer to the June 1992 issue of QSU, available from CEEM Information Services.*

---

**ENDNOTES**
[1]    Nordeen, D. L., *Harmonization of Quality Standards: A Perspective from the American Automotive Industry Community*, SAE International Governments/Transportation/Industry Conference, 1992.
[2]    *Measurement Systems Analysis Reference Manual*, AIAG Press, October 1990.

# REVIEW AND REVISION OF ISO STANDARDS

BY DONALD MARQUARDT

## INTRODUCTION

ISO directives provide for review and revision or reaffirmation of standards approximately every five years. In the case of the ISO 9000 series, the ISO Technical Committee 176 has developed a two-phase strategy for the first two review and revision cycles.

The first section of this chapter contains a reprint of an article entitled *Vision 2000: The Strategy for the ISO 9000 Series Standards in the 90s*. This article describes the two-phase strategy and the concepts upon which it is based. It was first printed in *Quality Progress* magazine, May 1991.

Later portions of this chapter describe the various other standards that TC 176 has published or is preparing. Some key concepts developed in the TC 176 Working Group that is revising the ISO 9000 series standard are also summarized.

# VISION 2000: THE STRATEGY FOR THE ISO 9000 SERIES STANDARDS IN THE '90S

BY DONALD MARQUARDT, JACQUES CHOVE, K.E. JENSEN, KLAUS PETRICK, JAMES PYLE AND DONALD STRAHLE

This article is adapted from the report of the Ad Hoc Task Force of the International Organization for Standardization (ISO) Technical Committee 176 (TC 176). The task force was commissioned to prepare a strategic plan for ISO 9000 series architecture, numbering, and implementation. The task force report, which has become known as *Vision 2000*, was prepared by the authors of this article. TC 176 adopted unanimously the strategic principles of the report at its meeting in Interlaken, Switzerland, in October 1990. This article is part of a worldwide communication effort to gain broad acceptance of these principles and to influence standardization activities globally in the quality arena.

This article contains four major sections:

1.  The Stake

    - The ISO 9000 series standards
    - Global trends
    - The critical issues

2.  Basic Concepts

    - Generic product categories
    - Industry/economic sectors
3.  Analysis of the Marketplace

    - Preventing proliferation
    - Segmenting the markets

4.  Vision 2000

    - Migration to product offerings involving several generic product categories
    - Implications for standards development
    - Recommendations on implementation

## The ISO 9000 Series Standards

In the years just prior to 1979 when TC 176 was formed, quality was rapidly emerging as a new emphasis in commerce and industry. Various national and multinational standards had been developed in the quality systems arena for commercial and industrial use and for military and nuclear power industry needs. Some standards were guidance documents. Other standards were for contractual use between purchaser and supplier organizations.

Despite some historical commonalties, these various standards were not sufficiently consistent for widespread use in international trade. Terminology in these standards and in commercial and industrial practice was also inconsistent and confusing.

The publication of the ISO 9000 series in 1987, together with the accompanying terminology standard (ISO 8402), has brought harmonization on an international scale and has supported the growing impact of quality as a factor in international trade. The ISO 9000 series has quickly been adopted by many nations and regional bodies and is rapidly supplanting prior national and industry-based standards. This initial marketplace success of the ISO 9000 series is testimony to two important achievements of TC 176:

■ The ISO 9000 series embodies comprehensive quality management concepts and guidance, together with several models for external quality assurance requirements. Using an integrated systems architecture, the standards are packaged under a harmonized, easily memorized numbering system. These features have high value in meeting the commercial and industrial needs of current international trade.

■ The ISO 9000 series was published in time to meet the growing need for international standardization in the quality arena and the wide adoption of third-party quality systems certification schemes.

More recently, TC 176 has been preparing additional international standards in quality management, quality assurance, and quality technology. Some of these will become part numbers to the 9000 series, while others will be in a 10000 series that has been reserved by ISO for use by TC 176.

# Global Trends

## Global Competition

Globalization has become a reality in the few years since the ISO 9000 series was published. Today, all but the smallest or most local commercial and industrial enterprises are finding that their principal marketplace competitors include companies headquartered in other countries.

Consequently, product development and marketing strategies must be global to reckon with global competition. Quality continues to grow in importance as a factor in marketplace success.

## The European Community

The rapid implementation of the European Community (EC) single-market arrangement, targeted for full operation in 1992, has become a major driving force. EC 1992 has global significance in quality because it places new marketplace pressures on all producers worldwide that wish to trade with European companies or even compete with European companies in other markets.

The EC 1992 plan rests on the use of TC 176-produced standards as the requirement documents for its third-party certification scheme for quality systems registration, and for auditing compliance to the requirements.

Under such certification schemes, a company arranges to be audited by a single accredited independent (third-party) registrar organization. If the company's quality systems documentation and implementation are found to meet the requirements of the applicable ISO 9000 series international standard, the registrar grants certification and lists the company in its register of companies with certified quality systems. All purchasers of the company's products can then accept the third-party certification as evidence that the company's quality systems meet the applicable ISO 9000 series requirements.

Such a third-party certification scheme provides a number of benefits. Certification demonstrates that a company has implemented an adequate quality system for the products or services it offers. By this, better internal commitment as well as enhanced purchaser confidence can be achieved.

In the EC 1992 scheme, quality system certification often will be a prerequisite for product certification or product conformity statements. In addition, from a broader national viewpoint, the scheme will result in improvements in the quality capability of a large fraction of commercial and industrial organizations.

An important corollary benefit for any organization is reduction of the costs of multiple assessments by multiple trading partners. In practice, purchaser organizations often audit portions of the quality systems of their suppliers, but because of supplier quality system certification, the purchaser does not have to duplicate the, say, 80 percent that has already been audited by the third-party auditor.

## Quality as a Competitive Weapon

Quality assurance continues to be a competitive weapon for companies, even in markets where third-party certification has become widespread. The competitive advantage can be achieved by means of second-party (purchaser) quality system requirements and audits that supplement (i.e., go beyond) the requirements of the ISO 9000 series contractual standards. This approach can be carried another step by setting up mutually advantageous partnership arrangements between purchaser and supplier, supplementing third-party audits.

Such partnerships focus on mutual efforts toward continuous quality improvement and the use of innovative quality technology. In instances where purchaser-supplier partnerships are fully developed, third-party certification often plays an important early role but might become relatively less important as the partnership develops and progresses beyond the requirements of the ISO 9001, ISO 9002 or ISO 9003 contractual standards. Various quality awards conferred at the company, national, or multinational level also provide further motivation for excellence in quality.

# The Critical Issues

## Proliferation of Standards

The ISO 9000 series standards — in particular, those for contractual use (ISO 9001, ISO 9002 and ISO 9003) — are being employed in many industries for many different kinds of products and services. Some groups are evaluating or implementing local or industry-specific adaptations of the ISO 9000 series for guidance, for certification, for auditing and for documentation.

These include national or regional bodies (such as CEN/CENELEC, the European regional standardization organization) and international standards committees for industry sectors (such as other technical committees of ISO and IEC). These developments are indicators of success of the ISO 9000 series and indicators of concerns that TC 176 must address.

If the ISO 9000 series were to become only the nucleus of a proliferation of localized standards derived from, but varying in content and architecture from the ISO 9000 series, then there would be little worldwide standardization. The growth of many localized certification schemes would present further complications. Once again, there could be worldwide restraint of trade because of proliferation of standards and inconsistent requirements.

## Inadequacies of Existing ISO 9000 Series Standards

Careful study of the ISO 9000 series standards by certain major groups of users or potential users has identified a number of needs that are not easily met with the ISO 9000 series contractual standards in their present form. One example of such users or potential users is large companies, such as electric power providers or military organizations that purchase complex products to specific functional design.

These users request, for example, a requirement for a quality plan to document how the generic requirements of the ISO 9000 series standards will be adapted to the specific needs of a particular contract. The requirement for a quality plan can improve the consistency of audits.

The position of such purchasers in the supply chain and their size enable their actions to expedite or hinder the worldwide implementation of harmonized external quality assurance standards. Moreover, there appears to be a large number of other users that would optionally want some of the same changes to the standards.

At the same time, it is important to preserve simplicity of ISO 9000 series application for smaller companies.

At its meeting in Interlaken, Switzerland, in October 1990, TC 176 took actions to reckon with these critical issues in formulating future policy for international standards.

To understand the basis for the TC 176 actions, some terminology and concepts must be introduced.

## A Terminology Distinction

A product can be classified in a generic sense in two separate ways. The task force has introduced two terms to describe this important distinction. The first term is *generic product category*. The second term is *industry/economic sector* in which the product is present.

## Generic Product Categories

The task force has identified four generic product categories:

- Hardware
- Software
- Processed Materials
- Services

These four generic product categories are described in Table 7-1. At the present time, Subcommittee 1 of TC 176 is developing formal definitions based on the descriptions of the four generic product categories in this table.

Subcommittee 1 has developed and submitted for international comment definitions for *product* and the generic product category *service*. *Product* is defined as the result of activities or processes. Notes to the definition point out that a product can be tangible or intangible or a combination thereof, and that, for practical reasons, products can be classified in the four generic product categories introduced in Table 7-1.

*Service* is defined as the results generated by activities at the interface between the supplier and the customer, and by supplier internal activities to meet the customer needs. Notes to the definition point out that the supplier or the customer may be represented at the interface by personnel or equipment, that customer activities at the interface may be essential to the service delivery, that delivery or use of tangible products may form part of the service delivery, and that a service may be linked with the manufacture and supply of tangible products.

We believe the four generic product categories are all the kinds of product that need explicit attention in quality management and quality assurance standardization.

## Industry / Economic Sectors

The term *industry/economic sector* applies to all sectors of the economy, including service sectors. The dual use of *industry sector* and *economic sector* recognizes that each term is used for the intended meaning in specific countries or languages. Such sectors include administration, aerospace, banking, chemicals, construction, education, food, health care, insurance, medical, retailing, telecommunications, textiles, tourism, and so forth. The number of industry/economic sectors and potential subsectors is extremely large.

An industry/economic sector can be described as a grouping of suppliers whose

---

## Generic Product Categories

**Hardware**

Products consisting of manufactured pieces, parts or assemblies thereof.

**Software**

Products, such as computer software, consisting of written or otherwise recordable information, concepts, transactions or procedures.

**Processed Materials**

Products (final or intermediate) consisting of solids, liquids, gases, or combinations thereof, including particulate materials, ingots, filaments or sheet structures.

**NOTE:** *Processed materials typically are delivered (packaged) in containers such as drums, bags, tanks, cans, pipelines or rolls.*

**Services**

Intangible products which may be the entire or principal offering or incorporated features of the offering, relating to activities such as planning, selling, directing, delivering, improving, evaluating, training, operating or servicing a tangible product.

**NOTE:** *All generic product categories provide value to the customer only at the times and places the customer interfaces with and perceives benefits from the product. However, the value from a service often is provided primarily by activities at a particular time and place of interface with the customer.*

---

*Table 7-1: Generic product categories.*

offerings meet similar customer needs and/or whose customers are closely interrelated in the marketplace.

## Required Combinations of Generic Product Categories

Two or more of the generic product categories have to be present in the marketplace offerings of any organization, whatever the industry/economic sector in which the organization operates.

An electric power utility is an example where the offering combines many characteristics of a service with delivery of a form of processed material (electric current) via a conducting cable.

Project management is another example where the offering typically combines many characteristics of a service with production and/or delivery of a hardware and/or software product.

Analytical instruments are examples where hardware, software, processed materials (such as titrating solutions or reference standard materials), and services (such as training) might all be important features of the offering.

## Confusion Due to Intermixing of Terms

It has been common practice to intermix the terms for generic product categories and the terms for industry/economic sectors. The result has been confusion and misunderstanding.

A prime example involves the terms "process industries" and "hardware industries." In retrospect, these terms are seen to be collective names for the industry/economic sectors where processed materials and hardware, respectively, are the primary kinds of product. All products are produced by processes.

People in the process industries know from experience that the classic quality management approaches, especially the quality control techniques and quality technology from the hardware industries, are not adequate to deal with the complexities they regularly encounter in the production processes and measurement processes for processed materials. In the language of ISO 9001 and ISO 9004, almost all processes in the process industries are special processes. These differences are crucial matters of degree and emphasis in a quality systems sense.

Terms such as *process industries* and *hardware industries* will continue to be useful when discussing collections of industry/economic sectors. However, for purposes of standardization in the quality arena, we recommend precise use of the four generic product category terms in written documents and oral communication.

## Goals for the ISO 9000 Series and Related Standards

The Ad Hoc Task Force of the International Organization for Standardization Technical Committee 176 (TC 176) set forth four strategic goals for the ISO 9000 series standards and their related ISO 10000 series standards developed by TC 176:

- ○ Universal acceptance
- ○ Current compatibility
- ○ Forward compatibility
- ○ Forward flexibility.

In the following table, informal illustrative tests are described for each strategic goal. These tests are not meant to be strict requirements but only examples of indicators as to whether a strategic goal has been satisfied adequately.

These goals and tests are intended to apply particularly to standards used for external quality assurance. They are important but less critical for quality management guidance documents.

These four strategic goals for TC 176-developed standards will require constant managerial attention by the participants in TC 176 as well as affected user communities. Proposals that are beneficial to one of the goals might be detrimental to another goal. As in all standardization, compromises and paradoxes might be needed in specific situations. Experience continues to show that, when all viewpoints are put forth objectively, a harmonized standard can result, providing benefits to all parties.

**Strategic Goals and Illustrative Tests for TC 176 Standards**

| Goal | Tests |
|------|-------|
| Universal acceptance | ○ The standards are widely adopted and used worldwide.<br>○ There are few complaints from users in proportion to the volume of use.<br>○ Few sector-specific supplementary or derivative standards are being used or developed. |
| Current compatibility | ○ Part-number supplements to existing standards do not change or conflict with requirements in the existing parent document. |

*(continued on next page)*

## Goals for the ISO 9000 Series and Related Standards
*(continued from previous page)*

    ○ The numbering and the clause structure of a supplement facilitate combined use of the parent document and the supplement.

    ○ Supplements are not stand-alone documents but are to be used with their parent document.

Forward compatibility   ○ Revisions affecting requirements in existing standards are few in number and minor or narrow in scope.

    ○ Revisions are accepted for existing and new contracts.

Forward flexibility   ○ Supplements are few in number but can be combined as needed to meet the needs of virtually any industry/ economic sector or generic category of products.

    ○ Supplement or addendum architecture allows new features or requirements to be consolidated into the parent document at a subsequent revision if the supplement's provisions are found to be used (almost) universally.

**Market Need**

In managing the ISO 9000 series standards during the 1990s, market need also must be kept in focus. There is no value in a standard that is not wanted or not used in the marketplace. We encourage TC 176 to expedite the process of identifying and balloting internationally proposed new work items for new standards documents to meet new market needs. TC 176 must always apply the test of market need before embarking on a new standards project, however.

## Analysis of the Marketplace for the ISO 9000 Series Standards

### Preventing Proliferation

The strategy regarding proliferation of supplementary or derivative standards must face up to a political and marketplace reality. TC 176 cannot legislate that industry groups, regional bodies, or other standards organizations will not produce supplementary or derivative documents.

This implies that to continue to influence the marketplace it serves, TC 176 must design its products and provide them in a timely way to prevent (or at least minimize) unhealthy proliferation of industry/economic sector schemes based upon supplementary or derivative documents.

Fortunately, the current global trends are driving many standard users toward strategic recognition that they need and should conform to international standards. This suggests that the marketplace will resist proliferation if TC 176 meets the marketplace needs in a timely way.

It is easy to see why people in various industry/economic sectors would be motivated to create supplementary or derivative documents when confronted with implementing the initial ISO 9000 series standards published in 1987. The initial series is truly generic in scope and is applicable to all four generic product categories.

Nevertheless, the language and many details refer mainly to products in the hardware generic category. People in industry/economic sectors that involve products in the other generic product categories could easily conclude that what they need is a supplementary or derivative document for their specific industry/economic sector. This turns out, in our opinion, to be the wrong solution for the right problem.

We believe the proliferation of supplementary or derivative documents and industry-sector-specific schemes can be prevented or minimized by recognizing criteria that segment the markets for standardization in quality management and external quality assurance.

We recommend a development path for ISO 9000 series architecture that mirrors these market segmenting criteria. This path will allow sufficient flexibility in the ISO 9000 series to meet the needs of users in all generic product categories and all industry/economic sectors. There are, in our view, three criteria that are important to segment the markets.

## Market-Segmenting Criterion 1: Generic Product Categories

Having distinguished generic product categories and industry/economic sectors as ways of classifying, we found an unanticipated commonalty of our viewpoints on standardization policy. The members of the *ad hoc* task force represent a variety of national standards systems, generic product categories, industry/economic sectors, areas of personal experience, and current functional roles within our own organizations.

From all these points of view, we conclude that:

■ Guidance standards written by TC 176 should explicitly deal with the special needs of each generic product category. In fact, at the October 1990 meeting of TC 176, supplementary documents (guidelines) for services and software were advanced to international standard status and work continued on a supplementary document for processed materials. Only these four generic product categories are represented by such formal work items. This reflects, we believe, a heretofore unarticulated international consensus on generic product categories.

■ Neither TC 176 nor other groups should write supplementary or derivative standards (whether guidance standards or quality assurance requirements standards) for specific industry/economic sectors. In fact, experience in several nations has been that their industry-specific schedules or guidance documents have soon fallen into disuse because they had only transient tutorial value.

## Market-Segmenting Criterion 2: Complexity of Purchaser Need and Product and Process Characteristics

A second dimension that segments the market for quality management and quality assurance standards has to do with the differing complexities of purchaser need and product characteristics as well as the differing complexities of designing and operating the process for producing and delivering the product or service. These differences are most obvious in external quality assurance situations.

The existing ISO 9000 series deals with this market-segmenting criterion by having three levels or models for external quality assurance requirements (ISO 9001, ISO 9002 and ISO 9003) and by providing guidance for selecting the appropriate model (ISO 9000, Clause 8.2) and for tailoring the model within a particular contract (ISO 9000, Clause 8.5.1).

In some industry/economic sectors, the options available in the existing ISO 9000 series are felt to be insufficient to meet all the critical needs. These deficiencies, for example, underlie the unmet needs of certain large organizations that purchase complex products to specific functional design, as discussed previously.

We believe that modest additions and revisions of the existing ISO 9000 series contractual standards can resolve these unmet near-term needs while preserving the necessary compatibility and flexibility.

## Market-Segmenting Criterion 3: Contractual vs. Noncontractual

For completeness, we remark that the distinction between contractual and noncontractual situations is a fundamental market segmenting criterion. The distinction is built into the existing ISO 9000 series architecture: ISO 9001, ISO 9002 and ISO 9003 are contractual requirements for quality assurance, and ISO 9004 provides guidance to a producer for implementing and managing a quality system. We believe the existing architecture meets the needs of this market-segmenting criterion.

## Combined Use of the Market-Segmenting Criteria

Market-segmenting criteria 1, 2 and 3 currently provide an opportunity for many options of requirements to meet the needs of the various industry/economic sectors. When the recommendations of the *ad hoc* task force report are implemented, additional options will be provided. We believe that the need for sector-specific supplementary or derived standards and schemes will disappear with this added flexibility of implementation.

# Vision 2000

The background, analyses, and goals discussed in the previous sections provide the basis for anticipating some critical features of standardization in the quality arena by the year 2000. We call this *Vision 2000*. We believe our recommendations will enhance progress toward *Vision 2000*.

## Migration to Product Offerings Involving Several Generic Product Categories

Underlying *Vision 2000* is recognition of where current marketplace trends are leading. In all industry/economic sectors, there is an across-the-board migration toward product offerings that are combinations of two or more of the generic product categories (hardware, software, processed materials, and services).

For example, many products today involve the production of processed materials that are then incorporated into manufactured parts and into hardware assemblies in which computer software also is an incorporated feature and the service aspects of selling, delivering, and servicing are important features of the total offering. A related example is firmware, where computing software is an integral part of the hardware of a product.

During the 1990s this migration will continue. This means that organizations will have to learn about and must implement the quality management and quality assurance terminology, skills, and emphases for all four generic product categories.

Global competition will be a powerful driving force in this process. Various requirements of society will also be a driving force, including laws, statutes, rules and regulations, codes, environmental considerations, health and safety factors, and conservation of energy and materials.

The boundaries for standardization program responsibilities will have to be worked out as a strategic issue in the 1990s. In this context, government agencies are one group representing the society as a customer whose needs and requirements must be satisfied and for whom appropriate quality management and quality assurance tools must be available.

Today, there is the impression that quality management and quality assurance for hardware, software, processed materials, and services are substantially different from each other. It is true that the relative emphases of quality system elements might differ and the sophistication of the quality technology being applied might differ, but the underlying generic quality system elements and needs are the same.

Today, there is the impression that quality systems and quality technology for hardware products is most mature because that has been the predominant kind of product in earlier standards and quality technology literature. However, we believe that the most rapid development of new quality technologies will occur in the other three generic product categories during the 1990s.

## Implications for Standards Development

The standards now under development by TC 176 include a generic guidance document for implementing ISO 9001, ISO 9002, ISO 9003, and guidance documents for software, processed materials, and services. All of these reflect, in their detailed content, the migration we have described. All of these are expected to be published within a couple of years. It can be expected that the 1990s will be a transition period in standards development. During the early 1990s, we will need these separate documents for the various generic product categories.

As product offerings continue to migrate toward combinations of two or more generic product types, suppliers will find it increasingly necessary for employees in different functional activities to refer to different (but interrelated) supplementary standards, each written in a somewhat different style and format. Organizations have the managerial task of achieving compatibility in their quality systems for their offerings containing combinations of several generic product categories. This will be state-of-the-art and acceptable for the early 1990s, but a more strategic approach is needed for the longer term.

We envision that, by the year 2000, there will be an intermingling, a growing together, of the terminology, concepts, and technology used in all four generic product categories. This vision implies that, by the year 2000, the need for separate documents for the four generic product categories will have diminished. Terminology and procedures for all generic product categories will be widely understood and used by practitioners, whatever industry/economic sector they might be operating in.

Consequently, our *Vision 2000* for TC 176 is to develop a single quality management standard (an updated ISO 9004 that includes new topics as appropriate) and an external quality assurance requirements standard (an updated ISO 9001) tied together by a road-map standard (an updated ISO 9000). There would be a high degree of commonalty in the concepts and architecture of ISO 9004 and ISO 9001. The requirements in ISO 9001 would continue to be based upon a selection of the guidance elements in ISO 9004. Supplementary standards that provide expanded guidance could be provided by TC 176 as needed.

Multiple models of external quality assurance (now exemplified by ISO 9001, ISO 9002 and ISO 9003 in accord with the complexity criterion) might still be needed.

ISO standards must be reaffirmed or revised at approximately five-year intervals. At its October 1990 meeting, TC 176 adopted a two-phase strategy to meet the needs for revision of the ISO 9000 series. The first phase is to meet near-term needs for the (nominal) 1992 revision, with no major changes in architecture or numbering. Work on the second phase will begin during 1991, with the intent of implementing *Vision 2000*.

The target date is 1996 — intentionally earlier than the nominal five years for the second cycle of revision. Working groups were set up within TC 176 to do these revisions. Formal comments have already been received from many nations as a basis for the revisions. Additional comments are being received as well.

*Vision 2000* emphatically discourages the production of industry/economic-sector-specific generic quality standards supplemental to, or derived from, the ISO 9000 series. We believe such proliferation would constrain international trade and impede progress in quality achievements. A primary purpose of the widespread publication of this article is to prevent the proliferation of supplemental or derivative standards.

It is, however, well understood that product-specific standards containing technical requirements for specific products or processes or describing specific product test methods are necessary and have to be developed within the industry/economic sector.

## A Visual Portrayal of International Quality Standardization

Figure 7-1 shows graphically how the evolving system of standards meets the combined needs for quality management and quality assurance from both the producer's and the purchaser's viewpoints during the early 1990s.

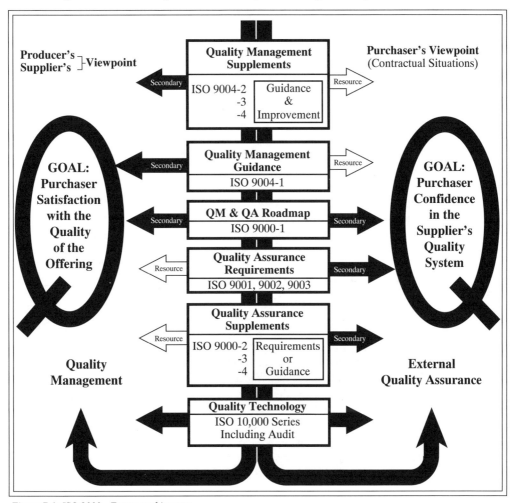

*Figure 7-1: ISO 9000—Future architecture.*

## Recommendations on Implementation

This section discusses some recommendations that are not entirely within the responsibility of TC 176. Nevertheless, reasonable conformance to these recommendations will be critical to success of the ISO 9000 series in the 1990s international environment:

■ TC 176 is encouraged to prepare standards that might be needed for an intermediate period for the four generic product categories. At the same time, TC 176 and all other standards-writing bodies are discouraged from writing standards for specific industry/economic sectors. The rationale for this recommendation was given earlier in this article.

Comment: This recommendation is not intended for standards dealing with technical requirements for specific products, processes or measurements that are outside the scope of TC 176.

■ Quality system certification schemes worldwide should register suppliers only to ISO 9001, ISO 9002, ISO 9003, and other ISO 9000 series requirements documents that might hereafter be published and to their national equivalents translated exactly from the ISO 9000 series.

There should be no industry/economic-sector-specific external quality system standards used as the assessment documents for such certification schemes. This recommendation applies to both third-party and second-party accredited assessment organizations.

■ Auditor accreditation (certification) schemes worldwide should be based on the ISO 10011 series audit standards.

■ Auditors should be accredited (certified) generically, not on an industry/economic-sector basis. Each audit team should include at least one person knowledgeable in the industry/economic sector(s) involved in a particular audit. This knowledge might reside in the accredited auditors on the team or in technical experts on the audit team.

■ TC 176 should help promote the development of mutual recognition arrangements among national quality system certification schemes worldwide. Fairness and consistency must be satisfied adequately, but failure to accomplish mutual recognition could severely restrain trade.

■ The European Community has adopted a series of European standards (EN 45000 series) dealing with general criteria for operation, assessment and accreditation of laboratories; certification bodies relating to certification of products, quality systems, and personnel; and suppliers' declaration of conformity.

Pre-existing ISO/IEC guides also deal with these topics. Implementation of the ISO 9000 series and ISO 10000 series standards interfaces with such criteria. At the October 1990 meeting, TC 176 requested its chairman and secretary to investigate the desirability and options to harmonize the European standards in the EN 45000 series and the relevant ISO/IEC guides and transform the results into international standards.

## Acknowledgments

*We acknowledge our indebtedness to R.N. Shaughnessy, TC 176 Chairman, for his early appreciation of the strategic issues and his leadership in causing this task force to be formed, and to K.C. Ford, TC 176 Secretariat, for his continuing and incisive support for our work. We also acknowledge the suggestions made by H. Kume and K. A. Rutter. Many other people have contributed indirectly through participating in other TC 176 activities or through contacts with task force members.*

*Donald Marquardt, Du Pont, United States; Jacques Chove Conseil, France; K.E. Jensen, Alkatel Kirk A/S, Denmark; Klaus Petrick, DIN, Germany; James Pyle, British Telecom, United Kingdom; and Donald Strahle, Ontario Hydro, Canada, are members of the Ad Hoc Task Force of the International Organization for Standardization Technical Committee 176. Marquardt is the Chairman of the task force.*

# CONCEPTS INTRODUCED IN THE PHASE-ONE REVISION — COMMITTEE DRAFT OF ISO 9000

The first-phase revision of ISO 9000 (1992) is intended to contain guidance concepts not included in the original 1987 version. The additional concepts are needed for effective understanding and current application of the entire ISO 9000 series.

The additional concepts also are planned for complete integration into the architecture and content of the ISO 9000 series second-phase future revision (1996). Two of these additional concepts are summarized briefly here.

## Stakeholders and Their Expectations

Every organization is a supplier of products to customers. The organization may be a commercial or industrial business, a service institution, an academic institution, or a government agency. The supplier organization has five principal groups of stakeholders (vested interest groups): its customers, its employees, its owners, its sub-suppliers and society.

The supplier needs to meet expectations and needs of all its stakeholders. (Table 7-2)

## Concept of a Process

The International Standards in the ISO 9000 series are founded upon the understanding that all work is accomplished by a process. Every process has inputs. The outputs are the results of the process. The outputs are products, tangible or intangible. The process itself is (or should be) a transformation that adds value.

---

### Stakeholders and Their Expectations

| Supplier's Stakeholders | Typical Expectations or Needs |
| --- | --- |
| Customers | Product Quality |
| Employees | Career/Work Satisfaction |
| Owners | Investment Performance |
| Sub-suppliers | Continuing Business Opportunity |
| Society | Responsible Stewardship |

*Table 7-2: Stakeholders and their expectations.*

## Concept of a Process

| Type | Examples |
|---|---|
| **Product-related** | O Raw materials<br>O Intermediate product<br>O Final product<br>O Sampled product. |
| **Information-related** | O Product requirements<br>O Product properties and status data<br>O Support function communications<br>O Feedback on product performance and needs<br>O Measurement data from sampled product. |

*Table 7-3: Concept of a process.*

Every process involves people and/or other resources in some way. An output may be, for example, an invoice, computing software, gasoline, a clinical device, a banking service or an intermediate product. There are opportunities to make measurements on the inputs, and at various places in the process, on the outputs. Inputs and outputs are of several types, as shown in Table 7-3.

The supplier functions in a supply-chain relationship to a sub-supplier and a customer. In this supply-chain structure the various inputs and outputs need to flow in various directions. It is emphasized that in this context *product* includes all four generic product categories (hardware, software, processed materials, services).

Quality management is accomplished by managing the processes in the organization. It is necessary to manage a process in two senses:

- Structure and operation of the process itself within which the product or information flows
- Quality of the product or information flowing within the structure.

Every company or organization exists to accomplish value-adding work. The work is accomplished through a network of processes. The structure of the network is usually not a simple sequential structure, but is typically quite complex.

# NEW ADOPTED AND DRAFT STANDARDS

This section looks briefly at newly adopted standards, draft standards and other proposed guidance documents in the ISO 9000 series. Two of the standards: *ISO 9004-2: Guidelines for Services* and *ISO 9000-3: Guidelines for software development* are discussed in greater detail.

The United States is in the process of adopting three ISO standards as national standards. ISO 9004-2, ISO 9000-3 and ISO 10011 (*Guidelines for auditing*) should become US national standards by the end of 1992.

---

## ISO/TC 176 Standards Issued and Being Developed

The numerical sequencing of ISO standards has been designated by the International Organization for Standardization. Approved and published ISO standards are designated ISO XXXX. Because of the importance of the ISO 9000 series, the ISO Central Secretariat has set aside a block of numbers in the 90xx range beginning with 9000, and a block of numbers in the 100xx range beginning with 10001 to be used by TC 176 as new standards are formulated.

Drafts of proposed standards go through several stages. Initially, while the Working Group is developing a standard, it is called a *Working Draft (WD)*. When the Working Draft is circulated internationally for formal ballot, it is called a *Committee Draft (CD)*. When sufficient consensus is achieved to seek approval as an international standard, the document is called a *Draft International Standard (DIS)* and is circulated internationally for ballot and approval. This process is illustrated in Figure 7-2.

The architecture of the ISO 9000 series maintains ISO 9001, ISO 9002 and ISO 9003 as standards with no "Part Numbers." Therefore their numerical designations do not have dashes and part number identifiers after the main number. ISO 9000 itself does have a number of supplementary "parts" which are:

❍ External quality assurance guidance for the proper use of ISO 9001, ISO 9002 and/or ISO 9003
❍ Potential supplemental quality management guidance to ISO 9000 itself
❍ Potential optional external quality assurance requirements that are supplemental to the requirements in ISO 9001, ISO 9002, or ISO 9003.

Part 1 (ISO 9000-1) has been reserved for the designation of successive revisions of ISO 9000 (1987) itself.

ISO 9004 has a number of supplementary "parts" which are expanded quality management guidance that relates to the existing or potential subject matter of ISO 9004. Part 1 (ISO 9004-1) has been reserved for the designation of successive revisions of ISO 9004 (1987) itself.

The ISO 100xx series is reserved for quality technology standards.

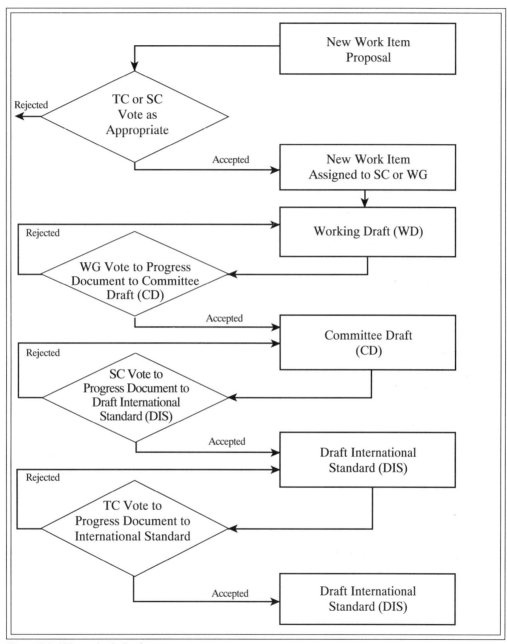

*Figure 7-2: ISO standards development process.*

## Status of Each Document as of Mid-1992

**Existing Standards**

○ ISO 8402: *Quality - Vocabulary* (1986)

○ ISO 9000: *Quality management and quality assurance standards*

  ● ISO 9000 - Part 1: *Guidelines for selection and use* (existing standard ISO 9000-1987)

  ● ISO 9000 - Part 2: *Generic guidelines for the application* of ISO 9001, ISO 9002, and ISO 9003 (approved, publication 1992/3)

  ● ISO 9000 - Part 3: *Guidelines for the application of ISO 9001 to the development supply and maintenance of software* (1991)

  ● ISO 9001: *Quality systems - Model for quality assurance in design/development, production, installation and servicing* (1987)

  ● ISO 9002: *Quality systems - Model for quality assurance in production and installation* (1987)

  ● ISO 9003: *Quality systems - Model for quality assurance in final inspection and test* (1987)

  ● ISO 9004: *Quality management and quality system elements*

    ISO 9004 - Part 1: *Guidelines* (existing standard ISO 9004-1987)

    ISO 9004 - Part 2: *Guidelines for services* (1991)

○ ISO 10011: *Guidelines for auditing quality systems*

  ● Part 1: *Auditing* (1990)

  ● Part 2: *Qualification criteria for quality systems auditors* (1991)

  ● Part 3: *Management of audit programs* (1991)

○ ISO 10012: *Quality assurance requirements for measuring equipment*

  ● Part 1: *Management of measuring equipment*

**Work in Progress**

○ ISO DIS 8402 - *Vocabulary*

○ ISO 9004 - Part 3 (CD): *Guidelines for processed materials*

○ ISO 9004 - Part 4: (CD): *Guidelines for quality improvement*

○ ISO 9004 - Part 5: (CD): *Guidelines for quality plans*

○ ISO 9004 - Part 6: (CD): *Guidelines for configuration management*

# Status of TC 176 Work Items

**Subcommittee 1 - Working Group 1 (ISO 8402)**
Title: *ISO 8402-1: Quality Systems Terminology*
Purpose: Revise ISO 8402 (1986) and add new terms
Status: Draft International Standard

**Subcommittee 2 - Working Group 2 (System Guidelines)**
Title: *ISO 9004-3: Guidelines for processed materials*
Purpose: Guidance for applying the concepts of ISO 9004 to processed materials
Status: Draft International Standard

**Subcommittee 2 - Working Group 4 (System Integration)**
Title: *ISO 9000-2: Guidelines for the application of ISO 9001, ISO 9002, and ISO 9003*
Purpose: Provide generic guidance on application
Status: Approved as international standard; publication expected 1993

**Subcommittee 2 - Working Group 5 (Software Quality Assurance)** (disbanded; work completed)
Title: *ISO 9000-3: Application of ISO 9001 to software*
Purpose: Guidance for use of ISO 9001 for external quality assurance of computer software products
Status: Standard published 1991

**Subcommittee 2 - Working Group 6 (Services)** (disbanded; work completed)
Title: *ISO 9004-2: Guidelines for services*
Purpose: Guidance for service applications
Status: Standard published 1991

**Subcommittee 2 - Working Group 8 (Project Management)**
Title: *ISO 9004-X: Project Management*
Purpose: Quality management guidelines for project management applications
Status: Being drafted

**Subcommittee 2 - Working Group 9 (Quality Improvement)**
Title: *ISO 9004-4: Guidelines for Quality Improvement*
Purpose: Develop process improvement concepts
Status: Draft International Standard

*(continued on next page)*

# Status of TC 176 Work Items (continued)

**Subcommittee 2 - Working Group 10 (ISO 9000 Revision)**
Title: *ISO 9000-1: Guidelines for the selection and use of the ISO 9000 series standards*
Purpose: Revise current ISO 9000 for both first-phase and second-phase revisions
Status: Committee Draft (CD)

**Subcommittee 2 - Working Group 11 (ISO 9001, 9002, 9003 Revision)**
ISO 9001, ISO 9002, ISO 9003 External quality assurance requirements
Purpose: Revise current ISO 9001, ISO 9002, ISO 9003 for both first-phase and second-phase revisions
Status: Committee Draft (CD)

**Subcommittee 2 - Working Group 12 (ISO 9004 Revision)**
ISO 9004-1: System elements
Purpose: Revise current ISO 9004 for both first-phase and second-phase revisions
Status: Committee Draft (CD)

**Subcommittee 2 - Working Group 13 (Quality Plan)**
Title: *ISO 9004-X: Quality plans*
Purpose: Develop a stand-alone document and/or quality plan requirements language for incorporation into ISO 9001, or quality planning guidance for incorporation into ISO 9004
Status: Committee Draft (CD)

**Subcommittee 2 - Working Group 14 (Configuration Management)**
Title: *ISO 9004-6: Configuration management*
Purpose: Develop configuration management guidelines
Status: Committee Draft (CD)

**Subcommittee 3 - Working Group 15 (Metrology)**
Short Title: *ISO 10012: Metrology*
Purpose: Develop standards for measuring equipment
Status: Part 1 of standard published, Part 2 being drafted

*(For further information, contact the Standards Administrator, American Society for Quality Control, Milwaukee, WI, (414) 272-8575.)*

## ISO 10011: Guidelines for Auditing Quality Systems

ISO 10011: *Guidelines for auditing quality systems* consists of three parts:

- 10011-1: *Auditing*
- 10011-2: *Qualification criteria for quality systems auditors*
- 10011-3: *Management of audit programs.*

An important feature of the ISO 9000 series is the provision for maintaining continuity of the quality system. This is necessary to avoid situations in which organizations establish appropriate quality practice, but then permit deterioration over time, so that it becomes ineffective.

Clause 4.17 of the ISO 9001 standard requires establishment of an internal quality audit system. An important value of regular internal quality auditing is the identification of system elements whose procedures are not being followed.

In addition, Clause 4.1.3 of the standard provides for a periodic management review. A footnote points out that this normally includes assessment of the results of internal quality audits by or on behalf of management. ISO 10011 provides guidance for

---

### Key Definitions in ISO 10011

**Quality Audit:** A systematic and independent examination to determine whether quality activities and related results comply with planned arrangements and whether these arrangements are implemented effectively and are suitable to achieve objectives.

(**NOTES:** The quality audit typically applies to, but is not limited to, a quality system or elements thereof, to processes, to products, or to services. Quality audits are carried out by staff not having direct responsibility in the areas being audited but, preferably, working in cooperation with the relevant personnel. Quality audits can be conducted for internal or external purposes.) (ISO 10011-1, 3.1)

**Auditor (quality)**: A person who has the qualification to perform audits. (**NOTES:** To perform a quality audit, the auditor must be authorized for that particular audit. An auditor designated to manage a quality auditor is called a *lead auditor*.) (ISO 10011-1, 3.2)

**Auditee:** An organization to be audited. (ISO 10011-1, 3.5)

establishing a quality audit system. The guidance of ISO 10011 Parts 1, 2 and 3 has been widely accepted internationally, and thus in effect enlarges the requirements of ISO 9001.

The three parts of ISO 10011 address the audit process, auditor qualifications and managing audit programs.

With the wide adoption of the ISO standard and the growth of the registration process, quality system auditing takes on new importance. No longer is auditing limited to the internal audit function; now the auditing process as described in ISO 10011 becomes a set of ground rules for procedures to be followed by registrars.

ISO 10011 has been adopted with minor changes by the European Community. The registration process thus provides a third level of assurance that the quality system has continuity; registrars typically review quality systems at six-month intervals. While the ISO 10011 standards are guidelines and not mandatory requirements, they are an excellent resource for establishing consistent audit practice worldwide.

## ISO 10012-1: Quality Assurance Requirements for Measuring Equipment — Part 1: Management of Measuring Equipment

ISO 10012 provides requirements for a detailed metrological confirmation system for measuring equipment. This standard contains quality assurance requirements for a supplier to ensure that measurements are made with the intended accuracy. It contains guidance on implementing requirements. The standard specifies the main features of the confirmation system to be used for a supplier's measuring equipment.

ISO 10012-1 is applicable to measuring equipment used in demonstration of compliance with a specification; it does not apply to other items of measuring equipment.

The standard is applicable to testing laboratories, including those providing a calibration service; this includes laboratories operating a quality system in accordance with *ISO Guide 25: General requirements for the competence of calibration and testing laboratories*. It is applicable to suppliers of products who operate a quality system in which measurement results are used to demonstrate compliance with specified requirements, and to other organizations where measurement is used for the same purpose.

Key sections of this standard are:

- Measuring equipment
- Confirmation system

- Periodic audit and review of the confirmation system
- Planning
- Uncertainty of measurement
- Documented confirmation procedures
- Records
- Nonconforming measuring equipment
- Confirmation labeling
- Intervals of confirmation
- Sealing for integrity
- Use of outside products and services
- Storage and handling
- Traceability
- Cumulative effect of uncertainties
- Environmental conditions
- Personnel.

Most sections contain valuable guidance toward applying the standard.

This standard has not become used routinely, but is called up in some two-party contractual situations. A Part 2 is under development, which would expand the perspective to recognize that measuring is itself a process and that the assurance of measurement integrity requires more than management of measurement equipment.

---

## Key Definitions in ISO 10012-1

**Metrological confirmation:** Set of operations required to ensure that an item of measuring equipment is in a state of compliance with requirements for its intended use. (**NOTES:** Metrological confirmation normally includes calibration, any necessary adjustment or repair and subsequent recalibration, as well as any required sealing and labeling.) (ISO 10012-1, 3.1)

**Measuring Equipment:** All of the measuring instruments, measurement standards, reference materials, auxiliary apparatus and instructions that are necessary to carry out a measurement. This term includes measuring equipment used in the course of testing and inspection, as well as that used in calibration. (ISO 10012-1, 3.2)

**Measurement:** The set of operations having the object of determining the value of a quantity. (ISO 10012-1, 3.3)

# ISO 9000-3: GUIDELINE FOR
# QUALITY ASSURANCE IN SOFTWARE

BY JEFFREY TUTHILL

In 1990, the International Organization for Standardization (ISO) Technical Committee 176 (TC 176) approved a 15-page quality assurance guideline, ISO 9000-3, for software operations.

This document should not be confused with the ISO 9003 standard, *Quality systems—Model for quality assurance in final inspection and test*. The ISO 9000-3 document, *Guidelines for the application of ISO 9001 to the development, supply and maintenance of software*, is intended to be used in conjunction with the ISO 9001 standard for the assessment and registration of software operations.

---

### Software Definitions in ISO 9000-3

**Software:** Intellectual creation comprising the programs, procedures, rules and any associated documentation pertaining to the operation of a data processing system. (Software is independent of the medium on which it is recorded.)

**Software Product:** Complete set of computer programs, procedures and associated documentation and data designated for delivery to a user.

**Software Item:** Any identifiable part of a software product at an intermediate step or at the final step of development.

**Development:** All activities to be carried out to create a software product.

**Phase:** Defined segment of work.

**Verification (for software):** The process of evaluating the products or a given phase to ensure correctness and consistency with respect to the products and standards provided as input to that phase.

**Validation (for software):** The process of evaluating software to ensure compliance with specified requirements.

---

ISO 9000-3 is a guideline, not a standard. Its original purpose was for use as a stand-alone document for the purpose of software products quality system implementation and improvement. Only three of the ISO 9000 series standards are intended to be used for registration: ISO 9001, ISO 9002 and ISO 9003. However, even before its publication, the UK had begun development of a registration scheme for software. This is now operating and is called *TickIT* (discussed ion more detail below). TickIT now has effectively made 9000-3 mandatory. However, the registration standard is ISO 9001.

Guidelines similar to ISO 9000-3 likely will be produced for assessing and register-ing other specialized areas to the ISO 9001, ISO 9002 and ISO 9003 standards. Service industries are also covered by a guideline document, ISO 9004-2. ISO 9004-2 is not yet formalized into a registration scheme.

## Contents of ISO 9000-3

The ISO 9000-3 guidelines are cross-referenced to the clauses of the appropriate ISO standard in informative annexes. ISO 9000-3, Annex A cross-references the guideline's clauses to those of the ISO 9001 standard. Conversely, ISO 9000-3 Annex B cross-references ISO 9001 clauses to guideline ISO 9000-3 (see box).

ISO 9000-3 contains 23 main clauses, numbered 4.1 to 6.9, and approximately 62 subclauses. Each refers to a particular quality discipline of software business. This unique application to software products is seen clearly in the Development Planning subclauses under Clause 5.4, where terminology such as *development phases*, *input*, and *output verification*, are used (see Table 7-4 on next page).

Software particulars are also highlighted in the Testing and Validation suggestions in Clause 5.7. ISO 9000-3, Clause 3, defines *software*, *software product*, *software item*, *development*, *phase*, *verification*, and *validation*. These definitions are helpful in assessing software operations to the requirements of ISO 9001.

In addition to the assessment of software companies, the ISO 9000-3 guideline is intended for use by computer and high technology corporations which have resident software as part of their business.

## Use of ISO 9000-3

Few software operations have been assessed to ISO 9001 using the ISO 9000-3 guideline, except in the United Kingdom. Most software businesses that have been registered in the European Community were assessed and certified to ISO 9002

## ISO 9001 and ISO 9000-3 Cross References

| ISO 9001 CLAUSE | QUALITY SYSTEM ELEMENTS | ISO 9000-3 CLAUSE |
|---|---|---|
| 4 | Quality System Requirements | 4, 5, 6 |
| 4.1 | Management Responsibility | 4.1 |
| 4.2 | Quality System | 4.2 |
| 4.3 | Contract Review | 5.1, 5.2 |
| 4.4 | Design Control | 5.2, 5.3, 5.5, 5.6, 6.1 |
| 4.5 | Document Control | 6.1, 6.2 |
| 4.6 | Purchasing | 6.7 |
| 4.7 | Purchaser Supplied Product | 6.8 |
| 4.8 | Product Identification/Traceability | 6.1 |
| 4.9 | Process Control | 5.5, 6.5, 6.6 |
| 4.10 | Inspection and Testing | 5.6, 5.7, 5.8 |
| 4.11 | Inspection, Measuring and Test Equipment | 5.6, 6.5, 6.6 |
| 4.12 | Inspection and Test Status | 6.1 |
| 4.13 | Control of Non-Conforming Product | 5.5, 5.6, 5.7, 5.9, 6.1 |
| 4.14 | Corrective Action | 4.4 |
| 4.15 | Handling, Storage, Packaging and Delivery | 5.8 |
| 4.16 | Quality Records | 6.3 |
| 4.17 | Internal Quality Audits | 4.3 |
| 4.18 | Training | 6.9 |
| 4.19 | Servicing | 5.9 |
| 4.20 | Statistical Techniques | 6.4 |

## ISO 9000-3 vs. ISO 9001 Cross Reference

| ISO 9000-3 CLAUSE | QUALITY SYSTEM ELEMENTS | ISO 9001 CLAUSE |
|---|---|---|
| 4.1 | Management Responsibility | 4.1 |
| 4.2 | Quality System | 4.2 |
| 4.3 | Internal Quality Audits | 4.17 |
| 4.4 | Corrective Action | 4.14 |
| 5.2 | Contract Review | 4.3 |
| 5.3 | Purchaser's Requirements Specification | 4.3. 4.4 |
| 5.4 | Development Planning | 4.4 |
| 5.5 | Quality Planning | 4.2, 4.4 |
| 5.6 | Design and Implementation | 4.4, 4.9, 4.13 |
| 5.7 | Testing and Validation | 4.4, 4.10, 4.11, 4.13 |
| 5.8 | Acceptance | 4.10, 4.15 |
| 5.9 | Replication, Delivery and Installation | 4.10, 4.13, 4.15 |
| 5.10 | Maintenance | 4.13, 4.19 |
| 6.1 | Configuration Management | 4.4, 4.5, 4.8, 4.12, 4.13 |
| 6.2 | Document Control | 4.5 |
| 6.3 | Quality Records | 4.16 |
| 6.4 | Measurement | 4.20 |
| 6.5 | Rules, Practices and Conventions | 4.9, 4.11 |
| 6.6 | Tools and Techniques | 4.9, 4.11 |
| 6.7 | Purchasing | 4.6 |
| 6.8 | Included Software Products | 4.7 |
| 6.9 | Training | 4.18 G |

*Table 7-4: ISO 9001 and ISO 9000-3 cross references.*

because no design and development functions existed at the facility. The first edition of ISO 9000-3 was released in 1991. Many companies are still reviewing the document.

According to Brian Hoy of the National Standards Authority of Ireland (NSAI) in Dublin, at least four companies in Ireland have incorporated the ISO 9000-3 guideline in their ISO 9001 registrations. Hoy reports that some US companies are including the ISO 9000-3 guidelines in ISO 9001 registration efforts. Yet it is important to stress that a company does not become **registered** to ISO 9000-3. If the guideline is used while undergoing ISO 9001 registration, that fact may be noted on the registration certificate.

No European Community directive specifically regulates software products. The EC Commission, however, does plan to address the software industry. When the EC established its new approach to directives in the mid-1980s, it indicated that the software and information technology industries would be two areas on its agenda. (See Chapter 8 for a discussion of EC directives.)

## Guidelines or Standard?

According to Jim Roberts of Bell Communications Research (Bellcore), the impetus for the ISO 9000-3 guideline came from a broad consensus of European software producers, purchasers, users and registrars who wanted a guidance document to aid in applying ISO 9001 to the software industry. Since the software industry is "technologically fast-moving and still young," differences exist on terminology and methodology when it comes to software quality, according to Roberts. Obtaining consensus in the TC 176 Working Group on these issues "was difficult and did not at the time justify writing a mandatory requirements documents," said Roberts. Therefore it was decided that it would be better to have a guideline rather than a prescriptive standard for this industry, although initially many Europeans expected the document to take the form of a prescriptive standard.

While Roberts doesn't favor a separate registration standard for software, he surmises that future use of the guidelines could necessitate a separate software standard. The software guidelines could also be incorporated into the ISO 9001 standard when it is revised in 1997. However, he said TC 176 will move cautiously in assessing how the guidelines are used and evaluating collective experience before deciding what future form the standard will take.

A future directive regulating software will likely mandate use of the European Community mark (EC mark) for software suppliers. A future directive will likely offer the conformity assessment modules for quality assurance as a means of compliance to the directive's essential requirements. The EC mark would be used only in connection with the certification of the product, not the quality system. The quality system will continue to be the registration standard.

Companies whose functions include software operations, preparing for any future EC directives regulating software, should consider registration to ISO 9001. These companies should also consider including the criteria of the ISO 9000-3 guideline in the registration effort.

## About the Author

*Jeffrey P. **Tuthill** is employed with L-CAD, Inc., a regulatory compliance engineering company providing ISO 9000 workshops, seminars, preliminary audits, and documentation assistance. Mr. Tuthill was previously employed by the National Standards Authority of Ireland and set up operations for this EC standards writing and certification body in the United States. During his two-year tenure with NSAI, he received an in-depth education on compliance with EC New-Approach directives. Mr. Tuthill now offers consulting services in the use of ISO 9000 registration as a compliance tool in the EC single market.*

# APPLICATION OF ISO 9000-3

According to Charles Cianfrani, Director of Corporate Quality Assurance for Fischer & Porter in Pennsylvania, "The degree of sophistication of US companies in the area of software quality assurance is much lower than with other elements of the quality system."

Fischer & Porter coupled the ISO 9000-3: *Guidelines for the application of ISO 9001 to the development, supply and maintenance of software,* with the ISO 9001 standard to form the company's own 75-page software development standard. Fischer & Porter became registered to ISO 9001 and, according to Cianfrani, found the ISO 9000-3 guidelines "very helpful" in creating a software standard and acquiring ISO 9001 registration.

"Software development needs to be viewed like any other product, not as an art form," said Cianfrani. He said many US auditors and registrars currently do not have the sophistication in software technology to do an adequate job of auditing. "They just make sure that there is a process," he stated.

US software developers need to look at the life-cycle cost of software after it is released. "The larger costs are unknown; people do not realize the quality costs associated" with the lack of a formal software quality assurance process, Cianfrani concluded.

Bell Communications Research (Bellcore), the research and technical support organization for the seven regional Bell telephone companies, is rewriting its technical reference for software quality systems to conform with both ISO 9001 and ISO 9000-3: *Guidelines for the application of ISO 9001 to the development, supply and maintenance of software*, according to Jim Roberts of Bellcore.

## United Kingdom's TickIT Program

The government of the United Kingdom has instituted a formal accreditation and registration program based on the ISO 9000-3 guidelines for software developers. The UK's Department of Trade and Industry (DTI) has developed a scheme, known as *TickIT*, based on the ISO 9000-3 guidelines, to tailor the use of ISO 9001 for both external and internal software developers.

The program applies to information technology "systems supply where software development forms a significant or critical part," according to the DTI's June 1991 issue of *TickIT News.*

The UK's TickIT initiative goes beyond the ISO 9000-3 guidelines because it awards a TickIT mark for companies registered under the program. This means the UK is "in effect, using the guidelines as a mandatory guidance standard," said Jim Roberts. However, not all European Community national accreditation bodies for quality systems have agreed to adopt the current TickIT program.

Roberts called the UK program an interesting development, with good material based on much study in the United Kingdom. He added that it can serve as a good working document upon which to build consensus in the United States in the area of improving software quality assurance.

## US Software Quality System Registration

Currently, the United States lacks an infrastructure for software quality system registration. However, in September 1992, the Registrar Accreditation Board (RAB) formed a Software Quality Systems Registration (SQSR) committee. Chaired by Bellcore's Jim Roberts, the SQSR committee will study the need for a registration and accreditation system for the application of ISO 9001 to software. If the need is demonstrated, the committee will make recommendations to RAB for a system which will satisfy US market needs and also meet the requirements of the EC and other regions of the world.

# ISO 9004 - 2: QUALITY MANAGEMENT AND QUALITY SYSTEMS ELEMENTS GUIDELINES FOR SERVICES

BY IAN G. DURAND

The current ISO 9000 quality standards, published in 1987, are explicitly intended to apply to services as well as to all types of products. However, while the concepts in these standards are universal, the language and structure clearly focuses on the manufacture of discrete units of hardware.

The concepts also reflect the inspection-oriented approach to quality assurance prevalent in national quality standards in the 1970s. Generally, an inspection orientation is not applicable to services because services are rarely created and stored in advance of the need.

This concern was raised within ISO Technical Committee TC 176 in 1985; but rather than delay the release of the basic standards, a new Working Group was established to draft a supplement focusing on quality of services.

Unfortunately, the relevance of the original ISO 9000 standards has not been recognized by many managers in service organizations. In spite of this, a growing number of service organizations in the United States and Europe have already been registered to ISO 9001 and ISO 9002 without reference to the new *Guidelines for services*.

In response to marketplace needs, ISO 9004 - Part 2: *Guidelines for services*, a supplement to the 1987 issue of ISO 9004: *Quality management and quality system elements*, was published in September 1991 by the ISO. Plans are now underway to adopt ISO 9004-2 as a US national standard. Currently, copies of ISO 9004 - 2 may be ordered through ANSI headquarters. (See Appendix A.)

*Guidelines for services* is noteworthy in several respects: First, the focus is on services and service organizations. Second, the focus on service quality necessarily leads to explicit discussions of most aspects of Total Quality Management (TQM). (Careful scrutiny reveals references to some of these topics in the current standards, but they are covered more completely and coherently in ISO 9004 - Part 2.) In this sense, *Guidelines for services* presages the direction of future revisions and additions to the entire ISO 9000 series.

---

## Service Definitions in ISO 9004-2

**Service:** The results generated, by activities at the interface between the supplier and the customer and by supplier internal activities, to meet customer needs. (**NOTES:** The supplier of the customer may be represented at the interface by personnel or equipment. Customer activities at the interface with the supplier may be essential to the service delivery.)

**Service delivery:** Those supplier activities necessary to provide the service.

**Supplier:** An organization that provides a product or a service to a customer.

**Customer:** The recipient of a product or a service. (**NOTES:** A customer may be, for example, the ultimate consumer, user, beneficiary or purchaser. A customer is sometimes referred to as a "business second-party." A customer may be a unit within the service organization.)

---

## Highlights

Of particular note in the *Guidelines* is coverage of:

- Management of customer relations and measurement of customer satisfaction
- Dependence of service quality on employee knowledge, skills and motivation, especially those employees in frequent contact with external customers
- Strong emphasis on the critical need for process management throughout the organization, including across departments
- Importance of continuous improvement based on quantitative measurements.

Other TQM topics emphasized include:

- Employee involvement and teamwork
- Prevention-oriented systems (versus inspect-and-fix approaches)
- Self-inspection
- Planning
- Life-cycle management of services.

Although not the subject of any specific clause in ISO 9004 - Part 2, quality management of services is assumed to be an integral part of normal business operations.

## Application to All Organizations

The *Guidelines* were written to apply to all organizations, large or small, and whether services are primary market offerings or ancillary to a tangible product.

Publication of this standard underscores the reality that all organizations are service organizations, even if those services support only the sale, ordering, delivery and billing of products.

ISO TC 176 clearly intended that the ISO 9004 standards be used by management for **internal guidance** and **not** as the basis for third-party **registration**. Of course, once the standards are in the public domain, there is little control over their use in two-party contractual situations. For example, for several years, a few third-party quality assurance firms have used ISO 9004 as the basis for second-party audits.

More importantly, uninformed references have already appeared in the quality press about using ISO 9001, ISO 9002 or ISO 9003 **in conjunction with** ISO 9004 - Part 2 to assess service organizations for third-party registration. Such unintended use would significantly expand the intended requirements, scope and coverage of ISO 9001; it would obviate the differences among ISO 9001, ISO 9002 and ISO 9003. Such inappropriate use could also make TQM principles the *de facto* basis for registration — a development which could completely derail the third-party registration process.

## About the Author

*Ian Durand is President of Service Process Consulting, Inc., of Edison, New Jersey. He was a major contributor to the drafting effort of ISO 9004-Part 2 and was the lead US delegate to the ISO working group responsible for publishing ISO 9004-Part 2: Guidelines for services. Durand continues to be active in ISO TC 176 and is involved in updating and revision of the basic ISO 9000 standards. He was a senior examiner in 1990 for the Baldrige Award. He teaches a course, Using the ISO 9000/ANSI/ASQC Q90 Series to Design and Implement a Quality Management System, for the American Society for Quality Control (ASQC).*

## ISO 9004-2 — ISO 9004
## Cross-Reference of Quality System Elements and Clauses

| Clause (or Sub-Clause) in ISO 9004-2: 1991 | Title | Corresponding Clause (or Sub-Clause) in ISO 9004: 1987 |
|---|---|---|
| 4 | Characteristics of service | 7.2 |
| 4.1 | Service and service delivery, characteristics | 7.2 |
| 4.2 | Control of service and service delivery, characteristics | 11.4 |
| 5 | Quality system principles | 5 |
| 5.1 | Key aspects of a quality system | 5.1.1 |
| 5.2 | Management responsibility | 4 |
| 5.2.2 | Quality policy | 4.2 |
| 5.2.3 | Quality objectives | 4.2, 6.19 |
| 5.2.4 | Quality responsibility and authority | 5.2.2 |
| 5.2.5 | Management review | 5.5 |
| 5.3 | Personnel and material resources | 5.2.4 |
| 5.3.2 | Personnel | 18 |
| 5.3.2.1 | Motivation | 18.3 |
| 5.3.2.2 | Training and development | 18.1, 18.2 |
| 5.3.2.3 | Communications | 7.3 |
| 5.3.3 | Material resources | 5.2.4 |
| 5.4 | Quality system structure | 4.4, 5.2.1 |
| 5.4.2 | Service quality loop | 5.1 |
| 5.4.3 | Quality documentation and records | 5.2.5, 5.3, 17 |
| 5.4.3.1 | Documentation system | 5.3.2 |
| 5.4.3.2 | Documentation control | 17.2 |
| 5.4.4 | Internal quality audits | 5.4 |
| 5.5 | Interface with customers | 7.3 |
| 5.5.2 | Communication with customers | 7.3 |
| 6 | Quality system operational elements | 5 |
| 6.1 | Marketing process | 7 |
| 6.1.1 | Quality in market research and analysis | 7.1, 19 |
| 6.1.2 | Supplier obligations | 8.2.4 |
| 6.1.3 | Service brief | 7.2 |
| 6.1.4 | Service management | 8.7 |
| 6.1.5 | Quality in advertising | 0.4.2.2 |

*(continued on next page)*

*Table 7-5: Cross-reference of quality system elements and clauses.*

## Cross-Reference of Quality System Elements and Clauses *(continued)*

| Clause (or Sub-Clause) in ISO 9004-2: 1991 | Title | Corresponding Clause (or Sub-Clause) in ISO 9004: 1987 |
|---|---|---|
| 6.2 | Design process | 8 |
| 6.2.2 | Design responsibilities | 8.2 |
| 6.2.3 | Service specification | 8.1, 8.2, 8.3 |
| 6.2.4 | Service delivery specification | 10 |
| 6.2.4.2 | Service delivery procedures | 10.1 |
| 6.2.4.3 | Quality in procurement | 9, 12.1 |
| 6.2.4.4 | Supplier-provided equipment to customers for service and service delivery | 13.3 |
| 6.2.4.5 | Service identification and traceability | 11.2, 19 |
| 6.2.4.6 | Handling, storage, packaging, delivery and protection of customers' possessions | 16 |
| 6.2.5 | Quality control specification | 12.2 |
| 6.2.6 | Design review | 8.5, 8.5.2 |
| 6.2.7 | Validation of the service, service delivery and quality control specification | 8.4, 8.5.3, 8.7, 8.9 |
| 6.2.8 | Design change control | 8.8 |
| 6.3 | Service delivery process | 10, 12.3 |
| 6.3.2 | Supplier's assessment of service quality | 12 |
| 6.3.3 | Customer's assessment of service quality | 7.3 |
| 6.3.4 | Service status | 11.7 |
| 6.3.5 | Corrective action for nonconforming services | 11.8, 14, 15 |
| 6.3.5.1 | Responsibilities | 15.2 |
| 6.3.5.2 | Identification of nonconformity and corrective action | 14, 15 |
| 6.3.6 | Measurement system control | 11.3, 13 |
| 6.4 | Service performance analysis and improvement | 16.3 |
| 6.4.2 | Data collection and analysis | 15.5 |
| 6.4.3 | Statistical methods | 20 |
| 6.4.4 | Service quality improvement | 6 |

*Table 7-5: Cross-reference of quality system elements and clauses (continued).*

# Examples to Which This Part of ISO 9004-2 May be Applied

**Hospitality Services**
Catering, hotels, tourism, entertainment, radio, television, leisure.

**Communications**
Airports and airlines, road, rail and sea transport, telecommunications, postal, data.

**Health Services**
Medical staff/doctors, hospitals, ambulances, medical laboratories, dentists, opticians.

**Maintenance**
Electrical, mechanical, vehicles, heating systems, air conditioning, buildings, computers.

**Utilities**
Cleansing, waste management; water supply, grounds maintenance, electricity, gas and energy supply, fire police, public services.

**Trading**
Wholesale, retail, stockist, distributor, marketing, packaging.

**Financial**
Banking, insurance, pensions, property services, accounting.

**Professional**
Building design (architects), surveying, legal, law enforcement, security, engineering, project management, quality management, consultancy, training and education.

**Administration**
Personnel, computing, office services.

**Technical**
Consultancy, photography, test laboratories.

**Purchasing**
Contracting, inventory management and distribution.

**Scientific**
Research, development, studies, decision aids.

**NOTE:** *Manufacturing companies also provide internal services in their marketing, delivery systems and after-sales activities.*

*Table 7-6: Examples to which this part of ISO 9004-2 may be applied.*

# THE EUROPEAN COMMUNITY: DIRECTIVES, STANDARDS AND PRODUCT CERTIFICATION

BY JAMES KOLKA

## INTRODUCTION

This handbook has focused on the ISO 9000 series international standard and on the process of applying the standard in companies that seek ISO 9000 registration. ISO 9000 is a global phenomenon, and companies around the world are registering to one of the ISO 9000 standards. For many companies, however, EC 92 is a key impetus for ISO 9000 registration. Although ISO 9000 registration is required only for some regulated products, the European Community (EC) is stressing ISO 9000 registration as an integral part of its overall goals for product regulation. ISO 9000 represents one piece in a complex regulatory and product certification framework being developed by the European Community.

This chapter takes a closer look at the "big picture." It discusses the goals of the EC and describes its regulatory procedures in detail. For US companies seeking to do business in the European Community, it is important to keep up-to-date with the EC's efforts to establish Community-wide directives, standards and certification procedures.

# THE ORIGINS OF EC 92

In the early 1980s, the European Community became concerned that it would be overwhelmed by economic competition from the United States, Japan and the emerging economies of the Pacific Rim. In 1985 the EC Commission presented a program for establishing a single internal market which was almost immediately endorsed by the EC's executive body, the European Council. The proposal called for "action to achieve a single market by 1992" and called for a timetable for implementation.

The document that emerged from the 1985 discussions, known as the White Paper, stated that physical, technical and fiscal barriers to trade were the three major obstacles to achieving a single internal market. In the past, the EC had been praised for uniting separate economies after World War II, but criticized for not doing enough to eliminate country-by-country barriers to the movement of goods and services.

Part of the EC's protectionist economic stranglehold was broken earlier, in 1979, by the *Casis de Dijon* decision of the European Court of Justice which established the principle of mutual recognition. This principle states that products that meet the requirements of one EC member state could freely circulate in other member states, a concept similar to the interstate commerce clause of the US Constitution.

The White Paper drew upon the rationale of the Casis de Dijon decision. It laid out a timetable for abolishing these barriers among the 12 member states and set the end of 1992 as the deadline. The Paper said that, to achieve its major goal of economic growth for its members, the free internal movement of goods, services, people and capital from one member state to another is essential.

EC's plan to move to one internal market was further expedited by the Single European Act, adopted in February 1986. This Act amends the 1957 Treaty of Rome which is the founding charter of the European Community. The major goal of the Single European Act is the completion of a European internal market by the end of 1992. Its passage demonstrated the EC's commitment to become an important economic trading bloc.

# REMOVING TRADE BARRIERS

By far, the trade barriers of most concern to US companies wishing to do business with the EC are *technical barriers*. These include different standards for products, duplication of testing and certification procedures for products, and differences in the laws of EC member states. These restrict the free movement of products within the EC.

# The Maastricht Treaty

In June 1992, Denmark rejected the Maastricht Treaty. In September 1992, France ratified the treaty by a narrow margin. Denmark's refusal to adopt the EC's treaty, however, will not affect the timetable for the adoption of common technical standards, including the ISO 9000 series. According to EC experts, Denmark's disagreement with the EC relates to questions of political and fiscal union. Common technical standards are supported by a separate document, *Completing the Internal Market, White Paper from the Commission to the European Council.*

The White Paper does not deal with political issues such as sovereignty, monetary integration, the taxing power of member states or military integration. Instead it is a clear, concise technical statement put forth by the EC Commission. It contains approximately 300 pieces of legislation for adoption and a clear timetable.

The White Paper is a perfect working document for standards development. The Commission limited its scope to concerns that member states already had acknowledged formally and informally. No legislative changes were needed to implement the White Paper. It pledges to eliminate fiscal, technical and physical barriers.

Unlike the Single European Act of 1987 and the Maastricht Treaty of 1991, the White Paper does not require treaty approval. It was accomplished by a communiqué from the European Council (heads of state) to the EC Commission in 1985. Legal authority to implement the White Paper already exists.

At midnight on December 31, 1992, 12 members of the EC will join the seven members of the European Free Trade Association to create the European Economic Area (EEA). The inevitability of this union is supported by at least two factors:

○ EFTA is cooperating with the three principle technical standards organizations (CEN, CENELEC and ETSI), ISO and IEC to create and adopt new standards. It is a Europe-wide effort

○ EFTA and the EC will likely become one body because three of its members (Sweden, Finland and Austria) have already applied for EC membership.

Currently the Maastricht Treaty is proceeding with the assumption that the Danes will find a way to develop protocols allowing them to approve the Treaty.

The EC recognized that, as technical barriers were lowered, a new framework must replace them. The goal of this new framework would be to create confidence among the member states in the:

- Quality and safety of products sold in the EC
- Overall competence of manufacturers, including their quality procedures
- Competence of the testing laboratories and certification bodies that assess the conformity of products.

The new framework would involve EC-wide directives issued by the European Commission that would replace individual member state regulations.

## Directives and Standards

As mentioned in Chapter 1, in the European system products are classified into two categories: regulated products and nonregulated products. Most products sold in the EC are nonregulated products. The EC's strategy for removing technical barriers to nonregulated products is to rely on the principle of mutual recognition and on product certification by a third party.

Only a small percentage of the total number of products is regulated. (Regulated products, however, comprise approximately 50 percent—or $50 billion—of US exports to the EC.) They are those products that the EC believes are associated with significant safety, environmental or health concerns.

The EC Council of Ministers is working to remove technical trade barriers for regulated products by issuing Community-level directives. A *directive* is the official legislation promulgated by the European Commission and binds all members of the EC who are required to convert the directive into national legislation and regulations. Existing laws and rules which conflict with the directive are invalid and are superseded by EC directives. After a transition period, the regulated products must meet the requirements of the directive.

In addition to issuing directives, the EC is seeking to harmonize technical requirements by mandating the use of product *standards* drafted or adopted by its regional standards organizations. These include the European Committee for Standardization (CEN), the European Committee for Electrotechnical Standardization (CENELEC), and the European Telecommunications Standards Institute (ETSI).

## The EC in a Nutshell

The 12 nations that make up the European Community are bound by its regulations. The regulatory process begins with the European Commission. A proposal is drafted by the Commission and is sent to the European Parliament. The Parliament, with its 518 members, votes on the proposal. However, this vote is not binding on the European Council.

The European Council is comprised of many working groups, each of which consists of civil servants from the member states. These groups examine the proposals and, if necessary, make changes. The proposal is then forwarded to the Committee of Permanent Representatives, made up of civil servants from the member states. When this Committee reaches agreement, the proposal is forwarded to the Council of Ministers. The makeup of the Council depends upon the subject matter of the proposal. The Council of Ministers decides whether to adopt the legislative proposal. It acts by majority vote. The results of the process are Regulations and Directives.

Regulations are directly binding on the member states; they do not require any action on the part of each state. Directives do not create new law directly, but instruct member states to amend their national legislation, within a prescribed period.

The European Court of Justice has the role of judicial oversight. It interprets and applies European Community law.

## Old-Approach Directives and New-Approach Directives

Prior to 1989, the EC issued directives that are now known as *old-approach* directives. These directives were highly specific, detailing and defining all technical characteristics and requirements of a product. The problem with old-approach directives, many of which are still in force, is that they are complicated, compliance is expensive, and they are soon out-of-date due to technological advances.

Nevertheless, these directives are binding on all manufacturers. If a company's product falls within the scope of an old-approach directive, it must meet the directive's requirements.

The EC soon realized that the detailed blueprint it was drafting was slowing its progress in meeting the goals of EC 92. To expedite the process, the EC began issuing more "generic-type" directives, known as *new-approach* directives.

New-approach directives are based on four key elements:

- Essential environmental, health, and safety requirements
- Presumption of conformity
- Mutual recognition
- Voluntary standards.

## Essential Requirements

New-approach directives stipulate only the minimum environmental, health, and safety requirements a product must meet to be considered "safe" for the marketplace. Technical requirements, or the "how-to" specifications, are left to be spelled out by regional standards organizations and the member states themselves. Although the directives do not specifically list these technical requirements, they do provide references for all appropriate supporting technical documentation.

## Presumption of Conformity

If a product conforms to technical standards, it is assumed that the product conforms to the essential requirements contained in the applicable directive. For example, if a company declares that its product conforms to a CEN or CENELEC standard, the product is presumed to conform with the applicable EC directive.

## Mutual Recognition

The principle of mutual recognition says that member states must accept products that are lawfully manufactured in any other member state, provided that the product meets the minimum health, safety and environmental concerns of the receiving state.

The EC is seeking to apply this principle not only to the acceptance of products, but also to test results and certification activities. Further, it intends to push for Mutual Recognition Agreements (MRAs), among non-EC nations.

## Voluntary Standards

Within the EC directives, companies have various options regarding the way they comply with the essential requirements of the directive. These are the conformity-assessment procedures discussed below. Companies also have a choice in the technical standard(s) to which their product can conform.

Essentially, they have two choices:

■ They can comply with the technical standard referenced in the directive. Conformance to the technical standard may involve a third-party evaluation; it depends on the specific directive and the procedure chosen for conformity assessment.

■ They can conform to no European standard or to a non-European standard. In this case, the company still must demonstrate that its product meets the requirements of the directive. This is accomplished by submitting the product to a *notified body* (see below) for third-party evaluation. In cases where there is a low safety risk, directives will allow a company to self-certify its product. However most conformity assessment options require some third-party involvement in testing and certification.

# CONFORMITY ASSESSMENT

Not only do new-approach EC directives reference the appropriate technical standards, they also outline the full range of conformity assessment procedures required, including, in many cases, the procedure for quality system certification. *Conformity assessment* refers to all processes — such as testing, inspection certification, or quality system assessment — that may be used to ensure a product conforms to the directive.

To determine which conformity assessment procedure applies to a product, manufacturers must study the appropriate directive or directives, review the options for conformity assessment, and choose the preferred or acceptable option. Depending on the type of product and its potential safety risk, the choices can range from manufacturer self-certification to the implementation of a full quality assurance system.

## Requirements May Include Several Directives

It is possible that a company must conform to more than one directive. For example, in the February 1991 issue of *Business America*, Mary Saunders of the US Department of Commerce gives an example of a commercial air conditioning manufacturer that would have to meet the safety requirements of three different directives, Machinery Safety, Pressure Vessels and Construction Products (which covers equipment installed in buildings and building materials).

The EC has also issued other directives that apply across all industry sectors. These include directives on product liability and product safety. Manufacturers will be required to comply with these as well. (See Chapter 10 for a discussion of the product liability and product safety directives; Appendix A contains a list of major EC directives.)

## Transition Period

In the case of some directives, provisions have been made for a transition period between the implementation of the directive and the date by which companies must comply. For example, under the medical devices directives, transition periods have been established, ranging from two to three years from the date the directive is implemented. Although this allows manufacturers to continue meeting existing national standards during the transition, they can sell only to countries where they can comply with national standards. They cannot sell to the entire European Community.

Manufacturers that meet the new EC-wide standards immediately will be able to sell medical devices throughout the EC and European Free Trade Association (EFTA). Consequently a number of EC and US medical device manufacturers are ignoring the transition period and are moving to complete certification as soon as possible. This gives them an edge over competitors, allows them to advertise compliance with new EC safety standards, establish an EC-wide marketing presence, and increase their market share.

With other directives, such as construction products and personal protective equipment, there is no transition period. Manufacturers of these products must be certified by January 1, 1993. Since construction products covers a vast range of products and the system for product certification is not fully operational, the lack of a transition period is causing difficulties in that industry.

# NOTIFIED BODIES

Directives also list the appropriate government-appointed organizations, known as *notified bodies*, authorized to certify that a particular product has conformed to a directive's requirements.

A notified body is designated by the competent authority of a member state from among the bodies under its jurisdiction. A *competent authority* is the national authority in each member country that has overall responsibility for the safety of products.

A notified body might be a testing organization, testing laboratory, the operator of a certification system, or even a government agency itself.

The name *notified body* comes from the fact that member states notify the EC Commission as to which bodies in their country are qualified to perform the specific evaluations stipulated in individual directives. The EC Commission will, in turn, "notify" all other competent authorities.

The duties of notified bodies are clearly spelled out in each directive, and lists of notified bodies varies depending on the directive. Each EC country must accept the results of conformity assessments by notified bodies in all other EC countries unless there is cause to believe the product was improperly tested.

Frequently, notified bodies are required to take out liability insurance unless that responsibility is legally assumed by the appointing member state. In some cases, the notified body's logo must also be stamped on the product along with the EC mark.

### The Competence of Notified Bodies

Each member state must have confidence that its notified bodies are competent to declare conformity to a directive. In order to ensure members of the competence of notified bodies, the EC has developed the Community-wide EN 45000 series standards for certification and testing. The EC also is developing a Council regulation to guide the creation of notified bodies and their compliance with the EN 45000 series. (Chapter 9 discusses these standards in more detail.)

# THE EC MARK

A notified body is authorized to permit manufacturers to affix the *EC mark* (also known as the *CE mark)*, which signifies proof that a company has met the specific conformity assessment requirements to market its product in the EC.

The CE designation, French for *Conformite Europeene*, is required in order to sell any product manufactured or distributed under the new-approach directives. The EC mark will replace all national marks now used to show compliance with legislated requirements for regulated materials and products.

The requirements for affixing the EC Mark are set forth in each directive. (See Figure 8-1.) Basically, four steps are needed to obtain the mark. They are:

■ Conformance with the requirements of the appropriate EC directives
■ Where appropriate, official registration to the appropriate ISO 9000 standard (ISO 9001, ISO 9002 or ISO 9003), if required by the directive
■ Documentation of any test data required by the directives
■ Necessary certification by the appropriate notified bodies to verify compliance with the directive(s).

Each member state must allow products with the EC mark to be marketed as conforming to the requirements of the directive. The same rules apply regardless of the product's origin.

In some cases the EC Mark alone is sufficient for market acceptance. In other cases, however, market acceptance for materials and products sold in a member state after December 31, 1992, may well hinge on the appearance of one or more additional certification and/or quality marks issued by bodies in that member state.

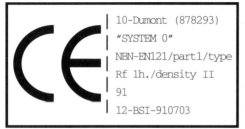

## Information to Accompany CE Mark by Manufacturers in European Community

| | |
|---|---|
| 10-Dumont (878293) | NAME OF PRODUCER AND PLANT |
| "SYSTEM 0" | COMMERCIAL NAME OF PRODUCT |
| NBN-EN121/part1/type | REFERENCE TO TECHNICAL STANDARD |
| Rf 1h./density II | CRITICAL PERFORMANCE DEFINITION |
| 91 | YEAR OF MANUFACTURE |
| 12-BSI-910703 | IDENTIFYING NUMBER OF EC CERTIFICATE |

*Figure 8-1: Information to accompany CE Mark by manufacturers in European Community.*

# TECHNICAL STANDARDS AND REGIONAL STANDARDIZATION ORGANIZATIONS

The essential requirements in the EC directives are broad guidelines only. The technical standards describe how these guidelines can be transformed into results. The task of developing specific technical standards to harmonize the many differing national standards of the EC countries into one set of common standards is carried out primarily by three European standard-setting organizations.

The largest and most important of the regional standards organizations is the European Committee for Standardization (CEN), followed by the European Committee for Electrotechnical Standardization (CENELEC), and the European Telecommunications Standards Institute (ETSI). A fourth organization, the European Organization for Technical Approvals (EOTA), assesses the technical fitness of construction products for their intended use, even when no EC-wide harmonized standard or national standard exists for that product.

These four organizations develop standards according to priorities set by the EC and its member states. They also consult with existing national standardization organizations.

CEN and CENELEC have negotiated agreements with the International Organization for Standardization (ISO) and the International Electrotechnical Commission (IEC) to develop new standards.

CEN and CENELEC will develop a new standard when:

- A standard does not already exist under ISO or IEC auspices,
- The standard cannot be developed at the international level, or
- The standard cannot be developed at the international level within a specific time frame.

All member states must conform to each standard once it is formally adopted.

## The Committee for European Standardization (CEN)

CEN is the Committee for European Standardization (or Normalization, hence the "N"). It is a non-profit organization, made up of delegates from 18 western European countries—the 12 European Community (EC) nations plus the six member nations of the European Free Trade Association (EFTA). CEN is composed of the national standardization institutes of these 18 countries.

CEN's mission is to prepare Europe for 1992 by helping to create a single market for goods and services. The goal of standards harmonization is to prevent technical barriers to trade. CEN's challenge is to prepare a single set of European standards in place of numerous national standards. CEN works to remove any standardization differences among its 18 members.

### Roles in Testing and Certification

CEN promulgates standards when the EC passes a directive. It also responds to EC requests to develop a standard when no directive has been issued. This is done in some cases to prevent trade barriers where there is a conflict between national standards and the corresponding certification requirements of member states or, in other cases, to cover products that are critical to the community's industrial policy.

When necessary, CEN promulgates new standards which the member countries are obligated to adopt as their own national standards. CEN promotes the implementation of international standards prepared by ISO or IEC. As far as possible, CEN avoids any duplication of work. CEN also creates and implements procedures for the mutual recognition of test results and certification schemes.

### CEN and ISO

In order to avoid duplication or conflict with other international standards, CEN adopts ISO standards whenever possible. CEN also works with ISO to draft new standards and has formal agreements with ISO for the exchange of information and for technical cooperation. CEN and ISO share common planning and have parallel votes during the development of standards.

### CEN Standards

CEN publishes its standards in one of three ways:
○ *European Standards* (EN) are totally harmonized and the 18 member nations of

*(continued on next page)*

**The Committee for European Standardization (CEN)** *(continued)*

CEN are obligated to adopt these standards as their own national standards. An EN must be implemented at the national level by being given the status of a national standard and by the withdrawal of any conflicting national standard.

Manufacturer compliance with European Standards is voluntary. But if an EN is met, it is presumed that this also fulfills the larger directive requirement. ENs for a new technology are prepared following specific requests from the EC and EFTA.

○ *Harmonization Documents* (HD) allow for some national deviations in standards. The HD must be implemented at the national level, either by the issuance of a corresponding national standard or, as a minimum, by public announcement of the HD number and title. In both cases, no conflicting national standard may continue to exist after a fixed date.

○ *European Pre-standards* (ENV) are guidelines for expected ENs or HDs, or guidelines for rapidly developing industries. ENVs may be established as prospective standards in all technical fields where the innovation rate is high or where there is an urgent need for technical advice. CEN members are required to make the ENV available at the national level in an appropriate form and to announce their existence in the same way as for ENs and HDs. However, any conflicting national standards may be kept in force until the ENV is converted into an EN.

*European Committee for Standardization*
*Rue de Stassart 36*
*B-1050 Bruxelles, Belgium*
*Tel: +32 2 519 68 11, Fax: +32 2 519 68 19.*

# THE EC'S GLOBAL APPROACH TO PRODUCT CERTIFICATION

The EC's overall, or "global," strategy for a unified market seeks to establish a comprehensive system that encompasses all aspects of product certification. This system has three major components:

■ EC-wide directives and harmonized technical standards

# European Committee for Electrotechnical Standardization (CENELEC)

The European Committee for Electrotechnical Standardization is CEN's sister organization and is also based in Brussels, Belgium. CENELEC is a non-profit technical organization working to harmonize standards among its 18 EC and EFTA member countries and is composed of delegates from those countries.

While CEN works closely with ISO to adopt standards on everything but technical issues, CENELEC works with its international counterpart, the International Electrotechnical Committee (IEC). CENELEC maintains an active working agreement with IEC, and 85 percent of the European standards adopted by CENELEC are IEC standards.

The procedures for the development of CENELEC standards are the same as those described for CEN. CENELEC publishes its standards in the same manner as CEN: as European Standards (EN), Harmonization Documents (HD), and European Pre-standards (ENV).

## CENELEC Priorities

CENELEC's areas of priorities for developing standards are low-voltage areas, other electric equipment, and agreed-upon mandates for standardization from EC and EFTA countries. Manufacturers can produce products that meet none of the CENELEC standards so long as the products fulfill the essential, more general EC directives. However, products which meet CENELEC standards are presumed also to fulfill the requirements of EC directives.

CENELEC is responsible for standard EN 45012, *General criteria for certification bodies operating quality system certification.* Implementation of this standard and the quality system management standard EN 29000 is the responsibility of the European Committee for Quality System Assessment and Certification.

■ Consistent conformity-assessment procedures
■ Competent certification and testing bodies.

The first component was discussed above; the second and third components will be discussed in more detail below.

---

# European Telecommunications Standardization Institute (ETSI)

The European Telecommunications Standardization Institute is the third sister organization in the CEN/CENELEC/ETSI regional triumvirate, promoting European standards for a unified telecommunications system.

ETSI membership is open to all relevant organizations with an interest in telecommunication standardization that belong to a country within the European Confederation of Posts and Telecommunications Administrations. Users, research bodies and others may participate directly in standardization work for Europe.

The process of publishing final ETSI standards is almost identical to the methods used by CEN and CENELEC. The three groups have formed a Joint Presidents Group to handle common concerns regarding policy and management. The three groups have also signed a cooperation agreement to prevent overlapping assignments and to work together as partners.

Non-European organizations interested in telecommunications are sometimes invited as observers to the technical work of ETSI. In addition, ETSI and the American National Standards Institute (ANSI), the US standardization body, have agreed to an exchange of information concerning their respective work.

---

## Conformity Assessment

In 1989, the EC developed a comprehensive or global approach to conformity assessment. The approach has three guiding principles:[1]

■ First, rather than adopting certification procedures on an *ad hoc* basis, directive-by-directive, as in the past, the EC will in the future choose from a set of detailed conformity-assessment procedures. These procedures are known as *modules*.

The modules range from a simple manufacturer's declaration of conformity, through third-party evaluation to individual production inspection. All future conformity assessment procedures will be based on one or more of these options.

■ Second, EC member states should be committed to common standards in the area of conformity assessment. Specifically these include the EN 29000 series standards for quality assurance and the EN 45000 series. The EN 45000 standards establish requirements for testing, certification, and accreditation bodies. These two standards form the backbone of the EC's system of mutual recognition.

■ Finally, there should be a testing and certification organization at the European level. This organization, called the European Organization for Testing and Certification (EOTC), would have the role of promoting mutual recognition agreements in the non-regulated sphere.

## Guidelines to the Modular Approach

The *modular approach* to conformity assessment provides for several procedures for a manufacturer to demonstrate compliance with directives. These range from a manufacturer's self-declaration of conformity to assessment of a quality system to type-testing of the product by a third-party, depending on the health, safety and environmental risks of the product.

| | MODULES | | | | | | |
|---|---|---|---|---|---|---|---|
| | **A** | **B+C** | **B+D** | **B+E** | **B+F** | **G** | **H** |
| PRODUCT SURVEILLANCE: Samples: | ○ | ○ | | | ● OR | | |
| Each Product: | ○ | | | | ● | ● | |
| Q.A. Surveillance: | | | ● EN 29002 | ● EN 29003 | | | ● EN 29001 |
| Type Testing: | | ● | ● | ● | ● | | ○ Design |
| Technical Documentation: | ① | ② | ② | ② | ② | ② | ③ |
| CE MARK AFFIXED BY: Manufacturer: | $C\epsilon$ | $C\epsilon$ | $C\epsilon$ ★ | $C\epsilon$ ★ | $C\epsilon$ ★ OR | | $C\epsilon$ ★ |
| Third Party: | | | | | $C\epsilon$ ★ | $C\epsilon$ ★ | |

○ Supplementary Requirements   ① Required to be available    $C\epsilon$    CE Mark

● Action by Third Party         ② Required by Notified Body    $C\epsilon$ ★ CE Mark with the Notified

                                    ③ Part of Quality System                        Body Identification Symbol

*Figure 8-2: Overview—EC 92 Conformity Assessment Procedures—The Modules.*

The EC Council outlines the combination of procedures it considers appropriate for each directive and sets the conditions of application. The manufacturers themselves, however, have the final choice as to which of the procedures they will follow.

Figures 8-2 and 8-3 illustrate the certifications options available to comply with the directives. If one or more directives is applicable to a particular product, the directives indicate whether a notified body must be involved, and if so, the extent of that involvement. Apart from Module A, the supplier has to involve a notified body for all other modules. The supplier is responsible for maintaining the conformity of its product to all relevant essential requirements.

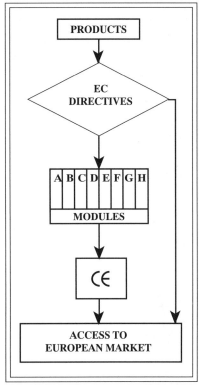

## Description of Modules in Modular Approach

There are two main phases in the modular approach: the design phase and the production phase. Both phases are covered by modules, which are further broken down into four types of examination:

- Internal control of production
- Type-examination
- Unit verification
- Full quality assurance — EN 29001.

*Figure 8-3: Conformity assessment process.*

These are examined in more detail below.

## Internal Control of Production

Internal control of production allows manufacturers to self-declare conformity to the specific standard. It is intended for simple, safe products. The manufacturers are required to keep technical documents so that they can be reviewed by national authorities upon request.

During the design phase, the manufacturer may carry out the procedure for conformity assessment itself. The manufacturer, however, must keep the technical docu-

| DESIGN | | PRODUCTION |
|---|---|---|
| **A. INTERNAL CONTROL OF PRODUCTION** | **Manufacturer**<br>• Keeps technical documentation at the disposal of national authorities<br>**Aa**<br>• Intervention of notified body | **A. Manufacturer**<br>• Declares conformity with essential requirements<br>• Affixes the CE-Mark<br>**Aa**<br>• Tests on specific aspects of the product<br>• Product checks at random intervals |
| **B. TYPE EXAMINATION** | **Manufacturer submits to notified body**<br>• Technical documentation<br>• Type<br><br>**Notified body**<br>• Ascertains conformity with essential requirements<br>• Carries out tests, if necessary<br>• Issues EC type-examination certificate | **C. CONFORMITY TO TYPE**<br>**Manufacturer**<br>• Declares conformity with approved type<br>• Affixes the CE-Mark<br>**Notified body**<br>• Tests on specific aspects of the product<br>• Product checks at random intervals<br><br>**D. PRODUCT QUALITY ASSURANCE**<br>**EN 29002 • Manufacturer**<br>• Operates approved QS-production & testing<br>• Declares conformity with approved type<br>• Affixes the CE-Mark<br>**EN 29002 • Notified body**<br>• Approves the QS<br>• Carries out surveillance of the QS<br><br>**E. PRODUCT QUALITY ASSURANCE**<br>**EN 29003 • Manufacturer**<br>• Operates approved QS-production & testing<br>• Declares conformity with approved type or essential requirements • Affixes CE-Mark<br>**EN 29003 • Notified body**<br>• Approves the QS<br>• Carries out surveillance of the QS<br><br>**F. PRODUCT VERIFICATION**<br>**Manufacturer**<br>• Declares conformity with approved type or with essential requirements<br>• Affixes the CE-Mark<br>**Notified body**<br>• Verifies conformity<br>• Issues certificate of conformity |
| **G. UNIT VERIFICATION** | **Manufacturer**<br>• Submits technical documentation | **Manufacturer**<br>• Submits product<br>• Declares conformity<br>• Affixes the CE-Mark<br>**Notified body**<br>• Verifies conformity with essential requirements<br>• Issues certificate of conformity |
| **H. FULL QUALITY ASSURANCE** | **EN 29001 • Manufacturer**<br>• Operates an approved QS for design<br>**EN 29001 • Notified body**<br>• Carries out surveillance of the QS<br>• Verifies conformity of the design<br>• Issues EC design examination certificate | **Manufacturer**<br>• Operates an approved QS for production & testing<br>• Declares conformity<br>• Affixes the CE-Mark<br>**Notified body**<br>• Carries out surveillance of the QS |

*Figure 8-4: Conformity assessment procedure modules.*

mentation available for the national authorities for at least ten years after production of the product. This way, assessments and checks can be carried out to determine whether the product complies with the directive.

The producer has to provide insight into the design, the manufacturing process and the performance of the product. The manufacturer must take all the steps necessary to ensure the manufacturing process guarantees that the product constantly complies with the essential requirements.

During the production phase, a notified body carries out testing on specific aspects of the product at random intervals. This module is designed for the manufacturer who chooses to produce, not in accordance with the European standards, but directly in accordance with the essential requirements of the applicable directive.

## Type-Examination

In type-examination, the design phase involves verification by a third party. In this module, the manufacturer has to present the technical documentation and one *product type* (typical example) to a testing organization of its choice. The testing organization assesses and draws up a declaration. This module must be supplemented by modules C, D, E or F.

### Conformity to Type (C)

The manufacturer can self-declare conformity to type with no quality system requirement. The manufacturer draws up a declaration of conformity for the approved type from module B, and keeps this for at least ten years after manufacture of the last product.

### Production Quality Assurance (D)

This requires third-party certification to ISO 9002. ISO 9002 includes the entire production process, except for design. The manufacturer's quality system for production is approved by a testing organization. Then the manufacturer declares that his product matches the approved type.

### Product Quality Assurance (E)

This requires third-party certification to ISO 9003, for inspection and testing. Module E is the same as Module D, except that the quality system concerns only the end-production checks.

### Product Verification (F)

This requires testing the product and certifying conformity by a third party. The manufacturer ensures that the production process guarantees the product meets the requirements. Then the manufacturer declares conformity. An approved testing organization checks this conformity. This can take place sometimes by testing each product separately and sometimes by random testing. Finally, the testing organization issues a certificate of conformity.

## Unit-Verification

Unit-verification requires the manufacturer to submit technical documents and a prototype product to regulatory authorities. A notified body must certify by checking the product that the production process conforms with essential requirements .

## Full Quality Assurance

Full quality assurance requires the manufacturer to operate an approved quality system for design, production and testing, and to be certified to the European quality standard EN 29001/ISO 9001 by a notified body. Manufacturers can avoid expensive, time-consuming product testing by instituting a full quality assurance system according to ISO 9001.

# DEGREE OF COMPLEXITY

As a general rule, the greater the safety risk associated with a product, the more complex the conformity assessment process. For example, in the EC Council *Directive on Personal Protective Equipment*, a manufacturer can probably choose to self-certify a product where the model is simple, the risks are minimal, and the user has time to identify those risks safely. Some examples are gardening gloves, gloves for mild detergent solutions, seasonal protective clothing, and gloves or aprons for moderate exposure to heat.

Manufacturers, however, must choose either ISO 9001, full quality assurance, or EC type approval plus EC verification in cases where personal protective equipment is of a complex design, "intended to protect against mortal danger or against dangers that may seriously and irreversibly harm the health…"

Given a choice between EC type approval plus EC verification or ISO 9001, most manufacturers will choose ISO 9001 registration. Under ISO 9001, the manufacturer submits the full quality system for approval, a preferable alternative to the more intrusive EC process of continuously submitting representative samples to a third-party for screening.

# ADDITIONAL REQUIREMENTS

In addition to using the basic framework of the ISO 9000 series, some EC directives have supplemental requirements. For example, to certify under the EC Construction Products directive, a manufacturer must also comply with the additional requirements of the EN 45000 series of standards. These standards apply to laboratory, testing, and certification organizations.

Other product sectors for which additional guidelines have been developed are medical devices (EN 46000) and aerospace products (EN 2000, EN 3042). Most likely, similar special requirements will be developed for other directives.

## Product Certification versus ISO 9000 Registration

To satisfy the conformity assessment requirements of most EC new-approach directives and to affix the EC mark, a company must receive third-party approval from an EC notified body. This product certification approval may not be the same as ISO 9000 registration by a registrar.

It is possible that at least two certifications may be necessary. For example, the new EC medical devices directives will require a registered ISO 9000 quality assurance system, augmented by compliance with the EN 46000 requirements. A simple registration to ISO 9001 will not suffice to fulfill the requirements of the directive. A company will require certification of its product to the EN 46000 requirements, in addition to the essential requirements set forth in Annex 1 of the directives. Similar essential requirements are set forth in each EC new-approach directive.

A February 27, 1992, notified body Working Paper is now being circulated by the EC Commission. When it is approved, it will outline the operating procedures and requirements for notified bodies.

# THE GLOBAL APPROACH TO CERTIFICATION AND TESTING

The third component of the EC's comprehensive framework for product standardization is the role of certification and testing bodies. The goal of the EC is to increase confidence by member nations in the work of these organizations so that the results of testing will be accepted throughout the EC.

In its 1989 presentation, entitled *The Global Approach to Certification and Testing,* the EC outlined the major elements of its program for certification and testing bodies:

■ The credibility of the manufacturer must be reinforced. This can be achieved by promoting the use of quality assurance techniques.

■ The credibility of and confidence in testing laboratories and certification bodies must be enhanced. This can be achieved by developing the EN 45000 series of standards to evaluate the competence of testing laboratories.

■ The competence of laboratories and certification bodies is established through an accreditation process based on EN 45000 standards. This accreditation process involves a third-party evaluation (and is discussed in more detail in Chapter 9).

According to this system, notified bodies must produce documentation proving they conform to the EN 45000 series. If these bodies are not formally accredited, the appropriate national authorities must produce documentary evidence that they do conform to the relevant standards of the EN 45000 series.

In addition, as mentioned above, the European Organization for Testing and Certification (EOTC) would have the role of promoting mutual recognition agreements in the **nonregulated** sphere.

## European Organization on Testing and Certification (EOTC)

The principle of mutual recognition, which allows the free circulation of goods among member states, does not, by itself, solve all the problems that arise. How can Country A be certain that goods offered for sale from Country B are really acceptable? How can member states have confidence that goods marketed in Europe do not present risks to health and safety? The manufacturer's declaration of conformity does not guarantee satisfactory answers to these questions. European standards provide agreements on specific technical criteria. But there must also be agreement on the testing and certification procedures used to assess conformity to those standards.

One possible answer to these questions may be the European Organization on Testing and Certification. EOTC was proposed by the European Commission for the purpose of dealing with conformity assessment issues. It was created in April 1990 to promote mutual recognition of test results, certification procedures, and quality system assessments and registrations in **nonregulated** product areas throughout the EC and EFTA. Its primary goal is to encourage equivalency of certificates and to avoid the duplication caused by multiple certifications.

The EOTC will also be responsible for providing technical assistance to the EC Commission in the implementation of some EC legislation, especially in the preparation of Mutual Recognition Agreements with non-EC countries.

EOTC is in an experimental stage at this time and will move to an operation phase as soon as guidelines for recognition of agreement groups and sector committees begin to be applied.

EOTC will be made up of a council, sector committees organized along industry disciplines, specialized committees along functional disciplines, and agreement groups. It is possible that agreement groups may include non-European groups. The agreement groups work out the specific issues and ensure their implementation. Members bind themselves by contract to recognize each other's test results.

## Recognition Arrangement for Assessment and Certification of Quality Systems in the Information Technology Sector (ITQS)

ITQS is one of several agreement groups that EOTC has formally approved. Agreement groups are set up along industry lines and allow companies to rely on just one test or assessment that will be accepted throughout Europe.

The assessments carried out by the certification bodies (registrars) cooperating in ITQS will be carried out in a harmonized way, using common standards, techniques and guidance material. As of Fall, 1992, nine certification organizations from seven European countries are participating in ITQS (see box). ITQS membership is open to any EC or EFTA organization, provided the organization accepts and applies ITQS regulations, including an auditor guide.

The ITQS auditor guide is "unique because instead of being a guidance document for the certification applicant, it is mainly designed to be used by the certification bodies," according to Paul Caussin of AIB-Vincotte. AIB-Vincotte is the ITQS secretariat.

The auditor guide "tells the auditors what to look for when auditing an information technology firm, covers software and hardware development, and production and service activities," said Caussin. The purpose of an auditing guide is to ensure that information technology firms certified by an ITQS member are assessed on an equivalent basis. Quality managers at some US information technology firms have cited a lack of experienced information technology auditors as one of the reasons the US does not, as of yet, have a strong, formalized system for information technology quality assurance.

Criteria for information technology auditors under the ITQS system include a professional education or training, or practical experience in information technology, as well as specific training in the understanding of quality control techniques applicable to information technology. "ITQS regulations also require that the auditors be evaluated on a regular basis by an evaluation panel, possibly from a professional society," according to Caussin.

## ITQS Members

The following registrars participate in ITQS:

| | |
|---|---|
| AFAQ | Paris, France |
| AIB-Vincotte, Secretariat | Brussels, Belgium |
| BSI-QA | Milton Keynes, Great Britain |
| Elektronik Centralen | Horsholm, Denmark |
| IMQ | Milan, Italy |
| N.V. KEMA | Arnhem, The Netherlands |
| RW-TUV | Essen, Germany |
| TUV-Bayern | Munich, Germany |
| TUV-Rheinland | Cologne, Germany |

**ITQS Chairman:**
Folkert Rienstra
N. V. KEMA, Postbus 9035
6800 ET Arnhem, The Netherlands
Tel: +31 85 56 62 23, Fax: +31 85 51 54 56.

**ITQS Secretariat:**
Marc de Feu
AIB-Vincotte, Koningslaan 157
B-1060 Brussels, Belgium
Tel: +32 2 53 68 211, Fax: +32 2 53 74 619.

**ITQS Liaison:**
Edgar Bier
RW-TUV, Im Teelbruch 122
D-4300 Essen, Germany
Tel: +49 2 01 825 51 14, Fax: +49 2 01 825 51 31.

# THE EC AND OTHER COUNTRIES

As the EC moves toward its goal of a unified market and maps out its comprehensive system for product regulation and certification, it is also defining its future relationship with other countries. One of the key components of this relationship is *nondiscrimination*. This means the same rules apply, regardless of the product's origin. A corollary to this is acceptance of test reports or certificates of conformity from countries outside the EC. These relationships, however, are still in a developmental phase.

## Subcontracting

Can notified bodies subcontract any of their activities to bodies outside the EC? The EC has proposed new rules for subcontracting and is moving to permit more extensive use of subcontracting. According to the EC's proposed general guidelines for subcontracting as stated in the February 27, 1992 Working Document:

- EC notified bodies will need to hold subcontractors to the EN 45000 series of standards, including the requirements to maintain records.

- Subcontractors must contract with notified bodies and test to the same standards as the notified body.

- EC notified bodies "cannot subcontract assessment and appraisal activities."

- EC notified bodies remain responsible for any certification activity.

## Mutual Recognition

Currently, US companies that achieve ISO 9000 registration obtain whatever recognition that their accrediting entity has in the country in which the accreditation entity (i.e., NACCB in the United Kingdom, RAB in the United States) is located. Other countries in the EC and elsewhere can voluntarily choose to recognize the registration certificate. The registration certificates are not yet governed by EC legislation and EC-wide recognition is not yet mandatory.

Presently, a few national accreditation entities are negotiating mutual recognition agreements to recognize one another's ISO 9000 registrations.

Although the term *mutual recognition agreement* fairly describes what has been

negotiated, it should not be confused with the EC legal term. The EC legal term —
*Mutual Recognition Agreement* — will be governed by an EC legal document and
will refer to product-sector Mutual Recognition Agreements, negotiated between the
EC and third countries (United States, Canada, Japan, etc.).

(Issues of registrar accreditation and the recognition of registration certificates are
discussed in more detail in Chapter 9.)

## Non-EC Notified Bodies

Under the EC system, only member states can designate only notified bodies from
within the EC. No subsidiaries or related enterprises located in a third country can
perform full third-party product certification and quality system registration **except
under a Mutual Recognition Agreement (MRA) with government authorities of**

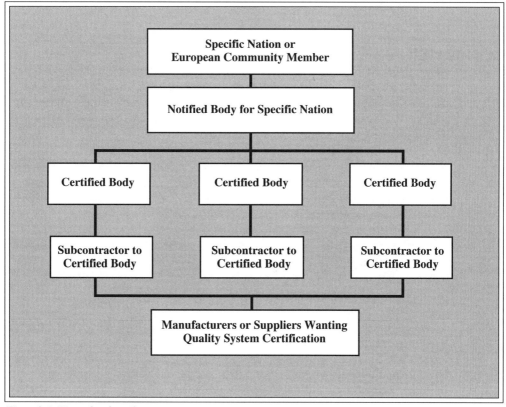

*Figure 8-5: Hierarchy of certification.*

**that country.** In addition, their competence must be assessed by third parties, according to the provisions of the EN 45000 standards.

At the present time, an EC Commission November 18, 1991, Working Document and a 1992 Commission Communication on MRAs on this issue are in circulation. When a directive is finalized it will state the general criteria for negotiating MRAs that allow notified bodies to reside in a non-EC country.

An MRA would allow US testing and certification organizations to act as notified bodies in the product areas covered by the MRA. In this way, non-EC notified bodies could award the EC mark for regulated products under the negotiated industry sector.

The uncertainty surrounding notified bodies is one of the larger problems facing US industry as it decides when and how to seek quality system registration.

# CONCLUSION

For those people reading about the European Community and its new structure for the first time, it probably seems like one of Bob Newhart's early comedy routines in which he has Abner Doubleday call a company that sells party games and try to describe his new idea, a game called "baseball."

Naturally, the description of a baseball diamond, outfield, batter, pitcher, home plate, three bases, balls, bats, outs, innings and nine players to a team sounded like total gibberish to the party game company. But what may have been gibberish in 1839 is now called our national pastime.

The EC's new game may seem confusing and unsettled. From our US perspective, it may not appear to be a level playing field. But it is becoming **the** playing field. Not understanding its dynamics could mean that a company's team is suited up for football only to discover that the other team is playing baseball.

To understand the EC system, it will be necessary to read the directives in depth and more than one directive or set of laws likely will be involved. Understanding the process will be crucial to becoming an effective competitor in what may become the world's largest market. For those companies that get there early and establish a presence, the monetary rewards could be substantial.

## About the Author

*James W. Kolka has a Ph.D. in political science/international affairs from the University of Kansas, and a J.D. with a background in product liability and environmental law from the University of Wisconsin-Madison. An international legal consultant, he has served as a full professor, published numerous articles, served as vice president both at Drake University and in the University System of Georgia. He has held senior management positions in the University of Wisconsin System, developed Wisconsin's statewide Adult Extended Degree Program and was instrumental in the creation of the Center for International Standards and Quality at Georgia Tech. Dr. Kolka has conducted seminars and consulted on product liability, product safety, services liability, EC product certification, comparative law, environmental planning, global liability, strategic planning and the integration of ISO 9000 quality assurance systems with preventative law programs and legal documentation for the US and the EC markets. Dr. Kolka is fluent in Spanish and conversant in German, Portuguese and Italian. He has worked throughout the United States, Canada, Europe and Latin America. (404/977-4049)*

**ENDNOTE:**

[1]    Farnell, J., Presentation made in 1990 to the EC Commission.

# THE REGISTRAR AND REGISTRAR ACCREDITATION

BY JOSEPH TIRATTO

As explained in earlier chapters, auditing a company's quality system may be performed by the company (self-audit), by the customer who requires quality system assurance (second-party evaluation), or by a third party. Third-party assessment of a company's quality system and registration to ISO 9000 standards is performed by an organization authorized by an accreditation body to conduct audits and to issue registration.

This chapter examines the:

■ Role of the registrar
■ Accreditation of registrars
■ Recognition of registration certificates
■ Criteria for evaluating the work of registrars
■ Developing European framework for registrar accreditation
■ US accreditation system and the work of the Registration Accreditation Board (RAB) and the National Institute for Standards and Technology (NIST).

This chapter specifically focuses on registration and accreditation in the EC and the United States and reviews the current developing relationship between the two. It also provides an overview of the many issues that are unresolved and highlights problems and differences that must be worked out along the road to mutual acceptance of registration and accreditation practices.

# ACCREDITATION AND RECOGNITION - INTRODUCTION

Accreditation of registrars and recognition of registration certificates are critical issues. Companies that enlist the services of registrars must be confident that the registrar is authorized by an accreditation agency to provide acceptable audit services and that the results of its audit — the registration certificate — will be accepted in those countries where the company seeks to do business.

The general requirements are straightforward. However, accreditation and recognition systems that will be accepted internationally are still developing. Europeans and Americans are currently working on these issues, which will take some time to be resolved.

The key issue is this: If a registrar performs a quality system audit based on the ISO 9000 series standards and subsequently registers a facility, how will that facility's registration be viewed in the rest of the industry and in the rest of the world? Will the registration be recognized by an accreditation body with direct traceability to an EC member state or to the European Community as a whole?

## The EC: Regulated versus Nonregulated Products

For products not regulated by the EC, any registration acceptable to a company's customer is appropriate, whether performed by a European or non-European entity. Customer acceptance is the sole criteria.

If a company is seeking ISO 9000 standards certification to fulfill requirements for **regulated** products, the registrar must be authorized to perform the audit by an EC notified body, or a body subcontracting to the notified body.

### Mutual Recognition of Registration Certificates in Europe

At this time, a registration obtained in one EC member state for a regulated new-approach product may not necessarily be accepted in other EC states on a bilateral basis. As discussed in Chapter 8, other countries in the EC can voluntarily choose to recognize the registration certificate.

### US Registrars

Under existing EC member state national laws, some registrars in the United States are subcontracted to perform ISO 9000 standards audits by agreement with European accreditation bodies. In addition, some accredited, European-based registrars have subsidiaries or offices in the United States.

## Other Questions

At this time, there are still many unresolved issues concerning international acceptance — that is, between the United States and the EC — of registration practices. Some of the outstanding questions include:

■ If the EC accepts ISO 9000 standards facility registration certificates issued by US registrars, is there any way to guarantee that the United States would recognize certificates issued by EC notified bodies?

■ Who in the United States would be required to recognize certificates issued by EC notified bodies?

■ What assurances could be provided by the EC regarding the competence of their notified bodies and vice-versa?

These and other questions surrounding registrar activities remain unsettled.

# REGISTRATION AND ACCREDITATION IN EUROPE

### Accreditation Bodies in Europe

Who accredits European registrars? In Europe, third-party assessors are regulated by governmental or quasi-governmental agencies. The Dutch Council for Certification (RvC) in The Netherlands and the National Accreditation Council for Certifying

Bodies (NACCB) in the United Kingdom are two quasi-governmental bodies that certify organizations to perform third-party quality system audits.

Other accreditation bodies in Europe include AFAQ in France, UNICEI in Italy, and AENOR in Spain. The RvC, the first body to be established, is the only accreditation body in Europe, at this time, that will accredit certification bodies outside of its own country.

## Mutual Recognition of Registration Certificates in Europe

It remains unclear how the mutual recognition of registration certificates will be worked out in Europe. If a company in the United States is registered to the ISO 9000 standards by a registrar that has been accredited by a European accreditation organization, the registration may appear to have a more formal pedigree and traceability to the EC. However, the issue is far from settled.

For **nonregulated** products, the mutual recognition of ISO 9000 registration in Europe may not be settled for some time because of political and national differences and barriers. The European Organization for Testing and Certification (EOTC), described in Chapter 8, has been charged with developing agreements on the mutual recognition of marks.

## Criteria for Accrediting Certified Bodies in Europe

How does a company that receives ISO 9000 series standard registration know that the notified body in Europe that awarded the registration is competent?

The EC is developing a framework for evaluating notified bodies, using the EN 45000 series of standards (see box). CEN/CENELEC adapted the EN 45000 series of standards from existing ISO/IEC guides to increase the level of confidence in the certification, inspection and testing bodies of the European Community.

Of this series, *EN 45012: General criteria for certification bodies operating quality system certification*, is important to companies seeking ISO 9000 series standard registration.

## EN 45012

Organizations that perform quality system certification activities must be evaluated against the requirements of EN 45012. These criteria address the requirements for certified bodies at a national or European level. Implementation of this standard is the responsibility of the European Committee for Quality System Assessment and Certification.

Further guidance related to EN 45012 implementation is contained in the *ISO/IEC Guide 40: General Requirements for the Acceptance of Certification Bodies*, and *ISO/IEC Guide 48: Guidelines for Third-party Assessment and Registration of a Supplier's Quality System*.

Not all quality system registrar accreditation bodies have adopted EN 45012, but US and European accreditation bodies are expected to adopt the standard by the end of 1992. Manufacturers or suppliers operating in the international marketplace should ensure that the quality system registrar with which they are working has been accredited according to EN 45012.

When the framework for evaluating notified bodies is in place, each notified body will be assessed by a third-party against the requirements of EN 45000, to ensure its notification within the Community. These standards will form the foundation for a system of mutual recognition within the EC.

## Certification of Auditors

A final issue of interest to companies who are considering registration to ISO 9000 standards is the qualification of auditors. Who certifies auditors and according to what criteria?

*ISO 10011: Guidelines for auditing quality systems*, has been accepted by ISO as the qualifications criteria for auditors. As one of the minimum conditions for registration, only certified lead assessors can lead the audit team and perform the assessment.

The Institute for Quality Assurance (IQA) in the UK is currently the only organization outside of the United States that governs and controls the assessor training and certification process. The US's Registrar Accreditation Board's (RAB) program for auditor assessor certification is discussed in the next section.

## The Developing Quality Systems Network

The EC is developing an organizational superstructure to better integrate the work of quality system certification bodies and to create equivalency in the certification process. Two key organizations include the European Committee for Quality System Assessment and Certification (EQS) and the European Network for Quality System Assessment and Certification (EQNET). (See boxes on pages 252 & 253.)

# The EN 45000 Series

The EN 45000 series consists of seven documents. These standards are aimed at ensuring that declarations of conformity, test results, and product and quality system certificates from different national testing labs and certification bodies are equivalent. Many of these standards are modifications of ISO Guides, listed on the next page. These guides were written to provide general guidance to countries worldwide, involved with certification of products.

**EN 45001:** *General criteria for the operation of testing laboratories,* details the issues that laboratories must address to demonstrate competence in product testing. These include: test personnel; equipment; test methods; test reports; quality systems; and conflict of interest.

**EN 45002:** *General criteria for the assessment of testing laboratories,* is designed for accreditation bodies that assess testing labs. EN 45002 incorporates the criteria of EN 45001. It also discusses other requirements for accreditation bodies, including: a written accreditation process, published assessment methods, a minimum reassessment period, an opportunity for applicant laboratories to comment on the inspection report, a possible requirement for laboratories to participate in proficiency testing, and rules involving subcontracting of testing.

**EN 45003:** *General criteria for laboratory accreditation bodies,* includes guidelines for organizations that want to become accreditation bodies. Requirements include, among others: free and open to access by applicants, independence of the accrediting body, the establishment of sectoral committees to advise the accreditation body, and an appeals procedure.

**EN 45011:** *General criteria for certification bodies operating product certification,* includes the criteria required for national or European recognition of a product certification body.

**EN 45012:** *General criteria for certification bodies operating quality system certification,* looks specifically at the issue of quality system registration (certification). Its basic criteria parallels that of EN 45011.

**EN 45013:** *General criteria for certification bodies operating certification of personnel,* applies to the certification of personnel, according to the same criteria as in EN 45011.

**EN 45014:** *General criteria for declaration of conformity,* goes into detail about the process of actually preparing the Declaration of Conformity to demonstrate conformance with a directive's requirements.

**EN 45019:** Guidance on specific aspects of testing and certification.

**EN 45020:** Definitions.

*[To obtain the above standards, contact the American National Standards Institute, (212) 354-3300.]*

# ISO/IEC Guides
## Pertinent To Certification, Registration and Accreditation

Guide 2     General terms and definitions concerning standardization and certification

Guide 7     Requirements for standards suitable for product certification

Guide 16     Code of principles on third party certification systems and related standards

Guide 23     Methods of indicating conformity with standards for third party certification systems

Guide 25     General requirements for the technical competence of testing laboratories

Guide 27     Guidelines for corrective action to be taken by a certification body in the event of misuse of its mark of conformity

Guide 28     General rules for a model third-party certification system for products

Guide 38     General requirements for the acceptance of testing laboratories

Guide 39     General requirements for the acceptance of inspection bodies

Guide 40     General requirements for the acceptance of certification bodies

Guide 42     Guidelines for a step-by-step approach to an international certification system

Guide 43     Development and operation of laboratory proficiency testing

Guide 44     General rules for ISO or IEC international third-party certification schemes for products

Guide 45     Guidelines for the presentation of test results

Guide 48     Guidelines for third-party assessment and registration of a supplier's quality system

Guide 49     Guidelines for development of a quality manual for a testing laboratory

Guide 53     An approach to the utilization of a supplier's quality system in third party product certification

Guide 54     Testing laboratory accreditation systems - General recommendations for the acceptance of accreditation bodies

Guide 55     Testing laboratory accreditation systems - General recommendations for operation

---

**European Committee for
Quality System Assessment and Certification (EQS)**

EQS was formed to achieve, among others, the following main goals:

○ Harmonization of rules for quality system assessment and certification
○ Overall recognition of quality system certificates
○ Efforts to permit mutual recognition of the certificates of quality system certification
   bodies.

The ultimate aim is to avoid multiple assessment and certification of an organization's
quality system and to develop confidence in quality system assessment and certification
carried out by competent bodies.

---

# REGISTRATION AND ACCREDITATION
# IN THE UNITED STATES

Until recently the United States did not have an accreditation system. However, there
were several important reasons to develop such a system:

■ To establish credibility for US-based registrars
■ To follow the precedent set by an EC resolution that calls for implementing
   accreditation bodies throughout the EC
■ To keep pace with the worldwide move to establish accreditation bodies in each
   country.

In response to these needs and to the proliferation of third-party certifiers in the United
States, the Registration Accreditation Board (RAB) was established as an affiliate of the
American Society for Quality Control (ASQC) in late 1989 to develop a joint ANSI/
RAB American National Accreditation Program for registrars of quality systems.

## Registrar Accreditation Board

The RAB is a national board that accredits those organizations in the United States
that perform third-party auditing against the ISO 9000 series standards. The RAB
performs initial audits of registrars, issues certificates of accreditation, performs
regular follow-up surveillance, and maintains a directory of accredited registrars.

---

## European Network for
## Quality System Assessment and Certification (EQNET)

Early in 1990, EQNET was founded by eight certification institutions:

○ AFAQ (Paris, France)
○ AIB-Vincotte (Brussels, Belgium)
○ BSI (Milton Keynes, Great Britain)
○ DQS (Germany)
○ DS (Denmark)
○ N.V. KEMA (Arnhem, The Netherlands)
○ SIS (Sweden)
○ SQS (Switzerland)

Other national certification institutions from the remaining EC and EFTA countries will join the EQNET as soon as they meet the requirements in conformity with EN 45012, and comply with the additional European harmonization criteria. The main tasks of EQNET include:

○ Close cooperation in order to recognize the certificates issued by other members on the basis of existing contracts and to promote the recognition of the certificates
○ Coordination of the certification of border-crossing groups of companies/organizations and the joint conduct of the said certifications in a competent and efficient way
○ Issuance of several certificates at the same time on the basis of joint certification audits.

For now, cooperation between individual members is based on analogous bilateral sets of agreements. The intention is to expand the EQNET network further with the aid of multilateral contracts as soon as possible.

---

The RAB has established a group of qualified auditors to perform the audits, an accreditation council to evaluate the audit results and to make accreditations, an operations council, a board of directors, and an administrative office.

## RAB Accreditation Criteria

The criteria used by RAB to accredit registrars are the same as those used by the EC and EFTA accreditation organizations. A common basis for accreditation will

enhance the mutual recognition of accreditation systems between the United States
and European countries and eventually with other US trading partners.

It is anticipated that mutual recognition of accreditations will lead to international
acceptance of individual supplier quality system registrations. The RAB has incorporated the following international criteria into its own criteria:

- **ISO 10011:** *Guidelines for auditing quality systems*
- **ISO/IEC Guide 40:** *General requirements for the acceptance of certification bodies*
- **ISO/IEC Guide 48:** *Guidelines for third-party assessment and registration of a supplier's quality system*
- **EN 45012:** *General criteria for certification bodies operating quality system certification.*

## RAB Recognition

The RAB is seeking formal recognition of its registrar accreditation scheme in both
the United States and in Europe. Since the system to establish broad mutual recognition of accreditation bodies throughout Europe is not functioning at this time, the
RAB has negotiated with European countries on a bilateral basis to achieve mutual
recognition of accredited registrars.

In August 1992, the RAB signed a Memorandum of Understanding (MOU) with the
Dutch Council for Certification (RvC) that its supporters say will eventually lead to
mutual acceptance of registrar accreditations performed on both sides of the Atlantic.

## NIST and the Proposed CASE program

In setting up its EC-wide accreditation structure, the European Community prefers to
work on a government-to-government basis. The RAB is not a government organization. The US Department of Commerce has designated the National Institute of
Standards and Technology (NIST) to establish criteria for conformity assessment in
the United States.

In March 1992, NIST proposed its own program for accrediting registrars — the
Conformity Assessment Systems Evaluation (CASE) program. The purpose of the
program is to establish criteria and a system to evaluate and recognize specified
conformity assessment activities, including the accreditation of quality systems
registrars and the recognition of the "accreditors" of quality systems registrars such
as the RAB.

## What is an MOU?

A Memorandum of Understanding (MOU) is a formal agreement between two or more parties to confer a mutual exchange of benefits. Unlike a legal contract, which involves a specific exchange of goods and/or services for monetary consideration, an MOU follows no specific legal requirements.

For example, an MOU could be an agreement between two parties in which one party, an American university, agrees to sponsor a series of seminars for two years to be taught by a non-profit organization from an EC member state. The exact details would be worked out seminar-by-seminar. Another example could be a situation in which two accrediting institutions from two countries agree to develop formal protocols to recognize each other's accredited companies for a specific number of years. In effect, they agree to agree.

While the shape of agreements and the types of participating parties are open to imagination, MOUs generally are used by organizations to confer mutual benefits. Naturally, the limits of an MOU are confined by the legal capabilities of the parties that sign the agreement.

*James Kolka*

The program is designed to accommodate conformity assessment bodies who need government recognition. According to the proposal, NIST will review all relevant national and international standards in order to establish its system. It is also reviewing similar systems in other countries to make the CASE program compatible with other assurance programs around the world.

CASE would be organized as a separate office within NIST. It would be fully funded by fees charged to accredit conformity assessment organizations. The nature of these fees has not yet been set. At the time of this writing, the CASE program is still at the proposal stage.

### Designating US Notified Bodies

Would the CASE program be authorized to designate notified bodies in the United States? The US government currently is awaiting an EC directive regarding MRAs that will address the question of notified bodies in foreign countries.

# RAB-RvC Memorandum of Understanding

The agreement was signed by the RAB, American National Standards Institute (ANSI) and the RvC. ANSI is the RAB's partner in the US ISO 9000 series quality system accreditation and registration scheme. According to RAB President George Lofgren, the RAB/RvC MOU will provide more confidence in the US registration and accreditation scheme since the RAB "now has something in writing that says we have these intentions."

## RAB/RvC Team

Part of the confidence may come as organizations applying for RAB accreditation realize that the RvC is actively participating in the registrar accreditation process. The RAB and RvC performed several joint assessments prior to signing the MOU. The agreement "means we will be doing more of the activities we are already doing."

According to Lofgren, each accreditation team will be made up of one representative each from RAB and RvC. The team will produce a joint report that will be evaluated independently by both organizations. He said that the MOU makes it possible for an organization to get both RAB and RvC marks simultaneously since the process is common through the issue of a joint report.

However, the final evaluation and issue of an accreditation certificate is handled separately. The current MOU arrangement will save time and considerable expense since a prospective registrar would not have to undergo two separate audit processes.

Lofgren said the arrangement will also allow a European organization seeking RAB accreditation to be evaluated in the same manner as a US organization seeking RAB/RvC accreditation. One representative from each organization will conduct the European audit and issue a single report.

## Not Final Goal

As confidence grows in the US system, European organizations will likely take advantage of this arrangement if export to the US market is the goal, Lofgren commented. He noted, however, that the MOU arrangement RAB signed is not an ideal system. "What we want to happen in the future is accreditation on a national basis that will be recognized internationally without the need for multiple accreditation." Lofgren said the RAB-RvC MOU is "just a point on a continuum" toward the establishment of this system.

"We have established this MOU because it is not currently possible to establish broader MRAs with a whole group of European accreditation bodies," Lofgren concluded.

The RAB is negotiating similar arrangements with the United Kingdom's National Accreditation Council for Certification Bodies (NACCB) and with the Standards Council of Canada (SCC). The SCC has only recently set up its registrar accreditation system. At least seven potential registrars have applied for acceptance by the SCC.

Until the directive is issued and until MRAs are negotiated along industry sector lines to allow US conformity-assessment bodies to act as notified bodies, the question of which US organization will be responsible for designating notified bodies will remain unanswered.

Since the EC has not yet defined the ground rules for naming US organizations as notified bodies, it is premature to speculate on the sort of role — if any — CASE or NIST may play in designating notified bodies.

## The Potential Conflict Between CASE and RAB

According to Bob Gladhill of the NIST Office of Standards Services, the CASE program "would not necessarily" undermine similar RAB efforts. CASE "could work in conjunction with" or "provide recognition to" RAB, he said.

---

### The CASE Program's Conformity Assessment Classification

The CASE program proposal classifies conformity assessment activities into conformity, accreditation, and recognition levels.

The *conformity level* addresses activities that provide the actual conformity of a product or of an organization, such as registering an individual manufacturer's quality system or product. Conformity-level activities are performed by testing laboratories, product certifiers, and quality system registrars. It is not anticipated that the government's CASE program will be involved in this type of activity.

The *accreditation level* involves evaluating and accrediting testing laboratories, certification bodies, or quality systems registrars. CASE will be involved on this level and plans to accredit registrars and award certificates. NIST/CASE accreditation will be a voluntary program open to "all entities which desire NIST recognition," according to the proposal.

The *recognition level* involves formally recognizing organizations that provide evaluation and recognizing organizations, such as RAB, that provide accreditation of registrars.

In the CASE proposal, the description of the accreditation level refers to "entities that evaluate and accredit…registrars." This statement is **incorrect** and should read "the accreditation level relates to evaluating…quality systems registrars," according to Bob Gladhill of NIST. CASE will indeed be involved in evaluating and recognizing "entities that evaluate…registrars," but this will happen on the recognition level, said Gladhill.

---

RAB, however, has taken the position that a registrar accreditation system run by the federal government would be inappropriate, duplicative, and possibly a serious conflict of interest.

RAB's argument against the government program is that no conformity assessment organization should be active on two different levels, as the CASE program plans to be. RAB accepts NIST's role in providing "recognition" to the accreditors of quality system registrars such as RAB, but does not think that the government should be directly involved in accrediting registrars.

RAB supports a government role in **recognition** activities but not **accreditation** activities. RAB argues that a government registrar accreditation program would unnecessarily duplicate RAB efforts. RAB estimates that the size of the registrar market could not support two accreditation bodies.

According to RAB, establishing the government as a direct competitor to RAB would weaken government/industry cooperation and could lead to government monopoly of accreditation services as registrars seek the status of government approval.

According to RAB, **accreditation** activities already in place within the private sector should be encouraged — not threatened — by the government. The government should not engage in **accreditation** activities in competition with the private sector.

## RAB Assessor Certification in the United States

RAB has developed and is using an assessor certification program, *Certification Program for Auditors of Quality Systems*. In addition, it has published a program to train ISO 9000 series auditors, *Requirements for the Recognition of an Auditor Training Course*.

US auditors with Institute of Quality Assurance (IQA) lead auditor training certification can meet RAB Lead Auditor criteria if they have successfully completed one of three training requirements:

- An IQA 36-hour Lead Auditor training course
- An ASQC Certified Quality Auditor (CQA) course, plus RAB approved 16-hour ISO 9000 series course
- Certification from RAB-recognized auditor certification body (such as IQA) as an ISO 9000 auditor.

## A Summary of RAB's Comments on the NIST Proposal

The CASE program would enable the Department of Commerce, acting through NIST, to provide assurance to foreign entities that US conformity-assessment activities related to laboratory testing, product certification and quality systems registration satisfy international guidelines.

Clearly, there is a need for US government assurance that designated conformity-assessment programs satisfy specified criteria. RAB supports NIST's role in providing the needed recognition as an appropriate function of government. However, evaluations of the competence of conformity-assessment bodies are best and more appropriately handled through private-sector accreditation programs. The reasons for this are:

○ **Conflict of Interest:** It is inappropriate for any entity to operate at more than one of the three levels of conformity assessment activities—*conformity*, *accreditation*, and *recognition*.

○ **Duplication of Efforts:** In the quality systems certification area, the NIST proposal duplicates the existing ANSI/RAB American National Accreditation Program for Registrars of Quality Systems.

○ **Weakening Government-Industry Cooperation:** The NIST proposal would establish government as a competitor with the private sector, thus weakening the cooperative relationship between government and industry.

○ **Market Size Analysis:** The market size for conformity assessment activities is not sufficient to justify establishing alternatives to current private-sector programs. Fewer than 100 companies are likely to become accredited to perform quality system registrations of supplier companies.

○ **Unnecessary Cost to Taxpayers:** NIST proposes that the program be fee-supported. However, while ongoing costs may well be covered by user fees, who would pay for the considerable expense of developing these new programs? Surely these development costs would be borne by taxpayers. Private-sector accreditation programs have been developed at no cost to taxpayers.

### Conclusion

RAB advocates letting government do what government does best and letting the private sector do what it does best. Because only the government can provide assurances to other governments, **recognition** activities should be a function of government. The **recogni-**

*(continued on next page)*

---

**A Summary of RAB's Comments on the NIST Proposal** *(continued)*

**tion** activities NIST proposes represent an opportunity for government to demonstrate its ability to cooperate with the private sector in providing a function that government is uniquely qualified to perform.

However, **accreditation** activities already in place within the private sector should be encouraged—not threatened—by the government. The government should not engage in **accreditation** activities in competition with the private sector. RAB therefore recommends that **accreditation** activities not be included in the proposed program.

*[Registrar Accreditation Board, 611 E. Wisconsin Ave., P.O. Box 3005, Milwaukee, WI 53201-3005, Tel: (414) 272-8575, Fax: (414) 272-1734.]*

---

Currently, only training offered by IQA-recognized training organizations will be accepted for the 36-hour Lead Auditor course. As of late 1992, the RAB-approved 16-hour course is not yet available. The RAB auditor certification program follows international guidelines similar to the IQA auditor training guidelines.

The Certified Quality Auditor rating currently offered by the American Society for Quality Control (ASQC) means that an applicant to the program has fulfilled requirements and has demonstrated knowledge of auditing.

The CQA rating does not exempt the candidate from required audit experience. A CQA rating, which is a 16-hour course, along with appropriate ISO 9000 training given by the RAB-approved training organizations, will exempt the candidate from the standard 36-hour course.

The CQA program will not be affected by RAB's new auditor certification scheme since RAB and ASQC are separate organizations.

# CONCLUSION

As the above discussion makes clear, registrar accreditation issues are far from settled. Companies considering seeking registration to one of the ISO 9000 standards should ask potential registrars some questions. Consultant Bud Weightman suggests, among others, the following:

■ What is the source of a registrar's accreditation?

■ Is the source of accreditation an EC member state or a body recognized by the EC?

■ If the accreditation entity is not yet recognized, when will it be recognized?

■ Has the accreditation entity adopted EN 45012?

■ If not, does it have plans to do so?

■ With which certifying bodies in the EC does the registrar have MOUs?

Acceptable answers to these questions should afford a company sufficient confidence to begin its path to ISO 9000 standards registration.

## About the Author

*Joseph Tiratto, Professional Engineer (PE), is an international consultant on quality systems, an Institute of Quality Assurance Lead Assessor (auditor) and a European Engineer (EUR ING). Tiratto is a member of the Registrar Accreditation Board (RAB), US Technical Advisory Groups (TAG) to ISO/TC 176 and several other international and national standards groups. He also directed the development of a registrar quality system that would meet both RAB and Dutch Council for Certification (RvC) requirements.*

# THE LEGAL LIMITATIONS OF ISO 9000 REGISTRATION AND EC PRODUCT LIABILITY AND PRODUCT SAFETY

### BY JAMES KOLKA AND GREGORY SCOTT

ISO 9000 registration is playing an increasingly larger role in global trade. Manufacturers are becoming aware that ISO 9000 registration is important, perhaps vital, to their company's compliance with EC directives.

Thousands of company sites worldwide have already become registered to one of the standards in the ISO 9000 series. Countless others are working toward registration. In this move toward registration, many companies may not have given enough consideration to the legal aspects of ISO 9000 registration. This chapter discusses some of the key legal issues raised by ISO 9000 registration. These include the following:

■ What is the legal role of ISO 9004?

■ What is the relationship between ISO 9000 requirements and those of the liability and safety directives?

■   Is ISO 9000 registration a legal defense to a product liability suit?

■   Is ISO 9000 registration a separate source of liability?

Finally, this chapter will discuss the role of product liability prevention. The EC has stated that its purpose in creating liability and safety directives is not to encourage lawsuits but to encourage companies to prevent possible lawsuits by manufacturing safe products.

# THE ROLE OF ISO 9004

The basic ISO 9000 series standard contains five distinct standards: ISO 9001, ISO 9002 and ISO 9003 are prescriptive registration standards; ISO 9000 and ISO 9004 are guidance documents. These standards do not contain prescriptive language; companies do not register to ISO 9004. Companies, however, should pay special attention to ISO 9004 from a legal standpoint.

## Voluntary Standard

Although ISO 9004 is a voluntary guidance standard, it is a component of the ISO 9000 series. US courts have admitted voluntary standards to establish a manufacturer's "duty of care." Failure to conform to voluntary standards does not constitute negligence *per se,* but it may be considered by the court as evidence of negligence or as evidence of a design defect. This means that plaintiffs' attorneys can present ISO 9000 standards as a whole, including ISO 9004, to the court.

The EC can be expected to adopt the same strategy and treat the entire ISO 9000 series standard as an integrated whole.

A company will be hard-pressed to explain to a court that it decided that ISO 9001 was important enough to comply with for registration purposes, but considered ISO 9004 to be purely voluntary and advisory. The money, time, and effort spent on obtaining ISO 9000 registration flies in the face of an argument that companies somehow deem ISO 9004 to be unimportant or non-binding.

The plaintiff's attorney will likely argue that ISO 9004 sets forth the proper conduct of a reasonable and safety-conscious company because it codifies what a company should do to deal with product liability issues.

The only safe and logical way for a company to deal with the critical issues of safety and liability is to develop a product liability prevention program that responds to the guidance language of ISO 9004 as well as to the prescriptive language of ISO 9001, ISO 9002 or ISO 9003.

# REGISTRATION AND ITS LIMITATIONS

Quality assurance registration can confer significant benefits, whether as a regulatory, contractual or market requirement. Registration to ISO 9000, however, is not a legal shield; it will not prevent lawsuits.

In this sense, ISO 9000 registration is a double-edged sword. On the one hand, an ISO 9000-registered company has a well-documented quality assurance program to help it defend itself in the event of a lawsuit. But this same documentation can expose it to attack. Evidence of a failure to comply with its documented quality assurance program may expose the company to liability.

Companies should consider the following issues concerning the legal character of ISO 9000 registration.

## All Registrars Are Not Equal

All registrars are not equal; their costs and quality can vary widely; and cost is no guarantee of quality. A neophyte auditing team can breeze through a complex operation, overlook problems, and register a company that otherwise would not comply with the standard.

A manufacturer who was led to believe that his registration was complete, only to be challenged or sued, can in turn sue the registrar and other appropriate parties to recover damages.

A quality system is only as good as its construction, and an audit only as competent as the auditors. Since these activities do not occur in a vacuum, parties who are financially injured will seek recompense for incompetence and/or sue quality assurance professionals for malpractice.

## ISO 9000 Is Not a Complete Defense to a Claim

Simply achieving ISO 9000 registration for a facility is not a complete defense to any product liability claim. Nor is it a defense to claims that a program was improperly certified, or that certain procedures which should have been employed as part of the quality process were not employed.

In a strict liability case, the question is whether the **product itself** is defective. The focus is on the product, not on the nature of the quality control process.

## The Potential Liability of Consultants and Registrars

If a consulting firm, registrar or notified body fails to inform a client fully about potential liability and safety issues, can they be sued for negligence or faulty performance?

Since there is no law exempting private firms from liability exposure in the United States and the EC, this issue may be raised by unhappy clients and courts will decide each claim on its merits. Misleading a client can occur in different ways, including implying that registration means more than it does or by failing to suggest that registration is a limited entitlement and that legal counsel should be sought to deal with questions of liability and safety.

An indication of the EC's viewpoint on this issue can be found in both new-approach EC medical devices directives. The language in these directives stipulates that notified bodies "must take out liability insurance unless liability is assumed by the state in accordance with national law, or the member state itself is responsible for controls." No less measure of responsibility can be expected from registrars and consultants whose work precedes the notified bodies.

## ISO 9000 Registration Does Not Cover Product Liability and Safety

The legal benefits of quality assurance registration do not cover the issues of product liability, product safety and services liability. These directives have separate legal requirements which will be used to judge whether a product is unsafe or defective.

For example, if a company is registered to ISO 9001 in the EC and a customer sues because a defective product causes injury, ISO 9000 registration will not preclude the lawsuit. The question will be: "Is the product defective?"

ISO 9000 plays virtually no direct role in such a case. The court will examine the

# ISO 9000 Registration and Compliance with US Laws and EC Directives

What does ISO registration mean for complying with US laws or with EC directives? This issue deserves careful study. In the case of US agencies, such as the DoD or the FDA, each agency provides quality assurance criteria with which companies must comply. A company's quality assurance program must be tailored to meet the agency requirements.

An approved quality assurance program that follows an agency's guidelines will not save a company from being sued for product liability and product safety. An agency such as the FDA, for example, monitors self-certification by companies seeking FDA approval. Self-certification is an imperfect process. An inadequate response that escapes the scrutiny of the FDA monitoring process can still lead to liability suits.

Similarly, ISO 9000 registration does not guarantee a perfect quality assurance program and does not offer absolute protection from a liability suit. Liability would exist and the question for a consumer that is suing would be whether to include the consultants and registrar along with the medical corporation in the lawsuit.

In the case of EC harmonized, new-approach directives, close study will be required of the specific directive(s) and standards drafted by CEN, CENELEC or ETSI (e.g., toy safety, active implantable medical devices, simple pressure vessels, etc.). This will reveal whether ISO 9000 is required or optional, and, if optional, it will reveal the range of options described by the Conformity Assessment Procedures.

For example, in the case of the Toy Safety directive it will be necessary to study *Annex II: Essential safety requirements for toys*, and *Annex IV: Warnings and indications of precautions to be taken when using toys*. In addition, Articles 3, 5, 8, 10 and 11 describe necessary steps for compliance and certification necessary to affix the EC mark. It also will be necessary to study standards EN 71 and HD 271 H1. Finally, since the Toy Safety directive provides for options, it will be necessary to study the appropriate conformity-assessment procedures.

As mentioned earlier, it may be necessary to meet more than one EC directive. In such an instance, ISO 9001 full-quality-assurance certification may be the only way to maintain control, satisfy the directives, and obtain approval from the appropriate EC-notified bodies.

provisions of key directives and standards drafted by CEN, CENELEC or ETSI in accordance with those provisions (e.g., toy safety, active implantable medical devices, telecommunications terminal equipment, etc.).

For a legal defense, a company should have ready the appropriate documentation that would allow the use of one of the legal defenses available under the Product Liability directive. Absence of this documentation could mean an automatic loss in the suit.

# EC LIABILITY AND SAFETY DIRECTIVES

This section briefly discusses the EC Product Liability, Product Safety, and Machinery Safety directives, and the proposed Services Liability directive.

## Product Liability Directive

The EC entered a new era when it adopted the Product Liability directive on July 24, 1985. Prior to this directive, EC product liability protection did not exist and European consumers were protected under only a few national laws. Generally, if a consumer was injured by a defective product, the old Latin principle of *caveat emptor* ("let the buyer beware") prevailed.

The Product Liability directive changes this situation radically. After 1992, if a consumer is injured and can prove that a defective product caused the injury, the manufacturer responsible for putting the product on the market is strictly liable, regardless of fault.

The Product Liability directive defines what is meant by a defective product and identifies the acceptable legal defenses a manufacturer could use to defend against a legal action. The fact that an EC mark exists, conformity assessment has been achieved, and that a product is ISO 9000-certified to an EC technical directive is irrelevant. The Product Liability directive will provide the legal authorization, logic and statutory language that will be used by an EC court to determine whether a product is defective.

The Product Liability directive will also provide the legal defenses a manufacturer will have to use to reject a consumer's claim that a product is defective. In short, it is the Product Liability directive that a manufacturer should study in conjunction with the applicable technical directive (e.g., toy safety, medical devices, construction products, etc.) to understand the nature of the manufacturer's product liability exposure.

The success of any possible lawsuit will depend on a company's ability to defend its actions under the Product Liability directive. While the EC will not allow jury trials or contingency fees, it will control damages for pain and suffering and has set upper limits for recovery. However, the upper limits are generous and strict liability may be easier to prove.

In a January 13, 1992, article in *Business America*, Sara E. Hagigh of the US Department of Commerce noted that under the EC system it is not necessary to prove that a product is both defective and unreasonably defective, leading some experts to suggest that proving a defect is easier under EC product liability law than under US product liability law.

## Product Safety Directive

The EC adopted a Product Safety directive on June 29, 1992. The European Community considers product safety a key requirement for creation of the single internal market. The directive lays out basic principles of product safety and is meant to complement the Product Liability directive.

The Product Safety directive should be read in conjunction with the specific new-approach directives and with the Product Liability Directive. Among its highlights, it defines what is meant by a *safe product*, provides that products shall not present "unacceptable risks," establishes product-labeling and monitoring requirements, and requires that manufacturers develop procedures for product disposal if the product is deleterious to the environment.

## Machinery Safety Directive

In 1989, the EC Council adopted the Machinery Safety directive. The directive creates uniform design and safety requirements for machinery. It has two purposes: to promote safety and to eliminate barriers to trade that arise from the differing safety standards of the member states.

When understood in conjunction with the EC Product Liability directive, the Machinery Safety directive has significant ramifications for American companies selling machinery in the EC. The directive requires manufacturers or their authorized EC representatives to certify that their products comply with Community standards in accordance with specified procedures. The precise certification procedures to be followed depend upon the type of product involved, with certain types of machines subject to more restrictive certification procedures.

In 1991, the EC adopted amendments to the Machinery Safety directive that expanded its scope. Unless a type of machine is specifically excluded and/or covered by a specific new-approach directive (e.g., commercial refrigeration equipment), it is covered by the Machinery Safety directive. Two classifications exist under the directive: *Annex IV Machinery* which requires special safety steps outlined in the directive, and *Non-Annex IV,* which might allow for self-certification. Of particular interest are the warnings, cautions, instructions, maintenance instructions, etc., spelled out in *Annex I*.

### Services Liability Directive

Finally, the EC has proposed a Services Liability directive. The service sector in Europe is seen as critical to the EC's economic success. The proposed directive seeks to protect consumers of services and to resolve legal differences between member states.

The proposed directive includes the concept of strict liability as the theory of recovery against service suppliers. The commentary to the preliminary draft directive made clear that the aim is to introduce objective liability on the part of the supplier of defective services, regardless of any concept of fault.

The directive applies to any commercial transaction whether or not payment was involved. The definition of a *supplier of services* under this directive is quite broad. Among the examples cited are engineers, electricians, mechanics, hotel-service providers and dry-cleaning establishments.

The proposed directive would be extended to damages from services provided by health clinics, doctors, quality assurance professionals, registrars, and notified bodies. (New directives will be developed in the future which may remove the liability of specific service sectors from this general rule and create new specific liability rules for these sectors (e.g., medical services).

# IMPLICATIONS FOR COMPANIES

These liability and safety directives have important implications for any company that exports to the EC. One implication is obvious: companies exporting to the EC must comply with the new EC directives as well as the national liability laws within each EC member state.

**These directives apply to all products, both regulated and nonregulated.** Each manufacturer of a regulated product must study the product liability and product safety laws in conjunction with the appropriate EC directive that applies to its products.

With these new liability and safety laws, the EC is becoming more consumer-oriented. The litigation climate can be expected to resemble that of the US more closely.

## ISO 9000 and Product Liability and Safety

As the above discussion indicates, ISO 9000 registration and legal issues of liability and safety will require specific responses to distinct laws. The parties involved in ISO 9000 registration (consulting firms, registered corporations, and ISO registrars) need to understand this clearly. A failure to address legal concerns of liability and safety, when a party knows or should have known, could be as risky as overtly leading a corporation to believe falsely that ISO registration provides liability protection.

It is possible, however, to synchronize the technical documentation required for ISO registration with the legal documentation required to comply with the product liability, product safety, machinery safety or services liability directives. Comprehensive documentation would provide a powerful legal defense against future legal claims. In the EC, such documentation would be invaluable and would help reduce liability exposure.

# ISO 9000 AND PRODUCT LIABILITY PREVENTION

## ISO 9004 Guidance

Section 19.0 of ISO 9004 specifically addresses product safety and liability. Because of its importance, it is set forth here in its entirety:

*19.0 Product Safety and Liability*
*The safety aspects of product or service quality should be identified with the aim of enhancing product safety and minimizing product liability. Steps should be taken both to limit the risk of product liability and to minimize the number of cases by:*

- *Identifying relevant safety standards in order to make the formulation of product or service specifications more effective*
- *Carrying out design evaluation tests and prototype (or model) testing for safety and documenting the test results*
- *Analyzing instructions and warnings to the User Maintenance Manuals and labeling and promotional material in order to minimize misinterpretation*
- *Developing a means of traceability to facilitate product recall if features are discovered that compromise safety and to allow a planned investigation of products or services that are suspected of having unsafe features (see 15.4 and 16.1.3).*

A plaintiff's attorney would argue that, even though Section 19 is guidance language, the steps set forth in it should be followed long before a company seeks to register under any other standard in the series. This type of analysis is basic to ensure the safety of a company's products.

A plaintiff's attorney would use this section to cross examine in-house engineers and quality people on precisely what the company did to comply with this clause. Attempting to defend noncompliance by arguing that ISO 9004 is advisory and non-binding might suit the drafters of the standard but probably will not play well with the court.

Section 19 and ISO 9004 in general seem to codify product liability prevention and describe the procedures necessary to create safe products. To the extent the court believes that this is nothing more than a codification of what a reasonable company would do, non-compliance could disastrous.

The prevention theme is echoed in other parts of ISO 9004. For example, Clause 5.2.5: *Operational Procedures,* provides in part that:

The management system should emphasize preventive actions that avoid occurrence of problems, while not sacrificing the ability to respond to and correct failures should they occur.

## Answering the Tough Questions

The guidance language in ISO 9004 raises several other questions that companies would do well to address when preparing to register to ISO 9001, ISO 9002 or ISO 9003:

■ What will the company be able to tell the court in terms of its quality manual (Clause 5.3.2.1), its quality plant (Clause 5.3.3.3), and its quality records (Clause 5.3.4)? The impact of not having these documents in place prior to registering to another part of the standard may be devastating.

■ What can the company tell the court about the customer feedback system established by it in compliance with Clause 7.3? Much of this information should be part of a good information-gathering network set up to monitor post-sale issues. This, too, is part of a good, well-designed prevention program.

■ What will the company be able to tell the court regarding its designers' obligation to give "due consideration to the requirements relating to safety, environmental, and other regulations including items in the company's quality policy which may go beyond existing statutory requirements?" (Clause 8.2.4.)

■ Can the company document its design function? Has it done a hazard analysis as part of a design process? Did it do prototype testing specifically focusing on the safety and environmental concerns?

■ Precisely what does it mean to give due consideration to "safety" and "environmental and other regulations?" Does this mean a company must also consider EC product liability-related directives such as the Directive on General Product Safety or the Machinery Directive?

■ What has the company done to consider "fitness for purpose" and "safeguards against misuse," as required in Clause 8.2.5?

■ In that same clause, what has the company done to analyze the reliability, maintainability and serviceability of the product through a reasonable life expectancy, including safe failure and safe disposability?

■ What can the company tell the court about the testing that it did under Clause 8.4 to evaluate the performance, durability, safety, reliability and maintainability under expected storage and operation conditions?

■ How could a company possibly register to ISO 9001 without first having complied with the provisions of Clause 8.4? Will the company be able to show the court that it performed the design reviews provided for in Clause 8.5.2? How did these requirements relate to ISO 9001?

■ Clause 8.7 provides for a market readiness review. The review includes the availability and adequacy of installation, operation, maintenance and repair manuals. Can the company document its efforts to review the manuals for its product as part of a market readiness review?

■ How can a company become registered to ISO 9002 without first having implemented the provisions of Clause 10.0 of ISO 9004 dealing with quality and production?

A company that decides to pay attention to the guidance language in ISO 9004 will face quite a task. It contains provisions that may greatly expand liability as well as provisions that seem to conflict with current liability. For example, the clause below 0.4, entitled *Risks, Costs, and Benefits*, seems to conflict with certain parts of the EC Product Liability directive. It states, in part:

> *Risk, cost, and benefit considerations have great importance for both company and customer (0.4.1)... Consideration has to be given to risks related to deficient products or services (0.4.2.1). Consideration has to be given to increased profitability and market share. (0.4.4.1)*

This language suggests some type of risk-benefit analysis. The EC Product Liability directive has specifically rejected a risk-benefit analysis in considering whether a product is defective and supports instead a consumer expectation test.

This raises significant issues as to whether what a company does under ISO 9004 will translate into an adequate defense under the EC Product Liability directive. Apparently, a company that complies with ISO 9004 might nonetheless find itself in trouble with the consumer expectation test under the EC Product Liability directive.

# PRODUCT LIABILITY PREVENTION

The European Community has made clear that its principal focus in the product liability arena is on product liability prevention, not on liability *per se*. In other words, the focus is on requiring manufacturers to prevent accidents, not on creating undue liability.

The preparation process for an ISO 9000 registration audit includes close analysis of a company's existing quality system. This is the perfect opportunity not only to document which procedures are currently being followed, but to analyze critically which procedures should be followed to prevent product liability problems.

Product liability prevention may entail a full-scale audit of the design process to determine whether appropriate procedures are followed, documents are kept, or tests are conducted. Or, it may focus on including appropriate information in instruction manuals or on warning labels.

Increasingly, product liability prevention is focusing on potential post-sale obligations and the creation of post-sale safety committees. These committees analyze and synthesize relevant data received on a daily basis from warranty returns, claims, lawsuits, and salespeople to determine whether some type of post-sale action is necessary. Product liability prevention also entails document retention policies that will allow the manufacturer to defend itself in litigation and take whatever post-sale action might be necessary.

## A Defense for Manufacturers

Documented preventive actions create defenses in the event of legal action. Updating warning labels and instruction manuals to current standards makes them much more difficult for the injured person's expert to criticize. The availability of data that was analyzed by an appropriate safety committee makes it much easier to defend against an allegation that the company failed to take some type of post-sale action.

Finally, prevention includes an analysis of the standards and laws that apply to a given product, which ensures that the company has identified all relevant standards and laws that apply to its product.

A prevention program can be a full-scale audit or a focused project (i.e., warning labels and instruction manuals). The most prudent approach for doing business on a global basis is to start with a full-scale product liability audit at the same time that ISO 9000 certification is achieved. Through periodic checks and periodic updates, the systems put into place following the audit can be updated.

# THE FUTURE

Obtaining ISO 9000 registration is becoming critical to selling products in a global marketplace. It will not, in and of itself, provide defenses to product liability claims. The implementation of thorough product liability preventive procedures will reduce the likelihood of accidents and place a company in an excellent position to defend product liability claims.

## About the Authors

*James W. Kolka has a Ph.D. in political science/international affairs from the University of Kansas, and a J.D. with a background in product liability and environmental law from the University of Wisconsin-Madison. An international legal consultant, he has served as a full professor, published numerous articles, served as vice president both at Drake University and in the University System of Georgia. He has held senior management positions in the University of Wisconsin System, developed Wisconsin's statewide Adult Extended Degree Program and was instrumental in the creation of the Center for International Standards and Quality at Georgia Tech. Dr. Kolka has conducted seminars and consulted on product liability, product safety, services liability, EC product certification, comparative law, environmental planning, global liability, strategic planning and the integration of ISO 9000 quality assurance systems with preventative law programs and legal documentation for the US and the EC markets. Dr. Kolka is fluent in Spanish and conversant in German, Portuguese and Italian. He has worked throughout the United States, Canada, Europe and Latin America. (404/977-4049)*

*Gregory Scott, Esq. is a lawyer with the firm of Popham Haik Schnobrich & Kaufman, Ltd., in Minneapolis, Minnesota. Mr. Scott specializes in product liability and advises clients worldwide on international product standards and on product liability prevention strategies. He is Chairman of the International Law Subcommittee of the Product Liability Committee of the American Bar Association. Mr. Scott is a frequent writer and lecturer on product liability and product liability prevention, in both the United States and in Europe. He has also given seminars in Japan and Korea. (612/334-8013)*

# ISO 9000 CASE STUDIES

## INTRODUCTION

This chapter presents 12 case studies of companies that have completed or are in the process of completing the registration process. Covering a range from computers to chemical processing, these companies include:

# AIRCRAFT BRAKING SYSTEMS CORPORATION

*Akron, Ohio* - Aircraft Braking Systems Corporation's (ABSC) ISO 9001 registration audit did not require radical change or additions to the company's existing quality programs. Yet the year-long effort did pay important dividends, according to vice-president of quality assurance Jim Swihart and quality audit manager Dean Powell.

ISO 9001 registration "principally helped define responsibility and authority," Powell said. "We re-issued a lot of procedures, not so much changing what we were doing, but more updating and clarification. It didn't mean that much change on the floor."

An equally important benefit, according to Swihart and Powell, is the company-wide ownership all employees felt after successfully completing ISO 9000 series registration. "Quality is not just a department anymore," Powell emphasized.

The smooth implementation of the ISO 9001 standard may be a result of the highly audit-driven environment that is typical of companies supplying parts and services to the aviation industry.

According to Swihart, the company is audited about 52 times a year by its customers, which include major aircraft manufacturers, the Federal Aviation Administration (FAA), the Department of Defense (DoD), and airline operators. ABSC's quality system conforms to DoD's MIL-Q-9858A standard and FAA's FAR 21. The company also has an active Total Quality Management (TQM) program in place.

## Setting The Standard

ABSC, a manufacturer of wheel and brake systems for many major military, commercial and business aircraft, also participated in a pilot FAA quality system auditing program called Aircraft Certification Systems Evaluation Plan (ACSEP). The ACSEP quality system approach is scheduled to replace the old hardware-inspection-driven program, Quality Assurance Systems Analysis Review (QASAR), this summer.

## The Old Days

The documented ABSC quality successes, evidenced by ISO 9000 registration, is a distinct change from the company's operations in 1985 when its biggest customer at the time, DoD, gave the company a rating known as "Method C."

Swihart, Powell, and senior vice-president Rob Crawford are quick to point out the company's previous quality problems. According to Swihart, prior to 1985 the company took a hardware inspection-driven approach that provided "minimal documentation of quality systems." He said that this "hardware approach and DoD's system approach collided, and we lost."

The immediate problem ABSC had after receiving its Method C rating was keeping its production lines open. The problem was solved by hiring more inspectors and producing more inspection plans. ABSC's inspection staff eventually grew to more than 110 on-site, full-time inspectors.

## MOA Beginning of Journey

In 1987, ABSC signed a Memorandum of Agreement (MOA) with DoD addressing the company's commitment to quality improvement. ABSC agreed to improve quality performance by 10 percent per year or face a penalty. Meeting this goal meant improving procedures, buying new machinery, and using more-efficient manufacturing methods. ABSC has signed a total of five MOAs, a record among DoD contractors. All improvement goals to date have been met or exceeded.

ABSC continued development of its TQM and Statistical Process Control (SPC) program through 1991. SPC was first used on the shop floor in 1988 and the TQM program began in earnest in 1989. Other improvements included pre-manufacturing agreements signed by the design, manufacturing, and quality engineering departments—a process that Swihart called an "engineered approach to quality."

The quality improvements put into place before ISO 9001 registration also included an In-Process Control (IPC) system that places the responsibility to monitor quality on the machine operator. Cellular manufacturing techniques are also used widely in the plant. The cellular concept puts the correct equipment and operators in one location and makes quality a part of an individual cell function.

## New Approaches

Swihart said that prior to using the cellular approach, the company was a job shop housing banks of lathes, mills and drills. Aircraft brake wheels passing through the manufacturing process were subject to frequent errors and damage. The total cellular manufacturing approach, including SPC, has meant an 87-percent quality improvement since 1987, Swihart said.

ABSC also ensured supplier quality before ISO 9000 series registration through an aggressive program that encourages suppliers such as carbon fiber, resin coating, and brake disk pattern manufacturers to work together. ABSC also hosts yearly supplier conferences and sends monthly report cards to suppliers on quality and delivery records.

The return for ABSC's five years of quality commitment has been greatly reduced costs and greater customer satisfaction. Swihart said that during the fiscal year ending March 31, 1992, the company spent more than $1.0 million less due to damaged or re-worked brakes and wheels than they had the previous year.

## Fewer Inspectors

ABSC now has 50 percent fewer inspectors. Delinquent sales are now less than .6 percent, rather than the former 18 percent record. The company used to be at the bottom of one major airline's rating system; now ABSC is number one on the list.

Swihart and Powell said ISO 9001 registration was a "natural" step for the company's quality improvement program. As a practical matter, Swihart said, ISO 9001 registration complemented the TQM concepts already in place. The business reasons may be more compelling: some of ABSC's European customers already require quality system registration.

Senior VP Crawford admitted that ABSC had come a long way on its quality journey. "We wanted to satisfy our customers and eliminate waste, and we think we have done that."

Crawford noted that the third-party registration has given the company new confidence that it can stand up to any audit team. Other quality awards are "largely public relations," Crawford added, calling ISO 9000 series registration a "real customer requirement."

## ABSC Gets Immediate ISO 9000 Registration Benefit

ISO 9000 series registration had an immediate benefit for ABSC, according to Jim Swihart.

Fokker, a major aircraft manufacturer based in the Netherlands, canceled its scheduled audit after learning of ABSC's successful registration audit. Another US airline customer reduced the scope of its audit requirements as a result of ABSC's ISO 9001 registered company status.

While Swihart said he was happy about the immediate return on the company's investment, he pointed out that reducing the number of yearly audits was only part of the reason to seek ISO 9000 series registration.

"We wanted ISO 9000 because it puts the emphasis back where it belongs: on the customer," Swihart said. He pointed out that some European contracts currently require ISO 9000 series registration. Swihart cited other reasons to seek ISO 9001 registration, including market advantages and the possible use of ISO 9000 as a regulatory requirement. The ISO 9000 series also complemented the company's continuing TQM Program.

## Registrar Chosen

ABSC began investigating ISO 9000 series registration in January 1991. By January 1992, the company was ready for a document review by its chosen registrar, Intertek Technical Services, Inc., of Fairfax, VA.

Dean Powell headed the registration effort, gathered information, and advised on where ABSC's system did not meet the ISO 9001 criteria. The 20 elements in the standard were assigned to a single quality engineering department engineer charged with preparing a compliance book for that section.

Each compliance book contained a copy of the ISO 9001 section specifications. All supporting documentation to prove a procedure existed and examples of those procedures were also included in the compliance book. Swihart said he did not intend for the auditors to rely on the detailed books for their audit, but pointed out that the books educated both the ABSC internal auditors and ISO 9000 auditors about the quality system.

## Quality Manuals

Powell said the quality manuals were not set up strictly around the ISO 9000 structure. While procedures were added where necessary, Powell said that defining responsibility and authority was one of the main benefits of registration.

"If we were speaking to another group on ISO 9000 series registration, defining authority would be a number one priority," Powell said. "You have to define who gives you the authority to do what you're doing and what are those responsibilities." ISO 9001 registration also ensured that all relevant procedure manuals are circulated through Powell's office.

Both Swihart and Powell agreed that existing documentation needed only to be "ISO-ized" for the ISO 9001 registration effort. "We were surprised how well our existing documentation dovetailed with the ISO requirements," Powell said. Nevertheless, getting ready for registration took more than 100 plant floor audits, Swihart pointed out.

Another benefit of registration was the dose of reality it gave the company, Swihart said. "It's good to have a third-party audit without a stake in the outcome, " he said. "It helps you get your feet back on the ground and lets you find out if you are as good as you think you are."

---

# Aircraft Braking Systems Corporation
## 63 Years of Aviation History

Aircraft Braking Systems Corporation (ABSC) has existed for only three years as a separate company, yet the company's ties to the aerospace industry extend to 1929 when Goodyear Tire & Rubber Company entered the aircraft tire and wheel market. Through the years, the Aircraft Wheel & Brake Division of Goodyear Aerospace Corporation evolved.

Loral Corporation, an international electronics corporation and a major US Department of Defense (DoD) contractor, acquired Goodyear Aerospace in 1987. In 1989, ABSC and another Goodyear Aerospace Division, Engineered Fabrics, were spun off as a new company, K&F Industries.

ABSC has almost one-third of the total worldwide market in aircraft wheels and brakes. The company dominates the general and military aviation markets. ABSC is second in the commercial transport market, with total annual sales of more than $250 million.

### Reduced Military Budgets

The reduction in military budgets worldwide and growth of international commercial business has had a major effect on ABSC's market. In 1988, about 45 percent of the company's business was military. ABSC's current market is about 20 percent military and 80 percent commercial.

Jim Swihart, vice-president of quality assurance, said that ISO 9000 series registration will help address the increasingly competitive world market. He noted that aircraft brake manufacturers may not recoup up-front costs from new aircraft program investments for 15

*(continued on next page)*

## **Aircraft Braking Systems Corporation** *(continued)*

years or more. In many cases, wheel and brake assemblies are provided at a loss to aircraft manufacturers and investment is recouped supplying spare parts for worn-out brakes.

ABSC products include:

○ Wheel and Brake Systems (carbon brakes; steel brakes; and main and nose wheels)
○ Brake Management Systems (digital and analog antiskid; automatic braking; brake-by-wire; and brake temperature monitoring).

Major ABSC aircraft manufacturer customers include:

○ Douglas (DAC) Aircraft
○ General Dynamics
○ Canadair
○ Gulfstream
○ Grumman
○ SAAB
○ Beech
○ Fokker
○ Airbus*
○ Dornier
○ Lockheed
○ Sikorsky
○ Lear
○ Rockwell
○ Boeing
○ Fairchild
○ Bell
○ Cessna.
*\* ABSC is the sole source for the new Airbus A321 program.*

# AMOCO PETROLEUM ADDITIVES COMPANY

*Wood River, IL* - Amoco Petroleum Additives Company's Natchez, MS, plant may not be Amoco Chemical's largest facility, but the 61-employee specialty chemical plant is leading a march to ISO 9000 series registration that should ultimately include the entire US Amoco Petroleum Additives Company business unit.

According to Elizabeth Bild, an Amoco Petroleum Products Company quality administrator who is coordinating the registration effort, ISO 9000 registration is part of the company's five-year-old total quality process. The journey began with implementation of total quality concepts that included management commitment, a statistical process control system and a supplier quality program.

"A lot of these things [quality initiatives that parallel the ISO 9000 series standard elements] had been initiated before [ISO 9000], but what was missing was an overall system," Bild said. She added that the ISO 9000 series has become a standard that has won over both management and plant operators.

## Audit Strategy

The ISO 9000 registration approach taken by the Amoco Petroleum Additives Company division sounds deceptively simple. According to Bild, the strategy began with auditor training for qualified individuals at each divisional facility. After setting up internal audit systems, audits were performed. When corrective action was complete, audits were performed again.

Amoco Petroleum Additives Company, which manufactures additives that enhance the performance of fuels and lubricants, also chose an informal administration approach for the ISO 9000 registration effort that involved as many employees as possible.

Bild heads a corrective action team made up of one person from each of the company's sites, but leading ISO 9000 registration activities was just one of its functions. "This isn't a full-time job for me [or anyone at Amoco Petroleum Additives Company]," Bild said. "We have had people work on ISO on special assignment for a few months, but the whole approach has been very decentralized... and we got lots of people involved."

Frank Sidorowicz, site coordinator for the Natchez registration, was on special assignment for a few months prior to the registration audit to coordinate completion of all internal audit action items. After the registration audit, Sidorowicz monitored ISO 9000 compliance for two months to verify that all systems continued to operate independently. Systems must continue to be able to operate effectively since registrars may perform unscheduled surveillance audits.

Natchez plant manager Bruce Newman said the audit/re-audit approach allowed a unique solution to aligning a chemical process industry facility to ISO 9000 guidelines. "We started from the bottom up writing operating, lab, and maintenance procedures."

Newman said the first two-day internal audit at the Natchez facility yielded a list of corrective actions that took about six months to complete. Tasks to correct the Natchez ISO 9000 nonconformities were then delegated at monthly meetings and tracked with reports back to the committee.

Bild said sharing information quickly after the audits was an important element of the registration effort. A portable personal computer used for the audits provided plant managers with a detailed list of findings, including the standard element, the ISO 9000 document reference for the finding, specific evidence and comments, the auditor name as well as the organizational representative verifying the audit results. Bild said the detailed audit results helped facility managers determine how to begin corrective action.

Other ISO 9000 compliance came a little easier. "We were in pretty decent shape for management responsibility (Clause 4.1)," Bild said. "And our Quality Administrative Teams (QAT) were already in place to satisfy management review (Clause 4.1.3) requirements and for monitoring the progress of the standards." In addition, employee training requirements (Clause 4.18) had been satisfied early in the registration process.

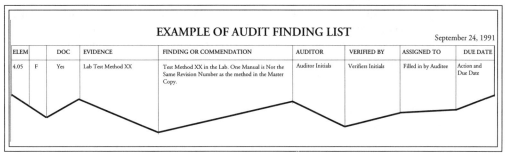

*Figure 11-1: Example of audit finding list.*

## Quality Manual

Bild, who is an American Society for Quality Control (ASQC) Certified Quality Auditor, said the top-tier quality manuals are organized according to the ISO 9001 elements. Some, such as Du Pont Electronics' Clearfield, PA, site plant, have used the existing quality manual and referenced sections for the auditors. The bottom two quality manuals contain detailed procedures for the operation and calibration of equipment.

Natchez plant manager Newman said that one of the benefits of ISO 9000 registration was a critical look at equipment preventive maintenance practices. He said that before ISO 9000 registration, Natchez had seen the manufacturing process in terms of raw materials through finished product. He said a team designed a preventative maintenance program for critical equipment and outside technicians were hired to write procedure and calibration manuals. Newman said the company's work force could not spare company personnel for the technical writing tasks.

Once the Natchez quality system was in place, Quality System Registrars (QSR) was contracted to perform a pre-assessment evaluation three weeks before the formal audit, which they also performed on July 8-10, 1991.

Bild said QSR's knowledge of the chemical process industry was a driving factor in the registrar selection process for the Natchez ISO 9002 registration. She added that QSR's lack of current direct European accreditation was of some concern to the company, but she considers QSR's intention to receive Dutch Council for Certification (RvC) accreditation a good insurance policy.

## Benefits of ISO 9000 Registration

The critical equipment maintenance program has meant a drastic reduction in emergency calls to maintenance staff, Newman said. ISO 9000 registration also highlighted critical equipment spare part inventory problems. "We will have to take the process one step further and work on the parts supply for critical equipment maintenance." In addition, Newman said, the variability index (product consistency) has been improved.

Newman said Mississippi's workers have an undeserved poor reputation which "we don't find to be true." He noted that, "we at the Natchez plant can meet international quality standards, and feel pride in that accomplishment."

## Amoco Petroleum Additives Company

Amoco Petroleum Additives Company manufactures additives that enhance the performance of fuels and lubricants. The specialty chemical company is a subsidiary of Amoco Chemical Company, which is the worldwide chemical manufacturing and marketing arm of Amoco Corporation.

Products include additives for passenger car, two-stroke, and heavy duty engine lubricants (heavy duty engines are used in trucks, locomotives and other large equipment applications); gasoline additives that control deposits in engine carburetors, fuel injectors and intake systems; distillate fuel additives that improve performance in cold weather; and automatic transmission fluid additives.

The company has its headquarters in Clayton, MO, and a research center in Naperville, IL, Amoco Petroleum Additives Company plant locations include Natchez, MS, and Wood River, IL.

## Chemical Process Industry
## ISO 9000 Registration Requires Specific Auditing Skills

Auditing the chemical process industry is not the same as auditing a parts manufacturing facility. That may seem an obvious statement, but many quality assurance managers who work in the chemical process industry say finding ISO 9000 consultants and registrars who understand the difference is surprisingly difficult.

Walking around tank clusters connected by pipes, pumps and measuring devices at the Amoco Petroleum Additives Company's Wood River plant, it is easy to see why it may be difficult to audit standards. Traditional product-manufacturing auditing concepts must be translated to ISO 9000 series document control, supplier assessment, traceability, and inspection and testing requirements of the chemical process industry.

Elizabeth Bild, an Amoco Petroleum Products Company quality administrator who coordinated the Natchez, MS, registration effort, said her initial research into both ISO 9000 registrars and consultants led her to some individuals who thought that the chemical process industry made heavy use of calipers. Despite this early frustration, Bild said, ISO 9000 registration has brought about new insight into the efficient running of a chemical process plant.

## Complex Process

The chemical process industry relies on complex chemical reactions that require the mixing of precise amounts of different chemical products within exact temperature and time guidelines.

Once these chemical processes begin, testing is performed to exacting tolerances and is continuously monitored. Viscosity is tested, percentages of chemical components are tracked and changes noted and corrective action initiated. It is an exact science that is more computer print-out than physical measurement and observation.

Bild pointed out green ISO 9000 signs attached to various meters, noted instruments that record and monitor critical ISO 9000 compliance criteria. In the testing lab, a robotic arm measures a vial of sampled liquid against a control standard while a computer records each test. ISO 9000 auditors must cross-check the standard number, against which the sampling equipment checks its measurements, with a master standards document.

## Document Control

A large, bottom-tier quality control book references a master list of correct testing procedures. Operators and the ISO 9000 auditors must ensure that the current index matches the one in the master document by date, number and process. A middle-tier book in a quality control manager's office references ISO 9002 criteria directly. (See Figure 11-2.) In another office, files of product acceptance criteria and acceptable tolerances must also be audited.

In another part of the plant, operators watch computer screens displaying colorful diagrams of tanks, pipes and valves. Bild pointed out that all the set points represented on the screen have to be documented to meet the ISO 9000 standard. Meters and control valves that mix the chemicals must also be calibrated.

Bild said some of the less critical work procedures at the plant were not documented before ISO 9000 registration. "ISO 9000 brought it all down to paper," she said. "If someone had been doing a job a long time, the exact procedure was not written down." She said that the method may not have damaged quality, but the system did not provide for the possibility that the employee may not always be around to perform that procedure.

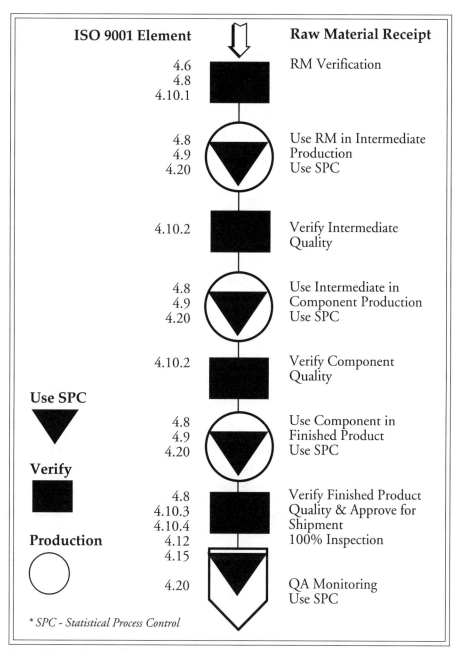

*Figure 11-2: Quality plan flow chart.*

# DATA GENERAL CORPORATION

*Apex, NC* - The real complexity of Data General Corporation's principal US computer manufacturing operations, like the mainframe and desktop computer systems it produces, is not readily apparent at first glance.

Rows of bright blue printed circuit board assembly machines go about selecting and installing various memory chips and other electronic wizardry from plastic feeder sleeves. Shiny metal boxes containing 18x18-inch blank circuit boards travel swiftly around the plant on stainless steel rollers.

A giant, 300-foot-long ominous-looking automatic storage and retrieval system nicknamed the "cornfield project" dominates the central core of the 300,000-square-foot facility. Metal boxes containing blank circuit boards disappear through doors at the base of the machine and then reappear elsewhere in the manufacturing line. The fanciful scene could be a movie set were it not that real computer equipment is being loaded on the trucks at the far end of the plant.

## Center for US Operations

Ralph Hudson, divisional vice president of worldwide manufacturing operations, said the consolidation of three other US sitesbrought a great deal of the technology and machinery to the ten-year-old facility. All US computer system assemblies and system integration operations are now performed at the Apex facility, including the final systems integration for the Eclipse MV and Avion family of computers.

Hudson said the decision to seek ISO 9002 registration was driven by a large international customer base — 50 percent of the total, 35 percent European — and by Data General's goal of achieving a defect ratio of 3.4 defects per million. The quality process by which this defect ratio is attained is usually referred to as *six sigma*. The next step on Data General's quality path is ISO 9001 registration that will involve the design community. Hudson said the company will eventually tackle the challenge of winning the more elusive Malcolm Baldrige Quality Award.

For the time being, however, Hudson and quality assurance director Rodney Gilvey are pleased with ISO 9002 registration. Both said the registrars contracted to perform the final audit, Underwriters Laboratories (UL), were "tough, but fair." UL has an agreement with the British registrar, British Standards Institution (BSi). Gilvey said he had scheduled a full year to prepare for and pass a certification audit. The process took only seven months. Data General passed on the first audit.

Adding to the marketing ammunition amassed to compete in the international computer market, the ISO 9002 registration allowed Data General's quality staff to update its procedures and documentation system. According to Hudson, a "major area of concern" was scheduled calibration of manufacturing machinery. "It was a surprise to see how far we had to go."

# Complex Process

More than 2,000 individual components must be attached to most printed circuit board cards produced by the dozens of assembly machines on the plant floor. Each component is tested by the assembly machine's robotic arm before installation. The machine also makes sure that the electronic components picked from the feeder sleeves match customer order specifications. Assembly machine operators, all trained in statistical process control (SPC), monitor a defect rate of about 500 defects per million insertions. Automated visual inspection reduces the defect ration to 25 defects per million.

A sophisticated failure analysis lab equipped with an electron microscope analyzes and documents defects from both the plant floor and the field. Ten percent of the plant's production output is taken off the production line and audited. Any defects found trigger a root cause analysis that may result in a design change.

A tracking system allows the quality manager to trace printed circuit board history during both manufacturing build and field repair in addition to supplier component performance in design applications.

# Sophisticated Testing

Assembled computers are tested by *Watchdog*, a software program that automatically checks orders against sales department records and verifies the computer system configuration to individual customer orders. The test equipment also simulates the presence of a hard disk (if one is not already installed) to make sure that future hardware upgrades will perform as promised.

The complexity of the process and documentation is as much a challenge for the auditors as it is for the company seeking certification. Auditors must be selective in their choice of areas to scrutinize. Gilvey said the three UL auditors chose to look at the extremes of the process as well as the exceptions. "If you have the exceptions under control," Gilvey said, "and you've got your mainstream [documentation and process] under control, you have a better chance of [knowing] you have the whole [system] under control."

Despite the vast amount of computer documentation at the Data General facility, Gilvey said paper is still a principal means of documentation. The copy machine at the plant was kept so busy during the days leading up the formal audit that the service technician was engaged to stay on site.

Gilvey said another Data General facility has a computer-based documentation system that was adopted by the Apex facility. The Apex facility chose to keep its system in place until after the registration. However, Apex will import this electronic documentation control system after the other Data General location gains registration. Gilvey hopes to reduce paper use by 90 percent as the company moves toward ISO 9001 registration.

## Data General's Registration Effort

Data General's aggressive approach to ISO 9000 series standard registration was prompted by market forces and a competitive spirit.

Rodney Gilvey said that prior to his company's ISO 9002 registration, Data General sales representatives around the world had reported a growing emphasis on quality system registration.

"We were losing relative position in bids because of our ISO status," Gilvey said. Now that the company has received its registration certificate, the tables have turned. The company has begun demanding that its suppliers become ISO 9000 series-registered.

---

## The 10 Steps of ISO 9002 Implementation

1. Create Management Awareness and Commitment
2. Establish ISO Task Team
3. Assess Quality System Against ISO Standard
4. Develop Action Plan
5. Update Management Weekly
6. Revise Quality Policy and Quality Systems Procedures
7. Create Employee Awareness and Commitment
8. Initiate Internal and Self-Audit Programs
9. Implement Corrective Action System
10. Include Total Plant Involvement

The personal challenge came after a pre-assessment audit conducted by Underwriters Laboratories. "We went through pre-assessment and were told that calibration and documentation problems would probably cause us to fail our registration audit," Gilvey said. "We took that as a challenge."

## Pre-Assessment Value

Gilvey admitted that reading the 18 sections of the ISO 9002 series standards (which remain posted on a wall in the plant) made him feel confident about Data General's pre-registration compliance. "We were doing internal compliance," Gilvey recalls, "but after the pre-assessment, we realized that we didn't have much objective evidence."

Originally, Gilvey thought the six-person task force assembled would require only 10 to 20 percent of a typical workday. After the pre-assessment, all six members were assigned full-time to the project. An additional ISO 9000-experienced team

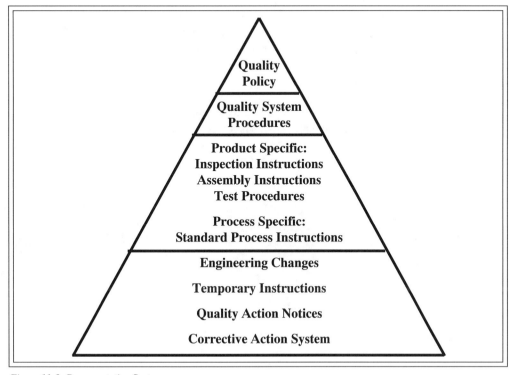

*Figure 11-3: Documentation System.*

member was brought in from a Pacific Rim facility. Data General has facilities in the Philippines, Thailand and Singapore.

Much of the work for the registration audit was already in place, including a basic workmanship policy and documented work instructions (assembly instructions). The company quality policy was edited to a single page. Middle-tier standard operating procedures and documentation for departmental relationships were upgraded.

Internal auditing requirements were enhanced using on-site audit training classes supplied by a consulting firm. Gilvey said Data General's on-going program of self-audits now includes an ISO audit component that references the 18 sections of the standard. Lead assessor training will be provided for one Certified Quality Auditor selected from each facility.

## ISO 9001 Next Goal

Like all successful ISO 9000 quality systems road maps, the Data General map began with management awareness and commitment. Now that the company has achieved its first goal of ISO 9002 registration, Hudson have successfully lobbied for management commitment to involve the design and research and development communities. Data General recently received backing from its company president to pursue ISO 9001 registration.

According to Gilvey, printed circuit board assembly defects have dropped 80 percent as a result of the registration process. The defect reduction is part of an ultimate goal of reducing defects by 50 percent per year for existing products and by 90 percent for new products.

# DU PONT ELECTRONICS

*Clearfield, PA* - According to Du Pont Electronics quality assurance manager Robert Craig, many companies embarking on a registration effort worry too much about details, and not enough about major roadblocks to registration.

"We didn't get too excited [during the early stages of ISO 9000 preparation] whether or not a specific document needed an initial or a full signature," Craig said. "If you start out [trying to correct the whole system at once] everyone is overwhelmed. That's when people get turned off and complain that the goal is not achievable. If you start at the top with the big issues, most of the details will be fixed by the time you get to that level."

Worrying first about big issues also helps the quality department get past the first signpost on the road to registration, management commitment and involvement. "You don't get much resistance when management can see a business reason for registration such as improving documentation control," Craig observed.

## Quality Steering Committee

The Quality Steering Committee was the vehicle that guided Clearfield registration implementation plans. Craig chaired the 12-member committee which included the Clearfield site manager and staff. Training and management review of the ISO 9000 effort was conducted through the committee's weekly meetings.

During the quality committee meetings, Craig (the committee's designated ISO 9000 coordinator) provided each area manager a review of each section of an applicable standard. A list of self-assessment questions for area managers was also provided that enabled each area manager to compare standards in his or her own area.

The questions and answers from the exercise resulted in a list of ISO 9000 standard *action items*. This "to-do" list distilled in a standard form what action was required, the person responsible for corrective action, when the corrective process began, a commitment date for completion, and a final completion date.

Craig said these action items were discussed at the quality committee meetings. The open discussion aided the registration effort by allowing for common problem-solving and implementation. "We never had five different solutions to the same problem," Craig noted.

An overview of ISO 9000 was presented to Clearfield employees during a single session that centered on the general implications of the standards. "We didn't try to make every individual on site an expert on standards," Craig said.

Clearfield focused its worker training instead on how ISO 9000 would affect specific jobs in the plant. For example, an operator "would know that document control is important, but the operator would be hard-pressed to explain what the standard says about document control."

Clearfield employees were kept informed weekly of registration effort progress through managers in specific areas of the facility. In addition, a monthly newsletter was created detailing the ISO 9000 preparation process and other on-going quality efforts at the Clearfield site.

## Quality Documentation

Craig recommended a tiered approach to quality documentation. The top-level manual should reflect ISO standards and overall quality policy. Department manuals should define organizational responsibility that accomplishes company policy. Each department manual should be supported by specific process documentation, calibration and inspection/test instructions and flow charts.

Clearfield's approach to its top-level quality manual focused on the efficient use of existing documentation. Craig said the Clearfield site quality manual was a detailed document before the ISO 9000 registration process began. Instead of changing the successful document to conform to ISO 9000 language and structure, Craig decided to cross-reference the existing manual.

ISO 9000 requirements met by different sections of the manual were listed in the appendix. Some ISO 9000 requirements, such as purchasing, required six separate section references in the quality manual.

Craig said cross-referencing made auditing more difficult for its auditor, Lloyd's Register Quality Assurance, Ltd. (LRQA), but he noted that "we didn't view the task [of registration] as making the site easy to audit." He said the auditors "didn't focus on specific terminology, but [all the ISO 9000 requirements] had to be [addressed] in your quality manual."

LRQA acceptance of Clearfield's quality manual cross-referencing scheme is a good example of ISO 9000 registration mythology. Before beginning the registration process, Craig understood via industry grapevines that changes to a company's quality manual required LRQA approval.

Craig said LRQA keeps its official copy of the Clearfield site's quality manual in his office. Changes to the manual are allowed any time without prior LRQA approval. Changes are reviewed during LRQA's twice-a-year surveillance visits of the company.

## Internal Auditing

The internal auditing system at Clearfield was an established part of the business before the ISO 9000 registration effort. LRQA considers a company's internal auditing system one of the most important elements of a quality system. Registrars sometimes accept internal audit findings versus auditing a specific section of a company. However, an overall audit is always performed.

Clearfield had established a two-year auditing cycle before registration. Craig said potential problem areas of the facility were pushed to the top of that schedule. LRQA had been impressed with the Clearfield site's auditing practices during its pre-assessment visit. The favorable impression "was a plus" during the actual ISO 9000 registration, Craig said.

Craig recommends training and using company employees as internal auditors rather than hiring outside consultants. Clearfield's two internal auditors accompanied LRQA auditors during their visit. The arrangement resulted in a more valuable learning experience for the internal auditors, Craig said.

The final signpost on the Clearfield road map to registration was the establishment of a corrective action system. An effective corrective action system, says Craig, is the engine that drives an ISO 9000 registration

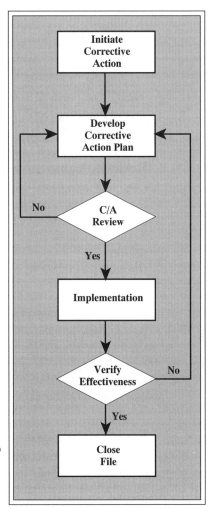

*Figure 11-4: Corrective action procedure.*

preparation effort. The system should be management-driven and involve all employees. Key elements should include a description of the condition needing correction, root cause of condition, a corrective action plan, a verification system, and a closure date for corrective action.

Du Pont Electronics quality management system at Clearfield was issued its ISO 9002 certificate of approval from LRQA on April 3, 1991.

## Registration Effort Focuses on Simplicity...Business Value

Robert Craig said the Clearfield quality team used a strictly pragmatic approach to direct the ISO 9002 quality system registration effort at the site.

"We tried to look for the simplest possible solution to accomplish the intent [of ISO 9002]," Craig said. "The simpler, the better. The ideal state is to avoid creating another piece of paper." Du Pont Electronics at Clearfield produces interconnectors for the data processing and telecommunications industries.

### Business Value

Craig said that at every juncture along the registration road map he sought to use the company's established quality system to meet ISO 9000 requirements. "We did nothing that did not have business value," Craig said. "We always weighed any decisions we made against this criterion. If the ISO requirement didn't have business value for Du Pont, then we probably had misinterpreted the requirement. The whole objective [of ISO 9000] is to make business more effective, not more cumbersome and rigid."

Craig's straightforward approach to achieving ISO 9000 registration influenced all the decisions he and the 12-member Quality Steering Committee made during the one-year registration process. Registration forced few changes to the existing quality manual. ISO 9000 training for the work force focused on individual operator tasks, not creating ISO standards experts. Documentation control problems were sometimes solved by purchasing a few rubber stamps and ink pads.

### Registration Myths

The registration process also put to rest common myths about quality system registration. Craig said the registration team from Lloyd's Register Quality Assurance, Ltd. was thorough and professional. "We had heard stories about cold, rigid assessors, but the approach [of the Lloyd's assessors] put everyone at ease," Craig said. "The problems they pointed out were truly oversights on our part, not nit-picking technicalities." He said the assessors were also sensitive to the production environment, sometimes changing schedules to accommodate critical work at the plant.

Cost of the registration process is another common myth. Craig said that the true out-of-pocket expense for the Clearfield accreditation was about $30,000. No new employees were hired, nor were any Clearfield employees dedicated full-time to the registration effort.

## Positive Changes

Clearfield's registration has forced a number of positive business management changes. Before registration, the Clearfield plant did not consider contract review to be part of site responsibility. Traditionally, contract review was handled by the marketing department at the home office in Wilmington, DE. ISO 9000 registration required Clearfield to review its system to ensure both a manufacturing capability and an ability to deliver the product on time. An improved system was put in place to address this registration requirement.

ISO 9000 registration also streamlined and improved purchasing procedures. The quality of suppliers was controlled before ISO 9000 registration, but the system was not documented. Purchasing was viewed as an off-site responsibility. ISO 9000 registration forced part of that responsibility — supplier selection and control — back to the Clearfield site. Craig said the work of generating and maintaining a list of quality suppliers was split among several employees to avoid adding new layers of bureaucracy.

Clearfield management strongly believes registration was a key element in enhancing business effectiveness.

Marketing advantages are also found in registration. Some Clearfield customers already accept ISO 9000 registration in lieu of a formal audit. The help Craig sometimes provides to customers seeking ISO 9000 registration is a value-added service that can differentiate Clearfield products from those of competitors.

## Constructive Feedback

Despite the sophistication of the Clearfield site's quality assurance program, Craig admitted the facility did not pass its ISO 9000 assessment in December 1990. When the assessors returned six weeks later, the issues pinpointed by the LRQA assessment had been addressed. LRQA approved Clearfield for ISO 9002 registration in February 1991.

Craig said Clearfield's first unsuccessful registration attempt was not perceived by employees or management as a personal or company defeat, but rather as "constructive feedback to further improve our quality system." He said the "frenzy of activity" surrounding registration attempts by some companies undermines the purpose of the ISO 9000 series standard.

"Some companies tend to go overboard and do things that don't have business value," Craig said. "You have to realize that whatever system you put in place, you must maintain it. Why use a sledge hammer when a tack hammer will do?"

---

### Du Pont Electronics' Clearfield Site, Interconnector Producer

Du Pont Electronics' Clearfield site is one of Connector Systems Division's major manufacturing locations providing state-of-the-art, high-reliability interconnect products.

Highly sophisticated connectors manufactured by the Clearfield site are used throughout the electronics industry to connect electrically circuit board to circuit board and wire and cable communications to circuit boards.

Many Clearfield products find their way into very demanding applications within data processing and telecommunication systems requiring very high dependability. Clearfield is viewed as a strategic supplier to such companies as AT&T, Compaq, Digital Equipment, Hewlett Packard, IBM, Motorola, Northern Telecom and many others.

Clearfield site began operations in 1966 under the direction of Berg Electronics (which was subsequently acquired by Du Pont in the early 1970s). The site began as a tool shop with nine employees to support Berg Electronics connector manufacturing facilities in the Harrisburg, Pennsylvania area. From this humble beginning, Clearfield has grown continuously over the years. Today the site is one of the area's largest companies having approximately 500 employees and occupying 140 million square feet of manufacturing space used to produce products for a global electronics marketplace.

# Du Pont Electronics' Clearfield Site, Registration Road Map

1. Create Management Commitment/Involvement
2. Establish a Quality Steering Committee
3. Train Management and Employees
4. Communicate Registration Plans
5. Develop Implementation Plans
6. Establish an ISO 9000 Referenced Quality Manual
7. Establish an Internal Auditing System
8. Establish a Comprehensive Corrective Action System

# ETHYL CORPORATION

*Baton Rouge, LA* - Ethyl Corporation's materials management group faced a daunting task on the road to ISO 9002 registration.

Instead of registering a single site, the group sought to have purchasing and logistics facilities in six states and Canada audited simultaneously for inclusion under one quality system certificate.

The strategy meant overcoming complex coordination obstacles involving joint team meetings and the preparation of common procedures. "Initially, there was skepticism [about quick, successful registration] because of the number of different facilities and procedures involved," said Don Tieken, general manager of the group.

The group includes both the logistics and purchasing departments. The headquarters for purchasing is located in Baton Rouge. The purchasing departments are located at manufacturing sites in Pasadena, TX; Magnolia, AR; Sauget, IL; St. Louis, MO; Orangeburg, SC; and Sarnia, Canada. Logistics encompasses transportation and the customer service departments. Ethyl Corporation produces petroleum additives, flame retardants, alpha olefins and numerous intermediate chemicals. Ethyl is the only producer of ibuprofen in the United States.

## 50 Percent of Sales Outside United States

The company views registration to the ISO 9000 series as one of the requirements for doing business in Europe. Over 50 percent of the company's sales are overseas. According to Tieken, the materials management group's desire for registration was initially "driven by our manufacturing organizations." Ethyl's Feluy, Belgium manufacturing facility received registration in 1990, and its Sauget, IL facility in Spring 1991.

A production unit in Pasadena was registered in December 1990. Tieken noted that the materials management group's involvement in these registration efforts highlighted a need for more up-front coordination to prevent duplication of effort between departments. "Since we needed to get ourselves prepared to be part of certification efforts [in Sauget and the other manufacturing facilities], we asked 'why not go after certification ourselves?'" said Tieken.

Instead of producing "as-requested" documentation for manufacturing facilities involved in registration efforts, the materials management group decided to pursue its own registration and to standardize procedures at all purchasing and logistics facilities.

## Beginning The Process: Teamwork and EQIP

In February 1991, the materials management group decided to seek ISO 9000 series registration and to complete the effort by December 31, 1991.

Team development was the first priority, according to Tieken. Five teams (which included one person from each plant) were arranged around common responsibilities at each site. For example, individuals dealing with raw materials at the different facilities formed one team.

Once teams were established, the materials management group used video-conferencing facilities to hold long-distance meetings. However, teams also met in person. "The travel budget went up considerably in 1991" due to registration efforts, Tieken noted.

Tieken pointed out that part of Ethyl's Quality Improvement Process (EQIP), begun in the mid-1980s, called for "commonalty" among the different purchasing facilities. He said that many existing procedures from that effort translated to the ISO 9002 registration initiative. Many procedures required only "putting them into the proper format and making sure they were implemented," Tieken observed.

Yet Tieken said that the ISO 9002 registration spotlighted the benefits of the international standard. Another benefit of Ethyl's established EQIP program was employee familiarity with team concepts used in the registration effort.

Tieken is proud that the documentation work for the ISO 9000 registration did not require hiring additional employees. "You need people who actually do the work to write the manuals, because they know how the work is done," he said. Only contract typing and binding help were needed during final preparation for the registrar site visit.

## Registration Responsibility

As general manager, Tieken was ultimately responsible for all registration efforts. Mike Haywood, manager of materials management's systems and economics, was assigned to spearhead and coordinate the effort. Part of his job involved checking to make sure diagrams and manuals from various sites were uniform. About 75 percent of Haywood's time was devoted to ISO activities throughout the process. Logistics director Jim Crane and manager of quality assurance Laddie McVicker led the logistics effort.

## Consultants, Internal Audits, and Pre-Assessment

Consultants from Excel Partnership, Inc., spent a week at the facility to see if "things tied together right," according to Tieken.

In mid-June, an internal audit team from Ethyl's Sauget facility visited Baton Rouge. The team said the materials management registration effort was 80 percent complete. Tieken declared that the thorough self-examination gave him confidence that materials management was well on its way to registration.

The Belgian certifying organization, AIB-Vincotte, had registered other Ethyl facilities both in Belgium and the United States. The materials management group also chose Vincotte as its registrar. After Vincotte's July 1 - 2, 1991, pre-assessment audit, the Excel consultants returned to double-check the quality manuals and documentation.

Vincotte performed a week-long final audit in late September 1991. Ethyl's materials management group was recommended for ISO 9002 certification and received its certificate on November 6, 1991. Vincotte officials said they believe Ethyl's materials management organization is the first registered as a separate department.

## Benefits of ISO Registration

Tieken said one of the most important benefits of registration is a standard procedure for supplier noncompliance. Before registration, a noncomplying supplier could face several different procedures from Ethyl facilities. Now, all Ethyl facilities have a uniform system to track and close out noncompliances. Ethyl also has a set of current supplier/buyer specifications and a "request-for-improvement" procedure. The system allows internal personnel to request changes that must receive a response.

Registration has also added more professionalism and a common direction to scattered programs, said Tieken. "Certification inspires confidence in our customers," added Ethyl senior economic analyst Bernard Maristany.

Finally, ISO has allowed Ethyl to integrate various quality programs into a unified whole and to achieve the sought-after goal of commonalty among sites.

## ISO 9000 Part of Continuous Improvement

Even though Tieken does "not view ISO as an ongoing process" other than making sure the procedures are followed, Ethyl's quality efforts and striving for continuous improvement do not end with ISO 9000 registration. Currently, 20 teams in materials management are responsible for specific activities and are investigating process improvements such as paperless purchasing.

---

# Ethyl System Overcame Barriers to Multi-Site Registration

Don Tieken says the Ethyl Materials Management Group had four advantages when the ISO 9002 registration process began:

## 1. Reorganized Purchasing Department

Ethyl's purchasing department, reorganized in 1987, now uses lead buyers for common items. For example, a buyer specializing in a particular item working from Ethyl's Pasadena facility buys that item for the entire company. One lead buyer purchases any specific raw material. In addition, purchasing departments at all the various facilities report through central purchasing in Baton Rouge.

## 2. Strategic Supplier Program

Ethyl's strategic supplier program, developed in 1986 with 14 of its most important suppliers, was already in place when the ISO 9002 registration process began. Tieken said the program also includes a formal quality survey that has resulted in a close working relationship between Ethyl and its suppliers.

## 3. Ethyl's Quality Improvement Process (EQIP)

This internal system, initiated in the mid-1980s, gave Ethyl a formal plan for continuous improvement. Tieken said the procedural standardization effort among all purchasing and logistics sites grew out of the EQIP effort. ISO 9000 registration affirmed a need for commonalty and also provided the impetus to achieve it. EQIP also uses a team approach to problem-solving used by Ethyl during the registration effort.

## 4. Familiarity with ISO Registration

Tieken's work group aided ISO 9000 registration efforts at various Ethyl manufacturing sites and contributed documentation during the audit and registration process. The familiarity provided by this process gave materials management a head start on its own registration effort.

# THE FOXBORO COMPANY

*Foxboro, MA* - The Foxboro Company's director of corporate business quality, John Rabbitt, says his company's successful certification to the ISO 9001 standard began as a search for a recognized world-class quality management standard to complement its own Total Quality Management (TQM) program.

"Our initial decision [to adopt the ISO 9000 standard] was to use it," Rabbitt said, "not go for it." The scope of ISO use in the company's manufacturing sector quickly grew to encompass the entire Foxboro organization. Rabbitt pointed out that Foxboro, a manufacturer of industrial process-control equipment and systems, had been actively pursuing a quality and customer satisfaction improvement program since the late 1980s in response to a pattern of decreased productivity, increasing waste and customer dissatisfaction.

## Quality Improvement Process

Foxboro adopted Florida Power and Light Company's Quality Improvement Process (QIP) as part of a TQM program and began to address quality at Foxboro.

QIP is built around five elements: customer satisfaction, management by fact, structured problemsolving, respect for people, and continual improvement.

The structured, team approach to quality improvement includes a QIP storyboard that allows each quality team to display written and graphic details of its quality successes.

Rabbitt said this tcam approach has the additional benefit of preparing team leaders for future management positions. He said 1,000 of the company's 5,000 employees have already completed training for this program.

The QIP program allowed Foxboro to begin a culture change to the concept of continual improvement throughout the company. At the same time, Foxboro restructured and simplified its facilities, sometimes slicing a single facility into five separate plants. It was the Manufacturing Quality Council that first suggested the need for an ISO 9000 quality system "strategic alignment" tool for Foxboro.

## The Certification Process

By the time Foxboro decided to seek ISO certification, its quality system's overhaul made the job "not such a big jump for us." Rabbitt tempered his confidence by pointing out that the auditing team from DnV Industries, Inc., a Norwegian registering agent, was very thorough. "We had three DnV auditors here for three weeks," Rabbitt recalled with a smile. "It was the longest three weeks of our lives."

Despite the difficulties of certification, Rabbitt praised DnV's fairness during the auditing process. He said the Norwegian certification scheme allows for minor changes in a company's quality system, even after the auditing team arrives and begins its audit.

Rabbitt said DnV found a missing document describing a procedure establishing a specification for a weld. DnV not only allowed Foxboro to write the specification, but assisted the department in doing so. The three ISO 9001-registered plants in Foxboro achieved an average of 97 points. A company must score at least 75 points to pass.

Since achieving its ISO 9000 Certificate of Conformity from DnV, Rabbitt has been in great demand to share his knowledge of the ISO certification process. He has written several articles on the subject and regularly accepts speaking engagements.

Asked if he has any advice for companies considering ISO 9000 certification, Rabbitt offered two short admonitions: "If you think you can hide anything from the auditors, forget it, and make sure you can do what you say in the company quality policy statement."

## Foxboro's Formula: Certification Success

The Foxboro Company's 14-point plan for ISO 9000 certification calls for company-wide commitment to the certification process to start with management. It suggests setting up mechanisms to train employees, identify problems, and take corrective action. The following plan is a sample nine-month program.

### 1. Obtain Senior Management Commitment

Success in achieving ISO 9000 certification begins at the top. It is the senior managers who will approve the resources and assign responsibly to achieve the ISO certification. Without their commitment, the process would take longer and be more painful than it has to be.

### 2. Establish an ISO Steering Council

The Steering Council is the focal point for all ISO 9000-related matters. Its principal energies should be aimed at establishing a comprehensive ISO development program and ensuring that it is adequately funded.

## 3. Educate the Council on ISO 9000

Understanding ISO 9000 and its elements is critical to the success of any certification road map. The members of the Council should include senior members from every area of the company's organization. It is vital to establish a body of experts operating by consensus. Rabbitt suggested using standard questionnaires developed by certifying agencies to assess organizational readiness for ISO certification.

Rabbitt noted that the Council should be a respected body within the company. Its members will be required to answer questions and suggest strategies to correct quality weaknesses.

## 4. Evaluate and Select a Registrar

Rabbitt said the most important qualification for a registrar is its worldwide recognition status, especially within the EC. He suggested a company consider how a registrar scores its audits. The British Standards Institution (BSi) uses a pass/fail system, while DnV (the Norwegians) uses a point system. In addition, Rabbitt suggested finding a registrar that understands the business it is auditing as well as becoming acquainted with the lead auditor, if possible.

Finally, negotiate both a primary audit date and a follow-up date. Registrars are booked months in advance. If the possibility of failure is not considered, a company could wait months for a return engagement from the auditing team.

## 5. Define Quality Responsibility

The ISO Steering Council should delegate quality responsibility throughout the company organization. Rabbitt pointed out that this responsibility does not have to be full time, but the organization must demonstrate that all those involved in quality have taken proactive steps. This participation must also be documented.

## 6. Establish Procedure Structure

Rabbitt suggested developing three layers of procedures to restructure an existing system. The corporate level may be vague and focused on supported quality standards, including an approach to ISO 9000 requirements and a definition of corporate assurance responsibilities.

At the plant level, documentation is still fairly vague but may define how ISO 9000 is consistent with corporate quality assurance. The detailed procedure documentation is most evident in departmental operations. Foxboro re-tabbed or referenced every procedure to ISO 9000. The company made 9,000 changes — most of them by employees who actually performed the tasks.

Spreading the work among employees took care of both workload and alignment issues. The people who performed the task also documented they were doing the task. This documentation supported the training records requirement for ISO.

## 7. Define Documentation Standards

The primary goal here was to make one document serve as many purposes as possible and to standardize all other documents for efficiency.

## 8. Educate All Employees on ISO 9000

Registering a company to ISO 9000 standards required full participation from all employees. Education reduced resistance to change and prepares employees to meet the auditors with confidence. Training, along with an in-house ISO 9000 newsletter, portrayed ISO 9000 registration as a competitive tool.

## 9. Develop Operational ISO Management Teams

Vehicles were developed to disseminate information about documentation and standards that will motivate employees to execute elements of the quality program. The ISO management team should consist of senior members from each company organization and include supervision from each group. Any questions should be directed to the ISO Council for resolution. Rabbitt said this process should be managed weekly and that compliance should be monitored.

## 1O. Procedure Upgrades

This process examined the existing procedures and developed corrective actions for deficient areas. It began when management outlined the process flow and identified the procedure documents and required records.

## 11. Establish Corrective-Action Tracking

In-plant audit teams should be developed to discover areas of noncompliance. The findings can be documented with a quality corrective-action request. This team approach provides confidence for the ISO registration and tracks how quickly problems are remedied. Rabbitt said this system uncovered 417 noncompliant procedures at Foxboro before the DnV auditors arrived.

## 12. Train Internal Audit Teams

Members from different parts of the organization, once trained in the requirements of ISO 9000, can act as a mini-audit team when joined by a certified lead auditor. These internal auditors can also assist ISO 9000 auditors during the actual audit.

## 13. Use Corporate Audit Teams to Verify Compliance

The corporate audit team sweeps behind the plant mini-audit teams to verify standards compliance. The ISO standard requires a formal review of the organization and its compliance to procedures. ISO auditors often ask to review past audits. The ISO auditors look for any open findings or recurring problems. Rabbitt said the auditors from DnV discovered a few open findings at Foxboro.

## 14. Registration Audit

The certification process takes from one to three weeks to complete. Set aside a designated space for the auditors. Include copies of all the documents needed for the audit. The Steering council members should escort and assist the auditors, meet daily during the audit to review the previous day's results, and implement corrective action plans.

Finally, it is important to promote an open, friendly atmosphere. According to Rabbit, the auditors want companies to succeed since both the reputation of the company and the auditor are at stake.

# LUTRON ELECTRONIC COMPANY

*Coopersburg, PA* - The success of Lutron Electronic Company, Inc.'s ISO 9001 registration audit is testimony to the flexibility of both the international quality management standard and the management team directing the nine-month effort.

Lutron is an international lighting control manufacturing company with a solid reputation for quality products and service. Yet the company uses no specific quality management program such as Total Quality Management (TQM). Instead, the company has developed its own quality system that has a continuous improvement philosophy as its root.

Quality assurance manager Dennis Capewell and technical services manager Richard Wagner said that the company's unique approach to quality management did not hinder the registration effort or minimize the overall benefit of ISO 9000 series standard registration.

## Benefits of Registration

"Quality has always been part of our culture," Capewell said. "We saw the ISO 9000 [series standard] as a mechanism for continuous improvement and as a means to formalize that process."

Both Capewell and Wagner said the benefits of achieving ISO 9001 registration go beyond the practical pursuit of enabling the company to compete on a level playing field in Europe. Customers in the United Kingdom are beginning to make inquiries about Lutron's ISO 9000 series standard registration status.

Wagner said the process both surprised and delighted him. He was surprised to find that few written procedures were being followed consistently in the plant. On the other hand, Wagner was "pleasantly surprised" by the amount of existing, detailed procedure documentation, which provided direction and organization for the registration effort.

## Beginning the Process

Lutron's journey to ISO 9001 registration began with a three-day ISO 9000 seminar in November 1990. By December, Wagner, Capewell, and senior QA specialist Dennis Anthony had gone through existing documents and a formal internal audit had been completed by the manufacturing manager. Eventually, Anthony devoted nearly all his time to the registration effort. All other members of the lead team added the registration effort to existing responsibilities.

A consultant was hired to perform an informal audit and to educate corporate headquarters managers about the registration process. Before the consultant left, a preliminary organization of the manual was completed and an implementation plan devised.

Underwriters Laboratories (UL), the registrar chosen to perform the final registration, arrived in February to perform a pre-assessment audit. Wagner said Lutron worked toward the pre-assessment as if it were the final registration audit. Although UL is prevented from making any specific suggestions, he said, general discussions offered by UL about "paper trails" needed to meet ISO 9000 series standard requirements were helpful.

After the UL auditors left, Capewell, Wagner and Anthony spent the next five months implementing an overall registration strategy that included weekly meetings, drawing up action plans, and tracking each department's progress. Wagner said strategy stressed departmental "ownership" of the quality and procedure manuals. A single UL auditor visited Lutron in June to assess progress in key areas. An August final assessment date was set.

## Aggressive Time Frame

Capewell said that the resident quality system at Lutron helped the registration effort. He was challenged by both the process of registration and the company's desire to retain a flexible approach to managing its employees and its quality system.

The principal challenge for Lutron was to shift the culture to follow written procedure and to avoid erecting barriers to communications. Specific implementation plans evolved as the process moved along. Milestones such as pre-assessment and manual audits were charted and specific action items issued. Lutron's lack of formal communication protocols allowed for open dialogue during the process, Capewell said.

"We had to be careful not to turn ourselves into a bureaucracy," Wagner said. "That's not how Lutron became a successful company. I think the biggest challenge of the process was not to build walls [with procedures] or have people look at [ISO 9000 compliance] as a cookbook for success."

## Payback for Registration

Capewell said the benefits of ISO 9001 registration are just beginning to be realized. He said engineering efficiency and new product cycle time has improved. The quality assurance process has improved using ISO 9001 registration lessons. "We see it as a major strategy for continuous improvement," Capewell said, "since it allows us to change more rapidly and be specific about those changes."

## ISO 9001 Registration
## Closing the Loops at Brookdale Plant

Evidence of ISO 9001 registration at Lutron Electronics Company, Inc.'s Brookdale, PA facility is not hard to find.

A complete set of quality manuals is neatly shelved on the top of a row of file cabinets under a bright blue sign marked "Documentation." Although Rich Wagner, manager of technical services, said the sign refers to the file cabinets and not specifically to the quality manuals, he noted that manuals contain procedures from plant operation to product rejection procedures.

The Brookdale plant is a manufacturing facility, but it also serves engineering and custom product production needs. ISO 9001 registration affected everything from instrument calibration to the procedure used to ferret out defective stock.

Wagner pointed to a "for reference only" sticker attached to the front of a voltage meter. He said that the meter is used only to make sure that a product is working. Other meters are used for more precise measurements. He said the UL auditor suggested that the sticker be displayed to avoid any confusion.

Meters used for precise product testing also have stickers that include calibration dates and reference numbers. If an out-of-calibration meter is found, tracking down affected shipped products is possible. Revision levels are also included on all documents.

Before ISO 9001 registration, it was difficult to track raw material problems and make corrective actions. Now department quality managers can communicate that information back to the vendors and purchasers. Establishing this paperwork trail was both cost-effective and will ultimately result in significant savings, Wagner said.

## Stock Sweeps

Defective vendor products are difficult to purge from any manufacturing facility warehouse. But ISO 9001 registration has allowed Lutron to tackle the problem.

According to Brookdale quality control supervisor, Donald Ponge, problems with defective parts traditionally resulted in a "stock sweep" of all Lutron facilities. A memo sent out would purge defective products from warehouse facility shelves, but the sweep did not track enroute defective parts sent before a sweep was ordered. The system also did not track how defective parts were purged.

A procedure is now in place that tracks not only the defective part, but what action was taken to ensure that the problem does not happen again.

Wagner said most of the quality system used by Lutron before registration was effective, but ISO 9001 registration provided a paper trail that is ultimately more comfortable for a company with a worldwide quality record to maintain.

# MEMC ELECTRONIC MATERIALS

*Moore, SC*—The ISO 9002 registration of MEMC Electronic Materials, Inc., is clear evidence that quality and customer satisfaction are determining factors in today's interrelated, high-technology, global economy.

The MEMC site, once a US-owned textile knitting operation, now manufactures silicon wafers used for computer chips and semiconductor devices, and sells its product around the world. MEMC was registered to ISO 9002 by Quality Systems Registrars in October 1991 and will undergo its second certification audit in Fall 1992.

Located near Spartanburg/Greenville in northwest South Carolina, the German-owned MEMC considered ISO registration about two years ago after receiving inquiries from some of its European customers, according to quality improvement manager H. L. "Dunk" Hale, Jr. US customers such as Honeywell also began mentioning ISO 9000 registration as part of supplier certification programs. MEMC's German parent company, Huls, also had ISO 9000 registration on its agenda, said Hale.

Based on these preliminary inquiries, MEMC began to understand that ISO 9000 "was coming along on the horizon pretty strong," said Hale. "Our European customers did not say point blank, 'You have to do this,' but it was pointed out that [ISO 9000] was something we should be thinking about."

## ISO 9000 Equals Common Sense, Satisfies Customers

After studying the requirements of ISO 9000, Hale said MEMC realized "that there is nothing in ISO but good common sense, and things we wanted to do anyway." He said MEMC also realized that many of the required procedures had already been written.

Plant manager Dan Hargett said MEMC identified ISO registration as a means to "ensure the consistency that our customer base was looking for, as well as to signify to ourselves and to our customers that we had an evaluation system" to check that consistency. Since the common sense principles of an ISO-based system had been in practice at MEMC for years, preparing for registration "was more evolutionary than revolutionary," said Hargett.

Proof of MEMC's ability to satisfy customers is showcased in a plant trophy case that contains customer quality awards from Mitsubishi, Motorola, NCR, and Honeywell, among others. The customer plaques are now joined by MEMC's ISO 9002 certificate.

## Industry Drives Innovation

Because it sells its silicon wafers to high-technology computer chip and semiconductor device manufacturers, MEMC is forced to stay on the leading edge of quality initiatives in order to satisfy a demanding customer base. "We are in a business that drives us," said Hargett. "Our customers are on the leading edge of what's new and different from a quality and technology perspective, so that tends to drive us a little faster and harder than it does other industries."

Hale agreed that a demanding customer base is critical to quality improvement. "That is always going to be your primary driving force: you have got to satisfy your customer," he said. "If your customer is not driving you, you are going to go along at your own speed."

## Support Groups Gain Most From ISO Audit

The demands of customers, including numerous customer audits, prepared MEMC for its ISO registration. "People always ask me, 'How did you prepare for ISO?'" said Hale. "I tell them we began preparing 12 years ago when the plant opened."

Preparing for the ISO audit was not a major undertaking. Work-force attitude change, as well as the required documentation necessary for ISO registration, had been accomplished *five to seven years ago,* Hale said. MEMC did not use any consultants for its registration effort, did not undergo a preliminary assessment, and passed its registration audit on the first try.

MEMC's manufacturing area was already very disciplined and had detailed procedures before ISO registration. The MEMC facility possess an impressive documentation center, with five seven-foot bookshelves filled with binders on how to run plant machinery. All of the documentation existed prior to the ISO effort. All procedures are revised yearly. Operators must pass both a written exam and a hands-on test to be certified to operate equipment, and every employee is re-certified each year.

"Most of the improvements or enhancements from ISO registration have come in the support groups, such as purchasing, accounting, or human resources," said Hale. The purchasing department, for example, had to write desk procedures for its activities, according to contract coordinator Becky Lewis.

One advantage of the ISO 9000 registration audit is that it emphasizes non-manufacturing departments as well as manufacturing, said purchasing manager Bob

Hambrick. He pointed out that before ISO 9000 registration, customer audits did not emphasize the support groups to document procedures, "whereas ISO 9000 emphasizes both manufacturing and non-manufacturing departments," said Hambrick.

Prior to ISO registration, purchasing followed plant procedures, but did not have departmental procedures. Purchasing now has departmental procedures and adds to them continuously. "When somebody from the plant comes to [purchasing] to ask a question that there is no guideline on, we now say, 'Let's do a procedure on that,'" said Lewis.

## Benefits

For a company with few written procedures, an ISO registration effort can be a difficult, time-consuming process. For MEMC, however, the process was relatively easy given the strides the company had made over the last decade and the rigor of its customer audits. Hale still sees the ISO registration effort as extremely beneficial.

A company "may think [ISO 9000 registration] is a lot of money and ask, 'What are we going to get for it?'" said Hale. "I'm convinced ISO 9000 registration is money well-spent because you know that you have got to stay sharp, and there is a real incentive to do that."

He also likened the visit of ISO auditors to a consulting visit. "Even though the registration audit is an evaluation, you still get some benefit of a consulting-type visit because you learn about your operation," he said. Between the South Carolina facility and a sister plant in Missouri, MEMC receives about 50 customer audits a year. "ISO certification may mean customers will not audit as often, or maybe not at all," said Hale. Just recently, a customer auditing MEMC spent his visit discussing future improvements and long-range plans; his curiosity about the present was satisfied by the ISO 9000 registration.

Hale's emphasis on customer satisfaction is also met with ISO registration. "ISO registration cannot help but build confidence with your customers," he said. Hale also sees ISO 9000 registration as a stepping stone to other quality programs such as the Malcolm Baldrige Award. MEMC applied for the Baldrige Award in 1991 and will do so again in 1993. Hale has been a Baldrige examiner for three consecutive years. "ISO certification is a great stepping stone to Baldrige," he said.

## Ripple Effect of Quality

Initially, MEMC received inquiries about ISO 9000 registration from its European customers. In the future, MEMC hopes to establish a system that will require its own suppliers to be ISO certified. Under such a system, supplier audits conducted by MEMC could then be performed in a manner similar to Baldrige audits. "We will have the best of both worlds," says Hale. "We will know the supplier has the fundamental systems in place because they are ISO-certified, then we could focus on performing a Baldrige-type audit and focus on management leadership, quality results, and customer satisfaction."

The ripple effects of ISO-based quality have already been put into motion thanks to MEMC's 9002 registration. Joe Dawson works with the incoming quality assurance group and is also on one of MEMC's supplier audit teams. These teams of trained employees work with and audit key suppliers. Undergoing an ISO 9000 registration "helps in auditing suppliers and shows you what to look for when auditing suppliers," Dawson said.

---

### MEMC, Formerly Owned By Monsanto, Now Has German Parent

MEMC Electronic Materials, Inc.'s Moore, SC facility is one of six MEMC facilities worldwide that are part of a German conglomerate, Huls, which is owned by another German company, VEBA. German and Japanese companies lead the silicon wafer industry, according to MEMC quality improvement manager H. L. "Dunk" Hale, Jr. Hale said there are no longer any major US-owned companies that manufacture silicon wafers for outside sale. Silicon wafers are the foundation for computer chips and semiconductor devices.

Other MEMC facilities are located in St. Peters, MO; Malaysia; Japan; and two in Italy. With the exception of the Italian plants, all of the MEMC facilities were once owned by Monsanto, which sold MEMC to Huls in 1989, according to Hale. MEMC's Missouri facility is also registered to ISO 9002 by Quality Systems Registrars. The two Italian sites have been registered by an Italian registrar, and the Malaysian facility underwent an ISO 9000 audit in late June 1992. MEMC employs 4,900 people worldwide, and approximately 1,000 work at the South Carolina facility.

# MONSANTO CHEMICAL COMPANY

*Sauget, IL* — Monsanto Chemical Company's W. G. Krummrich facility used a rigorous internal auditing schedule to prepare for ISO 9002 registration.

Thirty-two internal audits were performed in less than a year using ISO 9000 criteria. The company hired Bywater of the United Kingdom to perform in-house auditor training. Fourteen Krummrich employees are now auditors approved by the Institute for Quality Assurance (IQA).

The Krummrich facility, just across the Mississippi River from St. Louis, achieved ISO 9002 registration November 7, 1991, after a final audit by British Standards Institution (BSi). The registration was for the manufacture and distribution of Santoflex, ACL, and chlorobenzenes.

Krummrich is the first Monsanto Chemical Company facility in North America to be ISO 9002-registered; a facility in Canada recently received ISO 9001 registration and several European sites also have ISO 9002 registration.

Krummrich's pride in registration is evidenced by the advertisements developed to explain the ISO achievement to customers and by the lapel pins reading "W. G. Krummrich ISO 9000 Registered" that are given to plant visitors.

## Beginning the Process

When a pair of Europeans transferred to the St. Louis headquarters to head the Rubber and Process Chemicals division's quality and manufacturing departments, the Krummrich facility was urged to become registered as a model for other US facilities, according to Tom Kreinbrook, Krummrich's quality services leader.

In May 1990, plant manager Bill Boyle hired Kreinbrook, who had previous ISO 9000 experience, to implement a quality system and to lead the facility to ISO registration.

"Initially, our driving force was external (and) we thought we'd need to do this to compete in the European Economic Community," said Boyle, noting that Krummrich's chemical products are shipped all over the world. However, once the benefits of ISO were realized, the value of the system itself, and not the market implications of registration, became the driving force.

"We would have continued (implementing ISO) even if there were no registration or if the European Economic Community disintegrated," said Boyle. "It's great that it has some customer implications as well, but its value is in doing it and in getting very good at it, independent of whatever publicity you might get out of it," he said.

## Gaining Commitment

From May until early Autumn 1990, Kreinbrook met with every unit at the Krummrich facility to explain ISO and "to gain commitments to be involved in the registration effort." The facility employs 600 workers.

The Krummrich site is composed of six distinct manufacturing units. Kreinbrook met with all six in October 1990 to set up timelines and delegate responsibility for ISO registration. Development of the procedures that describe the quality system also began.

In late 1990, "we were not making significant progress toward registration," said Kreinbrook. ISO coordinators were designated and made the "focal point for the implementation of a quality system."

An ISO coordinator was named in all six manufacturing units as well as in each of the service units (purchasing, distribution, laboratory, and the maintenance group). Nearly 80 percent of these coordinators' time was spent on ISO activities leading up to registration.

In addition, each of the units had a full-time trainer who spent approximately 50 percent of his or her time on ISO activities before registration. The trainers are operators whose responsibilities include training employees and updating operating instructions in the respective units.

## Quality Systems Launched

On January 15, 1991, Krummrich's quality system was implemented through the launching of the quality system manual. The system included ISO criteria but was much more inclusive, Kreinbrook said. "For the next three months, all units began training people in the manual procedures and looking at the procedures to see if that is really the way the work was performed."

After a three-month grace period, internal audits began in March 1991. Along with the extremely close scrutiny of the system came the inevitable revisions to the procedures.

Scharringhausen has made the updating of statistical process control (SPC) charts a job definition. "It's no longer just someone's hobby," he said. Implementing ISO also has led to a better appreciation and understanding of others' jobs within the same unit, he said.

# NORTHERN TELECOM

*Research Triangle, NC*—The five-member team assigned in January 1991 to plan and manage registration to ISO 9001 for Northern Telecom's Public Networks division faced two daunting challenges—simultaneously registering four facilities and getting the cooperation of 8,000 employees. If that wasn't enough, the main facility in Research Triangle Park followed a largely untraveled road, since few other telecommunications companies in the United States have completed the registration process.

Despite these intimidating facts, team member and senior assessment engineer Greg Lilly said his initial reaction to the standard was one of confidence. "However, I didn't think the scope was going to be as large as it turned out to be," he said. It was only with the commitment of senior management and management at all levels, from all sites, that this could be accomplished. The team found top-down support and commitment through all phases of preparation and assessment.

Now that the North Carolina facility has received its ISO 9001 registration, it joins a company-wide effort that will include 75 ISO 9000 series registrations around the world by the end of 1993. Northern Telecom currently has registered 36 facilities at various worldwide locations. According to Paul Grooms, public networks facility team leader, networks sites have also received ISO 9002 registration.

## A Complex Process

The complexity of satisfying ISO 9001 registration requirements within a 660,000-square-foot office and manufacturing facility is obvious. Many different printed circuit packs are manufactured or supported by 4,000 employees located at this one site. One type of circuit pack produced is called a line card, with production of these topping more than seven million annually. These are just one part of many units produced at the site to create the primary product—a digital switching system. The line cards convert telephone voices (analog signal) into digital electronic information.

Thousands of these cards move swiftly along conveyor tracks through automated stations that insert electronic chips and solder them into place. Highly trained employees inspect and test each card. The cards eventually end up in one of the company's refrigerator-size digital switching units, either the DMS-10 or DMS-100. The DMS-10 can handle 10,000 individual telephone lines, and the DMS-100 can handle up to 100,000 individual telephone lines.

The completed units, after undergoing a series of reliability and customer requirement tests, are shipped to telecommunications customers throughout the world. In
the United States major customers of the public networks division include all seven
regional Bell holding companies, major independent telephone companies and
interexchange carriers, and the US government.

## Little Fundamental Change

Despite the complexity of the operation, Grooms and the other four members of the
implementation team agreed that registration forced little change in the existing
system. However, registration did increase the participation level of groups involved
in the quality process, such as test engineering, new product introduction and
production planning.

Jeff Harpe, senior manager of new products, said that "while ISO 9001 didn't
significantly change the process for introducing new products, it did require that the
process be better defined and documented." Registration also forced a closer look at
the quality aspects of marketing and support activities.

Some activities, such as customer support, had already carefully considered their
mission. For example, Northern Telecom customers visiting the public networks
facility have been able to use a computer monitor to locate quickly the exact location
of an order in the system test area. In addition, a quality assessment facility is used to
simulate exact customer requirements to make sure that particular installation
configurations will perform as expected.

## Internal Quality

Quality inside the plant includes a world-class calibration lab that oversees 6,000
pieces of equipment and maintains on-time calibration schedules for four facilities.
An in-plant inspection facility for incoming products can be used on-site to test for
defects using state-of-the-art chemical and physical analysis and electron micros-
copy. All employees are carefully monitored for electrostatic discharge (ESD)
caused by normal friction of shoes on concrete floors. ESD can cause serious
problems in sensitive electronic equipment.

Recent changes in robotic technology allow for a 50-percent increase in manufacturing floor space, and have also led to increased quality by allowing for immediate
correction of problems in the production line.

## Certified Vendor Program

In addition to these internal quality criteria, Northern Telecom's Certified Vendor Program ensures strict compliance to existing quality standards. Grooms pointed to a number of blank nameplates on a board listing certified vendors, indicating that a supplier had been taken off the approved list. He said registration to the ISO 9000 series is requested of all Northern Telecom suppliers and will be required in the future.

While the ISO 9001 registration process did broaden quality system participation in non-manufacturing groups such as marketing, an increasing sense of quality process ownership by all Northern Telecom employees was a major benefit of the process. A large banner hangs in the manufacturing facility, with the slogan: Northern Telecom, Raleigh area, is 9001 Registered. Keep the *Excellence!* Momentum."

## Additional Benefits

Quality system engineer Charles Fodell, who handled much of the communications job for the registration effort, noted that the ISO 9001 audit encouraged a higher level of performance from all public networks facility employees. He said a natural tendency exists for organizations to prepare for most audits as a one-time event, after which standards become relaxed.

"With ISO 9000, things were not going back to the way they were after the audit," Fodell said. "People started seeing things improve that they always knew needed addressing. The top-down drive to get things done and changes that made sense to employees resulted in a new enthusiasm [from employees]."

Grooms agreed, noting that before ISO 9001 registration, it was a quality function to prepare for an audit and take care of all the details. "Production was doing production, and we were responsible for quality," he said. "What ISO 9001 registration did was make it a team effort since the job was so large and the impact on the total system so great. It took everyone working together." Senior assessment engineer Lilly added that ISO 9000 registration transformed the team from "quality cop to a quality resource."

# Five-Person Team Directed
# ISO 9001 Registration Effort During Year-and-a-Half Journey

The process resulting in the successful ISO 9001 registration audit April 28-30, 1992, of Northern Telecom's public networks division began in January 1991.

According to Paul Grooms, leader of the registration effort, the five-member team was the "focal point" for registration activity. All training, communications and awareness activities, registrar interface and standard interpretation advice emanated from the team.

Charles Fodell was largely responsible for public liaison work, logistics and, along with senior assessment engineer Al Crowle, responsible for the overall awareness training throughout the four facilities covered by the registration.

Fodell was asked to participate in the company's training sessions for New Product Introduction (NPI). All NPI personnel were trained to the elements, requirements and significant changes to their process that the standards would produce. Senior assessment engineers Gill Preddy and Greg Lilly, along with Crowle, acted primarily as element experts charged with interpreting the standards and performing the internal systems audits.

## Three-Tiered Approach

The team developed a three-tiered approach to managing the complex documentation required by the facility. The team developed a top-level document that gives an overview of quality requirements in a particular area. Details described by the top-level document are found beginning with the second-tier documents. The more detailed work instruction documents are found only in the third-level documentation.

According to Grooms, the three-level approach headed off a potential documentation bottleneck. "With a multi-facility registration, we had a test engineering function in three other facilities," Grooms pointed out," and all three did different types of tests. If we tried to address all those procedures in the top level, then it would be a very cumbersome document. Any changes in the third-tier would invalidate the top-tier quality manual."

Creating a second-tier level that drove the third level of documentation solved this potential problem. The quality manual remains valid throughout any revisions so that it is ready for top-level audits.

## Solving Complex Problems

The initial knowledge for solving these complex problems came from related quality assessment training such as the American Society for Quality Control's (ASQC) Certified Quality Auditor (CQA) courses. The team members also observed auditor training classes lead by Excel Partnership, Ltd., a Connecticut-based consulting and training organization. The three-day class was attended not only by quality department employees, but by representatives from other key areas affected by registration effort.

Communicating the importance of ISO 9001 registration to four sites and 8,000 employees was accomplished by an internal newsletter, orientation seminars, banners and an information hotline. Some of the functions led individual informal training seminars. Crowle and Fodell made more than 75 presentations to various Northern Telecom departments. Spot awards were given to individuals who made outstanding contributions to the registration effort.

Leon Britt, operations project manager assigned to work on preparing for ISO, said, "All sites were involved with administering and communicating standards to the production workers."

## Daunting Audit Job

The actual job of auditing all four facilities covered by the ISO 9001 registration fell to Lilly, Preddy and Crowle. The auditing process identified action items that were maintained in action registers by Crowle. The registers included implementation dates and closure dates for the appropriate facilities.

When the chosen registrar, Underwriters Laboratory (UL), arrived for the audit, the team accompanied the auditors as the official Northern Telecom representatives.

The initial UL audit of the public networks facility was performed October 20-November 2, 1991. A re-assessment took place April 28-30, 1992. According to Grooms, the initial five-day, four-auditor visit was "a learning experience." Much of the return visit by two UL auditors involved direct responses to corrective actions and visits to specific sites to ensure compliance.

## UL Choice

While the long process was difficult, team member Crowle said he was pleased with Northern Telecom's performance. "I feel we were tested by the best," he said. "They did a very thorough audit that taught us a lot of useful audit techniques."

Grooms noted that the choice of UL as registrar had both a practical and business sense side. UL has a North Carolina office near the Northern Telecom facility. In addition, Grooms said that co-registration with British Standards Institution Quality Assurance (BSi QA) was a desirable option.

Official plans for pursuing other quality initiatives beyond the ISO 9000 series have not been formalized, Grooms said. However, he did agree that ISO 9001 registration is a "good stepping stone in that direction."

## Future Plans

In the meantime, the company plans to continue developing its own internal program known as *Excellence!* and to pursue the quality goals stated in *Vision 2000* (see box).

Grooms noted that the activity currently is sustaining a high level of attention to quality. The facility is establishing self-audit programs for all functions as a practical and functional matter. "Obviously, five people can't sustain an organization as large as Northern Telecom," Grooms said. "It takes everyone working together."

---

### Company Profile: Northern Telecom

Northern Telecom, Inc., is the second largest telecommunications manufacturer in the United States and a subsidiary of Northern Telecom, Ltd., the third largest in the world. The corporation employs about 57,000 people worldwide and had 1991 revenues of $8.18 billion.

Northern Telecom is headquartered in Nashville, TN, and operates 55 manufacturing plants around the world. The 660,000-square-foot facility in Research Triangle Park, NC, opened in 1980. The facility, which employs 4,000 people, manufactures the DMS family of digital switching systems for the public telephone network.

Northern Telecom owns or leases more than 2.2 million square feet of office, manufacturing and warehouse space in the Raleigh-Durham area. This includes the Technical Education Center which offers almost 200 courses to train more than 18,000 telephone company employees a year. The Center also provides technical and professional development courses for Northern Telecom employees.

---

# Global Business Strategy

Northern Telecom's global business strategy was defined in 1988 as *Vision 2000*. The goals of the company are expressed in six core values: excellence, teamwork, customers, commitment, innovation and people.

NT says that companies often use the word *global* to mean they do business in several countries. But at NT, *global* means designing products capable of operating in world markets.

NT's Meridian 1, for example, is a system that will be used to connect the national telephone networks of England and France. The telephone switching system will be wired through the soon-to-be-completed Anglo-French Eurotunnel. It uses software that is totally compatible with the different networks.

NT also is looking ahead to the next advance in cellular phone technology. Soon, people will be able to carry lightweight telephones in their pockets or briefcases wherever they go. At home, the phones will ring simultaneously with wired phones so we can answer whichever one is most convenient. NT plans to play a fundamental role in developing and marketing this new telecommunications service.

# RICE AIRCRAFT

*Hauppage, NY* - A New York-based aircraft fastener distributor became the first US aircraft product supplier to achieve ISO 9002 certification as a registered stockist.

According to Paula Rice, Rice Aircraft, Inc. decided to seek ISO registration after a major European aerospace company advised the company early last year that worldwide supplier bases would be drastically reduced as a direct result of European Community ISO 9000 quality system conformance requirements.

Rice said the small Hauppauge, NY company decided to change the "paradigm" for US aircraft fastener suppliers. Before ISO 9002 certification, Rice Aircraft's quality program had been product-driven. The company inspection system conformed to DoD's (Department of Defense) MIL-I- 45208 inspection system requirements. No distribution companies were required to conform to DoD's stricter quality system standard, MIL-Q-9858.

DoD is considering the possible replacement of its MIL-Q-9858 and MIL-I-45028A standards with the ISO 9000 series standard for all new contracts. Formal recognition of the standard was issued in February 1991. In addition to expected formal quality system registration demands from DoD and the EC, Rice Aircraft president Bruce Rice emphasized that his company's decision to seek ISO 9000 registration was driven by an even more important factor.

## Registration "Market-Driven"

"Our registration was market-driven," Rice wrote in a recent statement about the registration effort. "We had to verify and demonstrate adherence to the strict international requirements our EC and Pacific Rim customers demand."

Rice Aircraft's management of over 75,000 different parts manufactured by dozens of suppliers may seem an easily manageable task on the surface. However, aircraft stockists must meet rigorous documentation and service requirements. Each order processed by the company must be carefully inspected to ensure that it meets customer specifications. All Rice inspectors have been trained by the American Society for Quality Control's certified technician program.

Fasteners shipped by the company must meet the specific requirements of each customer and require absolute labeling accuracy. Manufacturer certifications and test reports are included with many customer shipments. Finally, orders must be transported quickly and accurately to meet "just-in-time" requirements used by the aircraft industry.

ISO 9002 registration transcends the historical definition of a product stockist, Rice noted. ISO conformance ensures maintenance of process controls throughout the quality system, including internal auditing (to ISO 10011 guidelines), quality cost data management, document control, and review of corrective actions. ISO 9000 series requirements for training and statistical process control, in regard to returned goods procedures and analysis, and sales and purchasing operations, are clearly traceable aspects of the system.

## Benefits of Registration

Rice said the definitive customer acceptance of ISO 9002 registration, along with the company's commitment to an ongoing program for quality improvement, are already paying benefits.

Bruce Rice said that during a recent second-party audit by a major airline carrier, the auditors were surprised. "As soon as they saw our documentation system," he said, "the auditors said they felt a comfort level far above what they had seen at other stocking distributors." ISO 9002 registration is also a newly acquired competitive tool. He noted that major customers have begun to include a question on their quality surveys for ISO 9000 registration among the listings for applicable quality systems such as MIL-Q-9858 and MIL-I-45208.

ISO 9002 registration may pay big benefits in Pacific Rim countries. The company's Singapore representative said the registration will allow the company to compete for business in the large airline overhaul shops expected to proliferate in the area.

The ISO 9000 series standard is also an international language. At a recent air show in Canada, aircraft manufacturer representatives from China and Indonesia noticed Rice Aircraft's prominently-displayed ISO 9002 certificate. Rice said the level of credibility offered to prospective customers by ISO 9000 series certification may lead to new business relationships that would not have been possible before registration.

## Rice Aircraft Registration "Home-Grown"

Rice Aircraft, Inc., decided to use a "home-grown" approach when it began preparing for its ISO 9002 registered stockist certificate status, according to Paula Rice. After deciding that the company should pursue ISO 9000 series certification to compete in a shrinking international marketplace, Rice Aircraft signed up top management for ISO 9000 training. Rice took lead assessor training and soon after, the company's quality team began developing a time line for ISO 9002 certification.

## Nine Months to Accreditation

In November 1990, Bruce Rice and the Quality Improvement Process (QIP) team decided to initiate the ISO 9002 implementation program within their own corporate "culture." The QIP team spent several months assessing and documenting every company process in a set of 30 procedures that, after corrective action implementation, fulfilled all the requirements of the ISO 9002 standard and MIL-Q-9858.

In March 1991, the company contracted with The Victoria Group, a management consulting firm, to perform a pre-assessment audit against ISO 9002. The consultants also audited Rice against the British Standards Institution (BSi) *Specification for Application of BS 5750 Part 2/ISO 9002/EN29002* for stockist of assessed capability, System Requirements, Level A: Quality Ensured Material with source lot traceability.

## Audit Reports

The consulting auditors spent two days at Rice Aircraft, generating seven "audit reports" that documented discrepancies in processes and procedures. After corrective action was taken, Rice contacted Lloyd's Register Quality Assurance (LRQA) to perform the formal assessment. LRQA offers an auditing scheme program for "registered stockists."

LRQA auditors initially conducted a complete documentation review and returned two weeks later to review ISO 9002 implementation. Nonconformances to the standard cited on the first visit were corrected before the auditor returned. Rice Aircraft received its Certificate of Approval from Lloyd's (National Accreditation Council for Certification Bodies) and the Dutch Council for Certification (RvC) on July 31, 1991. Lloyd's reciprocal arrangement with the RvC allows for the additional certification if requested by the customer.

Rice said her company's next quality hurdle is the New York State Excelsior Award, which is based upon the Malcolm Baldrige Award. She said a team from Rice plans to visit other companies to provide benchmarks for the company's effort to achieve Baldrige status.

# TAYLOR-WHARTON CYLINDERS

*Harrisburg, PA* - The manufacture of high-pressure cylinders is a hands-on operation. Square billets of highly refined steel are plucked by a masked worker one-by-one from a huge furnace, before an army of skilled workers shapes, cuts, inspects, cleans, x-rays, tests, paints, and loads the finished products onto trucks.

Taylor-Wharton Cylinders vice-president and general manager Clark Hall believes that ISO 9000 series registration is also a hands-on operation. He said the decision to seek ISO 9001 registration was driven not only by pressing European Community product and quality system compliance requirements, but by the committed involvement required of every employee successfully to complete a quality system registration effort.

## Management Involvement

"I feel very strongly that [the drive for the ISO 9000 effort] must come from management, " Hall said. Delegating and directing the effort is not enough. Management must "participate in and lead" the effort. He said too many "fundamental business decisions are made during the registration process that should not be delegated to the quality assurance department."

Hall admits that he was the "chief cheerleader" for Taylor-Wharton's registration drive. But his enthusiasm for the ISO 9000 series' common sense standard had a practical side. He said he liked the procedure and documentation discipline offered by ISO 9000 series registration. In addition, high-pressure vessels, like medical products and several other product categories, will require quality system assurance to enter the EC market. "It was obvious that ISO 9000 [quality system] certification was coming and we wanted to do it sooner rather than later," Hall said.

Currently, a "substantial" portion of Taylor-Wharton's production is exported to Europe. Taylor-Wharton also has a related cryogenic cylinder manufacturer located in Husum, Germany. The Germany connection made the choice of TUV Rheinland of North America, Inc., the logical registrar for the facility. TUV Rheinland also verifies conformance to various German product codes at the Harrisburg site, along with other US government and third-party inspectors verifying domestic product code enforcement such as Department of Transportation codes.

## CEN Regulations

The European Committee for Standardization (CEN) is working on cylinder standards that may reduce inspection requirements by relying on ISO 9000 series quality system registration to ensure product standard conformance. However, the ISO 9001 certificate Taylor-Wharton received from TUV is driven by increasing customer demand for registration, and by a desire to change basic company management practices.

"What is attractive about ISO 9001 are requirements for documentation and self-auditing that ensure you do what you say you're doing," Hall said. The quality system base offered by ISO 9000 series registration will assist Taylor-Wharton's stated goal of creating a world-class manufacturer that manages quality using ISO 9000 and Total Quality Management (TQM) principles.

## Procedures and Documentation

At Taylor-Wharton, the ISO 9000 series registration effort revealed that the company's written procedures and process documentation were not adequate. "Before [registration] virtually everything was verbally communicated and much of the training [of hourly workers] was done by other hourly workers," Hall said. All training is now performed by supervisors who use a controlled, centralized document.

The transition from verbal to formal documented procedures was difficult for some supervisors, but most were able to meet the challenge. Hall said the ISO 9000 review committee was "pleasantly surprised" with the procedures and other documentation created by the supervisors.

Reaction from the plant workforce was also positive as audit teams from different departments learned how co-workers contributed to the overall production and quality control process. He noted that any resistance to the process came from supervisors who had to make radical changes to a system that had not previously required extensive documentation.

## World Class Company

The effort required to achieve ISO 9001 registration will significantly pay off as the company moves toward its world-class aspirations. The inspection-driven quality assurance department is using more process controls, despite the large number of required inspections for high-pressure vessels.

The bottom-line result of Taylor-Wharton's quality improvement efforts will be increased profitability, Hall pointed out. "We have put in considerable time figuring out the cost of quality and the consequences of not doing it right the first time. We have a good idea what those costs are. No one in the organization needs to be convinced of that."

# Taylor-Wharton Registration
# A Fast-Track Effort

Taylor-Wharton Cylinder's ISO 9000 registration effort began "in earnest" in mid-August 1991. The background work and planning began earlier. "I am not sure that I would recommend it [a fast-track registration drive]," Hall said. "It was an intense couple of months." The company received its ISO 9000 certificate from German ISO 9000 series registrar TUV Rheinland of North America, Inc., in December 1991.

During the months before Taylor-Wharton's ISO 9000 series full-court-press registration effort, a review committee coordinated task identification and duty assignments that created a policy and quality manual as well as manuals for procedures and control documents. The process also created an extremely long "to-do" list for procedure documentation.

Hall chaired the review committee along with quality assurance director Rick Close, plant superintendent Jack Muth, engineering director Ben Keller, and manager of product technology Rick Grande.

## "To-Do" List

The procedures "to-do" list was broken down into assignments. Two guide procedures were written to give managers and supervisors a model to create their own procedure documentation for every item on the assignment list.

All the procedures were submitted to Rick Grande, who served as editor for the review committee. After all members of the review committee were satisfied that the procedures matched the job described, these procedures became part of the official procedure manual. Policy and control documents were created using the same methodology.

Hall said regular Friday management staff meetings were used to keep the process on track and to provide information about the registration process. Some managers used monthly meetings with the workforce as a platform to explain registration requirements. "It was almost a constant training and communications process," Hall said.

## Auditing

After the preparatory procedure and documentation work was accomplished, auditing teams examined the entire company. In October 1991, two employees took an ISO 9000 auditing training course from Excel Partnership, Ltd. An internal auditing program was written. Over the months leading up to registration, five three-member teams made sure that the new quality policies implemented remained in effect. The auditing effort allowed employees from diverse divisions of the company to audit each other. "It made everyone learn about the entire company's operations," Hall said.

The internal auditing process was such a success that about 85 percent of the nonconformances found by TUV auditors reviewing submitted completed manuals were matched by Taylor-Wharton auditors.

When Hall felt the registration effort was nearly complete, he called TUV in for a pre-assessment. He said that a pre-assessment audit any earlier or at the beginning of the process would not have been an effective use of the company's or auditor's time. "In the beginning we were just too far away."

The TUV auditor spent two days interviewing managers and reviewing the process. Two meetings were held with key managers. The first, at the beginning of the process, brought more information about the registration process. The second meeting, after the audit was complete, pointed out nonconformances found.

Two TUV Rheinland representatives, one from Germany and one from the Connecticut office, spent one week at the Taylor-Wharton facility. The company received the recommendation of the auditors for ISO 9001 registration on Friday, December 13, 1991.

# ABOUT THE CONTRIBUTORS

The following contributors were cited in the interpretive articles in this handbook:

**Dennis R. Arter** is a Senior Member of ASQC and is active in the new Quality Audit Division. His book, Quality Audits for Improved Performance, was published by Quality Press in 1989. Arter teaches two courses for the ASQC Professional and Technical Development series: Quality Audits for Improved Performance, and Auditing to the ISO 9000 Standards.

**Robert W. Belfit** is President and Chairman of Omni Tech International, Ltd., quality systems consultants. He was actively involved for twenty years at Dow Chemical in the design and implementation of Dow's global quality systems. Dr. Belfit developed and leads OTI's ISO 9000 seminars. He is an ASQC Certified Quality Auditor and an IQA Provisional Assessor.

**Clyde Brewer** is Vice-President of the first RAB-accredited registrar, Quality Systems Registrars, Inc. He is a Registered Professional Quality Engineer and holds a Masters Degree in Quality Systems from the University of Dallas. During his 40-year career, Brewer has participated in the development and implementation of several quality system certification programs, including the US military's MIL-Q-9858 and the UK's BS-5750.

**Robert D. Bowen** is President of r. bowen international, inc. He has spent more than 18 years as a quality professional with the DuPont Corporation. He is certified by the ASQC as a Quality Engineer and Quality Auditor and sits on the Electronics Industry Association (EIA) Committee for Quality and Reliability Engineering.

**Garnett Davis** is Operations Supervisor for the Quality System Certification department of Det Norske Veritas Industry, Inc. (DnV). He is responsible for all activities related to the auditing of DnV clients, from scheduling of audits to the assignment of audit teams. Garnett is also a certified DnV Lead Auditor, and has led audits for clients in a myriad of industries.

**Ian Durand** is President of Service Process Consulting, Inc., of Edison, New Jersey. He was a major contributor to the drafting effort of ISO 9004-Part 2 and was the lead US delegate to the ISO working group responsible for publishing the ISO 9004-Part 2: Guidelines for Services. Durand continues to be active in ISO TC 176 and is involved in the updating and revision of the basic ISO 9000 series of standards. He was a senior examiner in 1990 for the Baldrige Award. He teaches *Using the ISO 9000/ANSI/ASQC Q90 Series to Design and Implement a Quality Management System* for the American Society for Quality Control (ASQC).

**Terry Heaps** is Project Administrator, QA Services for Vincotte USA, Inc., a Houston-based ISO 9000 series quality systems auditing company. Vincotte USA is a subsidiary of AIB-Vincotte, the leading certification body of Belgium.

**David L. Johnson** is Audit Manager, AT&T Quality Registrar.

**Joseph Klock** is Manager, ISO Registrations at AT&T. Mr. Klock is an ASQC member and certified quality engineer.

**Charles McRobert** is President of Quality Practitioners, Inc., which provides training and consulting in the application of the ISO 9000 series. McRobert has successfully developed and implemented ISO 9000 systems and helped companies secure ISO 9000 registration. He is an accredited auditor in the United States and Canada, with auditing experience in both countries.

**David Middleton** is Vice-President of Excel Partnership, Inc., an international training and consulting organization with offices in the UK and Connecticut.

**Joseph Tiratto,** Professional Engineer (PE), is an international consultant on quality systems, an Institute of Quality Assurance (IQA) Lead Assessor (auditor) and a European Engineer (EUR ING). Tiratto is a member of the Registrar Accreditation Board (RAB), US Technical Advisory Groups (TAG) to ISO/TC 176 and several other international and national standards groups. He also directed the development of a registrar quality system that would meet both RAB and Dutch Council for Certification (RvC) requirements.

**The Victoria Group** is a management consulting company in the quality field. Established in the UK in 1989, The Victoria Group offers public programs, in-house training and private consulting on all aspects of the ISO 9000 series of standards and Lead Auditor training. The principals in the Group include **Roderick Goult, Graham Hill and Steve Nicholas.**

# Appendix A

# STANDARDS AND DIRECTIVES

## ISO 9000 STANDARDS

To order the ISO 9000 standards and other quality systems standards, send a letter including the request and a check to:

> **ANSI**, Attention: Customer Service
> 11 West 42nd Street, New York, NY 10036
> Tel: (212) 642-4900; Fax: (212) 302-1286
> (Some orders require a 7% handling charge.)

**ISO 9000 Compendium**
Includes the entire ISO 9000 (1987) series, 10011 and 10012 series standards, 8402 vocabulary standards, draft standards, guideline documents and *Vision 2000, A Strategy for International Standards Implementation in the Quality Arena during the 1990's*. 224 pages. $135.

**ISO 9000 (1987):** *Quality Management and Quality Assurance Standards—Guidelines for Selection and Use.* ANSI version ANSI/ASQC Q90 (1987). $25.

**ISO 9001 (1987):** *Quality Systems - Model for Quality Assurance in Design/Development, Production, Installation and Servicing.* ANSI version ANSI/ASQC Q91 (1987). $28.

**ISO 9002 (1987):** *Quality systems - Model for quality assurance in production and installation.* ANSI version ANSI/ASQC Q92 (1987). $25.

**ISO 9003 (1987):** *Quality Systems - Model for Quality Assurance in Final Inspection and Test.* ANSI version ANSI/ASQC Q93 (1987). $21.

**ISO 9004 (1987):** *Quality Management and Quality System Elements—Guidelines.* ANSI version ANSI/ASQC Q94 (1987). $40.

**ISO 9000-3 (1991):** *Quality Management and Quality Assurance Standards—Part 3: Guidelines for the Application of ISO 9001 to the Development, Supply, and Maintenance of Software.* $40.

**ISO 9004-2 (1991):** *Quality Management and Quality System Elements—Part 2: Guidelines for Service.* $43.

The **ANSI/ASQC Q90-94 (1987)** Series on Quality Management and Quality Assurance Standards (Item T30) is sold as a set for approximately $45 for members and approximately $53 for non-members by:

**American Society for Quality Control**
611 East Wisconsin Avenue, Post Office Box 3005
Milwaukee, WI 53201
Tel: (414) 272-8575 or (800) 248-1946

Or, order from the ANSI address noted on previous page.

# EUROPEAN COMMUNITY DIRECTIVES

Demonstrating conformity with a directive or with a European standard is not a straightforward process, mainly because the European product standards and certification system is not fully in place. Despite the uncertainties, it is a good idea to develop a strategy for learning about standards and directives that affect your products and how to comply with them.

A good place to start is to obtain, read, and understand A Global Approach to Certification and Testing (COM (89)209), the policy statement of the European Commission referred to in Chapter 8 of this handbook. (Available from ANSI). This useful document will help you understand the specific conformity assessment sections in particular directives.

In its report, ANSI Global Standardization News Volume 2, ANSI provides strategy and tactical recommendations for complying with all EC requirements. Key questions to consider and steps to follow in the strategy include the following:

● First, is your product regulated or unregulated, based on EC requirements?

- If it is regulated, is there an EC directive that will affect your products? If so, obtain the directive and analyze it.

- How many directives apply?

  Contact your industry's trade association to determine EC 92 activities or contact the US Department of Commerce, Office of European Community Affairs, for lists and status reports on EC directives.

- Does the scope of the directive include your product?

- What are the essential requirements invoked by the directives?

- What are the required methods for demonstrating conformity? Review the conformity assessment section of the directive. This is usually section 8.

- What is the effective date? What grandfathered provisions have been made for products on the market at the time of implementation?

- If the directive is final, has the EC Commission published any lists of related standards? If not, determine whether the Commission has mandated the preparation of any European standards.

- For final directives, determine how member states have implemented the directive and what organizations have been named as notified bodies.

- If the product is regulated in the United States, consult ANSI, your trade association, the US Department of Commerce, Office of European Community Affairs, the National Institute of Standards and Technology*, or the applicable regulatory agency in the United States to determine if there are any official agreements completed or in process which would permit you to comply with the European requirements as a by-product of complying with the applicable regulations.

- If the product is not regulated in the United States, consult the same sources mentioned above and any applicable private sector testing organization(s) in the United States to determine whether there are any private-sector agreements between testing and certification bodies and their counterparts in Europe, such that certificates from the private body could be used to demonstrate conformity with the European requirements.

(*Addresses and phone numbers of these organizations are listed after the following tables.)

## Selected EC New Approach Directives

| | Implementation Date | Transition Period |
|---|---|---|

**Adopted Directives**

| | | |
|---|---|---|
| Toys | 1/1/90 | None |
| Simple Pressure Vessels | 7/1/90 | 7/1/92 |
| Construction Products | 6/27/90 | Indefinite |
| Electromagnetic Compatibility | 1/1/92 | 12/31/95 |
| Gas Appliances | 1/1/92 | 12/31/95 |
| Personal Protective Equipment | 7/1/92 | 12/31/92 |
| Machinery | 12/31/92 | 12/31/94 |
| Non-Automatic Weighing Instruments | 1/1/93 | 1/1/2003 |
| Active Implantable Medical Devices | 1/1/93 | 12/31/94 |
| Type Approval of Telecommunications Terminal Equipment | 11/6/92 | None |

**Proposed Directives**

| | | |
|---|---|---|
| Medical Devices | 7/1/94 | 6/30/97 |
| Elevators | 1/1/95 | 12/31/97 |
| Equipment for Use in Explosive Atmospheres | 7/1/93 | 12/31/2002 |

**Planned Directives**

In-vitro Diagnostics
Flammability of Furniture
Pressure Equipment
Measuring and Testing Instruments
Recreational Craft
Cable Ways
Amusement Park and Fairground Equipment
Playground Equipment (includes sports equipment)
Used Machinery
Fasteners

*Table A-1: Selected EC new-approach directives.*

# EC Product Directives

## Referencing ISO 9000 (EN 29000) Standards As a Component of the Product Certification Process

ISO 9000 (EN 29000) Reference

**Adopted Directives**

Construction Products ...................................................29002 or 29003
Gas Appliances ..............................................................29002
Personal Protective Equipment ......................................29002 or 29003
Non-Automatic Weighing Instruments ..........................29002
Active Implantable Medical Devices .............................29001 or 29002
Telecommunications Terminal Equipment ....................29001 or 29002

**Proposed Directives**

Medical Devices ...........................................................29001 or 29002
Elevators .......................................................................29001 or 29002
Equipment for Use in Potentially Explosive
Atmospheres (mines, surface extractions) .....................29001 or 29002

**Planned Directives**

Flammability of Furniture .............................................29002
Pressure Equipment ......................................................29001 or 29002
Measuring and Testing Instruments ...............................29001, 29002 or 29003
Recreational Craft .........................................................29001 or 29002
Cable Ways Equipment ..................................................29001
Amusement Park and Fairground Equipment .................29003
Fasteners .......................................................................29002

*Table A-2: EC product directives referencing ISO 9000 (EN 29000) standards as components of the product certification process.*

## EC Legal Requirements for
## Industrial Equipment and Consumer Goods

| Directive | Citation Number | Official Journal | Date of OJ | Current Status | Date of Implem. |
|---|---|---|---|---|---|
| **General** Extension of information procedures on standards and technical rules | 83/189 | L 100 | 4/26/83 | Adopted | |
| (Amendment to Directive 83/189, L 80) | 88/182 | L 81 | 3/26/88 | Adopted | 1/1/89 |
| Green Paper on European Standardization Action for a faster technological integration in Europe (L 247) | (91) 521 | | 11/27/91 | Proposal | N/A |
| **Appliances** Appliances burning gaseous fuels (L 223) | 90/396 (88)786 (88)459 | L 196 C 42 C 260 | 7/7/90 2/21/89 10/13/89 | Adopted Common Position Amendment | 1/1/89 |
| **Civil Aviation** Council regulation on technical requirements in civil aviation | 3922/91 | L 373 | 12/31/91 | Adopted | 1/1/92 |
| **Construction Products** (L 140) | 89/106 | L 40 | 2/11/89 | Adopted | 6/28/91 |

*(continued on next page)*

*Table A-3: EC legal requirements for industrial equipment and consumer goods.*

# EC Legal Requirements for
## Industrial Equipment and Consumer Goods *(continued)*

| Directive | Citation Number | Official Journal | Date of OJ | Current Status | Date of Implem. |
|---|---|---|---|---|---|
| **Electrical Equipment** | | | | | |
| Electrical equipment for use in potentially explosive atmospheres/certain types of protection - standards and marking (amends 79/196) Certificates of conformity (L 147) | 84/47 | L 31 | 2/2/84 | Adopted | 1/1/85 |
| | 88/571 | L 311 | 11/10/88 | Adopted | 12/31/89 (see also L 382,88/665) |
| | 90/487 | L 270 | 10/2/90 | Amendment | |
| | 82/490 | L 218 | 7/27/82 | Recommendation | |
| Low Voltage: electrical appliances: standards (L 185) | 73/23 | L 77 | 3/26/73 | Adopted | 8/75 |
| Commission communication on notified bodies, marks and standards | 88/C168/02 | C 168 | 6/27/88 | Communication | |
| **Electromagnetic compatibility** | | | | | |
| Radio Interference (L 127) (Electromagnetic compatibility) | 89/336 | L 139 | 5/23/89 | Adopted | 7/1/88 |
| Reference Standards | 92/C44/10 | C 44 | 2/19/92 | Communication | |
| | 92/C90 | C 90 | 4/10/92 | Communication | |
| Amendment - Transition Period | | L 126 | 5/12/92 | Adopted | 10/28/92 |
| **Instruments** | | | | | |
| Non-automatic weighing instruments (L 213) | 90/384 | L 189 | 7/20/90 | Adopted | 7/1/92 |

## EC Legal Requirements for
## Industrial Equipment and Consumer Goods *(continued)*

| Directive | Citation Number | Official Journal | Date of OJ | Current Status | Date of Implem. |
|---|---|---|---|---|---|
| Council Directive on Measuring Instruments and methods of metrological control (L 315) | 71/316 | L 202 | 9/6/71 | Adopted | 3/26/73 |
| | 83/575 | L 332 | 11/28/83 | Amendment | 1/1/85 |
| | 87/355 | L 192 | 7/11/87 | Amendment | 12/31/87 |
| | 87/354 | L 192 | 7/11/87 | Amendment | 12/31/87 |
| | 72/427 | L 291 | 12/28/92 | Amendment | 1/1/73 |
| | 88/665 | L 382 | 12/31/88 | Amendment | Immed. |
| **Lifts** Standards applied to electrically operated lifts (amends 84/329/EEC) (L 226) | 90/486 | L 270 | 10/2/90 | Adopted | |
| Proposal for a Council Directive on safety requirements for lifting appliances for persons | COM(92)35 | C 62 | | 3/11/92 | Proposal |
| **Medical Devices** Active Implantable Medical Devices (L 212) | 90/385 | L 189 | 7/20/90 | Adopted | 7/1/92 |
| Proposal for a Council Directive concerning medical devices (C 328) | (91) 287 | C 237 | 9/12/91 | Proposal | 12/31/93 |
| **Product Liability** Directive on liability of defective products (L 110) | 85/374 | L 210 | 8/7/85 | Adopted | 7/1/88 |
| **Safety** Household Appliances: airborne noise (L 50) | 86/594 | L 344 | 12/6/86 | Adopted | 12/4/89 |

*(continued on next page)*

## EC Legal Requirements for
## Industrial Equipment and Consumer Goods *(continued)*

| Directive | Citation Number | Official Journal | Date of OJ | Current Status | Date of Implem. |
|---|---|---|---|---|---|
| (Noise Standards) | 90/C28/20 | C 28 | 2/7/90 | Amendment | |
| Lawnmower noise | 84/538 | L 300 | 11/19/84 | Adopted | |
| (L 79) | 88/180 | L 81 | 3/27/88 | Adopted | 7/1/91 |
| Safety of Toys (including chemical properties and electrical toys) | 88/378 | L 187 | 7/16/88 | Adopted | 6/30/89 |
| | (88)201 | C 155 | 6/23/89 | | |
| Reference Standards | | C 154 | 6/23/90 | | |
| List of Notified Bodies | 90/162/14 | C 162 | 7/3/91 | Communication | |
| (L 85) | 90/278/03 | C 278 | 11/6/90 | Communication | |
| | 90/320/03 | C 320 | 12/20/90 | Communication | |
| | 90/32/06 | C 32 | 2/7/91 | Communication | |
| | 90/68/03 | C 68 | 3/16/91 | Communication | |
| | 91/155 | L 76 | 3/22/91 | Extension | 6/18/91 |
| | 91/307/03 | L 321 | 11/21/90 | Corrigendum | |
| | 91/279/04 | C 307 | 11/27/91 | Communication | |
| | | C 279 | 10/26/91 | Communication | |
| Machine Safety (L 128) | 89/392 | L 183 | 6/29/89 | Adopted | 12/31/92 |
| Amendment to include Mobile Machinery | 91/368 | L 198 | 7/22/91 | Amendment | 1/1/93 |
| Amendment - lifting/ loading | COM(91) 547 | C 25 | 2/1/92 | Proposal | 7/1/94 |

*(continued on next page)*

## EC Legal Requirements for
## Industrial Equipment and Consumer Goods *(continued)*

| Directive | Citation Number | Official Journal | Date of OJ | Current Status | Date of Implem. |
|---|---|---|---|---|---|
| Minimum safety and health for work equipment used by workers at the workplace (second directive under 89/391/EEC) (L 187) | 89/655 | L 393 L 59 | 12/30/89 | Adopted Corrigendum | 12/31/92 |
| Minimum safety and health for personal protective equipment in the workplace (third directive under 89/391/EEC) (L 188a) | 89/656 | L 393 L 59 | 12/30/89 | Adopted Corrigendum | 12/31/92 |
| Commission communication for implementing Directive on safety aspects of personal protective equipment (L 188b) | 89/328/02 | C 328 | 12/30/89 | Commun. | 12/31/92 |
| Council Directive on laws relating to personal protective equipment | 89/686 | L 399 | 12/30/89 | Adopted | 12/1/91 |
| Reference standards - respiratory protective devices (L 181) | | C 44 | 2/19/92 | Commun. | 12/1/91 |
| Minimum safety and health on visual display units (Visual Display Units - CRT) (L 220) | 90/270 | L 156 | 6/21/90 | Adopted | 12/31/92 |
| Approximation of laws concerning general product safety (C 181) | (89) 162 (90) 259 | C 193 C 156 | 7/31/89 6/27/90 | Proposal Proposal | |

*(continued on next page)*

## EC Legal Requirements for
## Industrial Equipment and Consumer Goods *(continued)*

| Directive | Citation Number | Official Journal | Date of OJ | Current Status | Date of Implem. |
|---|---|---|---|---|---|
| Proposal for a Council Directive on safety requirements for equipment for use in potentially explosive atmospheres | COM(91) 516 | C 46 | 2/20/92 | Proposal | 7/1/93 |
| Proposal for a Council Directive on safety of recreational craft | COM(92) 141 | C 123 | 5/15/92 | Proposal | |
| **Simple Pressure Vessels** (L28) | 87/404 | L 220 | 8/8/87 | Adopted | 7/1/90 |
| Amendment-Transition period | 90/488 | L 270 | 10/2/90 | Adopted | 7/1/92 |
| Reference Standards | 92/C104 | C 104 | 4/24/92 | Communication | |
| **Telecommunications terminal equipment** Directive on the initial stage of the mutual recognition of type approval for telecommunications terminal equipment (L 96) | 86/361 | L 217 | 8/5/86 | Adopted | 7/24/87 |
| Approximation of member state laws concerning telecommunications terminal equipment, including mutual recognition of conformity (L 280) | 91/263 | L 128 | 5/23/91 | Adopted | 11/6/92 |

---

### **Informal Draft EC Commission Documents**

1.  Council directive on furniture flammability safety requirements

2.  Essential requirements for safety in pressure equipment

3.  Interpretation of standards for construction products: Eurocodes

4.  European standards for procurement

5.  Directive on safety requirements for used machinery

6.  Safety requirements for cableway equipment

7.  Safety requirements for amusement park and fairground equipment

8.  Safety requirements for playground equipment (includes sports equipment)

9.  Safety requirements for in vitro diagnostics

10. Safety requirements for measuring instruments

11. Safety requirements for fasteners

---

## Where to Get EC Directives

### European Community Depository Libraries in the US

The EC has established a network of libraries in the United States to provide access to all official EC publications. All depositories automatically receive, free of charge, one copy of each EC institution's periodical and non-periodical publications. The collection is available to the public during the library's regular working hours, free of charge and without any conditions. Many of the libraries also offer interlibrary loan services. The libraries listed below are included in this network.

Of particular importance for businessmen and lawyers is the Official Journal of the European Communities (OJEC), the equivalent of the Federal Register. The "C" section of the OJEC includes proposed legislation and other important notices; the "L" section has the final texts of legislation. Annual indexes and the Directory of Community Legislation in Force provide subject and numeric reference access to legislation. Depository collections also contain the legislative proposals and communications of the Commission in their original, "COM" document form, as well as reports and debates of the European Parliament, opinions of the Economic and Social Committee, and decisions of the Court of Justice.

Subscriptions to the Official Journal are available in the US and Canada through UNIPUB, the North American representative of the EC for all publications. Daily publications of the Official Journal are sent to subscribers at the close of each week's business. The annual subscription costs for the L. and C. Series are $595.00 surface mail and $1465.00 airmail. The Journal is also available on microfiche.

**UNIPUB**
4611-F Assembly Drive
Lanham, MD 20706-4391
(800)274-4888 (USA)
(800)233-0504 (Canada)

**European Community Depository Libraries**

**American University**
Law Library
4400 Massachusetts Avenue, NW
Washington, DC 20016

**Arizona, University of**
International Documents
University Library
Tucson, AZ 85721

**Arkansas, University of**
Documents Department, UALR Library
33rd & University
Little Rock, AR 72204

**California, University of**
International Documents
Public Affairs Service
Research Library
Los Angeles, CA 90024

**California, University of**
Documents Department
General Library
Berkeley, CA 94720

**California, University of**
Documents Department
Central Library
La Jolla, CA 92093

**Chicago, University of**
Government Documents
Regenstein Library
1100 E. 57th Street
Chicago, IL 60637

**Colorado, University of**
Government Publications
University Library
Box 184
Boulder, CO 90309-0184

**Council on Foreign Relations, Library**
58 East 68th Street
New York, NY 10021

**Duke University**
Public Documents Department
University Library
Durham, NC 27706

**Emory University**
Law Library
School of Law
Atlanta, GA 30322

**Florida, University of**
Documents Department
Libraries West
Gainesville, FL 32611

**George Mason University**
Center for EC Studies
4001 N. Fairfax Drive
Suite 450
Arlington, VA 22203

**Georgia, University of**
Law Library
Law School
Athens, GA 30602

**Harvard University**
Law School Library
Langdell Hall-Law 431
Cambridge, MA 02138

**Hawaii, University of**
Government Documents
University Library
2550 The Mall
Honolulu, HI 96822

**Illinois Institute of Technology**
Law Library
77 South Wacker Drive
Chicago, IL 60606

**Illinois, University of**
Law Library
School of Law
504 E. Pennsylvania Avenue
Champaign, IL 61820

**Indiana University**
Government Documents
University Library
Bloomington, IN 47405

**Iowa, Universityh of**
Government Publications Library
Iowa City, IA 52242

**Kansas, University of**
Govt. Documents and Maps
University Library
6001 Malott Hall
Lawrence, KS 66045

**Kentucky, University of**
Government Publications
Margaret I. King Library
Lexington, KY 40506

**Library of Congress**
Serial Division
Madison Building
10 First Street, S E.
Washington, DC 20540

**Maine, University of**
Law Library
246 Deering Avenue
Portland, ME 04102

**Michigan State University**
Documents Department
University Library
East Lansing, MI 48824-1048

**Michigan, University of**
Serials Department
Law Library
Ann Arbor, Michigan 48109-1210

**Nebraska, University of**
Acquisition Division
University Libraries
Lincoln, NE 68588-0410

**New Mexico, University of**
Social Science Coll. Dev.
Zimmerman Library
Albuquerque, NM 87131

**New Orleans, University of**
Business Reference
Earl K. Long Library
New Orleans, LA 70148

**New York Public Library**
Research Library, Ecn & Pub Aff.
Grand Central Station
PO Box 2221
New York, NY 10017

**New York, State University of**
Government Publications, Library
1400 Washington Avenue
Albany, NY 12222

**New York, State University of**
Government Documents
Lockwood Library Building
Buffalo, NY 14260

**New York University**
Law Library
School of Law
40 Washington Square South
New York, NY 10012

**Northwestern University**
Government Publications
University Library
Evanston, IL 60201

**Notre Dame, University of**
Document Center
Memorial Library
Notre Dame, IN 46556

**Ohio State University**
Documents Division
University Library
1858 Neil Avenue Mall
Columbus, OH 43210

**Oklahoma, University of**
Government Documents
Bizzell Memorial Library
Room 440
401 West Brooks
Norman, OK 73019

**Oregon, University of**
Documents Section
University Library
Eugene, OR 97403

**Pennsylvania State University**
Documents Section
University Library
University Park, PA 16802

**Pennsylvania, University of**
Serials Department
Van Pelt Library
Philadelphia, PA 19104

**Pittsburgh, University of**
Gift and Exchange
Hillman Library G 72
Pittsburgh, PA 15260

**Princeton University**
Documents Division, Library
Princeton, NJ 08544

**Puerto Rico, University of** *
Law School Library
Rio Piedras PR 00931

**South Carolina, University of**
Documents/Microforms
Thomas Cooper Library
Columbia, SC 29208

**Southern California, University of**
International Documents
Von Kleinschmidt Library
Los Angeles, CA 90089

**Stanford University**
Central Western European Coll.
The Hoover Institution
Stanford, CA 94305

**Texas, University of**
Law Library
School of Law
727 East 26th Street
Austin, Texas 78705

**Utah, University of**
International Documents
Marriott Library
Salt Lake City, UT 84112

**Virginia, University of**
Government Documents
Alderman Library
Charlottesville, VA 22903

**Washington University**
John M. Olin Library
Campus Box 1061
1 Brookings Drive
St. Louis, MO 63130

**Washington, University of**
Government Publications
University Library FM-25
Seattle, WA 98195

**Wisconsin, University of**
Documents Department
Memorial Library
728 State Street
Madison, WI 53706

**Yale University**
Government Documents Center
Seeley G. Mudd Library
38 Mansfield
New Haven, CT 06520

*Established in 1990, may not be complete.*

# EC STANDARDS

To find out whether your product is covered by harmonized (EC-wide) standards, first call:

**Office of European Community Affairs**
**International Trade Administration**
Department of Commerce
Room H-3036
Washington, DC 20230
Tel: (202) 482-5276

Charles Ludolph, Director, Office of European Community Affairs
Mary Saunders, Director of Single Internal Market Information Services

The office will send the standard to you if it is in the EC office files. If the standard is in the "proposal and commentary stage," it will be necessary to examine *Information and Notices,* an almost daily publication of the Official Journal of the European Community. This publication can be found in any state EC full depository library or any partial depository library. The Official Journal can also be found in many law libraries. For the nearest location, call (202) 862-9500.

For information on various aspects of EC activities related to standardization, contact the Office of European Community Affairs at the Department of Commerce above or:

**National Center for Standards & Certification Information (NCSCI)**
TRF Building, Room A163
Gaithersburg, MD 20899
Tel: (301) 975-4040; Fax: (301) 926-1559

**Office of the US Trade Representative**
Technical Barriers to Trade
Winder Building, 600 17th St., NW, Room 513
Washington, DC 20506
Tel: (202) 395-3063

**European Community Information Service**
2100 M St., NW, Suite 707
Washington, DC 20037
Tel: (202) 862-9500

**European Community Information Service**
305 East 47th St.
3 Dag Hammarskjold Plaza
New York, NY 10017
Tel: (212) 371-3804

Other sources for EC standards and standardization information are listed below.

**United States and Canada**
**The American National Standards Institute (ANSI)**
11 West 42nd St., 13th Floor
New York, NY 10036
Tel: (212) 642-4900; Fax: (212) 302-1286.

Other ANSI offices:

**ANSI Brussels Office**
Avenue des Arts 50
BTE 5, 1040 Brussels, Belgium
Tel: 011 322 513 6892; Fax: 011 322 513 7928

**ANSI Washington Office**
655 15th St., NW, Suite 300
Washington, DC 20005
Tel: (202) 639-4090; Fax: (202) 347-6109

**American Society for Quality Control (ASQC)**
611 E. Wisconsin Ave.
Milwaukee, WI 53202-4606
Tel: (414) 272-8575 or (800) 248-1946

**Canadian Standards Association**
178 Rexdale Blvd.
Rexdale, ON M9W 1R3 Canada
Tel: (416) 747-4000; Fax: (416) 747-4149

**Compliance Engineering**
629 Massachusetts Ave.
Boxboro, MA 01719
Tel: (508) 264-4208

**Document Center**
1504 Industrial Way, Unit 9
Belmont, CA 94002
Tel: (415) 591-7600; Fax: (415) 591-7617

**Global Engineering**
1990 M St., NW, Suite 400
Washington, DC 20036
Tel: (202) 429-2860 or (800) 854-7179; Fax: (202) 331-0960

**Information Handling Services (IHS)**
PO Box 1154
15 Inverness Way East
Englewood, CO 80150
Tel: (303) 790-0600 or (800) 241-7824

**Intertek Technical Services**
9900 Main St., Suite 500
Fairfax, VA 22031
Tel: (703) 591-1320

**Standards Sales Group (SSG)**
9420 Reseda Blvd., Suite 800
Northridge, CA 91324
Tel: (818) 368-2786 or (800) 755-2780; Fax: (818) 360-3804

**European Community**
In Europe, the principal point of contact for the European Community is:

**Commission of the European Communities Directorate-General**
Information, Communication
Culture Rue de La Loi 200 B-1049
Brussels, Belgium
Tel: 235 11 11

**European Committee for Standardization (CEN),**
**European Committee for Electrotechnical Standardization (CENELEC),**
**European Organization for Testing and Certification (EOTC)**
2 Rue de Brederode, Boite No. 5
1000 Brussels, Belgium
Tel: 011 32 25 196811; Fax: 011 32 25 196819

**European Telecommunications Standards Institute (ETSI)**
C-O/CEPT
Telecommunication
CMSN
British Telecommunications International
BT 1-10
120 Holborn, London
E C1N, UK

**International Electrotechnical Commission (IEC)**
3 Rue de Varembe
Case Postale 131
CH-1211 Geneva 20, Switzerland
Tel: 011 41 22 7340150; Fax: 011 41 22 7333843

**International Organization for Standardization (ISO)**
Rue de Varembe 1
CH-1211 Geneva 20, Switzerland
Tel: 011 41 22 7490111; Fax: 011 41 22 7333430

**GATT**
Centre William Rappard
154 Rue de Lausanne
1211 Geneva 21, Switzerland

For further information on European standards, the National Institute of Standards and Technology has prepared a more extensive summary of the EC initiatives on standards and other related materials. These can be obtained by contacting:

**Department of Commerce**
**National Institute of Standards & Technology**
**National Center for Standards and Certification Information (NCSCI)**
TRF Bldg. Room A163
Gaithersburg, MD 20899
Tel: (301) 975-4040; Fax: (301) 926-1559

NCSCI provides assistance in obtaining current standards, regulations and certification information for the manufacture of products.

# ON-LINE DATABASE SERVICES

**Lexis/Nexis - Europe Library**
The Lexis/Nexis network offer the Europe Library, which includes the following items:

- European Community treaties
- Amendments to the treaties
- Secondary legislation (regulations, directives, decisions, etc.)
- Preparatory acts (proposals for legislation, decisions of the European Court of Justice)
- EC-related news from 30 different sources
- Financial information on European companies
- Analytical reports
- Summaries of EC-related information.

For information, contact your local Lexis/Nexis office or call (800) 346-9759, or (800) 543-6862 for customers in the legal community.

# EC HOTLINE

This hotline reports on draft standards of the European Committee on Standardization (CEN), the European Committee for Electrotechnical Standardization (CENELEC) and the European Telecommunications Standards Institute (ETSI). It also provides information on selected EC directives. The recorded message is updated weekly and gives the product, document number and closing date for comments. The hotline number:

Tel: (301) 921-4164 (Not toll free)

# GATT HOTLINE

This hotline provides current information, received from the GATT Secretariat in Geneva, Switzerland, on proposed foreign regulations which may significantly affect trade. The recorded message is updated weekly and gives the product, country, closing date for comments (if any) and Technical Barriers to Trade (TBT) notification number. The hotline number is:

Tel: (301) 975-4041 (Not toll-free)

# EC 1992 SINGLE MARKET INFORMATION

For information on the 1992 Single Market program, background information on the European Community, or assistance regarding specific opportunities or potential problems, contact the Office of European Community Affairs' Single Internal Market Information Service (202-482-5276).

In addition, Department of Commerce industry experts assigned to the 1992 Single Market program are indicated below. Write to the Department of Commerce, Washington, DC 20230:

**Aerospace,** Juliet Bender, Office of Aerospace, Room 2122, Tel: (202) 482-4222

**Autos,** Stuart Keitz, Office of Automotive Affairs, Room 4036, Tel: (202) 482-0669

**Chemicals, Construction Industry Products, and Basic Industries,** Mary Ann Smith, Office of Basic Industries, Room 4043, Tel: (202) 482-0614

**Construction Projects and Industrial Machinery,** Bob Tibeault, Office of Capital Goods and International Construction, Room 2001B, Tel: (202) 482-2474

**Consumer Goods,** Harry Bodansky. Office of Consumer Goods, Room 4317, Tel: (202) 482-5783

**Industrial Trade Staff,** Ted May, Room 3814, Tel: (202) 482-3703

**Information Technology, Instrumentation and Electronics,** Myles Denny-Brown, Office of Telecommunications, Room 1001A, Tel: (202) 482-4466

**Service Industries,** Fred Elliott, Office of Service Industries, Room 1124, Tel: (202) 482-1134

**Textiles and Apparel,** Office of Textiles, Apparel and Consumer Goods Industries, Room 3100, Tel: (202) 482-3737

**US & Foreign Commercial Service,** Room 3802, Tel: (202) 482-5777; District Office: (800) 343-4300, ext. 940

# ADDITIONAL US GOVERNMENT CONTACTS

Additional US government contacts for information on European Community matters include:

**Office of the US Trade Representative**
600 17th St., NW
Washington, DC 20506
Tel: (202) 395-3320/6120

**European Commission**
**Delegation of the European Communities**
2100 M St., NW
Washington, DC 20037
Tel: (202) 862-9500

**Department of Agriculture**
**Foreign Agricultural Service**
14th & Independence Ave., SW
Room 4647, South Building
Washington, DC 20250
Tel: (202) 720-8732

**Small Business Administration**
**Office of International Trade**
409 3rd St., SW, 6th Floor
Washington, DC 20416
Tel: (202) 205-6720 or (800) 827-5722

**Department of State**
**Office of European Community and Regional Affairs**
Room 6519
Washington, DC 20520
Tel: (202) 647-2395

**Department of State**
**Office of Commercial, Legislative, Public Affairs**
Room 6822
Washington, DC 20520
Tel: (202) 647-1942

**US Export-Import Bank**
811 Vermont Ave., NW, Room 1203
Washington, DC 20571
Tel: (202) 566-8990

For advice or information about any aspect of exporting to the EC, contact a local International Trade Administration (ITA) District Office or speak to the appropriate desk officer at the US Department of Commerce's International Trade Administration:

**Belgium, Luxembourg, Netherlands**
(202) 482-5401

**Denmark**
(202) 482-3254

**France**
(202) 482-6008

**Germany**
(202) 482-2434

**Greece, Portugal**
(202) 482-3944

**Ireland, Italy**
(202) 482-2177

**Spain**
(202) 482-4508

**United Kingdom**
(202) 482-3748

# Appendix B

# ISO 9000 REGISTRARS

This section contains profiles of registrars that offer third-party auditing services and registration to the ISO 9000 series standards. These registrars meet one of the following criteria:

● They are accredited to issue ISO 9000 certificates by a European accreditation entity and/or the Registrar Accreditation Board in the United States.

● They have an agreement such as a Memorandum of Understanding (MOU) with another registration organization to mutually recognize ISO 9000 certificates.

## ABS QUALITY EVALUATIONS, INC. (ABS QE)

**Overview**    Headquartered in Houston, American Bureau of Shipping Quality Evaluations (ABS QE) is a subsidiary of the American Bureau of Shipping. Founded in 1862, the American Bureau of Shipping is one of the world's leading ship classing societies, with more than 200 offices in 92 countries.

ABS diversified outside of the marine industry and has offered a wide variety of third party quality system assessment services since 1973. In 1990, ABS Quality Evaluations, Inc. was formed as a subsidiary of ABS to handle all third party assessment and certification to a wide range of new and existing quality system certification programs, including ISO 9000.

**Scope**    ABS QE is accredited to certify in many industries, including:

● Electrical equipment
● Engines and gears
● Industrial machinery
● Marine and offshore products
● Pressure vessels

- Ship management companies
- Structural and mechanical metal products

ABS continues to expand its scope to better serve customer needs in various industries.

**Accreditation**      ABS QE is accredited by both the Dutch Council for Certification, Raad voor de Certificatie (RvC), and the Registrar Accreditation Board (RAB) in the United States to provide the ISO 9000 certification. ABS QE's sister company in London, ABS QE Ltd., is seeking accreditation from the United Kingdom's National Accreditation Council for Certification Bodies (NACCB).

ABS QE ISO 9000 audits are led by Institute of Quality Assurance (IQA) registered lead assessors. To ensure consistency and credibility, audit team members are employed by ABS and have passed an IQA-approved lead auditor course.

**Address**      263 North Belt East
Houston, TX 77060

**Contact/Phone**   Patti Wigginton
Tel: (713) 873-9400; Fax: (713) 874-9564

# AFAQ — FRENCH ASSOCIATION
# FOR QUALITY ASSURANCE

**Note:**      *For more information on the French scheme for ISO 9000 registrations, see the American European Services (AES) entry.*

**Overview**      AFAQ was founded in 1988 in France to perform third party certification of quality management systems against the requirements of the ISO 9000/EN 29000 series of standards. Since 1988, more than 600 companies have been certified within the AFAQ scheme. AFAQ staff assessors, operating throughout the world, are selected according to the ISO 10011-2 qualification criteria for auditors. As a non-profit organization, AFAQ is interested only in maintaining the highest level of confidence in the market place.

**Scope**      The AFAQ scheme works in accordance with European standard EN 45012, *General criteria for certification bodies operating quality system certification.*

As required by EN 45012, the Board of Management of AFAQ is made up of representatives and organizations with a wide interest in certification but without any one interest predominating. The accredited scope of AFAQ's certification program covers almost every standard industrial classification. AFAQ is an EC Notified Body for a number of mandatory certifications.

**Accreditation**  AFAQ, AENOR (Spain), QMI (Canada), and SQS (Switzerland) recognize each other's evaluation of an organization's quality system for certification to the ISO 9000 series through a Memoranda of Understanding (MOU).

**Address**  Tour Septentrion Cedex 9
92018 Paris La Defense
France

**Contact/Phone**  Sylvie Rolland
Tel: (33) (1) 47 73 49 49; Fax: (33) (1) 47 73 49 99

# ASOCIACION ESPAÑOLA DE NORMALIZACION Y CERTIFICACION (AENOR)

**Overview**  AENOR has been offering quality system registration services since 1989, and has registered more than 90 businesses thus far.

**Scope**  AENOR is a third party registering body performing multi-sectorial activities.

**Accreditation**  AENOR complies with European Norm 45012 and has been a member of E-Q-NET network since 1990. AENOR has also been recognized as an accredited body for carrying out the tasks provided for in several European Directives.

**Address**  Fernandez de la Hoz, 52
28010 Madrid
Spain

**Contact/Phone**  Isabel Ramirez
Tel: 34 1 410 4851; Fax: 34 1 410 4976

# AMERICAN EUROPEAN SERVICES, INC. (AES)

**Note:**          *Although AES is not a registrar, this entry has been included so readers may better understand the French scheme of accreditation.*

**Overview**       The APAVE Group, established more than a century ago, and AES, Inc., its American subsidiary in Washington, DC, provide technical services to companies operating in all major industries.

Active in both the public and private sectors, APAVE serves more than 130,000 customers from offices in more than 100 locations in France and Europe, and from more than 35 other countries around the world. These services include:

- Quality assurance audits, vendor surveillance, and equipment inspection
- Certification to French codes for American manufacturers exporting to France (including electrical equipment, machinery, and pressure vessels)
- Assistance to US investors and builders in Europe in the area of environmental regulatory compliance and permitting
- Regulatory safety and building code compliance for companies building facilities in Europe

APAVE played a role in creating the French Quality Assurance Association (AFAQ), a European registrar. APAVE representatives hold positions on various AFAQ committees. AFAQ grants certification to companies that demonstrate compliance to the ISO 9000 series. It has certified 400 companies and has mutual recognition agreements with DQS (Germany), SQS (Switzerland), and QMI (Canada).

SEQUAL, a wholly owned subsidiary of APAVE, was formed in 1987 as a quality system assessor and assists companies in achieving AFAQ certification to ISO 9000. SEQUAL engineers conduct safety and quality related assessments for three types of certification: product, company, and personnel accreditation. SEQUAL provides the formal assessment to ISO 9000 criteria and processes the necessary documentation for final AFAQ approval and certification.

**Scope**         AFAQ grants certification to companies in the automobile, electronic, and chemical industries.

**Address**  1054 31st Street, NW, Suite 120
Washington, DC 20007

**Contact/Phone**  Eric Thibeau
Tel: (202) 337-3214; Fax: (202) 337-3709

# AMERICAN ASSOCIATION FOR LABORATORY ACCREDITATION (A2LA)

**Overview**  The American Association For Laboratory Accreditation (A2LA) is a non-profit scientific membership organization dedicated to the formal recognition of testing organizations which have achieved a demonstrated level of competence. Accreditation is available to all laboratories regardless of whether they are owned by private companies or government bodies. Quality system registration is available for suppliers of reference materials.

**Scope**  A2LA has offered laboratory accreditation services for virtually all types of tests since 1980 and has been offering quality system registration services to environmental reference materials suppliers since 1991. A2LA has provided service to more than 400 laboratories and five suppliers.

**Accreditation**  A2LA has four mutual recognition agreements: with Australia's NATA; Hong Kong's HOKLAS; New Zealand's TELARC; and with the Naval Sea Systems Command Naval Shipyard Laboratory Accreditation Program.
A2LA has also signed a Memorandum of Understanding with the EPA's Environmental Monitoring Systems Laboratory at Cincinnati (EMSL-Cincinnati) effective June 1991, which establishes a relationship between A2LA's Certification Program for A2LA Certified Reference Materials and EPA's Cooperative Research and Development Agreements (CRADA) for EPA Certified Reference Materials.

**Address**  656 Quince Orchard Road, #304
Gaithersburg, MD 20878-1409

**Contact/Phone**  Peter Unger
Tel: (301) 670-1377; Fax: (301) 869-1495

# A.G.A. QUALITY, A DIVISION OF A.G.A. LABORATORIES

**Overview**        A.G.A. Laboratories was founded in 1925 for the primary purpose of testing
gas appliances and related accessories. Product testing capabilities also
include electric and oil fired products. As the principal US approvals agency
for equipment used in the residential and commercial sector, A.G.A. engineers
have evaluated hundreds of production plans for appliances and conducted
thousands of in-plant inspections of US, European, Asian, and South American facilities. More than 500 manufacturers participate in the A.G.A. certification program prior to sale. More than 200 million appliances in the US and
abroad bear A.G.A.'s symbol of certification, a star seal.

To respond to the needs of manufacturers requiring independent auditing and
verification to ISO 9000 standards, A.G.A. Laboratories formed A.G.A.
QUALITY to conceive, develop, and market a quality system registration
program.

**Scope**           A.G.A. performs quality system registration in the fields of gas appliances and
related accessories. A.G.A. has registered and is currently auditing several
non-gas product manufacturers in the following areas:

- Aerospace
- Business
- Professional services
- Chemicals
- Other process areas
- Distribution
- Electrical
- Electromechanical products
- Mechanical products and processes
- Nuclear
- Printing
- Publishing
- Test laboratories

**Accreditation**   Over the past two years, A.G.A. has formed mutual recognition agreements
for quality system registration services with counterpart agencies in France,
Germany and The Netherlands. Similar agreements with other international
registration bodies are under negotiation. A.G.A. is pursuing accreditation
from the Registrar Accreditation Board in the US.

A.G.A. has participated in four US delegations that met with European Community officials to coordinate matters related to quality assurance programs.

A.G.A. personnel serve on the board of directors and other committees of the American National Standards Institute engaged in the development of a US strategy to respond to European Community initiatives in international standards development, product testing and quality assurance registration.

**Address**          8501 E. Pleasant Valley Road
                     Cleveland, OH 44131

**Contact/Phone**    Steve Gazy
                     Tel: (216) 524-4990; Fax: (216) 642-3463

# AT&T QUALITY REGISTRAR (AT&T QR)

**Overview**    AT&T Quality Registrar has registered quality systems using the ISO 9000 standards since June 1991. Before 1991, AT&T QR's auditors performed hundreds of second party audits for AT&T using ISO 9000 standards, ANSI Z1.15 standards, AT&T and Bell System Quality standards, and military standards.

AT&T QR has principal offices in New Jersey, Pennsylvania, California, Hong Kong, Singapore, Taipei, Tokyo, Ireland, and Brussels. Satellite offices are located in New York, Massachusetts, North Carolina, Georgia, Florida, Ohio, Illinois, Oklahoma, and Colorado.

**Scope**    AT&T registers companies in the following industries:

- Chemicals
- Communications equipment and systems
- Computer software
- Distributors of electrical and electronic products.
- Electrical equipment
- Electronics
- Fabricated Metal Products
- Industrial machinery and computer equipment
- Instruments and related products

- Primary metals
- Printing and Publishing
- Rubber and Plastic products
- Textiles

**Accreditation**    AT&T QR received its accreditation from the Registrar Accreditation Board in June 1991.

**Address**
**Contact/Phone**    To reach AT&T Quality Registrar, call 1-800-521-3399 or contact one of the following:

David Swasey
AT & T Quality Registrar
1090 E. Duane Avenue
Sunnyvale, CA 94086
Tel: (408) 522-5377;
Fax: (408) 522-4436

Sann Rene Glaza
AT & T Quality Registrar
1945, Chaussee de Wavre
1160 Brussels, Belgium
Tel: (322) 676-3596;
Fax: (322) 676-3812

John Malinauskas
AT & T Quality Registrar
650 Liberty Avenue
Union, NJ 07083
Tel: (800) 521-3399

Johnson Cheng
AT & T Quality Registrar
23rd Floor, 3 Exchange Square
8 Connaught Place
Central Hong Kong
Tel: (852) 846-2823;
Fax: (852) 810-0564

# BRITISH STANDARDS INSTITUTION QUALITY ASSURANCE (BSi)

**Overview**    BSi QA has operated product certification schemes for nearly 90 years and for more than 10 years has operated a Registration System for company capability assessment against the requirements of BS5750/EN29000/ISO 9000. BSi is also the United Kingdom Standards Body.

**Scope**    The accredited scope of BSi's quality assurance registration program covers almost every Standard Industry Classification.

**Accreditation**    BSi QA is accredited by the National Accreditation Council for Certification

Bodies (NACCB) and the Dutch Council for Certification [Raad voor de Certificatie (RvC)].

**Address**   BSi Quality Assurance
PO Box 375
Milton Keynes MK14 6LL
United Kingdom

**Contact/Phone**   Business Development Enquiries
Tel: 0908-220-908; Fax: 0908-220-671

# BUREAU VERITAS QUALITY INTERNATIONAL (NORTH AMERICA) INC. (BVQI)

**Overview**   Bureau Veritas Quality International (BVQI) is a third party assessor and registrar of quality management systems headquartered in London. Founded in 1988, BVQI is represented in 31 countries.

BVQI is a subsidiary of Paris-based Bureau Veritas. Bureau Veritas was founded in 1928 as a ship classification agency. It is now represented in 131 countries and employs 5,000 people in the fields of marine inspection, commodities inspection, aircraft survey and classification, civil engineering and construction works inspection, industrial sector support, and quality system registration.

Bureau Veritas Quality International (North America) was founded in 1991 to meet the growing needs for quality system registration in North America. With headquarters in Jamestown, NY, BVQI (NA) has affiliated operations through Bureau Veritas offices in Montreal, New York, Miami, Houston, Los Angeles, and Vancouver.

**Scope**   BVQI has a comprehensive scope in most major manufacturing and service areas. The Control System of BVQI has been designed to meet the requirements of European Norm (EN) 45012 and ISO 9001.

**Accreditation**   BVQI is accredited by the United Kingdom's National Accreditation Council for Certification Bodies (NACCB), by the Dutch Council for Certification [Raad voor de Certificatie (RvC)] and by the Registrar Accreditation Board

(RAB) in the United States. BVQI has accreditation pending with the Registrar Accreditation Board (RAB) in the United States, as well as in Sweden, Switzerland, Denmark, Belgium, Germany, Italy, and Australia-New Zealand.

**Address**        North American Central Offices
509 North Main Street
Jamestown, NY 14701

**Contact/Phone**  Greg Swan
Tel: (716) 484-9002; Fax: (716) 484-9003

# CERAMIC INDUSTRY CERTIFICATION SCHEME LTD. (CICS)

**Overview**       The Ceramic Industry Certification Scheme Ltd. (CICS) provides the ceramic industry and associated industries with an independent third party certification scheme for quality management systems and product conformity.

**Scope**          The scope of accreditation includes the following sectors of the ceramic and associated industries:

- Bathroom, sanitaryware and associated products
- Bricks, roofing tiles, and pavers
- Ceramic transfers
- Floor and wall tiles
- Raw materials suppliers and equipment manufacturers in the ceramic industry
- Refractory and industrial ceramics, including engineering ceramics
- Tableware
- Whiteware
- Colours, frits and glazes
- Clays

**Accreditation**  CICS is accredited by the National Accreditation Council for Certification Bodies (NACCB) in the United Kingdom.

**Address**          Queens Road
                     Penkhull
                     Stoke-on-Trent ST4 7LQ
                     United Kingdom

**Contact/Phone**   J. E. Leake
                     Tel: (44) 782-411008; Fax: (44) 782-412331

# DET NORSKE VERITAS INDUSTRY, INC. (DNVI)

**Overview**         Det Norske Veritas (DNV) was formed in 1864 as a ship classification society based in Norway. DNV has expanded and now offers other services, including quality system certification. These services have been performed for many years to earlier quality standards, and DNV received its first EC accreditation to perform ISO 9000 certification from the UK's NACCB in 1989.

                     DNV certification services in the United States are performed by the Quality System Certification department of DNV Industry, Inc. (DNVI), created in 1991, and based in Houston. East and West coast DNV offices supply additional auditors for audits in those regions.

**Scope**            Due to activities in many different industries, the NACCB and RvC scopes of accreditation awarded DNV are among the most extensive issued. DNV has issued more than 330 certificates worldwide as of June 1992, encompassing industries such as chemical processing, electronics and instrumentation, and the manufacture of oilfield equipment.

**Accreditation**    DNV is accredited to perform quality system registration by seven European bodies:

●   NACCB (United Kingdom)
●   RvC (Raad voor de Certificatie, The Netherlands
●   UNI CEI (Italy)
●   SWEDAC (Sweden)
●   DAO (Denmark)
●   NiB (Norway)
●   Belgium's accreditation body

German and US accreditations are expected before the end of the year.

DNV's direct accreditations relieves it from relying on memorandums of understanding, as the company can issue its own certificates without relying on a sub-contracted registrar. DNV Industry, Inc. of Houston acts on behalf of whichever sister company's accreditation is required.

**Address**        16340 Park Ten Place, Suite 100
                   Houston, TX 77084

**Contact/Phone**  Yehuda Dror or Steve Cumings
                   Tel: (713) 579-9003; Fax: (713) 579-1360

# ENTELA LABORATORIES, INC.

**Overview**       ENTELA, Inc. was originally founded in 1974 as a Michigan Corporation specializing in structural steel inspection. In 1981, equipment and personnel were added to initiate an in-house materials laboratory. Originally, ENTELA Engineering Services contained structural engineering, field service inspection, asbestos inspection, and geotechnical engineering departments. Laboratory division growth led to the formation of ENTELA Laboratories, a testing consulting company providing services to the manufacturing industry. Services include:

- Metals chemistry
- Simulated environmental testing
- Plastics/non-metals testing
- Product testing
- Electrical/electronics testing
- Metallurgy
- Mechanical engineering
- Third party certification programs
- Metrology
- Calibration

ENTELA, Inc. employs more than 75 individuals and has facilities in Grand Rapids, Michigan, and Taipei, Taiwan.

**Scope**          ENTELA Laboratories, Inc. has a comprehensive scope in most manufacturing and several service areas. The control system of ENTELA has been designed to meet the requirements of ISO 9001 and EN 45012.

**Accreditation**  ENTELA has accreditation pending with the Dutch Council for Certification (RvC). ENTELA is currently accredited by the American Association for Laboratory Accreditation. ENTELA is actively pursuing MOUs with Switzerland, Denmark, Belgium, Germany, Italy, Australia, New Zealand, and Taiwan.

**Address**  3033 Madison Avenue SE
Grand Rapids, MI 49548

**Contact/Phone**  Paul Riksen or Robert Kosack
Tel: (616) 247-0515, (800) 88-Tests; Fax: (616) 247-7527

# INTERTEK SERVICES CORPORATION

**Overview**  For nearly 20 years, Intertek has been providing quality contract services, including management services, consulting, training, systems development, audits/assessments, surveys, and inspections as well as supplier services. Intertek's client list includes companies in the aerospace, aircraft, automotive, computer, communications, electronics, medical, chemical, and utilities industries.

Headquartered in Fairfax, VA, Intertek also has a West Coast office near Los Angeles, ten regional offices throughout North America, and 9 international offices. A sister company, Intertek Technical Services, provides consulting services in preparation of quality management system certification.

**Scope**  Intertek is accredited to perform registration for the following industries:

- Aerospace
- Chemical
- Computer
- Electrical and electromechanical
- Electronic and microelectronic
- General manufacturing
- Pharmaceutical
- Telecommunications
- Machinery and equipment

Intertek has an on-going program for expanding its scope to meet its customers' needs.

**Accreditation**     Intertek was accredited in 1991 by the Dutch Council for Certification, Raad
                      voor de Certificatie (RvC), to perform quality management system registration
                      services. Intertek also provides in-house training services for auditing quality
                      management systems to ISO 9000, as well as lead assessor training courses.
                      Intertek operates a formal certification system that satisfies the requirements
                      of EN 45012 and ISO 10011, Part 2, and the criteria of National Accreditation
                      Councils.

**Address**           9900 Main Street, Suite 500
                      Fairfax, VA 22031

**Contact/Phone**     Frederick J. Becker
                      Tel: (703) 476-9000, (800) 336-0151; Fax: (703) 273-4124

# KEMA-USA, INC. (KEMA)

**Overview**          KEMA Registered Quality Inc. is a new subsidiary of the holding company
                      KEMA-USA, Inc., which is fully owned by N.V. KEMA in the Netherlands.

**Scope**             The main activities of KEMA Registered Quality Inc. are:

- Assessment of quality management standards according to ISO 9000
  standard series and comparable quality standards, and issuing the KEMA
  Q.M.S. certificate;

- Conformity assessments of products and production processes according
  to the essential requirements as described in the New Approach EC
  Directives, and issuing certificates of conformity for the CE Mark
  (applicable product areas are: medical devices, telecommunications
  terminal equipment, hazardous location products, electrical machines).

- Testing and certification of electrical appliances and installation materials
  according to international (IEC) and harmonized European (EN) standards and issuing the KEMA KEUR mark.

**Accreditation**     KEMA Registered Quality Inc. has cooperative arrangements with other
                      North American certification and registration organizations such as UL (USA)
                      and CSA/QMI (Canada) in order to facilitate the obtainment of multiple
                      certification and to reduce assessment and testing costs.

**Address**  KEMA-USA, Inc.
4379 County Line Road
Chalfont, PA 18914

**Contact/Phone**  Theo Stoop
Tel: (215) 822-4281; Fax: (215) 822-4271

# LLOYD'S REGISTER QUALITY ASSURANCE LTD. (LRQA)

**Overview**  Lloyd's Register Quality Assurance (LRQA) was founded in 1985 in Great Britain to perform third party certification of quality management systems. LRQA is a subsidiary of Lloyd's Register, which has carried out independent certifications since 1760.

Because of the affiliation to Lloyd's Register, LRQA has registered lead assessors throughout the world. Since 1985, LRQA has certified more than 2,000 companies worldwide, including more than 25 in North America last year.

**Scope**  LRQA's policy is to apply for accreditation in every new business it undertakes. LRQA offers a complete range of accredited services in:

- Architecture
- Civil engineering
- Consumer services
- Design
- Electrical appliances
- Electronic components
- Fabrication
- Food and drink producers, packagers, and distributors
- Installation of fixtures and fittings
- Lighting equipment
- Metallurgical
- Project management
- Steelwork erection
- Switchgear
- Telecommunications
- Textile dyes and pigments

**Accreditation**  In 1986, LRQA became the first third party certification body to be accredited for quality management systems in both the United Kingdom and The Netherlands, by the National Accreditation Council for Certification Bodies (NACCB) and the Dutch Council for Certification (Raad voor de Certificatie or RvC) respectively. LRQA will apply for accreditation in each country in which it is eligible to operate.

**Address**          33-41 Newark Street
                     Hoboken, NJ 07030

**Contact/Phone**  David Hadlet
                     Tel: (201) 963-1111; Fax: (201) 963-3299

# THE LOSS PREVENTION CERTIFICATION BOARD LTD. (LPCB)

**Overview**         The Loss Prevention Certification Board Ltd. conducts both product conformity certification and certification of supplier quality management systems. LPCB is an independent authority on whose board all interested parties are represented.

**Scope**            LPCB's scope comprises firms that provide fire protection and security products, systems and services.

**Accreditation**    LPCB is accredited by the National Accreditation Council for Certification Bodies (NACCB) in the United Kingdom.

**Address**          Melrose Avenue
                     Borehamwood
                     Hertfordshire WD6 2BJ
                     United Kingdom

**Contact/Phone**  Chris Beedel
                     Tel: 44-081-207-2345; Fax: 44-081-207-6305

# MET LABORATORIES, INC.

**Overview**         MET is an independent third party testing laboratory. As a nationally recognized testing laboratory, MET lists and labels products in accordance with

National Safety (ANSI/UL) Standards. MET Laboratories, Inc. has over three decades of testing and certification experience.

**Scope**　　　MET performs safety, performance, telecommunication, EMI/RFI, and environmental testing. Using the ISO Guides 9000 and ANSI/ASQC Q90 series documents as a basis, MET regularly conducts unannounced inspections of the manufacturer's facility in order to assure continuing compliance. MET certifies that the manufacturing process complies with ISO 9002 for the product certified.

**Accreditation**　MET is the first nationally recognized testing laboratory licensed by the Occupational Safety and Health Administration (OSHA) for safety certification, listing, and labeling. MET is accredited by the National Institute of Standards and Technology (NIST). Under OSHA regulations, MET maintains strict standards for testing and certification. Accreditation for ISO 9002 registration is part of the OSHA accreditation of a manufacturer's product certification.

**Address**　　914 W. Patapsco Avenue
Baltimore, MD 21230-3432

**Contact/Phone**　Joyce Holton
Tel: (410) 354-3300; Fax: (410) 354-3313

# NATIONAL QUALITY ASSURANCE LTD. (NQA)

**Overview**　　National Quality Assurance Ltd. (formerly National Inspection Council Quality Assurance, Ltd.) was formed in 1988 in the United Kingdom. NQA offers registration of quality management systems to ISO 9000, EN 29000, and BS 5750 (NACCB Category 1). NQA received its NACCB accreditation in early 1990. NQA has offices in Scotland, Northern Ireland, the United States of America and the United Kingdom. Worldwide expansion plans include India and Eastern Europe.

NQA registration services in the United States are performed by NQA, USA with IQA registered lead assessors. NQA, USA was created in 1991 and is based in Boxborough, Massachusetts, with additional offices in the East, West and Midwest sections of the United States supplying additional assessors for those regions.

**Scope**          It is NQA policy to obtain NACCB accreditation for all the quality system
                   registrations it offers. NQA's current scope of accreditation is among the most
                   extensive issued by the NACCB. NQA has issued more than 800 certificates
                   worldwide as of June 1992 including: building engineering services; design
                   and manufacture of heating elements; domestic appliance servicing; electro-
                   plating; manufacture of cutting tools; general process instrumentation;
                   manufacture, installation, connection, commissioning, maintenance, testing,
                   and hire of radio, telecommunications, and data systems; packing and blend-
                   ing of raw materials (such as chemicals, fertilizer), synthetics, and foodstuffs;
                   manufacture, installation, and maintenance of water pumps and their associ-
                   ated controls; and provision of catering services.

**Accreditation**  NQA is accredited to perform quality system registration by the United
                   Kingdom's National Accreditation Council for Certification Bodies
                   (NACCB).

                   NQA's direct accreditation relieves it from relying on memorandums of
                   understanding, as the company can issue its own certificates without relying
                   on a sub-contracted registrar.

                   A registered company that has met the requirements of the ISO 9000 series of
                   standards is entitled to display the relevant NQA registration logo together
                   with the mark of NACCB accreditation.

**Address**        1146 Massachusetts Avenue
                   Boxborough, MA 01719

**Contact/Phone**  James P. O'Neil
                   Tel: (508) 635-9256; Fax: (508) 266-1073

# NATIONAL STANDARDS AUTHORITY OF IRELAND (NSAI)

**Overview**       National Standards Authority of Ireland (NSAI) is a division of EOLAS. It is
                   the national standards body of Ireland. NSAI dates to 1946 and operates under
                   the Industrial Research and Standards Act, 1961, as well as the Science and
                   Technology Act, 1987, of the Irish government. NSAI's main office is in
                   Dublin, Ireland, with additional offices throughout Ireland. The North
                   American office is based in Merrimack, NH.

**Scope**        NSAI offers certification services in the area of quality systems certification to ISO 9000/EN 29000, product certifications to the Irish Mark of Electrical Conformity (IMEC), verified manufacturer's testing (VMT), standards membership scheme, and ISO 9000/EN 29000 workshops. As the Irish national standards body, NSAI is required by law to provide certification to all products and services and all NSAI lead assessors are registered to the Institute of Quality Assurance (IQA) in the UK. NSAI operates in accordance with EN 45012 *General Criteria for Certification Bodies Operating Quality System Certification.*

**Accreditation**   NSAI is accredited as a registrar by means of an Act of Irish Parliament and is notified to the EC by the Irish government. As a member of the European Quality System Certification Network (E-Q-Net), NSAI has reciprocal recognition for its certificates with all EC and EFTA member states. Companies registered by NSAI may obtain a registration in all EC and EFTA countries without further assessment upon payment of the necessary registration fees. NSAI also has a bilateral agreement with the Canadian General Standards Board (CGSB). Future bilateral national agreements are pending.

**Address**      North American Certification Services
5 Medallion Center (Greeley Street)
Merrimack, NH 03054

**Contact/Phone**   Richard Bernier
Tel: (603) 424-7070; Fax: (603) 429-1427

# NSF INTERNATIONAL (NSF)

**Overview**     NSF International has been offering product certification to companies involved in public health and the environment since 1944. NSF registers quality systems; develops and maintains consensus standards; tests and certifies products; inspects production facilities; and conducts special studies to support these services.

**Scope**        NSF is an independent, private, non-profit organization providing third party services through programs that focus on public health and environmental quality.

**Accreditation**   NSF has memorandums of understanding with Underwriters Laboratories Inc.

(UL) and the American Gas Association Laboratories (A.G.A.), and is actively working toward accreditation in 1992 by an internationally recognized accrediting organization.

NSF has American National Standards Institute (ANSI) accreditation as a consensus standards writer, as well as for its product certification programs.

**Address**        3475 Plymouth Road
PO Box 130140
Ann Arbor, MI 48113-0140

**Contact/Phone**  Garry Puglio
Tel: (313) 769-8010; Fax: (313) 769-0109

# QUALITY MANAGEMENT INSTITUTE (QMI)

**Overview**       QMI, a division of CSA, has offered quality system registration service in North America since 1979. QMI has five offices in Canada serving North America and overseas. QMI currently has 1,100 active applicants, 400 of which are registered. QMI has an internationally recognized auditor certification program that is compatible with IQA criteria. QMI offers related products and workshops presented by QMI certified auditors.

**Scope**          QMI's applicants are from across major industry segments, including telecommunication, petrochemical, chemical, electrical and electronics, pulp and paper, mechanical, mining and the service sector.

**Accreditation**  QMI has a network of registrars around the world including operational memorandums of understanding with the following:

- AFAQ, France
- BSI, Great Britain
- JMI, Japan
- SA, Australia

- TELARC, New Zealand
- SQS, Switzerland
- KEMA, Holland

Memorandums of understanding in development:

- DQS, Germany
- SIS, Sweden
- UL, USA

QMI has applied for accreditation under the Canadian registrar accreditation scheme developed by the Standards Council of Canada. Accreditation is pending, but expected sometime in 1992.

**Address**      Suite 800, Mississauga Executive Center
Two Robert Speck Parkway
Mississauga, Ontario, Canada L4Z 1H8

**Contact/Phone**  Catherine Neville
Tel: (416) 272-3920; Fax: (416) 272-3942

# QUALITY SYSTEMS REGISTRARS, INC. (QSR)

**Overview**     Quality Systems Registrars, Inc. (QSR) was established to provide quality system registration services to the ISO 9000 series standards. QSR was formed in February 1990 to provide a management-oriented American approach to quality program administration and certification. QSR is the first American owned company to be accredited to register ISO 9000 quality systems.

QSR staff obtained expertise from the nuclear and petroleum industry programs accredited by the American Society of Mechanical Engineers. QSR principals have more than 35 years of combined experience in quality system certification. The QSR Board of Governors has more than 65 years of experience in quality system certification.

QSR is proud to be affiliated with Baldrige winners/finalists and organizations that do not desire to revert to an inspection-driven quality system. QSR offers annual, fixed-price quotations to eliminate the mystery of plus expenses.

**Scope**       QSR is accredited to perform registrations in the following Standard Industrial Classifications:

● Air transportation
● Chemicals and allied products
● Computer equipment
● Electrical and electronic equipment and components
● Engineering, accounting, research, management, and related services
● Fabricated metal products

- Industrial and commercial machinery
- Lumber and wood products
- Measuring, analyzing, and controlling instruments
- Mining, quarrying
- Oil and gas extraction
- Paper and allied products
- Petroleum refining and related industries
- Pharmaceuticals.
- Photographic, medical, and optical goods
- Pipelines except natural gas
- Primary metal industries
- Rubber and plastics products
- Textile mill products
- Transportation equipment
- Wholesale trade of durable and nondurable goods

**Accreditation**   QSR was accredited by the Registrar Accreditation Board (RAB) in March 1991. In December 1991, QSR received accreditation by the Dutch Council for Certification, Raad voor de Certificatie (RvC).

**Address**   1555 Naperville/Wheaton Road, Suite 206
Naperville, IL 60563

**Contact/Phone**   Richard Kleckner
Tel: (708) 778-0120; Fax: (708) 778-0122

# SGS YARSLEY QUALITY ASSURED FIRMS (SGS YARSLEY)

**Overview**   Yarsley Quality Assured Firms was established in 1985 to meet the growing demands in all industry sectors for independent ISO 9000/EN 29000/BS 5750 quality system registration services. The SGS Group of Geneva, Switzerland, the world's largest independent inspection and testing company, acquired Yarsley Quality Assured Firms in 1990. The SGS Group operates in over 140 countries.

SGS Yarsley offers ISO 9000 registration services and quality systems training via regional centers in Redhill, United Kingdom; Hong Kong; and Hoboken, New Jersey. In North America, local offices in San Diego; Houston; Chicago; Daytona Beach, FL; and Fairfield, NJ, provide local services.

**Scope**          SGS Yarsley Quality Assured Firms has registered nearly 1,000 companies in
                   115 industrial/service sectors including:

- Building
- Chemicals
- Distribution
- Electronics and electrical
- Engineering
- Foodstuffs
- Plastics and rubber
- Stockholding
- Textiles
- Wood and paper

**Accreditation**  SGS Yarsley Quality Assured Firms has been accredited by the United
                   Kingdom's National Accreditation Council for Certification Bodies (NACCB)
                   since 1987.

                   SGS Yarsley is considering accreditation by the US Registrar Accreditation
                   Board. Certification from SGS Yarsley is formally recognized by all NACCB
                   registrars and their clients, as well as by SGS clients worldwide.

**Address**        1415 Park Avenue
                   Hoboken, NJ 07030

**Contact/Phone**  Ernani Pires
                   Tel: (201) 792-2400; Fax: (201) 656-0636

# SGS STANDARDS APPROVAL AND COMPLIANCE INC. (SGS CANADA)

**Overview**       Yarsley Quality Assured Firms was established in 1985 to meet the growing
                   demands in all industry sectors for independent ISO 9000/EN 29000/BS 5750
                   quality system registration services. The SGS Group of Geneva, Switzerland,
                   the world's largest independent inspection and testing company, acquired
                   Yarsley Quality Assured Firms in 1990. The SGS Group operates in more
                   than 140 countries.

Within Canada, SGS Yarsley operates as a division of SGS Standards Approval and Compliance Inc. SGS Yarsley offers ISO 9000 registration services and quality systems training via regional centers in Redhill, United Kingdom; Hong Kong; Hoboken, New Jersey; and Markham, Ontario, Canada.

**Scope**            SGS Yarsley Quality Assured Firms has registered nearly 1,000 companies in 115 industrial/service sectors including:

- Building
- Chemicals
- Distribution
- Electronics and electrical
- Engineering
- Foodstuffs
- Plastics and rubber
- Stockholding
- Textiles
- Wood and paper

**Accreditation**    SGS Yarsley Quality Assured Firms has been accredited by the United Kingdom's National Accreditation Council for Certification Bodies (NACCB) since 1987.

SGS Standards Approval and Compliance Inc. has applied to the Standards Council of Canada as an approved registration organization for the Canadian national system of ISO 9000. Certification from SGS Yarsley is formally recognized by all NACCB registrars and their clients, as well as by SGS clients worldwide.

**Address**          90 Gough Road, Unit 4
                     Markham, Ontario, Canada L3R 5V5

**Contact/Phone**    Raymond Grayston
                     Tel: (416) 479-1160; Fax: (416) 479-9452

# SIRA CERTIFICATION SERVICE/SIRA TEST & CERTIFICATION LIMITED (SCS)

**Overview**     Sira Certification Service (SCS) is the certification arm of Sira Test and Certification Ltd., which was formed in 1981 using the internal certification service of Imperial Industries plc, extant since 1946, as its nucleus. It is an independent company whose principal occupation is the certification of products for use in explosive atmospheres both above and below ground.

Its Quality Management Service was initially developed to support the Product Certification Service. Because of the increase in demand for Quality Management Certification, SCS now offers its QMS Certification service as a separate service to its Product Conformity activities.

SCS believes in global recognition. To this end, not only does it participate in international harmonization but it has also signed an agreement with Factory Mutual Research Corporation of Boston, leading to mutual acceptance of testing services which seek to bridge at least part of the Atlantic barrier.

**Scope**     SCS is accredited to certify electrical and electronic equipment including that for Potentially Explosive Atmospheres. The Product Conformity Certification scope of accreditation includes similar types of equipment.

**Accreditation**     SCS is accredited by the UK Secretary of State for Trade & Industry under the National Accreditation Council for Certification Bodies (NACCB) scheme to certify Quality Management Systems. It is the only UK organization accredited to issue ISO 9001 certificates in the field of Potentially Explosive Atmospheres.

In addition, SCS is one of only ten European Certification Bodies approved to issue Product Conformity Certificates for Explosive Atmosphere Electrical Equipment under EC Directive 76/117/EEC for surface industry and is one of the three bodies approved to issue similar certificates under EC Directive 82/130/EEC for mining equipment. These certificates carry a QMS requirement and are recognized throughout the EC.

**Address**     Saighton Lane
Saighton
Chester CH36EG
United Kingdom

**Contact/Phone**   Graham Tortoishell
                    Tel: Chester (0244) 332200, Fax: (0244) 332112

# STEEL RELATED INDUSTRIES
# QUALITY SYSTEM REGISTRAR (SRI)

**Overview**    Steel Related Industries (SRI) Quality System Registrar was established to
                respond to the growing need of basic manufacturing and service industries, the
                steel industry and its many suppliers to demonstrate that they possess a quality
                system that meets basic customer demands. SRI is a registrar for ISO 9000,
                providing independent third-party assessments of the quality systems of
                principal industry producers, processors and suppliers.

                SRI's professional staff has broad-based experience and is qualified to
                conduct quality system registrations of many major basic manufacturing,
                mining and service organizations. Its auditors come from a variety of industry
                backgrounds including steel producing and processing, foundry, metal
                fabrication, chemical, mining, equipment, machine shop, refractory, ferroalloy
                and engineering.

                SRI's lead auditors have performed hundreds of second and third party ISO-
                based audits throughout North America. Most also conduct second party TQM
                assessments for the Steel Industry Supplier Audit Process (SISAP).

                SRI operates as a not-for-profit, unincorporated, North America based, self-
                supporting entity, originally established as an affiliate of the American Iron
                and Steel Institute.

**Scope**       SRI performs quality system registration of basic manufacturing and service
                companies, in steel related industries.

                ● Mining and quarrying
                ● Chemicals and allied products
                ● Primary metals
                ● Stone, clay and glass
                ● Fabricated metal products
                ● Industrial machinery and equipment
                ● Motor vehicles and equipment

- Transportation and warehousing
- Research and management services
- Engineering and construction services
- Laboratory apparatus and instruments

**Accreditation**   SRI is accredited by the Registrar Accreditation Board (RAB) and at this writing (10/26/92) is completing the process of accreditation with a major European community accreditation body.

**Address**   SRI Quality System Registrar
Suite 450
2000 Corporate Drive
Wexford, PA 15090

**Contact/Phone**   Dr. Peter B. Lake, Director
Mr. James H. Bytnar, Operations Manager
Tel: (412) 935-2844; Fax: (412) 935-6825

# TUV AMERICA (TUV)

**Overview**   TUV America is a wholly owned subsidiary of TUV Bayern. Originally established in 1870, the TUV organization now employs more than 18,000 people worldwide. TUV Bayern represents the largest TUV subsidiary employing more than 4,500 people offering a wide range of expertise in almost every engineering and technical discipline.

**Scope**   TUV is an EC Notified Body for a number of mandatory and voluntary inspections, tests, and certifications. Technical expertise includes:

- Steam boilers and pressure vessels
- Nuclear power plants
- Refineries and pipelines
- Industrial machinery
- Subway systems
- Electrical equipment
- Control equipment and computers
- Medical equipment
- Automotive equipment
- Amusement park rides

**Accreditation**   TUV Bayern is a state-accredited European organization authorized to perform mandatory and voluntary inspections, testing, and certifications on behalf of the Federal Republic of Germany and the European Community.

TUV America offers ISO 9000 certification services under the guidelines of the German Certification Agency TUV CERT. Accreditations have been granted by the German Accreditation Board (DAR) under the auspices of the German Department of Commerce (BMWi). DAR is the German accreditation authority responsible for third party test laboratories, inspection agencies, and certification bodies.

**Address**        5 Cherry Hill Drive
Danvers, MA 01923

**Contact/Phone**  Manfred Popp or Mark Alpert
Tel: (508) 777-7999; Fax: (508) 777-8441

# TUV RHEINLAND OF NORTH AMERICA, INC. (TUVRHEINLAND)

**Overview**       TUV Rheinland of North America, Inc. has offered product testing and inspection services in North America since the early 1980s. Its parent company, TUV Rheinland e.V. in Koln, Germany, has offered these services since the late 1890s.

TUV Rheinland of North America has offered ISO 9000 services in North America since 1989. TUV Rheinland has over 40 offices worldwide and 11 offices in North America. It has provided testing and certification services to hundreds of companies in North America in the past decade. In addition to the ISO 9000 registrations offered to US companies, TUV CERT has registered dozens of manufacturers worldwide, with the majority in Western Europe.

**Scope**          In North America, TUV Rheinland specializes in auditing the following industries:

- Automotive
- Electronic
- Industrial
- Medical
- Pressure vessel and related

**Accreditation** TUV Rheinland is a member of the TUV CERT organization located in Bonn, Germany. TUV CERT is accredited by the official German Government Accreditation Council, the DAR (Deutschen Akkreditierungs Rat or German Accreditation Council). Therefore, the ISO 9000 registrations offered are in fact issued by TUV CERT.

**Address** 12 Commerce Road
Newtown, CT 06470

**Contact/Phone** Joseph DeCarlo
Tel: (203) 426-0888; Fax: (203) 270-8883

# UNDERWRITERS LABORATORIES INC. (UL)

**Overview** Underwriters Laboratories Inc. (UL) has offered quality system registration services since 1989. Through its Follow Up Services program, UL has conducted quality evaluations of manufacturers' quality systems for more than 70 years. UL has four major test facilities in the US and nearly 200 inspection centers throughout the United States and 59 other countries. UL has granted the Registered Firm Mark (signifying ISO 9000 registration) to more than 110 firms since the program was launched three years ago.

**Scope** Underwriters Laboratories Inc. conducts ISO 9000 registrations in a wide variety of industries, including:

- Chemicals and allied products
- Information technology equipment
- Electronic equipment
- Fabricated metal products
- Industrial and commercial machinery
- Measuring, analyzing and controlling instruments
- Paper and allied products
- Pipelines (except natural gas)
- Wholesale trade-durable goods industries

**Accreditation**    UL's ISO 9000 Registration Program received Raad voor de Certificatie (RvC) accreditation in August 1992.

Through a memorandum of understanding (MOU) with British Standards Institution (BSI), UL and BSI recognize each other's evaluation of an organization's quality system for registration to the ISO 9000 series standard.

UL has worked with BSI in various capacities since 1978. BSI is recognized in the fields of quality assurance, standards, testing, and certification. UL is known for its work in product testing, safety certification, quality assurance, and standardization.

In addition to the MOU with BSI, UL has built a network of relationships to help manufacturers get factory registration for the countries in which they do business. UL's network allows manufacturers whose facilities are registered to the ISO 9000 series standards to obtain additional registration(s) by the following registrars:

● JMI Institute (Japan)
● Standards Australia
● Standards Institution of Israel
● Quality Management Institute (Canada)
● American Gas Association Laboratories (United States)
● NSF International (United States)
● Bureau of Commodity Inspection and Quarantine (Taiwan)
● Singapore Institute of Standards and Industrial Research
● Standards and Industrial Research Institute of Malaysia

UL has been assessed to the appropriate portions of EN 45012 by BSI, which operates under the accreditation schemes of both the National Accreditation Council for Certification Bodies (NACCB) in the United Kingdom and the Dutch Council for Certification, Raad voor de Certificatie (RvC), in The Netherlands.

UL is the US National Supervising Inspectorate (NSI) for the International Electrotechnical Commission Quality Assessment (IECQ) System and serves as the Systems Supervising Inspectorate (SSI) for the National Electronic Components Quality Certification System (NECQ). Serving as NSI, SSI, and as a registrar to the ISO 9000 series allows UL to provide a variety of certifications without duplicating assessments.

**Address**      1285 Walt Whitman Road
             Melville, NY 11747-3081

**Contact/Phone**   Robert Zott
             Tel: (516) 271-6200 x837

# VINCOTTE USA, INCORPORATED (AV)

**Overview**      AIB has been established as a company concerned with safety and quality in the workplace since 1890. Vincotte has been performing the same type of work since 1872. These two firms merged in 1989 to form AIB-Vincotte (AV), which has eight offices in Belgium and one in Abu Dhabi in addition to the Houston office. AV has experience dealing with standardized quality systems since 1969.

**Scope**        AV employs more than 300 professionals in areas such as:

- Advanced technology systems
- Calibration of test and measuring equipment
- Chemical manufacturing
- Chemical, mechanical, and electrical testing
- Civil engineering projects
- Food
- Industrial projects
- Information technology
- Medical devices
- Nondestructive testing
- Nuclear safety
- Petrochemical equipment
- Power generation

**Accreditation**   AV is recognized by Belgian authorities and has audited the quality system of all suppliers (more than 600) of regulated equipment for the Belgian nuclear program. AV is also a notified body to the Commission of the European Communities (EC) in the framework of more than 50 European directives.

             AV is the leading certification body of Belgium and is the first company to be accredited under Belgium's newly established scheme for accrediting registrars, the NAC-QS system. AV has also signed a memorandum of under standing (MOU) with 14 leading certification bodies of Europe within the framework of the European Network for Quality System Assessment and Certification (E-Q-NET). Within E-Q-NET, AV has signed mutual recognition of certificate agreements with DQS of Germany and KEMA of The Netherlands.

Within the Recognition Arrangement for Assessment and Certification of Quality Systems in the Information Technology Sector (ITQS), AV has mutual recognition of certificate agreements with KEMA of The Netherlands; IMQ of Italy; EC of Denmark; BSI QA of Great Britain; AFAQ of France; and RW-TUV, TUV Rheinland, and TUV Bayern, all of Germany.

**Address**         Vincotte USA, Inc., a subsidiary of The AV Group
                    10497 Town & Country Way, Suite 900
                    Houston, TX 77024

**Contact/Phone**   Terry Heaps
                    Tel: (713) 465-2850; Fax: (713) 465-1182

# OTHER REGISTRARS

As of this writing, the following registrars are either seeking accreditation or their accreditation is pending with an accreditation body. For more information, contact each registrar directly.

### Canadian Gas Association

55 Scarsdale Road
Don Mills, Ontario
Canada M3B 2R3
Contact: John Wolf
Tel: (416) 447-6465; Fax: (416) 447-1026

## Canadian General Standards Board

Mailing Address:    Ottawa, Canada
K1A 1G6

Office Location:    9C1, Phase III
Place du Portage
11 Laurier Street
Hull, Quebec

Contact: James Littlejohn
Tel: (819) 941-8669; Fax: (819) 941-8706

## Quebec Quality Certification Group

70, rue Dalhousie, Bureau 220
Quebec (Quebec), Canada G1K 4B2
Contact: J.P. Lajeunesse
Tel: (418) 643-5813; Fax: (418) 646-3315

## Tri-Tech Services, Inc.

4700 Clairton Boulevard
Pittsburgh, PA 15236
Contact: Joseph Fabian or Raymond Luther
Tel: (412) 884-2290; Fax: (412) 884-2268

## Underwriters' Laboratories of Canada

7 Crouse Road
Scarborough, Ontario
Canada M1R 3A9
Contact: Howard Spice
Tel: (416) 757-3611; Fax: (416) 757-1781

## Warnock Hersey Professional Services Ltd

3210 American Drive
Mississauga, Ontario
L4V 1B3
Contact: Brian Rossborough
Tel: (416) 678-7820; Fax: (416) 405-0052

# Appendix C

# ISO 9000 Consultants

## INTRODUCTION

This section profiles 49 consultants who offer services related to ISO 9000. It is not a comprehensive list, but reflects those organizations who submitted information to QSU through September, 1992. As interest in ISO 9000 increases, so do the number of firms offering consultant services.

The qualifications and credentials of consultants are included in each listing. The following acronyms are used frequently:

> **CQA/CQE** - Certified Quality Auditor/Engineer. This is the American Society for Quality Control certification system.

> **IQA** - This is the United Kingdom's Institute for Quality Assurance, which registers auditors.

> Other useful acronyms are listed in the box on next page.

The ASQC's Registrar Accreditation Board has developed a Certification Program for Auditors of Quality Systems. It is patterned after the UK's IQA program.

*This listing is provided for your information and consideration. CEEM does not recommend or endorse any of the consultants included here. As with any decision of this nature, you must evaluate the needs of your company and the qualifications/experience of these and/or other consultants being considered and choose accordingly.*

## Acronyms Used by Consultants

AQP .............. Association for Quality and Participation
ASME .......... American Society of Mechanical Engineers
ASSE ............ American Society of Safety Engineers
ASTM ......... American Society for Testing and Materials
CMC ............. Certified Management Consultant
COAP .......... Certified Office Automation Professional
CQA ............. Certified Quality Auditor
CQE ............. Certified Quality Engineer
CRE .............. Certified Reliability Engineers
CSA ............. Canadian Standards Association
DOE ............ Design of Experiments
EMI ............. Electro Magnetic Compatability
FCC ............. Federal Communications Commission
IAEI ............. International Association of Electrical Inspection
IEEE ........... Institute of Electrical and Electronic Engineers
IIE ............... Institute of Industrial Engineers
NEQI ........... National Education Quality Initiative
PE ................ Professional Engineer
RFI .............. Radio Frequency Interference
TAG ............ Technical Advisory Group
TC ............... Technical Committee
UL ............... Underwriters Laboratories

# ADVENT MANAGEMENT ASSOCIATES, LTD.

**Address/Phone**   P.O. Box 3203
West Chester, PA 19381-3203
Tel: (215) 431-2196; Fax: (215) 431-2641

**Contact**   Hugh C. Lovell, Vice President

**Services**   Advent's services include a complete ISO 9000 package providing the client with all management assistance and training services necessary to prepare for certification. Since Advent is not involved in the actual certification, total energy is devoted to the implementation of the right mix of quality programs that make sense for the clients' business. Key elements of the service include:

- Initial assessment of current quality policies
- Management training in the fundamentals of ISO 9000
- Development of a total quality system
- Policies and procedures
- Auditor training and scheduling of internal audits
- Development of customer and market focus for the organization
- Development of implementation plans
- Training programs for company employees
- Assistance in application for certification
- Pre-assessment audit
- Post-assessment recap and corrective actions
- On-going consulting for recertification and continuous improvement beyond ISO 9000

**In Business**   14 years

**Clients Include**   Schenkers International Forwarders, Exidyne Instrumentation Technologies, Interconnect Systems Group, and NEPA Industrial Resource Center (10 Company Network) Montgomery Tank Lines

**Qualifications/ Certifications**   Advent consultants come from a broad range of backgrounds. Credentials include: PE, CQA Lead Auditor, COAP and CMC. Each ISO audit is headed by a trained Lead Auditor and supported by trained internal auditors and supporting specialists with a variety of credentials. Staff includes 10 Lead Auditors, 16 Internal Auditors and 20-plus consultants available for ISO work.

# ALLAN SAYLE ASSOCIATES

| | |
|---|---|
| **Address** | Redruth |
| | The Shrave |
| | Four Marks |
| | Hampshire GU 34 5BH |
| | United Kingdom |

**Contact**  Allan Sayle

**Services**  Allan Sayle Associates offers audits and assessments (internal and external), provides ISO 9000 compliance system development, integrates ISO 9000 systems with customers TQM program, and provides training and advice during implementation, as well as providing total quality programs. Self-audit training is available through videos and workbooks. Four-day quality assurance audit training course is available.

**In Business**  9 years

**Clients Include**  Digital Equipment, British Standards Institution, British Nuclear Fuels, New Zealand Dairy Board, Datachecker USA, Mobil, Sir Alexander Gibb & Partners, Norsk Air, Rolls Royce, Foxboro, James Williamson & Partners

**Qualifications/ Certifications**  Allan Sayle's qualifications include: BSc (Hons) from the University of Strathclyde, Fellow of the Institute of Quality Assurance, Member of the American Society for Quality Control. He has been a quality assurance professional for over twenty years and held positions of increasing seniority including Corporate QA Manager of a well known international engineering company.

An internationally-known speaker on quality management, he has had many papers published. Mr. Sayle still performs internal and external audits for clients all over the world. Until June 1991 he was a Member of Council of the Institute of Quality Assurance and a past member of its Editorial Committee. He is a member of the Editorial Board of Managerial Auditing Journal, a premier publication in that field; a member of the Canadian Standards Association's Auditing Standards Committee and of its Software Quality Assurance Standards Committee; and a member of the ASQC's Quality Audit Technical Committee. He is special adviser to the Singapore Quality Institute for its Assessor Registration Scheme and a member of its Board of Certification & Accreditation. A Lead Auditor qualified in accordance with the requirements of ANSI N45.2.23 since

1977, Mr. Sayle is also an accredited Lead Assessor with the British National Registration Scheme for Assessors of Quality Systems. Mr. Sayle is also one of the officially designated Lead Auditors for the Standards Association of New Zealand.

# APPLIED QUALITY SYSTEMS

**Address/Phone**  1379 Rice Creek Trail, Suite 16
Shoreview, MN 55126
Tel: (612) 783-1170; Fax: (612) 783-1171

**Contact**  Mark Ames, President

**Services**  Applied Quality Systems offers ISO 9000 and TQM consulting and training to clients in the manufacturing sector. Headquartered in Minneapolis/St. Paul, its professional staff provides services to clients from coast to coast. Applied Quality Systems is committed to tailoring its services to meet the unique needs of an organization. From planning and basic training to successful implementation, AQS is committed to its clients' success. Its approach to ISO 9000 focuses on employee knowledge and participation. This strategy is designed to impact productivity and achieve results in addition to compliance with ISO 9000. AQS's quality offerings include:

- Full service ISO 9000 implementation and training
- ISO 9000/TQM integration
- TQM implementation
- Basic concepts of quality, team building and strategic planning.

**In Business**  5 years

**Clients Include**  Colder Products Company, Houston Atlas (A Baker Hughes Company), Perkin-Elmer (Physical Electronics Division), Phoenix International, Ramsey Technology (A Baker Hughes Company), Seagate Technology, Spectrace Instruments (A Baker Hughes Company), Stonel Corporation, Texas Nuclear (A Baker Hughes Company), Young Manufacturing.

**Qualifications/ Certifications**  All staff members have degrees and extensive manufacturing experience, with half from engineering disciplines. Certifications include: CQE, CQA, and IQA lead assessor. All staff are ASQC members.

# ARCH ASSOCIATES

**Address/Phone**   15770 Robinwood Drive
Northville, MI 48167-2041
Tel: (313) 420-0122; Fax: Same

**Contact**   William M. Harral

**Services**   Arch Associates provides comprehensive, customized total quality support based on the ISO 9000 Series and applicable regional, national, industry, product, market sector and customer requirements to implement global competitiveness within client organizations which is aligned with their strategy, vision and culture.

Their scope of support services ranges from a complete cycle of strategic planning, quality system planning, development, documentation, training, implementation and ongoing oversight to specific projects for training, system enhancement or independent assessments against numerous standards. Assessments may focus on needs assessments, facilitate qualification/certification to different customer or public standards, or support EN45014 self-declaration for manufacturers of EC-regulated products.

**In Business**   9 years

**Clients Include**   Clients are primarily in the following industries:

Automotive, general manufacturing, basic metals, metal fabricating or forming, machinery/tools design and manufacture, electromechanical, plastic, microbiology, contracted design and other service industries. Client size ranges from small organizations such as Continental Carbide and McQuade Industries which have been featured in *Detroit Business* and *Nation's Business* as outstanding examples of small-organization, high quality-based growth during the recession, to the over 3000 person GM-Cadillac Grand Blanc Stamping Plant which received the Malcolm Baldrige National Quality Award.

**Qualifications/Certifications**   Arch Associates is a network of multidisciplinary professionals who typically possess over twenty years business experience, advanced degrees and appropriate certifications/registrations within their particular field. Most are very active within professional/technical societies and frequently present papers or speeches at various professional conferences or through professional publications. Some are MBNQA examiners or judges. William M. Harral, Director and Principal, serves as Total Quality Management Co-chair for the Quality Management Division of ASQC, is Truck Industry Liaison for the Automotive Division of ASQC and chairs both the ISO 9000 Committee and Supplier Qualifications/Certification Committee of the Continuous Quality Improvement Project Team of the Automotive Industry Action Group.

# ASSOCIATED BUSINESS CONSULTANTS, INC.

**Address/Phone**   201 E. Kennedy Boulevard, Suite 715
Tampa, FL 33602
Tel: (813) 223-3008; Fax: (813) 223-5406

**Contact**   Malcolm Harris
Steve Pearson

**Services**   Associated Business Consultants, Inc. provides consulting in ISO 9000 preparation, quality auditing, procedures development, and quality systems. Registered Lead Assessors from the United Kingdom and USA are on staff to perform quality system assessments. They provide consulting and training in SPC, ISO 9000 compliance, and auditing techniques.

**In Business**   6 years in the United Kingdom
1 year in the United States

**Clients Include**   Clients are involved in bulk materials, plastics, metals, wood, electronics, equipment, accounting, construction, distribution, and computers.

**Qualifications/**   Staff members are registered Lead Assessors, CQAs and CQEs.

# BQS, INC.

**Address/Phone**   110 Summit Avenue
Montvale, NJ 07645
Tel: (201) 307-0212, 800-624-5892; Fax: (201) 307-1778

| | |
|---|---|
| **Contact** | James C. Anderson |
| **Services** | Facilitation Services (Preparation for ISO 9000 - Consulting) |
| | Workshops - In-House (Internal Auditing Training Program, Document Control Workshop, Corrective Action workshop) |
| **In Business** | 6 years |
| **Clients Include** | Wang Laboratories, Sun Microsystems, James River Company, Hewlett Packard, NCR Corporation, BP Chemical, Allied Bendix Aerospace, Hoechst Celanese, ITT Cannon, Eastman Kodak. |
| **Qualifications/ Certifications** | BQS, Inc. is involved with various industries providing consulting services. BQS, Inc.'s expertise is in the following listed industries: Gear Manufacturing, Heavy Equipment, Computer, Paper, Chemical and related process industries. Each facilitator has specific training and background in assessment, installing and operating ISO 9000 registered systems. |

# BATALAS - HANDLEY-WALKER COMPANY

| | |
|---|---|
| **Address/Phone** | 17371 Irvine Blvd., Suite 250<br>Tustin, CA 92680<br>Tel: (714) 730-0122; Fax: (714) 730-0439 |
| **Contact** | Gary Crane or Rob Tucker |
| **Services** | Batalas - Handley-Walker offers a full range of consulting and training services, from initial adequacy audits through implementation assistance to pre-assessment audits. |
| **In Business** | Handley-Walker: 26 years<br>Batalas, Ltd.: 17 years |
| **Clients Include** | Advanced Cardiovascular Systems, Amdahl Computer, Apple Computer, Bausch & Lomb, Chesapeake Paper Products Company, Chevron International Oil Company, Emulex Caribe, Inc., NCR, Shell Oil Company, and Unisys Corporation |

| Qualifications/ Certifications | Part of the largest ISO 9000 consulting and training company in the world, Batalas - Handley-Walker Co. operates in the following countries: U.K., Ireland, Netherlands, France, Hungary, Hong Kong, Malaysia, India, Indonesia, Taiwan, Singapore, Australia, Curacao N.A., USA and Canada. Handley-Walker was established in 1966. Batalas, Ltd. was established in 1975 in the UK and quickly became a leading BS5750 consulting and training firm in Europe. |

# BOOZ•ALLEN & HAMILTON, INC.

| **Address/Phone** | 4330 East West Highway<br>Bethesda, MD 20814<br>Tel: (301) 907-4070; Fax: (301) 951-2255 |
| **Contact** | Joyce Doria |
| **Services** | Booz•Allen & Hamilton, Inc. provides consulting services for pre-registration assessment, registration support and strategic quality planning as well as training workshops. |
| **In Business** | 79 years |
| **Clients Include** | Fortune 200 firms, small and medium size companies, and all federal government agencies. |
| **Qualifications/ Certifications** | Booz•Allen & Hamilton, Inc. staff is composed of Lead Auditors, quality professionals, and subject matter experts from a wide range of industries and technologies located throughout the world. Booz•Allen & Hamilton, Inc. is not affiliated with any ISO 9000 Registrar. |

# BREWER & ASSOCIATES, INC.

| **Address/Phone** | 2505 Locksley Drive<br>Grand Prairie, TX 75050<br>Tel: (214) 641-8020; Fax: (214) 641-1327 |

**Contact**          Mike Cobb, Senior Vice President/CEO

**Services**         Brewer & Associates, Inc. has found that many programs being designed for
                     ISO 9000 introduce pressures and changes which are costly and unnecessary.

                     Brewer & Associates, Inc. offers a full range of quality consulting services,
                     with a specialty in design of quality systems to fit the organization and to
                     operate in conjunction with other quality enhancements, such as TQM,
                     Baldrige, etc.

**In Business**      9 years

**Clients Include**  Brewer & Associates, Inc. currently working with companies with ISO 9000
                     in the US, Canada, Mexico, Indonesia, Singapore and Malaysia. ALCOA,
                     Amtech Systems, Champion Technologies, Honeywell Micro Switch, Huffy
                     Bicycles, Lone Star Tool Company, Mushtag Pipe & Machinery, Occidental
                     Chemical Corporation, Paxton Polymer Corporation, Purna Bina Nusta

**Qualifications/**  Brewer & Associates, Inc. has been involved in quality system certification
**Certifications**   accreditation with the ASME program for Safety and Pollution Prevention
                     Equipment (SPPE) for Offshore Oil and Gas Operations for 14 years. They
                     created the original draft of the Q-1 Specification for a Quality System for the
                     American Petroleum Institute (API) in 1983.

# COLUMBIA QUALITY MANAGEMENT INTERNATIONAL (CQMI)

**Address/Phone**    P.O. Box 506
                     Orefield, PA 18069
                     Tel: (215) 391-9496; Fax: (215) 391-9497

**Contact**          J.P. Russell, President

**Services**         Columbia Quality Management International provides pre-assessment
                     evaluations and consultations by certified auditors. CQMI offers a wide range
                     of training programs and services for implementing ISO 9000.

**In Business**      5 years

**Clients Include** Allied Chemicals, American Cyanamid, Campbell Soup Company, Exxon Chemical Trading Inc., Internal Revenue Service, Northern Telecom, Owens/ Corning Fiberglass, Texaco Chemical, Coast Guard, Department of the Treasury

**Qualifications/** ASQC Certified Quality Auditors/IQA Lead Assessors
**Certifications**

# DONALD W. MARQUARDT AND ASSOCIATES

**Address/Phone** 1415 Athens Road
Wilmington, DE 19803
Tel: (302) 478-6695; Fax: (302) 478-9329

**Contact** Donald W. Marquardt, President

**Services** Donald W. Marquardt and Associates provides consulting and training in all phases of preparing for ISO 9000 certification. Consulting services and training also are provided in designing and analyzing experiments, and statistical process control using the Twin Metric improvement of Shewhart and CUSUM methods.

**In Business** 1 year

**Clients Include** Industrial companies and trade associations

**Qualifications/** Mr. Marquardt was with the Du Pont Company for 39 years. His assignments
**Certifications** included management of engineering services and consulting services. He organized and managed the Du Pont Quality Management and Technology Center. Mr. Marquardt is Chairman of the US Technical Advisory Group and leader of the US delegation to the ISO/TC176 committee, which developed the ISO 9000 series standards. He was chair of the ISO/TC176 international task force that prepared the Vision 2000 report establishing the strategic intent for implementing and revising the ISO 9000 series in the 1990's. He is a former President of the American Statistical Association, a Shewhart Medalist of the American Society for Quality Control, and has been a Senior Examiner for the Malcolm Baldrige National Quality Award. He has an IQA-approved lead assessor training certificate. He is a member of the Board of Directors of the Registrar Accreditation Board.

# DU PONT QUALITY MANAGEMENT & TECHNOLOGY CENTER

**Address/Phone**   Louviers 33W44
P.O. Box 6090
Newark, DE 19714-6090
Tel: (800) 441-8040 or (302) 366-2100; Fax: (302) 366-3366

**Contact**   Marg Bailey

**Services**   Du Pont Management & Technology Center offers a full range of services to help clients chart a successful course to ISO 9000 registration. The consultants can help a business start, or build on what it has already accomplished. Services include:

- ISO 9000 strategic planning consulting
- Quality system audits and auditor training (Internal audits and Pre-assessment audits)
- Quality manual evaluation
- Training seminars
- Training video package

**In Business**   30 years

**Clients Include**   Aluminum Company of America, AT&T Technology Systems, Atomic Energy of Canada Limited, The Bendix Corporation, Bethlehem Steel Corporation, Citgo Petroleum Corporation, The Clorox Company, Control Data, Adolph Coors Co., Corning Glass Works, R.J. Reynolds Tobacco Co.

**Qualifications/ Certifications**   Du Pont has been a leader in ISO 9000 implementation. Consultants in the Du Pont Quality Management & Technology Center have helped over 120 Du Pont businesses and many other businesses, large and small, prepare for ISO 9000 registration.

# EC TECHNICAL COMPLIANCE

**Address/Phone**   13 Westborn Drive
Nashua, NH 03062
Tel: (603) 880-8256; Fax: available on request

**Contact**   Jeffrey P. Tuthill

**Services**   EC Technical Compliance offers assistance in achieving ISO 9000/EN 29000 quality management system registration and referral of a quality registrar that will be recognized in the EC Single Market. It also offers assistance in documenting a quality system, providing preliminary audits and designing a company's internal audit function. EC Technical Compliance assists in developing awareness of the elements of the ISO 9000 series standards within a company, through seminars and workshops, which are customized to suit a corporation's needs.

**In Business**   Not available

**Clients Include**   G.W. Lisk Co., Exide Electronics, Union Specialists, Krebs Engineers, Ametek

**Qualifications/ Certifications**   Jeffrey Tuthill was previously employed with the National Standards Authority(NSAI) of Ireland and set up operations for NSAI in Merrimack, NH. During his two year tenure with NSAI, he received an in-depth education on compliance with the EC Single Market Technical Requirements. With this knowledge, he has developed a program of compliance with the essential requirements of EC "New Approach" Directives, utilizing the Firm Registration Scheme to ISO 9000/EN 29000 series standards. Mr.Tuthill offers additional consulting services related to this proactive program, using ISO 9000 registration as a compliance tool in the EC single market.

# FED-PRO, INC.

**Address/Phone**   5615 Jensen Drive
Rockford, IL 61111
Tel: (800) 833-3776; Fax: (815) 282-4304

**Contact**   Serge E. Gaudry

| | |
|---|---|
| **Services** | FED-PRO provides ISO 9000 training and offers computer software to assist in the preparation of an ISO 9001, 9002 or 9003 quality assurance manual. Services have included providing specialized on-site training on the US Department of Defense's MIL-Q-9858A and MIL-I-45208A specifications. To obtain timely information on the ISO standards, FED-PRO now has a representative based in London. |
| **In Business** | 10 years |
| **Clients Include** | Eli Lilly & Co., James River Corp., E.I. DuPont, GAF Building Materials, Allied Signal, TRW, Raytheon Corp., Fairchild Aircraft Corp., AT&T, General Electric |
| **Qualifications/ Certifications** | FED-PRO, Inc. has been providing quality assurance training services to the US Defense industry for the past ten years. FED-PRO consultants have written quality assurance manuals for firms ranging from twenty-person machine shops to Fortune 500 companies. FED-PRO has also been involved in quality-related projects with the US Navy nuclear program. During the past three years, they have taken an active role in assisting defense clients in adapting their quality program to the ISO 9000 standards. In 1991, FED-PRO published a video training program on ISO 9000 as well as a software program to assist its clients to prepare an ISO 9001, 9002 or 9003 quality assurance manual. |

# GILBERT EUROPE - GILBERT/COMMONWEALTH, INC.

| | |
|---|---|
| **Address/Phone** | P.O. Box 1498<br>Reading, PA 19603<br>Tel: (215) 775-2600; Fax: (215) 775-0221 |
| **Contact** | Kevin Kimmel |
| **Services** | Gilbert Europe, a wholly owned subsidiary of Gilbert/Commonwealth (G/C), was formed in 1981 to act as a focal point for international consulting services and provide auditing, training, and consulting services to companies as part of ISO 9000 quality system development and implementation. Gilbert Europe currently provides third-party assessment services as part of the UK Construction Steel Industry Certification Scheme. |

| | |
|---|---|
| **In Business** | 11 years |
| **Clients Include** | ARCO Chemical Company, EG&G, E.I. du Pont, Westinghouse, Department of Defense, Department of Energy, ARAMCO |
| **Qualifications/ Certifications** | Established in 1906, G/C has been providing design, consulting, project, and construction management services to a wide range of industries on a world-wide basis. |

# IQS, INC. (INTEGRATED QUALITY SYSTEMS)

| | |
|---|---|
| **Address/Phone** | 20525 Center Ridge Road, Suite 400 Cleveland, OH 44116 Tel: (216) 333-1344/(800)635-5901; Fax: (216) 333-3752 |
| **Contact** | John M. Cachat |
| **Services** | IQS provides consulting and training services, supported by a unique line of software products. IQS is a world leader in implementation-focused services and provides software tools to make it happen. |
| **In Business** | 6 years |
| **Clients Include** | Amoco Laser Company, Birmingham Metal Products, Gables Engineering, Honeywell, Inc., Kaiser Aluminum, Litton Industries Automotive, Parker Hannifin - Control, Rockwell - Rocketdyne Division, Union Carbide C&P Company Inc., and Westinghouse Electric |
| **Qualifications/ Certifications** | IQS has years of hands-on experience, backed by extensive academic credentials. IQS has helped several organizations prepare for and pass ISO 9000 assessments - faster and for less money. IQS' unique line of software product also helps clients with ISO 9000 certification maintain it. |

# INDEPENDENT QUALITY CONSULTANTS

**Address/Phone**  7480 W. Colorado Drive
Lakewood, CO 80232-6970
Tel: (303) 989-1210; Fax: (303) 989-1257

**Contact**  G.H. (Jay) Jones, Sr.

**Services**  Independent Quality Consultants' services include: ISO/TQM/SPC/MBNQA assessment, program development, training, and implementation

**In Business**  8 years

**Clients Include**  Coleman Outdoor Products, Coors Industries, Lear Siegler, Unocal 76 Corporation, Molycorp Inc., SAS Circuits, Defense Contract Management Command, Ohmeda Medical

**Qualifications/ Certifications**  Principal consultant, Jay Jones, is a graduate of California State University - Long Beach, a past Chairman of the Denver Section of the American Society for Quality Control, and a senior member of ASQC. He is a certified quality auditor, quality engineer, reliability engineer, and mechanical inspector.

# INFORMATION MAPPING, INC.

**Address/Phone**  300 Third Avenue
Waltham, MA 02154
Tel: (617) 890-7003; Fax: (617) 890-1330

**Contact**  Steve Gousie

**Services**  Information Mapping, Inc. (IMI) offers custom services for ISO 9000 in three areas:

- IMI experts work in close collaboration with clients to create documentation that meets ISO 9000 standards, with the goal of helping clients achieve ISO certification on their first attempt. This is a results-oriented service, based on Information Mapping's proprietary, research-based methodology for analyzing, organizing, and presenting information.

● IMI works with clients to establish a logical, structured ISO 9000 document control system. This ensures that employees, managers, and knowledge workers have quick, efficient access to all quality systems documentation.

● IMI's performance improvement specialists work with clients to implement quality management systems. This helps clients move beyond ISO 9000 certification to the organization-wide implementation of a quality management system, focusing on performance improvement by linking individual job performance to organizational goals.

**In Business** 25 years

**Clients Include** AT&T, Bell Atlantic, Dow Chemical Co., Dun & Bradstreet, Eastman Kodak, Intel Corp., Ricoh, Shawmut Bank, Shell Oil Co., US Postal Service

**Qualifications/ Certifications** IMI experts have made presentations at many ISO 9000/quality conferences, including ASQC regional conferences, BOSCON, Northeast Quality Control Conference (10/92), and the American Quality Congress national conference (5/92). IMI staff maintains membership in many ISO/quality organizations, including ASQC.

# INTERTEK SERVICES CORPORATION

**Address/Phone** 9900 Main Street
Fairfax, VA 22031
Tel: (703) ISO-9000; Fax: 7(03) 273-4124

**Contact** William Airey, Director of Special Programs

**Services** INTERTEK provides Quality Contract Services, which include management services, consulting, training, systems development, audits/assessments, surveys and inspections as well as key supplier services. INTERTEK is accredited to perform Quality Management System Certification and Registration and can provide in-house training services for Practical Auditing of Quality Management Systems to ISO-9000 and Lead Assessor Training Courses. INTERTEK's corporate headquarters is located in Fairfax, Virginia with their west coast office located in the Los Angeles area. INTERTEK has ten domestic regional offices, strategically located throughout North America, and nine international offices to support and satisfy our customer's requirements. INTERTEK's sister company, INTERTEK Technical Services, provides consulting services in preparation of Quality Management System Certification.

**In Business**      Nearly 20 years

**Clients Include**  Fortune 500 companies as well as smaller companies in the aerospace, aircraft, automotive, computer, communications, electronics, medical, chemical, utilities, and many other industries

**Qualifications/**  INTERTEK's certification and registration activities are accredited by the Dutch
**Certifications**   Council for Certification (Raad voor de Certificatie), to provide quality system certification and registration of quality management systems to firms seeking certification under one of the ISO-9000 international system standards. Accreditation by the RvC makes INTERTEK Services Corporation's certification mark directly traceable to an European governmental agency empowered to issue such certification. INTERTEK operates a formal certification system that satisfies the requirements of EN 45012, ISO-10011, Part 2 and the criteria of National Accreditation Councils. INTERTEK is accredited to perform certification and registration for the following industries: Electronic and Microelectronic Industry; Electrical and Electro-Mechanical Industry; Chemical and Pharmaceutical Industry; and General Manufacturing Industries.

# JOSEPH TIRATTO AND ASSOCIATES, INC.

**Address/Phone**    5 North Longview Road
                     Howell, NJ 07731-1701
                     Tel: (908) 367-0837; Fax: (908) 367-8898

**Contact**          Euring Joseph Tiratto, PE and President

**Services**         Services include: Quality Systems Consulting, Audits for ISO 9000 Series Standards, Auditor Training, Lectures/Seminars on ISO 9000 Series; Registration and Accreditation Systems.

**In Business**      1 year

**Clients Include** Machinery Manufacturers, Electrical Manufacturers, Electronic Manufacturers, Steel Mills, Forge Plants, Chemical Manufacturers, Service Industries, Shipping and Ship Building

**Qualifications/
Certifications** Joseph Tiratto has over 35 years of Engineering and Quality Management Service. He has BS Degrees in Naval Architecture & Marine Engineering and Mechanical Engineering. He has an MS Degree in Quality Management (December 1992). His qualifications also include Professional Engineer's License, Marine Engineer's License, Registered European Engineer (EC & EFTA Countries), Chartered Engineer (England), Registered Lead Assessor (IQA), Registered Lead Assessor Instructor, Member of Board of Directors of Registrar Accreditation Board (RAB), Member of ASQC Z-1 Committee on QA, and Member of TAG to ISO 176 Committee on QA.

# KOLKA & ASSOCIATES

**Address/Phone** 2193 Spear Point Drive
Marietta, GA 30062
Tel: (404) 977-4049; Fax: (404) 651-9185

**Contact** Dr. James W. Kolka, President

**Services** Services include:

- International legal consulting in product liability, product safety and services liability.

- Global Liability preventive law programs integrated with ISO 9000 Quality Assurance Programs designed to reduce liability exposure in US and EC markets.

- Certification for EC New Approach Directives, including Medical Devices Directives and new FDA ISO 9000 GMPs.

Kolka & Associates provides product certification programs, preventive law seminars, training workshops, strategic planning for manufacturers, engineering firms, services companies, law firms and insurance companies.

**In Business**     24 years

**Clients Include**  Georgia Tech Research Institute, Kaiser Aluminum & Chemical Corporation, Society for Automotive Engineers, International, Popham, Haik, Schnobrich & Kaufman, Ltd., National Electrical Manufacturers Association/Diagnostic Imaging Division, American Petroleum Institute, Quality Systems Update, Ministry of Education, Spain, Ministry of the Presidency, Costa Rica, US Office of Water Resources Research

**Qualifications/**  Dr. Kolka has a Ph.D. in Political Science & International Affairs; University
**Certifications**   of Kansas, a J.D. in Product Liability, Environmental Law; University of Wisconsin-Madison and a BS in Political Science (Economics/Chemistry), University of Wisconsin-Eau Claire. He is a member of the Wisconsin Bar Association, American Bar Association, and a Fellow at the American Council on Education, Ford Foundation. He served as full professor, published numerous articles, served as Vice President at Drake University and in the University System of Georgia. Dr. Kolka has held Senior Management positions in the University of Wisconsin System and developed Wisconsin's statewide Adult Extended Degree Program. He was instrumental in creating the Center for International Standards and Quality at Georgia Tech and has conducted seminars, workshops and programs throughout the United States, Europe and Latin America.

# L-CAD, INC.

**Address/Phone**   26 Keewaydin Drive
Unit A
Salem, NH 03079
Tel. (603) 893-3696; Fax. (603) 893-3544

**Contact**         Jeffrey P. Tuthill

**Services**        L-CAD offers assistance in the development of ISO 9000/EN 29000 quality systems, through initial training and assessment, documentation writing/editing, full preliminary assessment and internal auditor training, concluding with referral and arrangement of a European Quality Registrar for company Pre-License Assessment. L-CAD, Inc. will refer National Standards Authority of Ireland for Firm Registration, if a company does not have another preferred organization. L-CAD offers assistance in development of Testing Laboratory Accreditation to ISO/IEC Guide 25 or EN 45001 through training, assessment and Pre-License Audit by a European Laboratory Accreditation Body. L-CAD also provides product evaluation and testing to international, European and domestic Standards for TUV, CSA, UL, FCC and VDE Certifications.

| | |
|---|---|
| **In Business** | Consulting in Regulatory Compliance — 7 years<br>ISO 9000 consulting — 3 years |
| **Clients Include** | Exide Electronics, G.W. Lisk Co., KREBS Engineers, Ametec, Inc., Keithley Metrabyte |
| **Qualifications/<br>Certifications** | Qualifications include: BSi Lead Assessor Training and initial management of NSAI North American Certification Service in New Hampshire. L-CAD taught an ISO 9000 course for graduate studies class at Middlesex Community College in Lowell, MA, administered six ISO 9000 Workshops for NSAI in the United States, and held five in-house ISO 9000 workshops at various companies in 1992. L-CAD was involved with ISO 9000 Firm Registration of Beckman Instruments and Sun Microsystems. L-CAD employs experienced auditors for ISO 9000 and FDA Good Manufacturing Practice compliance and skilled technical writers for quality system documentation. |

# L. MARVIN JOHNSON AND ASSOCIATES, INC.

| | |
|---|---|
| **Address/Phone** | 822 Montezuma Way<br>West Covina, CA 91791<br>Tel. (818) 919-1728; Fax. (818) 919-7128 |
| **Contact** | L. Marvin Johnson, President |
| **Services** | L. Marvin Johnson and Associates, Inc. provides consulting services for quality management. It performs management, quality assurance and software system audits. It trains quality and evaluation auditors and ISO 9000 auditors. And, it provides various ISO 9000 seminars of varying lengths and costs. |
| **In Business** | 23 years |
| **Clients Include** | Bell Communications Research, South Carolina Electric and Gas, Johnston |

Pump Company, Western Gear Company, Rival Manufacturing Company, Burroughs, Western Precipitation (Joy Manufacturing), Memorex Corporation, Fluid Systems (Signal Company), Ford Aerospace, Stewart-Stevenson

**Qualifications/** L. Marvin Johnson and Associates, Inc. has been certified by the Governing
**Certifications** Board of the United Kingdom and the RAB of the United States for its ISO 9000 Quality Systems Lead Assessor courses.

# LEADS CORPORATION

**Address/Phone** PO Box 948217
Maitland, FL 32794
Tel. (407) 740-5444, 800-626-1832; Fax. (407) 740-5404

**Contact** F. R. "Bart" Bartolomei, Vice President

**Services** LEADS' consultants work closely with senior management to ensure their personal involvement and participation in: assessing their current quality and productivity status, establishing desired business-quality goals, developing a customized implementation plan and strategy, identifying specific improvement opportunities for immediate action, and defining and executing management actions which underscore their commitment.

**In Business** 9 years

**Clients Include** Arizona Department of Transportation, Department of Labor (OEUS), Office of Personnel Management, US Air Force Academy, Dow Corning, Empressa Naviera Santa, Hughes Simulation, Like Technologies, Inc., New York Telephone, Oxford Industries

**Qualifications/** The experience of the LEADS' consultants includes senior management
**Certifications** expertise in the service, manufacturing, human resources, aerospace, and engineering areas. LEADS Corporation is certified by the US Federal Government and the Arizona Department of Transportation to provide ISO 9000 consulting and training services. All consultants bring "hands-on" experience to every task and client.

# MCDERMOTT ASSOCIATES

**Address/Phone**  PO Box 1501
Arlington Heights, IL 60006
Tel. (708) 925-1707

**Contact**  Patrick J. McDermott

**Services**  McDermott Associates provides preliminary assessments for ISO 9000
certification as well as recommendations for achieving certification. They can
help organizations design and implement TQM processes. Associated training
services are provided in TQM, SPC and DOE. McDermott Associates
performs manual reviews for conformance to ISO 9000/Q90 series quality
systems standards. McDermott Associates also provides internal and external
auditing and seminars.

**In Business**  1 year

**Clients Include**  Specialization in medium and small businesses

**Qualifications/**  Patrick McDermott is President and Founder of McDermott Associates; an
**Certifications**  international consultancy. The firm was established in 1991, though the
principal has been engaged in the practice of quality since 1983. His experience in the quality field spans all phases of manufacturing, from electronic
switchboards to hand tools to plastics industries. Patrick McDermott is a
trained quality auditor and lead auditor to ISO 9000 standards. He holds a
Masters Degree in Management (MBA) and a BA Degree in Business/
Statistics. He is an active member of IIE and ASQC and a guest lecturer at
Governors State University on quality assurance.

# MEDICAL TECHNOLOGY CONSULTANTS EUROPE LIMITED (MTC EUROPE)

**Address/Phone**  Arndale House
The Precinct
Egham
Surrey TW20 9HN, UK
Tel: +44 (0) 784 432233; Fax: +44 (0) 784 470026

161 Boulevard Reyers
1040 Brussels
Belgium
Tel: +32 (0) 2 732 6070; Fax: +32 (0) 2 732 5575

**Contact**      Susan Whittle, Ph.D.

**Services**      MTC Europe offers assessment and auditing services and consulting on the
implementation of quality systems. The company recognizes that ISO 9001
(EN 29001) and ISO 9002 (EN 29002) will be the most efficient and satisfactory route to obtaining a CE Mark under the new European medical device
directives. MTC Europe has on its permanent staff an experienced UK
Department of Health lead assessor who can assess a manufacturer's present
quality status and advise on the steps required to satisfy quality standards.

**In Business**      3 years

**Clients Include**  Several of the world's top 20 healthcare manufacturers

**Qualifications/**  Medical Technology Consultants Europe, with its integrated advisory and
**Certification**    information service, is in an unrivaled position to offer accurate, objective, up-
to-date data and interpretation as well as practical guidance on what to do and
how to do it. Their team includes a former Director of the Scientific and
Technical Branch of the UK Department of Health, a Barrister and international businessman, an MD and PhD, a biochemical engineer, a qualified Lead
Assessor, a registered French pharmacist, an electronics engineer, and a
linguist. Team support includes a former director of the FDA Center for
Devices and Radiological Health, and a Professor of Cardiology.

# N.C. KIST & ASSOCIATES, INC.

**Address/Phone**  900 East Porter Avenue
Naperville, IL 60540
Tel. (708) 357-1180; Fax. (708) 357-3349

**Contact**      Robert E. Fisher

**Services**       N.C. Kist & Associates, Inc. offers a complete line of consulting services in
                   ISO 9000 including:

- Preparation of Quality Manuals and Quality Systems Procedures
- Quality Systems Auditor Training
- Training in ISO 9000 Requirements
- Implementation Assistance
- Pre-Registrar Assessment Audits
- Assistance during Registrar Assessment
- Periodic Quality Systems Evaluation.

**In Business**    20 years

**Clients Include** Aoki Industries Co., Ltd., Bakrie Pipe Industries, Crane Kemlite, FMC
                   Corporation, FRESA, International Computers, Ltd., Rhinelander Paper,
                   Sonoco Fibre Drum, Vallinox

**Qualifications/** N.C. Kist & Associates, Inc. specializes in developing cost-effective quality
**Certifications**  systems based on national and international standards. Since 1972 they have
                   assisted more than 250 clients worldwide. In 1987 they began to offer ISO
                   9000 consulting and have 30 ISO 9000 customers in the USA, Europe and the
                   Pacific Rim.

# OMNI TECH INTERNATIONAL, LTD.

Address/Phone    2715 Ashman Street
                 Suite 100
                 Midland, MI 48640
                 Tel. (517) 631-3377; Fax. (517) 631-7360

Contact          Douglas B. Todd

Services         Omni Tech International, Ltd. services include interpretation and implementa-
                 tion of manuals and procedures, adequacy audits and principles of auditing,
                 and ISO 9000 training. Omni Tech conducts ISO pre-certification (adequacy)
                 assessments. Once a client has determined that registration under an ISO
                 standard is needed, Omni Tech will assess the client's quality manual (if one
                 exists) and quality systems to determine how well they comply with the

criteria of the specific ISO standard. If these audits indicate that the client's manual and/or systems are not in compliance, Omni Tech will work with the client to develop the Quality Manual, and to implement the Quality Systems required.

| | |
|---|---|
| In Business | 6.5 years |

| | |
|---|---|
| Clients Include | Akzo Chemicals, BASF, Ferro Corporation, Franklin International, Hewlett-Packard, Monsanto, Occidental Chemical, Rhone-Poulenc, Texaco, Union Carbide |

| | |
|---|---|
| **Qualifications Certifications** | Omni Tech's qualifications include provisional RAB auditor, ASQC, CQA, provisional IQA assessor, IQA Lead Auditor, RAB Lead Auditor, member of ASQC-CQA Chemical Interest Committee, author of ANSI/ASQC Q90/ISO 9000 Guidelines, and 35-plus years experience with Dow Chemical Company. |

# PERRY JOHNSON, INC.

| | |
|---|---|
| **Address/Phone** | 3000 Town Center<br>Suite 2960<br>Southfield, MI 48075<br>Tel. (313) 356-4410; Fax. (313) 356-4230 |
| **Contact** | Bob Hammill |
| **Services** | Perry Johnson, Inc. (PJI) is a full-service TQM and ISO 9000 consulting, training and implementation firm. In addition to providing training courses, PJI is the world's largest creator and provider of proprietary TQM and ISO 9000 training support products, including programmed instruction workbooks, overhead transparency presentation packages, videotape presentations and computer software packages. |
| **In Business** | 9 years |
| **Clients Include** | 85% of the Fortune 500, including Johnson Wax, Mobil, Riverwood International, Northrop, US Navy, Graham Packaging, Heinz Pet Products, Ford Motor Company, Nabisco, Litton |

**Qualifications/ Certifications**   Since 1983 PJI has trained employees of more than 1,200 organizations throughout North America and Europe, implemented TQM in more than 500 facilities, presented seminars to more than 600,000 people and trained more than 1,300,000 others via its product catalog. PJI holds a contract awarded by the United States Office of Personnel Management to provide TQM services and products to agencies of the Federal government (OPM-89-2870). PJI is also a training contractor to the US General Services Administration (GS-02F-7576A).

# PROCESS MANAGEMENT INTERNATIONAL

**Address/Phone**   7801 E. Bush Lake Road, Suite 360
Minneapolis, MN 55439-3115
Tel. (800) 258-0313; Fax. (612) 893-0502

**Contact**   Pete Malkovich

**Services**   Process Management International (PMI), a leader in the consultation, education and training of Total Quality Management, offers a full range of ISO 9000 consulting and training services. PMI has teamed its TQM expertise with the ISO 9000 consulting experience of Optimum Systems for Quality (OSQ), based in Preston, United Kingdom. Together, PMI and OSQ have developed systems that make ISO 9000 consulting and training more effective, and more efficient. Based on more than five years of practice and research, these services assist companies with ISO 9000 registration and provide an effective means to enhance quality management within a company.

**In Business**   9 years

**Clients Include**   Zytec Corporation, Control Data, E-C Apparatus, Wales Scientific, BHP, Liquid Carbonics

**Qualifications/ Certifications**   PMI's ISO 9000 services combine its TQM expertise with that of OSQ. Results include:

● A proven ISO 9000 model, based on over 5 years of practice and research

● More than 50 organizations have achieved registration on their first attempt

- A network of experienced quality consultants nationwide who are able to integrate other TQM methods with ISO 9000

- Certified Lead Auditor training by consultants who know first-hand how internal auditing fits with the ISO 9000 effort and who have successfully worked with organizations for the past 8 years in improving the quality of their products and services.

# QUALITY MANAGEMENT CONSULTING SERVICES

**Address/Phone**  62 Murray Drive
Oceanside, NY 11572-5722
Tel. (516) 536-1859; Fax. Same as above

**Contact**  Dan Epstein

**Services**  ISO 9000 services include:

- Needs and Pre-audit Assessment
- Customized Quality Manuals and Procedures
- Motivational and Awareness Training
- Quality Management System Implementation.

For other quality related areas, services include:

- Motivational Training
- TQM and SPC initiatives
- Military Quality Systems Implementation
- Quality Improvement Tools
- Seminars/Workshops
- Problem Solving Tools.

**In Business**  1.5 years

**Clients Include**  Koehler Instrument Company, Davis Vision Systems, Technology Systems Corporation, ADEMCO, J. LeBoyer and Company

**Qualifications/**    Qualifications include more than 37 years experience in standards, reliability,
**Certifications**    quality control, safety, and motivational training. Prior to his present
consultancy, Mr. Epstein was a Senior Vice President, for 16 years, of a major
east-coast electronics manufacturer, with domestic and international responsibilities for product assurance, and responsibilities for overall manufacturing in
Japan and Taiwan. Mr. Epstein is an author and lecturer, has provided
testimony to Congress and is currently an Examiner for the Malcolm Baldrige
National Quality Award and has been certified as an ISO 9000 Lead Assessor/
Auditor by QMI Ltd. (UK).

# QUALITY PRACTITIONERS INC.

**Address/Phone**    417 First Street North
Indian Rocks Beach, FL 34635
Tel. (813) 596-2296; Fax. (813) 593-2192

                  **Contact**        Michael Hudson

**Address/Phone**    3100 Ridgeway Drive
Suite 2
Mississauga, Ontario L5L 5M5
Tel. (416) 569-6431; Fax. (416) 569-7651

                  **Contact**        Charles McRobert

**Services**    Quality Practitioners Inc. provides consulting and training services based on
the ISO 9000 and ISO 10011 quality standards. They specialize in the use of
these standards and are not involved with the application of other quality
philosophies. They provide in-house training, registration audits (on contract
basis), implementation training for system orientation and internal audit,
confidential pre-assessment audits and liaison with the registrar.

**In Business**    4 years

**Clients Include**    Russelsteel, Standard Machine, Prairie Machine, Doepker Industries, Amoco
Chemical Company, Amoco Performance Products, Inc., Iron Ore of Canada,
Petro-Canada, Lubplex, Novacor Chemicals, Ltd., Polysar Rubber Corporation

**Qualifications/** Staff is experienced in the use of the ISO 9000 standard and have assisted
**Certifications** companies to achieve ISO registration. Staff members are accredited auditors.

# QUALITY SCIENCES INSTITUTE

**Address/Phone** 3020 Issaquah-Pine Lake Rd
Suite 31
Issaquah, WA 98027
Tel. (206) 392-7573; Fax. (206) 391-9219

**Contact** K. C. Ayers

**Services** Services include ISO 9000 consulting, in-house training and public seminars.

**In Business** 1 year

**Clients Include** Advance Technology Laboratories (ATL), Allied Systems Company, Amfab
Resources, Carlton Company, Cyclo Products, Datatcom Technologies, Inc.,
Flir Systems, Inc., Radisys Corporation

**Qualifications/** ASQC Member; two members are ASQC Fellows. Course offerings are
**Certifications** endorsed by the National Education Quality Initiative and Association for
Quality and Participation.

# r. bowen international

**Address/Phone** 149 West Market Street
York, PA 17401-1314
Tel. (717) 843-4880; Fax. (717) 854-8591

**Contact** Robert D. Bowen

**Services** r. bowen international provides project planning, education, training, audits,
on-site resources, documentation services and supplier services.

**In Business** Since January 1, 1992

**Clients Include**  Electronics Industry, Food Processing Industry, Computer manufacturers, Micrographics, metallurgy

**Qualifications/**  Robert D. Bowen is ASQC certified as a Quality Engineer and Quality
**Certifications**  Auditor, with 15 years experience.

# ROBERT PEACH AND ASSOCIATES, INC.

**Address/Phone**  541 North Brainard Avenue
LaGrange Park, IL 60525
Tel. (708) 579-3400; Fax. (708) 579-1620

**Contact**  Robert W. Peach, Principal

**Services**  Robert Peach and Associates, Inc. evaluates quality management practices, conducts comprehensive quality fitness reviews, and makes in-depth analyses of quality systems. Assessments based on ISO 9000 and Baldrige Award criteria are used to develop quality manuals and documentation to meet customer requirements.

**In Business**  12 years

**Clients Include**  North American Philips, Inland Steel Company, Motorola, Inc., Corning, Inc., Sematech, Institute of Industrial Launderers, ASQC (As Administrator of Malcolm Baldrige Consortium), Management Association of Illinois, Georgia Institute of Technology, University of Wisconsin

**Qualifications/**  Robert Peach is a Certified Quality Engineer and a Registered Professional
**Certifications**  Engineer in Quality Engineering.

# R.P. COONEY & ASSOCIATES

**Address/Phone**  5868 East 71st Street
# 194
Indianapolis, IN 46220
Tel. (317) 845-0885

**Contact**          Ray Cooney

**Services**         R.P. Cooney & Associates help clients develop ISO-9000 conforming quality
                     management systems cost-effectively. Services include:

- Assistance in integrating ISO-9000 into existing TQM and continuous
  improvement efforts
- Management and staff training in the ISO-9000 standards
- Assessment of Quality Systems against ISO-9001, 9002, or 9003
- Gap analysis and corrective action assistance
- Facilitating ISO-9000 implementation planning and cost estimation
- Registrar selection and interface
- Pre-registration audit preparation.

**In Business**      First Listing

**Clients Include**  First Listing

**Qualifications/**  Raymond P. Cooney is a Business Consultant specializing in helping
**Certifications**   companies get rapid, bottom-line results from their TQM efforts. Mr. Cooney
                     has had extensive experience successfully implementing continuous improve-
                     ment while holding a variety of technical and managerial positions during 14
                     years with Exxon Chemical Company. Prior to joining Exxon, he worked for
                     Amoco, US Gypsum Co., and the Gillette Co. He received his Doctorate in
                     Chemistry from the University of Florida.

                     In 1991, Mr. Cooney received the Intermediates President's Award for leading
                     Exxon Chemical's first ISO-9000 registration in North America. He also
                     served in an advisory capacity for Exxon Chemical's second North American
                     ISO-9000 registration. His implementation efforts give him experience in
                     applying ISO-9000 in discrete and continuous manufacturing and service
                     situations. He has helped design and implement ISO-9000-conforming
                     auditing, corrective action, and document control systems, and quality
                     manuals. Mr. Cooney currently serves on the Reference Materials Committee
                     of the Accreditation Council of the American Association for Laboratory
                     Accreditation (A2LA). This Committee reviews and approves all of A2LA's
                     registration of reference materials suppliers' quality systems to ISO-9001 and
                     ISO 9002.

                     Mr. Cooney helped develop Exxon Chemical's Quality Principles Course and

Baldrige Award Management Self-Assessment Module. He is co-author of world class SQC software, and has helped design and implement a company-wide internal quality benchmarking network. He has started and led self-managed quality improvement teams and championed employee recognition and suggestion systems. Mr. Cooney has taken the 5-day BSI Lead Auditor and ASQC Quality Auditing courses. He is a member of ASQC, Organization Development Network, and the American Chemical Society, and has presented papers at national ASTM and world-wide Exxon TQM Conferences.

# SAFETY AND COMPLIANCE ENGINEERING, INC.

**Address/Phone**  25362 Shadywood
Laguna Niguel, CA 92677
Tel. (714) 363-1402

**Contact**  Gilbert Walter, President

**Services**  Services include: Product Safety, EMI/RFI, Quality Engineer & Technical Specification, Photography, Mechanical Engineering, Product Marketing, Component Engineering, and assistance to conformance to the Federal NISTIR4721 directive.

**In Business**  9 years

**Clients Include**  Information not available at time of publication

**Qualifications/ Certifications**  Safety and Compliance Engineering, Inc. (SCE) is a conglomerate of 25 senior engineering consultants. SCE has three trained ISO 9000 auditors. The founder of SCE is a state- and internationally-certified professional in product safety certification, a quality control engineer, California-certified professional engineer, California-licensed electrical inspector, member of IEEE, member of the American Society of Safety Engineers, and an international certified product safety manager.

# SANDERS QUALITY ASSOCIATES, INC.

**Address/Phone**   820 Gessner
Suite 940
Houston, TX 77024
Tel. (713) 465-8772; Fax. (713) 465-9742

**Contact**   Dr. Don Sanders

**Services**   Sanders Quality Associates, Inc., provides training and consulting in Continuous Quality Improvement and ISO 9000. Sanders offers courses on the implementation of a comprehensive quality program that integrates SPC and skills from the people side of quality as well as a comprehensive two-day course of ISO 9000 training in Leadership for Quality and Performance Enhancement.

**In Business**   11 years

**Clients Include**   VISTA Chemical, General Dynamics, Quanex Tube Group, Groth Corporation, Hollywood Marine, Mayer Electric, Industrial Distribution Group, PDVSA Services, Inc., PDVSA Services, BV, Bariven, SA.

**Qualifications/ Certifications**   Authors of the AMA Book/Course ISO 9000: A Step Guide to Registration, Sanders Quality Associates hold Ph.D.'s in statistics and are experienced Quality Auditors. Sanders Quality Associates, Inc. received its original lead auditor training via British Standards Institute approved courses.

# SCOTT TECHNICAL SERVICES

**Address/Phone**   34 Channing Street
Suite 400
Newton, MA 02158
Tel. (617) 527-7032; Fax. (617) 527-0618

**Contact**   Stephen Keneally or Otis Russell

**Services**   Services include: documentation and implementation of quality management systems per ISO-9000 guidelines; training in all levels of organizations in

Total Quality Management as continuous improvement. Scott Technical Services provides "hands-on, shirt-sleeve" operations management consulting to foster rapid organizational improvement.

**In Business**  7 years

**Clients Include**  Abiomed, Inc., Allied-Signal Aerospace Corporation (Bendix Communications Division), Cobra Industries, Inc., ELBIT Computer Ltd., GTE-Government Systems, Lavolin Corporation, MBTA-Mass. Bay Transportation Authority, Pacesetter Systems, Polymer Technology Corporation, Schwartzkopf Development Corporation

**Qualifications/ Certifications**  Qualifications include 100-plus years of combined experience in all phases of quality assurance and operations management. Initially focused on the Aerospace and Defense Industries, Scott Technical Services' experience now includes computers, telecommunications, medical electronics/devices, capital equipment, transportation and service.

# SERVICE PROCESS CONSULTING, INC.

**Address/Phone**  76 George Avenue
Edison, NJ 08820
Tel. (908) 321-0045; Fax. (908) 549-9117

**Contact**  Ian Durand, President

**Services**  Service Process Consulting, Inc. delivers customized consulting and training to service organizations and manufacturing companies to support their implementation of effective quality management systems. The firm also leads public workshops on behalf of trade and business organizations. The principals have particular expertise and experience in the ISO 9000 series of quality standards and in TQM.

**In Business**  3 years

**Clients Include**  Dorman-Roth Foods, Inc., Hexcel Corp., New Zealand Milk Products, Pittman, W.R. Grace, Delaware County Community College, Northeast Wisconsin Technical College

**Qualifications/ Certifications**   The president and principal consultant has been actively involved for more than 6 years in ISO 9000 series efforts. Mr. Durand has served as a senior examiner for the Malcolm Baldrige National Quality Award, and has studied and practiced in the areas of individual and group dynamics. Mr. Durand also has more than 30 years of experience in technical and management positions with AT&T, including developing a process quality and management methodology that is standard across the corporation. Other staff members have diverse experience in training, group dynamics, interpersonal skills, and process management. The firm recently created a comprehensive video seminar package on ISO 9000.

# SOFTWARE QUALITY ASSOCIATES

**Address/Phone**   2725 Coliseum Street
Los Angeles, CA 90018
Tel. (213) 292-5288

**Contact**   Edward L. Jordan

**Services**   ISO 9000 services consist of a pre-certification service in the area of software quality management and assurance and in the area of ISO 9000-3 software guidelines seminars. The firm also has capabilities on DoD Standards, such as 2167A, 2168, FDA Standards, GMPs; NATO Standards and IEEE Standards.

**In Business**   10 years

**Clients Include**   Eaton-Contel, McDonnell Douglas, Phoenix International Programming, DOD/US Air Force, DOD/US Navy

**Qualifications/ Certifications**   Edward Jordan has more than 30 years' experience in software engineering, specializing in software quality system management and quality assurance. He has developed and taught software quality assurance seminars for the DoD and other major firms, including AT&T and Ford Aerospace. He has developed seminars on various industry standards including DoD-STD-2167A, DoD-STD-2168, IEEE 730/983 and ISO 9000-3. Jordan received both his B.A. in Business Administration (1975) and M.B.A. in Management (1977) from Pepperdine University.

# STAT-A-MATRIX GROUP

**Address/Phone**   2124 Oak Tree Road
Edison, NJ 08820
Tel. (908) 548-0600; Fax. (908) 548-0409

**Contact**   Alan Marash, Vice President

**Services**   The STAT-A-MATRIX Group has been helping companies since 1968 in developing quality systems and in training personnel to meet the requirements of regulatory and consensus standards. Hence, their ISO 9000 activities are a direct outgrowth of prior successes in meeting nuclear, defense, FDA, and other quality requirements. They offer total consulting services, including initial baseline evaluation, top management orientation, action planning, quality system documentation and implementation, all levels of employee training, formal preassessment, support during third-party assessment, and follow-on services after registration. In addition, they offer public seminars in ISO 9000 overviews, lead assessor certification and internal auditor training, ISO 9000-3 and other specialized subjects such as documentation, FDA, DoD and the auto industry.

**In Business**   24 years

**Clients Include**   Fortune 500 companies, middle-market companies and small firms. References can be provided.

**Qualifications/**   STAT-A-MATRIX's worldwide staff of more than 60 includes approximately
**Certifications**   30 ISO 9000 management consultants, certified assessors and certified lead assessors. The average staff member has over 25 years of industry experience, plus an advanced degree and/or professional credentials, such as P.E., CQA, CQE, or IQA certification. STAT-A-MATRIX Group staff includes TC 176 members, ASQC fellows, and Baldrige Award examiners. They were the first US-based organization registered by the IQA, in London, England, to provide Lead Assessor Certification training and RAB registration is expected when the program is formalized. Members of their US, UK, Belgian, Japanese and Brazilian offices have assisted hundreds of companies to attain ISO 9000 registration.

# TQM CONSULTING

**Address/Phone**    Total Quality Management
2701 Revere St.
Suite 232
Houston, TX 77098
Tel. (713) 523-2312; Fax. (713) 520-0495

**Contact**             William E. Cox

**Services**            Total Quality Management (TQM) Consulting offers ISO 9000 quality
management systems design and implementation assistance and general
consulting on any quality improvement process based on principles of
Deming, Juran, Ishikawa, Crosby, TQM, SPC, the Baldrige award criteria, or
ISO 9000. Expertise includes the petrochemical industry, both services and
manufacturing, engineering and construction, research and development.

**In Business**        1.5 years

**Clients Include**   Exxon Chemical Co., Exxon Production Research Co., Callaway Chemical
Co., Cole Chemical & Distributing, Inc., Lyondell Petrochemical Co., Union
Carbide Chemicals & Plastics Co. Inc., Petrolite, KRC, Inc., Aztec Services,
Inc.

**Qualifications/**   William Cox has seventeen years experience in the petrochemical industry
**Certifications**     and seven years experience in quality management. He has been a member of
ASQC since 1987. Mr. Cox is an IQA-certified lead assessor (pending). He
has a BSChE degree from the University of Tennessee, 1975.

# THE TQM GROUP

**Address/Phone**    222 Berkeley Street, 15th Floor
Boston, MA 02116
Tel. (617) 236-8110; Fax. (617) 236-8120

**Contact**             Dan O'Brien, Partner

**Services**            The TQM Group's (TQMG) services take two basic forms: customized executive education and consulting services. Because of its roots in and affiliations with academia, The TQM Group can offer executive education that presents breakthrough concepts in compelling, high-impact executive sessions. Its executive workshops help senior managers understand the personal roles they must assume in order to lead a successful quality-improvement process, not just oversee one. The TQM Group's faculty members have presented executive seminars on a broad range of quality-related topics, including the Malcolm Baldrige Quality Award Framework, Building Leadership Competencies, Strategic Quality Planning and Goal Setting, Service Guarantees, Total Quality Management Systems, Setting Your Corporate Vision and Customer Retention.

In its consulting practice, TQMG employs a quality-assessment framework modeled on the Malcolm Baldrige National Quality Award methodology. Over the past three years, the award methodology has emerged as an international standard to assess quality performance. This assessment process includes:

- A thorough review of employee and customer data and other existing quality measurements
- Focus group interviews with senior and middle managers as well as with first-level supervisors and line employees
- In-depth review of past and existing quality practices
- A review of corporate and industry documents.

When an assessment is completed, TQMG also provides assistance with development of quality plans and the implementation of those plans.

**In Business** 4 years

**Clients Include** Automotive, Financial Services, Insurance, Hotels and Resorts, Telecommunications, Diversified Services, Software Development, Shipping and Freight, Airline, Retailing, Professional Services, Food Services

**Qualifications/ Certifications** The TQM Group was founded in Cambridge, Massachusetts in 1989 by a group of service professionals with roots at the Harvard Business School and with extensive experience in the application of quality-improvement strategies. The TQM Group's work is devoted exclusively to the design and implementation of total quality management systems. The TQM Group's expertise in the quality field is enhanced both by their own ongoing research and by their affiliations with quality experts in industry and academia.

# THORNHILL USA

**Address/Phone**   P.O. Box 3643
Wilmington, DE 19807
Tel. (215) 444-3998; Fax. (215) 444-1365

**Contact**   Ralph D. Schmidt

**Services**   Services include: Malcolm Baldrige, ISO 9001-2, Auto Standards, Supplier and Contractor Audits, SPC Training, Procedure and Manual Writing -- Resourcing Leadership on Strategy and Business Plans

**In Business**   1 year

**Clients Include**   Automotive Suppliers, Custom Plastic Resin, Compounders, and Major Chemical Companies

**Qualifications/**
**Certifications**   Each consultant has lead assessor training and over five years of "hands-on" quality system experience with Fortune 500 companies prior to joining the firm. IQA Registration is in process. Thornhill USA staff are ASQC members.


# UNC QUALITY MANAGEMENT SERVICES

**Address/Phone**   A Division of UNC Manufacturing Technology
67 Sandy Desert Road
Uncasville, CT 06382
Tel. (800) 628-6424, (203) 848-1511; Fax. (203) 848-2757

**Contact**   Craig R. Mesler, Director, Quality Services

**Services**
- ISO 9000 Training, Implementation, Consulting, and Preassessments
- Internal Quality Auditor Training
- Total Quality Management
- Process Improvement Programs
- Statistical Process Control Implementation and Training
- Quality System Implementation.

**In Business**   2 years

**Clients Include**   The J.M. Ney Co., The Ensign Bickford Co., The Thermo Electron Co., QualityAlert Institute, Mike Demma Inc., Tri Manufacturing, Inc., Chemical Dynamics, Inc., BQS, Inc., Analysis and Technology, Reflectone, Inc.

**Qualifications/ Certifications**   UNC employs certified ISO 9000 Auditors and Lead Auditors

# THE VERITY CONSULTING GROUP INC.

**Address/Phone**   12021 Wilshire Blvd.
Suite 825
Los Angeles, CA 90025
Tel. (213) 389-9700; Fax. (213) 389-9701

**Contact**   Charles Adams, Vice President

**Services**   Verity Consulting specializes in competitive analysis and competitive benchmarking. Its services include:

- Proprietary Studies (Benchmarking, Strategic-level Competitive Analysis, and Industry Attractiveness Studies)

- Seminars and Workshops (Hands-on Benchmarking Techniques, Implementing Benchmarking in Your Organization, Competitive Data Acquisition and Analysis, and Integrating Competitive Analysis into Strategic Plans)

- On-site Assistance (Building the Benchmarking Team, Competitive Data Acquisition and Analysis, Implementing Benchmarking Results, and Strategy Facilitation)

**In Business**   10 years

**Clients Include**   IBM, AT&T, Du Pont, Exxon, General Motors, United Airlines, Proctor & Gamble, Rockwell International, Pacific Gas and Electric Company, American National Standards Institute (ANSI)

**Qualifications/** Verity Consulting is the leading company in the field of competitive
**Certifications** benchmarking. The Directors of the company have completed hundreds of
proprietary benchmarking projects in a variety of different industries, including the following: Chemicals, Automotive, Pharmaceuticals, Gas and Electric
Utilities, Banking, Computers, Consumer Products, Airlines, Telecommunications, and Forest and Paper Products. Equally broad is its range of functional
experience. Verity has completed proprietary benchmarking studies in
virtually every functional area, including the following: Manufacturing,
Information Systems, Engineering, Human Resources, Sales, Research and
Development, Product Development, Marketing, Strategic Planning, Finance,
Training, and Purchasing.

# THE VICTORIA GROUP (MANAGEMENT CONSULTANTS) LIMITED

**Address/Phone**  PO Box 536
Fairfax, VΛ 22030
Tel. (703) 250-4990; Fax. (703) 250-5523

      **Contact**        Connie Johnson, USA Training Coordinator

**Address/Phone**  42 The Square,
Kelso,
Roxburghshire,
Scotland
Tel. +44 573 223399; Fax. +44 573 223701

      **Contact**        Ollie Young, Director

**Address/Phone**  13 High Street,
Billingshurst,
West Sussex, RH14 9PL
Tel. +44 403 785191; Fax. Same

      **Contact**        Rod Goult, CEO and USA Business Manager

**Services**  The Victoria Group (Management Consultants) Ltd. provides a full range of quality-related services. The company has unrivaled experience in implementing quality systems based on ISO 9000 or similar Standards; the principals and associates can claim well over 100 successful registrations. Services offered cover implementation planning and facilitation, executive orientation, staff and associate training in quality concepts, ISO and total quality management disciplines. The Victoria Group operates a Lead Auditor Training program which is recognized by the Governing Board of the Assessor Registration Scheme in the United Kingdom.

**In Business** 2 years

**Clients Include** The L.S. Starrett Company (Scotland) Ltd., Eastman Kodak, Hewlett-Packard, York International, Siemens Industrial Automation, Millipore Waters, Eli-Lilly, GTE, Coors, AT&T

**Qualifications/ Certifications** Most staff are Registered Assessors or Registered Lead Assessors within the British Government recognized scheme. All have been functionally responsible for the successful implementation and management of ISO 9001 or ISO 9002 based quality systems. They have extensive experience with many other industry and national standards, including MIL-Q-9858A, AQAP-1, Ford Q1, IBM and others.

# WRIGHT RELIABILITY/QUALITY PLANNING & SERVICES

**Address/Phone** 6 Susan Road
Marlborough, MA 01752
Tel. (508) 481-2631; Fax. Same

**Contact** Donald Wright

**Services** Services for any business wanting to improve product quality/reliability include:

- Automated data management system for planning ISO 9000 or TQM management systems
- Electronic equipment reliability projections to MIL-HDBK-217F or mathematical modeling of system
- Statistical Process Control (SPC)

- Charting and Graphing Statistics of Production Data
- Quality Function Deployment (QFD)
- Design of Experiments (Taguchi)
- Teaching in these areas.

**In Business**    2.5 years

**Clients Include**  Not available at time of publication.

**Qualifications/**    Donald Wright's qualifications include: Registered Auditor for ISO 9000,
**Certifications**     ASQC Reliability Engineering Certification RO1974, RCA Institutes in
Electronics (Audio/Video) 1960. He has a BGS Degree in Mathematics and
Science from Rollins College 1963, an MS in Systems Management from the
Florida Institute of Technology (Honors) 1970. Mr. Wright has thirty-plus
years experience as an engineer with training in design, all phases of Reliabil-
ity (physics and mathematical modeling), Statistical Process Control (SPC),
Quality (management, planning, and measures), writing software to teaching
reliability, and quality methods.

# Appendix D

# ISO 9000 RESOURCES

## BOOKS

*ISO 9000 Certification • Total Quality Management*
Author: Subhash C. Puri

This book discusses Total Quality Management and ISO 9000 certification. Subjects include:

- Developing a TQM Model
- TQM Model via ISO 9004
- Service Quality Model
- Software Quality Model
- Quality System Accreditation
- Quality System Standards
- Developing Quality Manuals
- Quality System Auditing, Guidelines, Checklist.

To order, send check for $40 (or Canada $45) plus $4 postage and handling to:

Standards-Quality Management Group
PO Box 66654
Washington Square
Washington, DC 20035
USA

PO Box 4146, Station "C"
Ottawa, Ontario K1Y 4P2
Canada
Tel:/Fax: (613) 820-2445

*ISO 9000 Explained, An Interpretation Guide*
    Author: Jack Kanholm

Published by:
    AQA Inc.
    334 Crane Blvd.
    Los Angeles, CA 90065
    Tel: (213) 222-3600; Fax: (213) 222-5239

This guide systematically interprets the ISO 9001, 9002 and 9003 standards. It explains the purpose, importance, scope and application of every requirement and offers illustrative examples of practical ways to achieve compliance. It also contains an exhaustive list of procedures and records needed to document an ISO 9000 system - $57 plus shipping.

**ISO 9000 Preparing for Registration**
    Author: James Lamprecht

Published by:
    Marcel Dekker, Inc.
    270 Madison Ave.
    New York, NY 10016

This book offers efficient ways to initiate an ISO 9000-based system from documentation through registration. Available from:

    ASQC Quality Press
    Customer Service Department
    PO Box 3066
    Milwaukee, WI 53201-3066
    Tel: (800) 248-1946; Fax: (414) 272-1734
    (ISBN 0-8247-8741-2/Item H0776) - $45 (ASQC member price: $40.50).

# ISO PUBLICATIONS

The following publications may be obtained from the American National Standards Institue or from the ISO Central Secretariat in Geneva, Switzerland.

### *ISO 9000 Compendium*

Includes the entire ISO 9000 (1987) series, 10011 and 10012 series standards, 8402 vocabulary standards, draft standards, guideline documents and Vision *2000, A Strategy for International Standards Implementation in the Quality Arena during the 1990's*...224 pages. $135. (Order form reference: ISBN 92-67-101 72-2, 1992.)

### *ISO Bulletin 7*

32 pages (Order form reference: ISBN 0303-805X, July 1991).

# ISO 9000 NEWSLETTERS

### *ISO Bulletin*

This newsletter is published monthly in English and French by the ISO Central Secretariat. It contains updates and articles as well as lists of published standards available. Prices may vary due to current exchange rate. For information write:

> Promotion and Press Department
> Case postale 56, CH-1211
> Genève 20, Switzerland
> Tel: +41 22 749 01 11; Fax +41 22 733 34 30

To order, contact US sales agents for ISO publications:

> ANSI
> 11 West 42nd St.
> New York, NY 10036
> Tel: (212) 642-4900; Fax: (212) 302-1286

### *ISO 9000 News Forum*

This newsletter on Quality Management Standards, is published six times a year in English and French by ISO. The newsletter is part of an "ISO Forum 9000" global package which also entitles Forum members to participation in ISO-organized application symposia, to new and revised editions of the ISO 9000 series and to sources of training material for company personnel, third party auditors and developing countries. Individual membership to the "ISO Forum 9000" global service is available through the ISO member body in a country or direct from the ISO Central Secretariat in Geneva:

| | | |
|---|---|---|
| 1 rue de Varembé | OR | ANSI |
| Case postale 56, CH-1211 | | 11 West 42nd Street |
| Geneve 20, Switzerland | | New York, NY 10036 |
| Tel: +41 22 749 01 11 | | Tel: (212) 642-4995 |
| Fax: +41 22 733 34 30. | | Fax: (212) 302-1286 |

### *Quality Systems Update*

An information service on all aspects of ISO 9000 and related issues. The service includes a newsletter, special bulletins on specific topics and the ISO 9000 Registered Company Directory. Subscribers also receive discounts on related publications and reports about ISO 9000 issues.

Full service subscription: $495/$520 outside US.
Newsletter only: $345/$370 outside US.
ISO 9000 Registered Company Directory Subscription: $195/$220 outside US

For information or to order, contact:

CEEM Information Services
10521 Braddock Rd.
Fairfax, VA 22032
Tel: (703) 250-5900; Fax: (703) 250-5313

# ISO 9000 TRAINING

The following organizations offer seminars and training materials in various aspects of quality management and quality assurance.

### Arch Associates

15770 Robinwood Dr.
Northville, MI 48167-2041
Tel: (313) 420-0122

**Contact**: Bill Harral

Arch Associates offers workshops including: *ISO 9000 Series Overview and Strategic Planning, Implementing Quality Standards, ISO Self-Audit and Management Review, Documenting Quality Systems*, and *Quality Standards-ISO 9000 Series Plus* In the last course mentioned, the workshop leaders- in addition to their separate qualifications- are both members of the Institute of Quality Assurance (IQA) in the UK and are ASQC certified as Quality Engineers, Reliability Engineers and Quality Auditors. British Standards Institute training and examination for IQA Lead Assessor certification.

### Batalas - Handley-Walker Co.

17371 Irvine Blvd., Suite 200
Tustin, CA 92680
Tel: (714) 730-0122; Fax: (714) 730-0439

Batalas - Handley-Walker Co. offers a full range of ISO-9000 training courses including: Lead Assessor (UK Registered), Implementation Training, Internal Audit, Documentation Preparation, and Management Overview. Handley-Walker was established in 1966. Batalas, Ltd. was established in 1975 in the UK and quickly became a leading BS5750 consulting and training firm in Europe.

### Brewer - Kleckner Education Services, Inc.

2505 Locksley Dr.
Grand Prairie, TX 75050
Tel: (214) 660-4575; Fax: (214) 641-1327

**Contact:** Laurie B. Miller

The B-K Education Services approach translates the course materials' significance into strategies and tactics to improve your effectiveness, while concentrating on techniques which have proven to be effective. The courses are presented by two or more highly qualified instructors with diverse backgrounds and experience in quality systems. Course designs are based on practical experience gained from designing, directing, implementing and measuring quality systems in a wide variety of businesses worldwide. Workshops include: Effective Quality Auditing Workshop (EQA), ISO 9000 Quality Management System Design (ISO 9000), ISO 10011-2 Lead Auditor Workshop (ISO 10011), Effective User Friendly SPC Workshop (SPC), Benchmarking for Quality Success Workshop (BQS), and ASQC (CQA and CQE Examination Refresher Courses).

**CEEM**
10521 Braddock Road
Fairfax, VA 22032-2236
Tel: (800) 745-5565, (703) 250-5900; Fax: (703) 250-5313

**Contact:** Leila Martin

CEEM's programs and information services cover a wide range of topics, including environmental management, ISO 9000 series quality system standards, and government regulatory compliance. Respected government and industry experts participate in discussions on topics such as the Environmental Protection Agency's (EPA) Superfund program, aboveground storage tanks, biotechnology, environmental permitting, workplace safety, risk assessment, and the Americans with Disabilities Act (ADA).

CEEM's ISO 9000 series quality system management courses, seminars and publications enjoy an international reputation. Course offerings include internal auditing processes, quality systems certification, laboratory quality assurance and automated management systems.

Conferences and seminars range from one to five days, depending on the topics and audience. While CEEM designs and sponsors many of its own course offerings, it also co-sponsors courses and seminars with respected national and international organizations.

Through its newsletters, guidebooks, handbooks, reports and videos, CEEM Information Services provides executives and managers with up-to-date information on an array of topics, including critical environmental issues, international product standards, laboratory certification, and ISO 9000 quality systems registration developments. CEEM's staff has extensive experience and expertise in conference management, journalism, marketing and training programs.

**DLS Quality Technology Associates Inc.**
108 Hallmore Drive
Camillus, NY 13031
Tel: (315) 468-5811

**Contact:** James A. Kalitta

DLS Quality Technology Associates Inc. has been in business for approximately one year and was established to be an ISO-9000 Registrar. At present they are working with the RAB to obtain certification as a registrar. Their Lead Assessors are both RAB and AQI certified and teach courses both at our client facilities and at the Onadaga Community College. Clients and potential clients include General Electric Co., DIL, SWS and Phillips. Courses include: *Introduction To IS-9000, Preparation For ISO-9000 Quality System Registration, ISO-9000 Quality System Documentation.*

## Du Pont Quality Management and Technology.

Du Pont, Louviers 33W44
PO Box 6090
Newark, DE 19714-6090
Tel: (800) 441-8040 or (302) 366-2100; Fax (302) 366-3366

Du Pont Quality Management and Technology conducts seminars including: a half-day management introduction, a two-day implementation seminar, a two-day audit seminar, a five-day lead assessor training seminar, a one-day quality manual preparation seminar and a 2 1/2 day experimentation seminar. Du Pont Quality Management and Technology has also produced a video: *ISO 9000: The First-Step to the Future.* The video provides a step-by-step orientation to the ISO 9000 standards. The two-module video program is 37 minutes long and includes a leader's guide and a "Roadmap to ISO 9000 Registration."

## FED-PRO, Inc.

5615 Jensen Dr.
Rockford, IL 61111
Tel: (815) 282-4300 or (800) 833-3776.

FED-PRO has produced a video training program and manual entitled *ISO 9000-9004 European QA Standards Video Training Program.* It provides clients with necessary basics to evaluate the compliance requirements. The video includes a 30-minute executive briefing and a 60-minute explanation of the compliance and certification requirements. The training program includes a reference and training manual. It also includes a complete copy of ISO 9000, 9001, 9002, 9003 and 9004. Cost: $245. To order, call the above number.

## Information Mapping, Inc.

300 Third Ave.
Waltham, MA 02154
Tel: (617) 890-7003; Fax: (617) 890-1339

**Contact**: Gretchen Sherman

With twenty-five years of experience, Information Mapping, Inc. (IMI) experts have made presentations at many ISO 9000/quality conferences, including ASQC regional conferences, BOSCON, Northeast Quality Control Conference (10/92), and the American

Quality Congress national conference (5/93). IMI staff maintains membership in many ISO/quality organizations, including ASQC. Seminars include: Documentation Skills for ISO 9000 and ISO Documentation: A Management Overview.

**Institute for International Research**
**American Institute**
437 Madison Ave., 23rd Floor
New York, NY 10022
Tel: (212) 826-1260 or (800) 345-8016; Fax (212) 826-6411

**Contact**: Sherry Baker

The Institute for International Research has produced an audio cassette training seminar "Implementing ISO 9000" (Item No. TZ264). The audio discusses the value of complying with ISO 9000. It also discusses the impact ISO 9000 will have on regulated industries, public procurement and customers in EC and EFTA countries, how to control the paperwork of ISO documentation, how to achieve quality and financial results from TQM efforts and the key role played by ISO 9000, and how to organize for ISO 9000 implementation. It includes eight 90-minute cassettes and a course manual.

**Learning Resources, Inc.**
700 Canal Street
Stamford, CT 06902-5921
Tel: (203) 637-5047; Fax (203) 637-2786

Learning Resources, Inc. provides generic and customary quality training in support of TQM, Implementation, and ISO 9000 registration. Through Bywater plc (a UK quality training and consulting firm), a series of video-supported training modules are available. Modules include video training material and model documentation. Titles include: TQM Strategy; Quality System Planning; Quality System Establishment; Quality System Audit; Quality Education; Quality Cost Measurement; and Quality Improvement. Costs range from $850 to $990 depending on package and quantity purchased.

**Perry Johnson, Inc.**
3000 Town Center, Suite 2960
Southfield, MI 48075
Tel: (800) 800-0450 or (313) 356-4410; Fax: (313) 356-4230

**Contact**: Carrie F. Hayden, National Sales Manager

Perry Johnson, Inc. conducts group seminars in its Michigan office, including: two-day introductory seminar (Cost: $650); two-day internal auditor training (Cost: $895); five-day ISO 9000 lead auditor training (Cost $1495); and five-day ISO 9000 implementation seminar (Cost: $1875). It also publishes a guide to ISO 9000, available free by contacting the above numbers.

**Process Management International**
7801 E. Bush Lake Road, Suite 360
Minneapolis, MN 55439-3115
Tel: (612) 893-0313 or (800) 258-0313; Fax (612) 893-0502

**Contact**: Julie Erler

Process management International conducts various seminars, including: one-day seminars on ISO 9000 registration; five-day seminars on ISO 9000 implementation; five-day seminars in training ISO assessors; two-day seminars on qualifying to be an ISO internal auditor.

**Quality Sciences Institute**
2030 Issaquah-Pine Lake Road SE, Suite 31
Issaquah, WA 98027
Tel (206) 392-7573 or (800) 756-5823

**Contact**: Jeff Kahl, Director of Marketing

Quality Sciences Institute conducts three-day workshops on implementation of ISO 9000 standards. The workshops include preliminary assessment, evaluation of strengths and weaknesses, instruction and role-playing. The company is developing a video-based ISO training series available in the Fall of 1992.

**Qualtyme, Incorporated**
4351 West College Avenue, Suite 503
Appleton, WI 54914
Tel: (414) 730-8868; Information Tel: (800) 526-0538; Fax (414) 730-1907

Qualtyme, Incorporated, in business over 15 years, offers several training videos on subjects including: Introductory SPC training, SPC chart interpretation, Basic and Advanced SPC training, Using SPC in the service sector and problem solving in the workplace.

**Rochester Institute of Technology**
**Center for Quality and Applied Statistics**
> Hugh L. Carey Building, PO Box 9887
> Rochester, NY 14623-0887
> Tel: (716) 475-6990; Fax: (716) 475-5959

The Center hosts two-day seminars entitled "ISO 9000: Quality System Registration for International Markets." The seminars teach participants to understand a variety of quality standards, the basics of quality systems, and to apply these standards to their own companies. Other seminars include: Software Quality Assurance, The ISO 9000 Seminar, and The BSI Quality Assurance Lead Assessor Course. They also offer *How To Prepare for the New International Quality Standards*, a comprehensive 10-hour video that addresses ISO 9000 history, basics, quality manuals, quality costs, how to register, a comparison with Malcolm Baldridge standards, a comparison with military standards, and case studies. A booklet with course materials, exercises, and overheads is also included. For specifics, please call Patrick McNenny at (716) 475-5261.

**Sanders Quality Associates, Inc.**
> 820 Gessner, Suite 940
> Houston, TX 77024
> Tel: (713) 465-8772; Fax (713) 465-9742

**Contact:** Dr. Judith A. Sanders or Dr. Donald A. Sanders, Directors.

Sanders Quality Associates, Inc. offers training in the "Continuous Quality Improvement" process. They use a four-step implementation, including: Orientation and Needs Analysis, Quality Training, On-Site Consulting, and Custom Design and Development. Sanders and Associates hosts week-long workshops on implementation of SPC and PSQ in the workplace. They also conduct two-day ISO 9000 implementation workshops.

## Additional Companies

The following contacts also offer seminars or training.

**American Productivity and Quality Center**
**Education and Training Division**
> 123 North Post Oak Ln.
> Houston, TX 77024-7797
> Tel: (800) 776-9676, (713) 681-4020

**American Society for Quality Control**
**Customer Service**
> PO Box 3066
> Milwaukee, Wisconsin 53201-3606
> Tel: (414) 272-8575, (800) 248-1946

**Association for Quality and Participation**
801-B West 8th St., Suite 501
Cincinnati, OH 45203
Tel: (513) 381-1959

**George Washington University
Continuing Engineering Education Program**
801 22nd St., NW, Room T 308
Washington, DC 20052
Tel: (202) 994-6106

**International Quality and Productivity
Center**
The Livery Building
209 Cooper Ave., Suite 7
Upper Montclair, NJ 07043-1850
Tel: (201) 783-4403, (800) 882-8684

**National Electrical Manufacturers
Association**
2101 L St., NW, Suite 300
Washington, DC 20037
Tel: (202) 457-8400

**Quality and Productivity Managment
Association**
300 North Martingale Rd., Suite 230
Schaumburg, IL 60173
Tel: (708) 619-2909

**Quality Source Company**
5 Town & Country Village, Suite 738
San Jose, CA 95128-2026
Tel: (408) 353-4921;
Fax: (408) 296-1432

**Society of Manufacturing Engineers**
One SME Dr.
PO Box 930
Dearborn, MI 48121-0930
Tel: (313) 271-1500

**Underwriters Laboratories Inc.**
1285 Walt Whitman Rd.
Melville, NY 11747-3081
Tel: (516) 271-6200

# COMPUTER SOFTWARE

**FED-PRO, Inc.**
5615 Jensen Dr.
Rockford, IL 61111
Tel: (815) 282-4300

*ISO 9000/MIL-9858A Quality Manual*
This program provides a generic quality assurance manual that covers all the basic
requirements stated in ISO 9004 and in MIL-Q-9858A. For relatively simple operations,
the manual can be used as written. In more complex situations, the word processsing
capabilities of the program will enable you to edit, add to, delete and/or modify the
content to meet the needs of your company.

Cost: $345. (UPS shipping included). Requires IBM compatible & WordPerfect or
Macintosh & Microsoft Word hardware/software.

## G.R. Technologies Ltd.
9011 Leslie St., Suite 211
Richmond Hill, Ontario L4B 3B6
Tel: (416) 886-1307; Fax: (416) 886-6327

### ISO 9000 Checklists
This program provides the auditor with a systematic and comprehensive method of conduct-ing an audit. An auditor can use the provided hardcopy workboook as is, or modify it to reflect the company's own requirements. The package contains a hard-copy workbook and a diskette containing three workbooks in WordPerfect format for ISO 9001, 9002 & 9003 respectively. Cost: $105, plus $7.50 shipping and handling.

## IQS, Inc.
20525 Center Ridge Rd., Suite 400
Cleveland, OH 44116-3453
Tel: (800) 635-5901 or (216) 333-1344; Fax (216) 333-3752

IQS,.Inc. software includes: *Customer Management, System Documentation, Product Documentation, Process Documentation, Preventive Maintenance, Calibration Manage-ment, Employee Involvement, Corrective Action, Supplier Managment.* Future releases include *Data Collection, SPC, Nonconformance Management, and Quality Costs.* Requirements: 386 IBM® or IBM compatible personal computer. Leasing Program available. Call IQS for detailed information or prices

## John A. Keane & Associates, Inc.
575 Ewing Street
Princeton, NJ 08540
Tel: (609) 924-7904; Fax (609) 924-1078

### QMS Programs® ISO-9000 Compliance Group
John A. Keane & Associates, Inc. offers QMS Programs that cover all three levels of ISO 9000. They provide a long-term solution to ISO data entry. Programs are horizontally integrated and work with other manufacturing software. They can be configured by the user to meet a company's needs. Call for prices or more specific information.

## Qualtyme, Incorporated
4351 West College Avenue, Suite 503
Appleton, WI 54914
Tel (414) 730-8868; Fax (414) 730-1907

Qualtyme, Incorporated offers real time SPC/SQC programs, Direct Numerical Control, manufacturing and industrial engineering planning and control systems, PC-based utility programs, preventive maintenance program and basic SPC software.

# FINANCIAL ASSISTANCE FOR ISO 9000 ACTIVITIES

The US Department of Commerce's Economic Development Administration has a Trade Adjustment Assistance program. Financial assistance is available for companies that require consulting services, including costs related to ISO 9000 certification. Companies that have experienced recent declines in sales and employment, due at least in part to increasing imports of competitive products, are eligible for the program. The government pays up to 75% of the cost of consulting services. The Trade Adjustment Assistance program funds the following 12 regional centers around the country.

**New England TAAC**
Richard McLaughlin, Director
120 Boylston St.
Boston, MA 02116
Tel: (617) 542-2395
[Connecticut, Maine, Massachusetts, New Hampshire, Rhode Island, Vermont]

**New Jersey TAAC**
John Walsh, Director
200 South Warren St.
CN 990
Trenton, NJ 08625
Tel: (609) 292-0360

**New York TAAC**
John Lacey, Director
117 Hawley St.
Binghamton, NY 13901
Tel: (607) 771-0875

**Mid-Atlantic TAAC**
William Gates, Director
486 Norristown Rd.
Suite 130
Blue Bell, PA 19422
Tel: (215) 825-7819
[Delaware, Maryland, Pennsylvania, Virginia, West Virginia, Washington, DC]

**Southeast TAAC**
Charles Estes, Director
Georgia Institute of Technology
Research Institute
151 6th St., O'Keefe Bldg., Room. 224
Atlanta, GA 30332
Tel: (404) 894-6106
[Alabama, Florida, Georgia, Kentucky, Mississippi, North Carolina, South Carolina, Tennessee]

**Southwest TAAC**

Robert Velasquez, Director
301 South Frio St., Suite 227
San Antonio, TX 78207-4414
Tel: (512) 220-1240
[Louisiana, Oklahoma, Texas]

**Mid-America TAAC**

Paul G. Schmid, Director
University of Missouri at Columbia
University Place, Suite 1700
Columbia, MO 65211
Tel: (314) 882-6162
[Arkansas, Kansas, Missouri]

**Great Lakes TAAC**

Margaret Creger, Director
University of Michigan
School of Business Administration
506 East Liberty St., 3rd Floor
Ann Arbor, MI 48104-2210
Tel: (313) 998-6213
[Indiana, Michigan, Ohio]

**Mid-West TAAC**

Howard Yefsky, Director
Applied Strategies International
150 N. Wacker Dr., Suite 2240
Chicago, IL 60606
Tel: (312) 368-4600
[Illinois, Iowa, Minnesota, Wisconsin]

**Rocky Mountain TAAC**

Robert L. Stansbury, Director
5353 Manhattan Cir., Suite 200
Boulder, CO 80303
Tel: (303) 499-8222
[Colorado, Nebraska, New Mexico,
North Dakota, South Dakota, Utah,
Wyoming]

**Northwest TAAC**

Ronald Horst, Director
Bank of California Center
900 4th Ave., Suite 2430
Seattle, WA 98164
Tel: (206) 622-2730
[Alaska, Idaho, Montana, Oregon,
Washington]

**Western TAAC**

Daniel Jimenez, Director, USC-WTAAC
3716 S. Hope St., Room 200
Los Angeles, CA 90007
Tel: (213) 743-8427
[Arizona, California, Hawaii, Nevada]

# STANDARDS AND CERTIFICATION INFORMATION

## US Government Publications

**The following reports are available from:**

Department of Commerce
Single Internal Market Information Service, Office of EC Affairs.
Tel: (202) 377-5276; Fax: (202) 377-2155

*EC Product Standards Under the Internal Market Program* **(December 1, 1991).**

*EC Testing and Certification Procedures Under the Internal Market Program* (November 1, 1991).

*Chemicals and European Community Directives* (October 1, 1991).

*EC Labor Policy and Workplace Safety - An Integral Part of 1992* (October 1, 1991).

*The EC Builds an Integrated, Modern Transportation System* (October 1, 1991).

*Intellectual Property Protection* (December 1, 1991).

*EC Telecommunications* (October 1, 1991).

*European Community's Policy and Regulations on Food and Beverages* (November 1, 1991).

*EC Single Market Law Affecting Exporting and Distribution: Agents, Distributors, Franchises* (December 1, 1991).

*European Community and Environmental Policy and Regulations* (October 1, 1991).

*The Export Yellow Pages*
Venture Publishing, Washington, DC, 1991. (Produced in cooperation with the International Trade Administration (ITA) of the US Department of Commerce)

Over 12,000 companies are listed by industry sector in this annual directory. Included are manufacturers and companies that provide services to exporters. Over 50,000 copies of the 1992 edition have been distributed free of charge by Commerce Department district offices in the United States and by American embassies and consulates overseas. *The Export Yellow Pages* is useful for US companies seeking export services and for foreign buyers seeking sources of US goods and services. Advertising space is available for companies listed in the directory. US companies interested in obtaining a copy of the directory or in listing their name in the directory (free of charge) should contact the ITA district office of the Department of Commerce in their area.

### *Business America*

This magazine is published bi-weekly by the US Department of Commerce and reports regularly on current developments affecting international trade and US exports. Subscription: $53 (US); $66.25 (International).

To order this magazine, send check or money order (payable to Superintendent of Documents) to:

Superintendent of Documents
US Government Printing Office
Washington, DC 20402
Tel: (202) 783-3238

## Publications from the National Organization of Standards and Technology (NIST)

The publications listed may be ordered from one of the following sources (see each listing for further instruction):

National Technical Information Service (NTIS)
5285 Port Royal Rd.
Springfield, VA 22161
Orders only: (800) 336-4700
Tel: (703) 487-4650; Fax: (703) 321-8547

Superintendent of Documents
US Government Printing Office (GPO)
Washington, DC 20402
Tel: (202) 783-3238; Fax: (202) 512-2250

Global Engineering Documents
2805 McGaw Ave., PO Box 19539
Irvine, CA 92714
Tel: (800) 854-7179; Fax: (714) 261-7892

Standards Code and Information Program (SCI)
National Institute of Standards and Technology, Administration Bldg., Room A629
Gaithersburg, MD 20899
Tel: (301) 975-4029
(When requesting information from SCI, please send a self-addressed mailing label)

***The ABC's of Standards-Related Activities in the United States*** (NBSIR 87-3576)
This report is an introduction to voluntary standardization, product certification and
laboratory accreditation.

Order as PB 87-224309 from NTIS.

***The ABC's of Certification Activities in the United States*** (NBSIR 88-3821)
This report, a sequel to NBSIR 87-3576, *The ABC's of Standards-Related Activities in the
United States*, provides an introduction to certification. It provides the reader with
information necessary to make informed purchases, and serves as background for using
available documents and services.

Order as PB 88-239793 from NTIS.

***Barriers Encountered by US Exporters of Telecommunications Equipment*** (NBSIR 87-3641)
This report addresses the perceived institution of unreasonable technical trade barriers by
major European trading partners to the export of telecommunications products and
systems by US companies.

Order as PB 88-153630 from NTIS.

***Directory of European Regional Standards-Related Organizations*** (NIST SP 795)
This directory identifies more than 150 European regional organizations, both governmental and private, that engage in standards development, certification, laboratory accreditation and other standards-related activities, such as quality assurance. Entries describe the
type and purpose of each organization; acronyms; national affiliations of members; the
nature of the standards-related activity; and other related information.

Order as PB 91-107599 from NTIS or as Cat. #0258-3 from Global Engineering Documents.

*Directory of Federal Government Certification Programs* (NBS SP 739)

This directory presents information on government certification programs for products and services. Entries describe the scope and nature of each certification program, testing and inspection practices, standards used, methods of identification and enforcement, reciprocal recognition or acceptance of certification, and other relevant details.

Order as PB 88-201512 from NTIS.

*Directory of Federal Government Laboratory Accreditation/ Designation Programs* (NIST SP 808)

This directory provides updated information on 31 federal government laboratory accreditation and similar type programs conducted by the federal government. These programs, which include some type of assessment regarding laboratory capability, designate sets of laboratories or other entities to conduct testing to assist federal agencies in carrying out their responsibilities. The directory also lists 13 other federal agency programs of possible interest, including programs involving very limited laboratory assessment and programs still under development.

Order as PB 91-167379 from NTIS.

*Directory of International and Regional Organizations Conducting Standards-Related Activities* (NIST SP 767)

This directory contains information on 338 international and regional organizations which conduct standardization, certification, laboratory accreditation, or other standards-related activities. It describes their work in these areas, as well as the scope of each organization, national affiliations of members, US participants, restrictions on membership, and the availability of any standards in English.

Order as PB 89-221147 from NTIS or order as Cat. #0258-3 from Global Engineering Documents.

*Directory of Private Sector Product Certification Programs* (NIST SP 774)

This directory presents information from 132 private sector organizations in the United States which engage in product certification activities. Entries describe the type and purpose of each organization, the nature of the activity, product certified, standards used, certification requirements, availability and cost of services, and other relevant details.

Order as PB 90-161712 from NTIS.

*Directory of State and Local Government Laboratory Accreditation/ Designation Programs*
(NIST SP 815)
This directory provides updated information on 21 state and 11 local government laboratory accreditation and similar type programs. These programs, which include some type of assessment regarding laboratory capability, designate private sector laboratories or other entities to conduct testing to assist state and local government agencies in carrying out their responsibilities. Entries describe the scope and nature of each program, laboratory assessment criteria and procedures used in the program, products and fields of testing covered, program authority, and other relevant details.

Order as PB 92-108968 from NTIS.

*GATT Standards Code Activities*
This brochure gives a brief description of NIST's activities in support of the Standards Code. These activities include operating the US GATT inquiry point for information on standards and certification systems; notifying the GATT Secretariat of proposed US regulations; assisting US industry with trade-related standards problems; responding to inquiries on foreign and US proposed regulations; and preparing reports on the Standard Code.

Order from SCI.

*GATT Standards Code Activities of the National Institute of Standards and Technology*
This annual report describes the GATT Standards Code activities conducted by the Standards Code and Information Program for each calendar year. NIST responsibilities include operating the GATT inquiry point, notifying the GATT Secretariat of proposed US Federal government regulations which may affect trade, assisting US industry with standards-related trade problems, and responding to inquiries about proposed foreign and US regulations.

Order from SCI.

Free handout material on office activities and standards-related information such as: government sources of specifications and standards; foreign standards bodies; US standards organizations; and a brochure on the National Center for Standards and Certification Information (NCSCI).

*Laboratory Accreditation in the United States* (NISTIR 4576)
This report, a sequel to NBSIR 87-3576 *The ABC'S of Standards-Related Activities in the United States* and NBSIR 88-3821 *The ABC'S of Certification Activities in the United*

*States,* is designed to provide information on laboratory accreditation to readers who are new to this field. It discusses some of the more significant facets of this topic, provides information necessary to make informed decisions on the selection and use of laboratories, and serves as background for using other available documents and services.

Order as PB 91-194495 from NTIS.

*A Review of US Participation in International Standards Activities* (NBSIR 88-3698)
This report describes the role of international standards, their increasingly significant importance in world trade, and the extent of past and current US participation in the two major international standardization bodies - ISO and IEC. The degree of participation covers the 20 year period 1966-1986.

Order as PB 88-164165 from NTIS.

*Standards Activities of Organizations in the United States* (NIST SP 806)
The directory identifies and describes activities of over 750 public and US private sector organizations which develop, publish, and revise standards; participate in this process; or identify standards and make them available through information centers or distribution channels. NIST SP 806, a revision of NBS SP 681, covers activities related to both mandatory and voluntary standards. SP 806 also contains a subject index and related listings that cover acronyms and initials, defunct bodies and organizations with name changes.

Order as PB 91-177774 from NTIS or order as Cat. # SP806 from Global Engineering Documents.

*A Summary of the New European Community Approach to Standards Development* (NBSIR 88-3793-1)
Summary of European Community plans to aggressively pursue goal of achieving an "internal market" by 1992 andstandards-related implications of such programs on US exporters.

Order from NTIS as PB 88-229489/AS.

*tbt News*
This newsletter provides information on government programs and available services established in support of the GATT Agreement on Technical Barriers to Trade (Standards Code). *tbt News* reports on the latest notifications of proposed foreign regulations; bilateral consultations with major US trade partners; programs of interest to US exporters; and availability of standards and certifications information. Subscription is free upon request.

Order from SCI.

*Technical Barriers to Trade*
> This booklet explains the basic rules of the international agreement on Technical Barriers to Trade negotiated during the Tokyo Round of the Multilateral Trade Negotiations (MTN), and describes Title IV of the US Trade Agreements Act of 1979 which implements the United States' obligations under the Agreement. The Agreement, popularly known as the Standards Code, was designed to eliminate the use of standards and certification systems as barriers to trade. The booklet describes the functions of the Departments of Commerce and Agriculture, the Office of the US Trade Representative, and the State Department on carrying out the US's responsibilities.
>
> Order from SCI.

*Trade Implications of Processes and Production Methods (PPMs)* (NISTIR 90-4265)
> This report discusses processes and production methods (or PPM's) and their relationship to trade, the GATT Agreement on Technical Barriers to Trade, and traditional product standards used in international commerce. The report provides background information on PPM's, a suggested definition, and the possible extension of their application from the agricultural sector to industrial products.
>
> Order as PB 90-205485 from NTIS.

*An Update of US Participation in International Standards Activities* (NISTIR 89-4124)
> This report presents updated information on the current level of US participation in ISO and IEC (reference: NBSIR 88-3698).
>
> Order as PB 89-228282/AS from NTIS.

## Other Government Reports/Guides

*Completion of the European Community Internal Market: An Initial Assessment of Certain Economic Policy Issues Raised by Aspects of the EC's Program* (December 1988).
> Available from the Office of the US Trade Representative, (202) 395-6120.

*Effects of Greater Economic Integration Within the European Community on the United States*
> US International Trade Commission, Office of the Secretary
> 500 E Street, SW
> Washington, DC 20436
> Tel: (202) 252-1809; Fax: (202) 252-1000

*Europe 1992: A Business Guide to Government Resources*
    United States Department of State
    Bureau of Public Affairs
    Tel: (202) 647-6575.

*Europe 1992 - A Practical Guide for American Business No. 3*
    US Chamber of Commerce. Cost: $20.
    Tel: (202) 463-5487

# EC PUBLICATIONS

Several of the subscriptions, books and other publications described below, and published by the European Community Office for Official Publications can be purchased from UNIPUB, a division of the Kraus Organization Limited. UNIPUB is the US distributor for many publications. Please contact UNIPUB at the following address:

    UNIPUB
    4611-F Assembly Dr.
    Lanham, MD 20706-4391
    Tel: (301) 459-7666, (800) 274-4888 (USA), (800) 233-0504 (Canada)
    Fax: (301) 459-0056

The European Community office in Washington, DC offers free documentation on a variety of European economic issues. For further information, contact:

    European Community (EC)
    Attn: Public Affairs - Free documentation
    2100 M Street, NW, 7th Floor
    Washington, DC 20037
    Tel: (202) 862-9500

To avoid unnecessary delay, please note that the European Community Office cannot accept telephone orders. Publications will be shipped only within the United States.

## Books/Reports

### *Countdown 1992*

An EC Directive Status Report issued periodically by the EC Committee of the American Chamber of Commerce in Belgium.
Contact: Laurent Barbet
Tel: 011 322 513 6892.

**For ordering and/or pricing information concerning any of the publications below, contact:**

ANSI
11 West 42nd St.
New York, NY 10036
Tel: (212) 642-4900; Fax: (212) 302-1286.

### *Compendium of ISO/IEC Guides for Conformity Assessment*

ISO and IEC* have published the second edition of their Compendium of conformity assessment documents. The 160-page volume contains 19 guides on requirements, methods, model rules, statements of policy and recommendations for efficient product certification, as well as reference documents and a set of definitions of relevant terms. These guides make due reference where appropriate to the ISO 9000 series of quality assurance standards issued in a companion publication (*ISO 9000 International Standards for Quality Management*). The new edition of the Compendium (Order form reference: ISBN 92-67-10170-6) which includes the new or revised ISO/IEC guides issued until 1991, is intended to become a complement to a new book, currently in preparation, on experience gained, and developments in the certification area since the early 1980's.
Cost: $75.

### *ANSI Global Standardization Report - Volume 1*

Report issued by ANSI's Brussels office in September 1989, containing information on results of first private sector meeting between delegations under ANSI's auspices, and CEN/CENELEC.

### *ANSI Global Standardization Report - Volume 2*

Issued in January 1990, this report contains information on how to access the European standards process; agreements (to date) between IEC and CENELEC, and ISO and CEN; a draft procedure for inputting comments on proposed European standards; and case studies giving examples of interaction among ISO, and CEN/CENELEC activities.

*ANSI Global Standardization Report - Volume 3*

This third in the series of the reports (published May 1990) issued out of ANSI's Brussels offices, updates standardization issues, and contains much information on testing, certification, and conformity assessment initiatives in Europe, including the formation of the European Organization for Testing and Certification (EOTC).

*ANSI Global Standardization Report - Volume 4*

Published in March 1991, this volume reports on meetings held in Brussels in October 1-2, 1990 between a delegation under the auspices of ANSI and CEN, CENELEC, EOTC, and the Commission of the European Communities, as well as meetings held on August 1-2, 1990 with European representatives of organizations involved with quality assessment activities that are based on requirements contained in the ISO 9000 series of standards. The IEC/CENELEC agreement regarding future cooperation on standards development work and ISO and CEN resolutions on furthering cooperation are also included.

*ANSI Global Standardization Report - Volume 5*

This fifth in the series of reports (published June 1991) reports on meetings held in Reston, Virginia in April 1991. between a delegation under the auspices of ANSI, and CEN, CENELEC, EOTC, and the Commission of the European Communities. It also contains the recently revised Agreement on Technical Cooperation between ISO and CEN, the EC Green Paper accompanied by ANSI's comments, as well as the latest information on testing, certification, and conformity assessment.

*ANSI Global Standardization Report - Volume 6*

Published in April 1992, this volume reports on meetings held November 6th and 7th, 1991 in Brussels with CEN,CENELEC, EOTC, ETSI and the European Commision.

*ANSI Global Standardization Report - Volume 7*

Published in August 1992, this volume reports on meetings held with CEN, CENELEC, ETSI, EOTC and European Commision on April 28-29, 1992 and May 26, 1992.

***CENELEC Report on Current Activities***

Contains information on policies and technical activities of CENELEC, including the listing of projects and stages of items, by committee.

***Completing the Single Internal Market: The Removal of Technical Barriers to Trade Within the European Economic Community.***

An introduction for foreign businessmen.

*EC-1992 and The Single Market In Europe - The Construction Products Directive.*
Prepared by Don Mackay, Manager of International Standards.
Air-Conditioning and Refrigeration Institute
4301 North Fairfax Dr., Suite 425
Arlington, VA 22203
Tel: (703) 524-8800; Fax: (703) 528-3816

*Europe of 1992*
Available from National Association of Manufacturers.
Tel: 202/637-3086
Cost: $25 for members or $50 for non-members.

*The European Communities 1992 Plan: An Overview of the Proposed Single Market*
Congressional Research Service. CRS Report 88-623 (September 1988). Available
through any local Senator or Congressional Representative.

*Panorama of EC Industry 1991/92*
European Community Commission, Brussels, 1991. The Panorama of EC Industry is a
unique work with a comprehensive and detailed picture of more than 180 sectors of
manufacturing and service industries within the European Community. It focuses on
structural changes, the effects of new technologies, environmental regulations, new or
forth-coming legislation, and changes in cost structures and forecasts.
Order from: UNIPUB.
Cost: $140.

*The 1992 Challenge from Europe: Development of the European Community's Internal
Market.*
Available from the National Planning Association.
Tel: (202) 265-7685
Cost: $15.

*Beyond 1992: Forces Shaping the New Europe.*
This report summarizes a February 22, 1991 conference focusing on how EC 92 will
affect US business. It includes an a survey taken the day of the event and an analysis of
changing opinions on EC affects on business. Order from:
Columbia Institute, Washington, DC
Tel: (202) 547-2470
Cost: $25.

*Effective Lobbying in the European Community.*
> Author: James Gardner.
> This how-to manual provides a full-scale analysis of the techniques of European lobbying from the practical perspective of the professional legislative advocate. Order from:
>> Kluwer
>> 6 Bigelow St.
>> Cambridge, MA 02139
>> Tel: (617) 354-0140; Fax: (617) 354-8595
>> Cost: $45.

*EuroMarketing A Strategic Planner for Selling into the New Europe, by Rick Arons.*
> Using the most current and accurate information available, this publication shows marketing executives of any size company how to market and sell products successfully in today's Europe. (May be available for a reduced rate for educational use according to specific qualifications.) For more information, call:
>> Probus Publishing Co.
>> Tel: (312) 868-1100
>> Cost:   $32.50.

*Faulkner & Gray's European Business Directory*
> This comprehensive resource guide for US companies doing business in Europe provides names, addresses, phone numbers and economic profiles of the 12 European Community and six Eastern European nations. The directory also has information on a wide variety of European service companies with expertise in banking, law, insurance, and accounting. For more information, contact:
>> Faulkner & Gray
>> Tel: (800) 535-8403
>> Cost: $295.

## Magazines/Newsletters

*ANSI Standards Action*

Published bi-weekly by ANSI, this newsletter lists proposed and recently approved American National Standards, ISO and IEC standards, CEN/CENELEC Standards activity, a registration of Organization names in the US, and proposed foreign government regulations. *Standards Action* is sold jointly with ANSI's montly newsletter, *The ANSI Reporter*, which reports on current activities of ANSI and the US voluntary standards community. The newsletters are provided to ANSI members at no charge and sold to other subscribers for $200 per year. To order, phone, fax or mail requests to:

Tel: (212) 642-9000; Fax: (212) 302-1286

Or mail request to:

American National Standards Institute
11 West 42nd Street
New York, NY 10036
Tel: (212) 642-4900; Fax: (212) 302-1286

*BSi News*

Published monthly
2 Park Street
London W1A 2BS
Tel: 071-629-9000; Fax: (Gr2/3) 071-629-0506.

Send address label to:

Manager, Membership Services
BSi Linford Wood Milton Keynes MK146LE
Tel: (0908) 220022; Fax: (Gr 2/3) (0908) 320856

BSi also publishes British Standards, withdrawn British Standards, changes to British Standards, as well as IEC, ISO, CECC, CEN, CENELEC, ENV and ETSI publications. For information call:

Tel: (0908) 221166

Or write to:

Enquiries and Sales
BSi Linford Wood
Milton Keynes MK146LE

*Consensus*

A quarterly publication, *Consensus* includes news and features on Canadian and international standards. Annual Subscription: $12 (Canada), $20 (outside Canada). Available in English and French by the Standards Council of Canada on behalf of the National Standards System. To order, contact:

Lucile Hildesheim
45 O'Connor Street, Suite 1200
Ottawa, Ontario K1P6N7
Tel: (613) 238-3222

*EC Brief*

Published bi-monthly by:
European Community office of Ernst & Young
Avenue Louise 523
1050-Brussels, Belgium
Tel: (32 2) 648-7666; Fax: (32 2) 640-9908

*EC Bulletin*

Published bi-monthly by:
Price Waterhouse
EC Services
Rue St. Lamberstraat 135
B-1200 Brussels, Belgium
Tel: (32 2) 773-4911; Fax: (32 2) 762-5100

*EC-US Business Report*

Published monthly. Subscription price: $200. Available from:
C&M International Ltd.
1001 Pennsylvania Avenue, NW
Washington, DC 20004-2595
Tel: (202) 624-2895

*Eurecom*

Published ten times a year. Available free from:
New York Delegation of the Commission of the European Communities
3 Dag Hammarskjold Plaza
305 East 47th Street
New York, NY 10017
Tel: (212) 371-3804

*Euronotes, European Law Developments Affecting International Business*
>Report published by:
>>LeBoeug, Lamb, Leiby & McRae
>>14 Rue Montoyer, 5th Floor
>>1040 Brussels, Belgium
>>Tel: 011 32 2 514 5650

*Europe*
>Published ten times a year by the Commission of the European Communities. Information and samples available. Contact the EC at (202) 862-9555. Subscription: $19.95 (US) or $29.95 (International). For subscriptions call (800) 627-7961.

*Europe Now*
>A newsletter published quarterly, free from:
>>US Department of Commerce
>>International Trade Administration
>>Office of European Community Affairs
>>Washington, DC 20230
>>Tel: (202) 482-5279

*Eurowatch: Economics Policy and Law in the New Europe*
>A newsletter published bi-monthly. Subscription: $797. Available from:
>>Buraff Publications
>>1350 Connecticut Ave., NW, Suite 1000
>>Washington, DC 20036-0990
>>Tel: (202) 862-0900

*The OECD Observer*
>Published bi-monthly in English and French. Cost: single copy: $4.50; annual subscription: $22. Contact:
>>Ulla Ranhall-Reyners, Editor.
>>OECD Publications Service
>>Château de la Muette
>>2, rue André-Pascal
>>F75775 PARIS CEDEX 16
>>Tel: (1) 45 24 82 00; Fax (33-1) 45 24 85 00

>To order subscription, call (1) 45 25 81 86.

*1992 Single Market Communications Review*
    This magazine is published quarterly by Kline Publishing, 6 Station Parade, Balham High
    Road, London SW12 9AD, England, Tel: (44 81) 675-6460; Fax: (44 81) 675-6466.

**Trade Winds**
    A monthly newsletter on information on standardization that effects global trade-$75.
    (Canada) or $85. (International). Contact:
        Sandy Watson
        Tel: (613) 238-3222, in Ottawa, Ontario.

# Online Databases

**EC On Line**
    The European Commission is offering an expanding family of on-line computer databases
    to obtain information about its activities.

    *INFO 92* is a database focusing on the progress of the EC toward a single market and
    includes summaries of EC legislation adopted and in preparation. The database is broken
    down into three areas: removal of physical barriers, removal of technical barriers, and
    removal of fiscal barriers. *INFO 92* also covers the incorporation of EC legislation into the
    Member States' own national law.

    The *RAPID* service includes press releases and information issued by the Spokesman
    Service of the European Commission. It contains the full text of all documents issued
    including memos, speeches and other key documents.

    *SCAD* provides EC proposals and acts, official publications and documents published by
    institutions, articles dealing with the EC, and statements and opinions from industry.

    *SESAME* watches R&D, demonstration and technology projects.

    [For more information write: EUROBASES, Commission of the European Communities,
    200 rue de la Loi, B-1049 Brussels 32 -2-235-00 01, 32-2-236-06 24.]

## European Free Trade Association Publications

The following is a partial list of publications available from:

**European Free Trade Association**
Press and Information Service
9-11 rue de Varembe, CH-1211
Geneva 20, Switzerland
Tel: 41-22-749-1111; Fax: 41-22-733-9291

*EFTA Bulletin*
Published quarterly in English, French, German, and Swedish/Norwegian editions.

*EFTA News*
Free newsletter published in English, French and German.

*The Stockholm Convention*
English/French bilingual edition.

*EFTA Annual Report, 1989*
Published in English, French and German.

*The Free Trade Agreements of the EFTA Countries With the European Communities*
Published in English, French and German.

*Compulsory Technical Regulations*
List of the competent national authorities in each EFTA country. Published in English only.

*EFTA: What it is, What it Does*
General information on the history and purpose of EFTA.

*EFTA Fact Sheets*
Facts and figures about EFTA including history, trade, activities and organization. Includes overview of the negotiations with the EC. Published in English, French or German.

*The European Free Trade Association*
In-depth history of the EFTA. Published in French, German and Norwegian.

*Money and Finance in European Integration*
    Notes from a 1988 seminar.

*EFTA Countries in a Changing Europe*
    Notes from a 1990 seminar.

*The EFTA Industrial Developement Fund for Portugal*
    General information about the fund and its statutes. Published in English.

*EFTA Trade 1990*
    Published in English.

*Handbook on EFTA Markets for Yugoslav Products*
    A guide to the markets of five EFTA countries. Published in English.

*Publications may be ordered by contacting the Press and Information service at the above address and phone numbers.*

# Appendix E

# ACRONYMS & GLOSSARY

## ACRONYMS

| | |
|---|---|
| AIAG | Automotive Industry Action Group |
| ANSI | American National Standards Institute |
| ASQC | American Society for Quality Control |
| BSI | British Standards Institution |
| CASE | Conformity Assessment Systems Evaluation |
| CD | Committee Draft |
| CE | Conformite Europeene (in French) |
| CEN | European Committee for Standardization |
| CENELEC | European Committee for Electrotechnical Standardization |
| CQA | Certified Quality Auditor |
| DIS | Draft International Standard |
| DoD | US Department of Defense |
| EC | European Community |
| EEA | European Economic Area |
| EFTA | European Free Trade Association |
| EN | European Norm |
| ENV | European Pre-standards |
| EOTA | European Organization for Technical Approvals |
| EOTC | European Organization for Testing and Certification |
| EQNET | European Network for Quality System Assessment and Certification |
| EQS | European Committee for Quality System Assessment and Certification |
| ETSI | European Telecommunications Standards Institute |
| FAR | Federal Acquisition Regulation |

GMP .......................... Good Manufacturing Practices (US Food and Drug Administration)

HD ............................. Harmonization Documents

IEC ............................ International Electrotechnical Commission
IQA ........................... Institute of Quality Assurance
ISO ........................... International Organization for Standardization
ITQS ......................... Recognition Arrangement for Assessment and Certification of Quality
                              Systems in the Information Technology Sector

MBNQA ................... Malcolm Baldrige National Quality Award
MOU ......................... Memorandum of Understanding
MRA .......................... Mutual Recognition Agreement

NACCB ..................... National Accreditation Coucil for Certifying Bodies (UK)
NIST .......................... National Institute for Standards and Technology
NSAI ......................... National Standards Authority of Ireland

OEM .......................... Original Equipment Manufacturers

RAB .......................... Registration Accreditation Board
RvC ........................... Dutch Council for Certification

SCC ........................... Standards Council of Canada
SPC ........................... Statistical Process Control

TC 176 ....................... Technical Committee 176
TQM .......................... Total Quality Management

WD ............................ Working Draft

# GLOSSARY

**ANSI** .............................. American National Standards Institute  Not a standards-writing body. Assures that member organizations which do write standards follow rules of consensus and broad participation by interested parties. ANSI is the US member of ISO.

**ASQC** ........................... American Society for Quality Control. A technical society of over 70,000 quality professionals. Individual members from throughout the world, but primarily from the US. Publishes quality-related American National Standards.

**Accreditation Mark** ..... An insignia that indicates accreditation. Only accredited certification bodies and the companies they certify are allowed to use an accreditation mark. Non-accredited certification bodies and the companies they certify may not.

**Assessment Body** .......... Third party which assesses products and registers the quality systems of suppliers.

**Assessment System** ....... Rules of procedure and management for conducting an assessment leading to issue of a registration document and its maintenance.

**BSi** ................................. British Standards Institution. This is the UK's standards-writing body.

**BSi QA** ........................... BSi Quality Assurance One of (at present) 15 accredited certification bodies (registrars) in the UK. Assesses suppliers for conformance to the appropriate ISO 9000 series standards; registers those which conform. Organizationally separate from BSi.

**CEN** .............................. European Committee for Standardization. Publishes regional standards (for EC and EFTA) covering non-electrical, non-electronic subject fields. (See also CENELEC.)

**CENELEC** ..................... European Committee for Electrotechnical Standardization Publishes regional standards (for EC and EFTA) covering electrical/ electronic subject fields. (See also CEN.)

**CE** ................................. The European Community mark of approval.  This mark signifies that the equipment complies with all applicable directives and product standards.

**Certified** ........................ The quality system of a company, location or plant is certified for compliance to ISO 9000 after it has demonstrated such compliance through the audit process. When used to indicate quality system certification, it means the same thing as registration.

**Company** ....................... Business unit; its purpose is to supply a product or service (first party).

**Conformity Assessment** .. Conformity assessment includes all activities that are intended to assure the conformity of products to a set of standards. This can include testing, inspection, certification, quality system assessment and other activities.

**Contractor** .................... The organization that provides a product to the customer in a contractual situation (purchaser) (Draft International Standard (DIS) 8402 Quality management and quality assurance - Vocabulary, Clause 1.12).

**Customer** ...................... The recipient of a product provided by the supplier (DIS 8402/1.9).

**DIN** ............................... Deutsches Institut fur Normung; Germany's standards-writing body.

**Design Review** ............... A formal, documented, comprehensive and systematic examination of a design to evaluate the design requirements and the capability of the design to meet these requirements and to identify problems and propose solutions (ISO 8402-1986(3.13).

**EC** ................................. European Community. The EC is a framework within which member states have agreed to integrate their economies and eventually to form a political union. Current members are Belgium, Denmark, France, Germany, Greece, Ireland, Italy, Luxembourg, Netherlands, Portugal, Spain, UK.

**EEC** .............................. The European Economic Community — this comprises the EC and EFTA countries.

**EFQM** ........................... European federation for Quality Management An organization of upper-level managers concerned with quality.

**EFTA** ............................ European Free Trade Association. A group of nations whose goal is to remove import duties, quotas and other obstacles to trade and to uphold non-discriminatory practices in world trade. Current members are Austria, Finland, Iceland, Norway, Sweden, Switzerland.

**EN 45000** ...................... A series of standards set up by the EC to regulate and harmonize certification, accreditation, and testing activities. National accreditation structures and inspection body standards are still being developed.

**EOQ** ............................ European Organization for Quality, formerly EOQC - European Organization for Quality Control. An independent organization whose mission is to improve quality and reliability of goods and services primarily through publications and conferences/seminars. Members are quality-related organizations from countries throughout Europe, including Eastern-bloc countries. ASQC is an affiliate society member.

**EOTC** ........................... European Organization for Testing and Certification. Set up by the EC and EFTA to focus on conformity assessment issues in the non-regulated spheres.

**EQS** ............................. European Committee for Quality System Assessment and Certification. The function of EQS is to harmonize rules for quality system assessment and certification (registration), facilitate mutual recognitions of registrations, provide advice and counsel to other committees in the EOTC framework on matters related to quality system assessment and certification.

**IEC** ............................. International Electrotechnical Commission. A worldwide organization that produces standards in the electrical and electronic fields. Members are the national committees, composed of representatives of the various organizations which deal with electrical/electronic standardization in each country. Formed in 1906.

**IQA** ............................. Institute for Quality Assurance. A British organization of quality professionals; Operates a widely recognized system of certification of auditors for quality systems.

**ISO** ............................. International Organization for Standardization. A worldwide federation of national standards bodies (87 at present). ISO produces standards in all fields, except electrical and electronic (which are covered by IEC). Formed in 1947.

**Inspection** ...................... Activities such as measuring, examining, testing, gauging one or more characteristics of a product or service and comparing these with specified requirements to determine conformity (ISO 8402-1986(3.14)).

**MOU** ............................. Memorandum Of Understanding; A written agreement among a number of organizations covering specific activities of common interest. There are a number of MOUs covering mutual recognition of quality system registrations in which one of the signatories is a non-European registrar.

**Modules** ......................... The EC has devised a conformity assessment system, consisting of modules, to handle the diversity of testing, inspection, and certification activities. Modules in the "modular approach" range from manufacturer declaration through a variety of routes involving design and type approval, to full third-party certification.

**NACCB** ......................... National Accreditation Council for Certification Bodies. This is the British authority for recognizing the competence and reliability of organizations which perform third-party certification of products and/or registration of quality systems. Formed in 1984, it is the world's second such organization.

**Nonconformity** .............. The nonfulfilment of specified requirements (ISO 8402- Quality - Vocabulary 1986, Clause 3.20).

**Notified Body** ................ A notified body is a competent organization, approved by the national government and notified to the European Commission and all other Member States.

**Organization** ................. A company, corporation, firm or enterprise, whether incorporated or not, public or private.

**Process** ........................... A set of interrelated resources and activities which transform inputs into outputs (DIS 8402, Clause 1.2).

**Product** ......................... The result of activities or processes (DIS 8402, Clause 1.4).

**Purchaser** ..................... The recipient of a product provided by the supplier in a contractual situation (contractor) (DIS 8402, Clause 1.11).

**Quality** ........................... The totality of characteristics of an entity that bear on its ability to satisfy stated and implied needs (DIS 8402, Clause 2.1).

**Quality Assurance** ........ All the planned and systematic activities implemented within the quality system, and demonstrated as needed, to provide adequate confidence that an entity will fulfill requirements for quality (DIS 8402, Clause 3.5).

**Quality Audit** ............... A systematic and independent examination to determine whether quality activities and related results comply with planned arrangements and whether these arrangements are implemented effectively and are suitable to achieve objectives (DIS 8402, Clause 4.9).

**Quality Control** ........... The operational techniques and activities that are used to fulfill requirements for quality (DIS 8402, Clause 3.4).

**Quality Management** ... All activities of the overall management function that determine the quality policy, objectives and responsibilities and implement them by means such as quality planning, quality control, quality assurance and quality improvement, within the quality system (DIS 8402, Clause 3.2).

**Quality Manual** ........... A document stating the quality policy and describing the quality system of an organization (DIS 8402, Clause 3.12).

**Quality Plan** ................. A document setting out the specific quality practices, resources and sequence of activities relevant to a particular product, project or contract (DIS 8402, Clause 3.13).

**Quality Planning** .......... The activities that establish the objectives and requirements for quality and for the application of quality system elements (DIS 8402, Clause 3.3).

**Quality Policy** .............. The overall intentions and direction of an organization with regard to quality, as formally expressed by top management (DIS 8402, Clause 3.1).

**Quality System** ............ The organizational structure, responsibilities, procedures, processes and resources for implementing quality management (ISO 8402, Clause,3.8).

**Quality System Review** ... A formal evaluation by top management of the status and adequacy of the quality system in relation to quality policy and new objectives resulting from changing circumstances (ISO 8402-1986, Clause 3.12).

**RAB** ............................. Registrar Accreditation Board. A US organization whose mission is to recognize the competence and reliability of registrars of quality systems, and to achieve international recognition of registrations issued by accredited registrars. A subsidiary of ASQC.

**RvC** ............................. Read voor de Certificatie (Dutch Council for Certification) The Dutch authority for recognizing the competence and reliability of organizations which perform third-party certification of products, accreditation of laboratories and/or registration of quality systems. The first such organization, formed in 1980.

**Registered** ..................... A procedure by which a body indicates the relevant characteristics of a product, process or service, or the particulars of a body or person, in a published list. ISO 9000 registration is the evaluation of a company's quality system against the requirements of ISO 9001, 9002, or 9003.

**Registration** .................. Inclusion of the supplier's particulars and field of assessed capability by the body in an appropriate public register or list.

**Registration Document** ... Documentation that a supplier's quality system conforms to specified standards. Issued by an assessment body.

**Service** ........................... The results generated by activities at the interface between the supplier and the customer and by supplier internal activities, to meet the customer needs (DIS 8402, Clause 1.5).

**Service Delivery** ........... Those supplier activities necessary to provide the service (ISO 9004-2:1991(E), Clause 3.6).

**Software** ....................... Intellectual creation comprising the programs, procedures, rules and any associated documentation pertaining to the operation of a data processing system (ISO 9000-3:1991(E), Clause 3.1).

**Software Product** ......... Complete set of computer programs, procedures and associated documentation and data designated (ISO 9000-3:1991(E), Clause 3.2).

**Sub-contractor** .............. The organization that provides a product to the supplier (DIS 8402, Clause 1.13).

**Supplier** ........................ The organization that provides a product to the customer (DIS 8402, Clause 1.10).

**Total Quality**
**Management** ................ A management approach of an organization, centered on quality, based on the participation of all its members and aiming at long term success through customer satisfaction, and benefits to the members of the organization and to society (DIS 8402, Clause 3.7).

**Traceability** .................. The ability to trace the history, application or location of an entity, by means of recorded identifications (DIS 8402, Clause 3.16)

**Validation**
**(for software)** ............... The process of evaluating software to ensure compliance with specified requirements (ISO 9000-3:1991(E), Clause 3.7).

**Verification**
**(for software)** ............... The process of evaluating the products of a given phase to ensure correctness and consistency with respect to the products and standards provided as input to that phase (ISO 9000-3:1991(E), Clause 3.6).

# Index

# I

# N

# O

# P

Peach, Robert W.  xvii
Perry Johnson, Inc.  424–425
Potts, Elizabeth A.  104
Process Management International  425–426
Product  21
Product Certification versus ISO 9000 Registration  235
Product Liability Directive  268
Product Liability Prevention  271,  274
Product Safety Directive  269
Publications  445
Purchaser  32

# Q

Q91 and MIL-Q-9858A  163
Quality  21
Quality Assurance  9,  22.
  Importance  6
Quality Concepts  24
Quality Control  22
Quality Management  9,  22
Quality Management Institute (QMI)  384–385
Quality Mangement Consulting Services  426–427
Quality Policy  22
Quality Practitioners, Inc.  427–428
Quality Sciences Institute  428
Quality System  22
Quality System Elements in ISO 9000  20
  Cross Reference  29
Quality Systems Registrars, Inc. (QSR)  385–386
Quebec Quality Certification Group  397

# R

r. bowen international  428–429
R.P. Cooney & Associates  429–431
RAB  252
Recognition  246
Registrar  7

## S